Conservation

Conservation

Economics, Science, and Policy

Charles Perrings and Ann Kinzig

OXFORD
UNIVERSITY PRESS

OXFORD
UNIVERSITY PRESS

Oxford University Press is a department of the University of Oxford. It furthers the University's objective of excellence in research, scholarship, and education by publishing worldwide. Oxford is a registered trade mark of Oxford University Press in the UK and certain other countries.

Published in the United States of America by Oxford University Press
198 Madison Avenue, New York, NY 10016, United States of America.

© Oxford University Press 2021

Library of Congress Cataloging-in-Publication Data
Names: Perrings, Charles, author. | Kinzig, Ann P. (Ann Patricia) author.
Title: Conservation : economics, science, and policy / Charles Perrings and Ann Kinzig, Tempe, Arizona.
Description: New York : Oxford University Press, 2021. |
Includes bibliographical references and index.
Identifiers: LCCN 2020046931 (print) | LCCN 2020046932 (ebook) |
ISBN 9780190613600 (hardback) | ISBN 9780190613617 (paperback) |
ISBN 9780190613631 (epub)
Subjects: LCSH: Conservation of natural resources. |
Conservation of natural resources—Decision making.
Classification: LCC S936.P47 2020 (print) | LCC S936 (ebook) | DDC 333.72—dc23
LC record available at https://lccn.loc.gov/2020046931
LC ebook record available at https://lccn.loc.gov/2020046932

DOI: 10.1093/oso/9780190613600.001.0001

1 3 5 7 9 8 6 4 2

Paperback printed by LSC Communications, United States of America
Hardback printed by Bridgeport National Bindery, Inc., United States of America

In memory of
Georgina Mace (1953–2020) and Karl-Göran Mäler (1939–2020)
two wonderful people
whose enduring contributions to science have influenced much
of our thinking

Contents

Preface

As we finalize this book, the world economy has been rocked by the emergence and spread of yet another novel zoonotic disease—COVID-19—with origins at the interface between humans, their domesticates, and wildlife. It reminds us that conservation is as much about the control of invasive pests and pathogens as it is about the preservation of endangered wild plants and animals. It also reminds us that every choice we make to promote or degrade life forms involves a social cost. In the COVID-19 case, the costs of our attempts to control the disease have involved major economic dislocation worldwide. The book starts from the premise that the conservation of any resource involves an opportunity cost—the benefits that could have been had by converting that resource to a different use. The conservation of natural resources, like the conservation of works of art, or historic buildings, involves trade-offs.

The book is, first, a study of how people decide to conserve or convert resources. Without worrying about the characteristics of particular resources, we ask when and for how long it may be optimal to conserve resources. In other words, we consider the general principles involved in making conservation decisions.

The book is, second, a study of the conservation of resources of the natural environment. This includes both directly exploited resources such as agricultural soils, minerals, forests, fish stocks, and the like, and the species and ecosystems put at risk when people choose to convert natural habitat, or to discharge waste products to water, land, or air. Conservation is as much about the problem of how much or how little to extract from the environment as it is about how much to leave intact.

The book is, third, a study of the context in which people make conservation decisions. Just as the decisions people make about investment in financial assets are influenced by the tax rules established in different countries, so too decisions about the conservation of natural resources are influenced by property rights, laws, and customs. This includes environmental regulations within countries, and environmental agreements between countries. We consider how conservation relates to environmental governance, and how governance structures have evolved over time.

We have aimed the book at three audiences. The first is graduate students in any of the disciplines bearing on conservation. While the arguments may be most familiar to those studying environmental, resource, or ecological economics, it is intended to be accessible to geographers, ecologists, conservation biologists, political scientists, those studying environmental law, and to those in the comparatively new field of sustainability science. The second audience we have in mind is conservation practitioners, and professionals whose remit includes the management of the natural environment and the use of natural resources. We hope that the book will help those charged with the conservation of the natural environment to think about the trade-offs involved, the better to balance the protection of endangered species and other societal goals, like economic development or poverty alleviation. The third audience we have in mind is the substantial environmentally informed and aware general public who are interested in digging beneath the superficial treatment of conservation often encountered in the media. For people who want to understand the balance that should be struck between preservation and exploitation, between the protection of beneficial species and the control of harmful species, the book offers a set of principles that can be applied in most circumstances.

By including a somewhat formal and fully general theory of conservation, we hope to show what is needed to make rational conservation decisions. By including applications to a range of environmental resource allocation problems, we hope to illustrate the many and varied factors that need to be taken account of in the process. While our discussion of the theory of conservation includes formal mathematical arguments, these are always paralleled by a nonmathematical development of the same arguments. We hope that readers will be able to select the approach that best suits them.

The first draft of the book was largely written while we on sabbatical in Italy and Greece in 2018, and we thank our hosts in Siena and Volos, Simone Borghese and George Halkos, for the opportunity to work in such congenial environments. We also thank our home institution, Arizona State University, for funding and logistical support during the preparation of the book. Our thinking has been influenced over the years by many wonderful people, too numerous to mention here. You know who you are, and we thank you.

Finally, the book is the culmination of many years of work on different aspects of the conservation problem, undertaken with the support of a range of funding agencies. Three projects undertaken with colleagues at a number of institutions have been particularly important: Advancing Conservation in a Social Context, funded by the Macarthur Foundation;

Modeling Anthropogenic Effects in the Spread of Infectious Diseases, funded by the National Institutes of Health (Grant 1R01GM100471); and Risks of Animal and Plant Infectious Diseases through Trade, funded by the National Science Foundation's Ecology and Evolution of Infectious Diseases program (Grant 1414374).

Charles Perrings and Ann Kinzig, July 2020

Figures

Tables

Abbreviations

AAFC	Atlantic Africa Fisheries Conference
ABS	Access and benefit-sharing
AFTA	ASEAN Free Trade Area
APFIC	Asia-Pacific Fisheries Commission
ASEAN	Association of Southeast Asian Nations
BSE	Bovine Spongiform Encephalopathy
CBD	Convention on Biological Diversity
CCAMLR	Commission for the Conservation of Antarctic Marine Living Resources
CCSBT	Commission for the Conservation of Southern Bluefin Tuna
CDC	United States Centers for Disease Control
CECAF	Fishery Committee for the Eastern Central Atlantic
CFC	Chlorofluorocarbon
CGIAR	Consultative Group on International Agricultural Research
CGRFA	Commission on Genetic Resources for Food and Agriculture
CI	Conservation International
CIAT	International Center for Tropical Agriculture
CIMMYT	Centro Internacional de Mejoramiento de Maíz y Trigo
CITES	Convention on International Trade in Endangered Species of Wild Fauna and Flora
CMS	Convention on Migratory Species of Wild Animals
CO2	Carbon Dioxide
COREP	Regional Fisheries Committee for the Gulf of Guinea
CRP	Conservation Reserve Program
CSIRO	Commonwealth Scientific & Industrial Research Organization,
CTMFM	Joint Technical Commission for the Argentina/Uruguay Maritime Front
CWA	Clean Water Act
CWP	Coordinating Working Party on Fishery Statistics
ECOWAS	Economic Community of West African States
ESA	Endangered Species Act
EU	European Union
FAO	Food and Agriculture Organization of the United Nations
FFA	South Pacific Forum Fisheries Agency
GATT	General Agreement on Tariffs and Trade
GBA	Global Biodiversity Assessment
GCM	General Circulation Model
GDP	Gross Domestic Product

GEF	Global Environment Facility
GFCM	General Fisheries Commission for the Mediterranean
GMO	Genetically modified organisms
GNP	Gross National Product
HDI	Human Development Index
HIV/AIDS	Human immunodeficiency virus/Acquired Immune Deficiency Syndrome
IAASTD	International Assessment for Agricultural Science, Technology and Development
IATTC	Inter-American Tropical Tuna Commission
IBSFC	International Baltic Sea Fishery Commission
ICCAT	International Commission for the Conservation of Atlantic Tuna
ICES	International Council for the Exploration of the Sea
ICRAF	International Centre for Research in Agroforestry (now the World Agroforestry Centre)
ICRISAT	International Crops Research Institute for the Semi-Arid Tropics
IHR	International Health Regulations
IITA	International Institute of Tropical Agriculture
ILRI	International Livestock Research Institute
IMF	International Monetary Fund
IMO	International Maritime Organization
INIBAP	International Network for the Improvement of Banana and Plantain
IOTC	Indian Ocean Tuna Commission
IP	Intellectual property
IPBES	Intergovernmental Science-Policy Platform on Biodiversity and Ecosystem Services
IPCC	Intergovernmental Panel on Climate Change
IPGRI	International Plant Genetic Resources Institute
IPHC	International Pacific Halibut Commission
IPPC	International Plant Protection Convention
IRRI	International Rice Research Institute
ITPGRFA	International Treaty on Plant Genetic Resources for Food and Agriculture
ITQ	Individual Transferable Quota
IUCN	International Union for Conservation of Nature
IWC	International Whaling Commission
KAZA	Kavango-Zambezi Transfrontier Conservation Area
LME	Large Marine Ecosystem
MA	Millennium Ecosystem Assessment
MDG	Millennium Development Goal
MEA	Multilateral Environmental Agreement
N	Nitrogen
NABRAI	National Biodiversity Risk Assessment Index
NAFO	Northwest Atlantic Fisheries Organization
NAFTA	North American Free Trade Agreement

NAMMCO	North Atlantic Marine Mammal Commission
NASCO	North Atlantic Salmon Conservation Organization
NDP	Net Domestic Product
NEAFC	North-East Atlantic Fisheries Commission
NGO	Nongovernmental organization
NNI	Net National Income
NNP	Net National Product
NPAFC	North Pacific Anadromous Fish Commission
OECD	Organization for Economic Co-operation and Development
OIE	World Animal Health Organization
OLDEPESCA	Latin American Organization for the Development of Fisheries
PES	Payment for environmental services
PGR	Plant Genetic Resources
PICES	North Pacific Marine Science Organization
PPS	South Pacific Permanent Commission
PSC	Pacific Salmon Commission
RECOFI	Regional Commission for Fisheries
REDD	Reducing Emissions from Deforestation and Forest Degradation
RFMO	Regional Fishery Management Organization
SEAFO	South East Atlantic Fishery Organization
SNA	System of National Accounts
SO2	Sulphur Dioxide
SPC	Secretariat of the Pacific Community
SPS	Sanitary and Phytosanitary Measures Agreement
SRCF	Subregional Commission on Fisheries
SWIOFC	South West Indian Ocean Fishery Commission
TBT	Agreement on Technical Barriers to Trade
TEEB	The Economics of Ecosystems and Biodiversity
TFCA	Trans Frontier Conservation Area
TFP	Total Factor Productivity
TNC	The Nature Conservancy
TRIPS	Trade-Related Aspects of Intellectual Property Rights
UK	United Kingdom
UN	United Nations
UNCCD	United Nations Convention to Combat Desertification
UNCED	United Nations Conference on Environment and Development
UNCLOS	United Nations Convention on the Law of the Sea
UNDP	United Nations Development Programme
UNEP	United Nations Environment Programme
UNFCCC	United Nations Framework Convention on Climate Change
UPOV	International Convention for Protection on New Plant Varieties
USA	United States of America
USDA	United States Department of Agriculture
USEPA	United States Environmental Protection Agency
USFDA	United States Food and Drug Administration

USMCA	United States-Mexico-Canada Agreement
WCMC	World Conservation Monitoring Centre
WCPFC	Western and Central Pacific Fisheries Commission
WECAFC	Western Central Atlantic Fishery Commission
WHO	World Health Organization
WIOTO	Western Indian Ocean Tuna Organization
WTA	Willingness to accept
WTO	World Trade Organization
WTP	Willingness to pay
WWF	World Wildlife Fund

1

Environmental Conservation and Environmental Change

> It must always have been seen, more or less distinctly, by political economists, that the increase of wealth is not boundless: that at the end of what they term the progressive state lies the stationary state, that all progress in wealth is but a postponement of this, and that each step in advance is an approach to it. . . . The richest and most prosperous countries would very soon attain the stationary state, if no further improvements were made in the productive arts, and if there were a suspension of the overflow of capital from those countries into the uncultivated or ill-cultivated regions of the earth.
>
> **John Stuart Mill,** *Principles of Political Economy,* **1848**

1.1 Introduction

In the fifth century BC Heraclitus of Ephesus observed that the only constant in the universe is change, and yet to manage change people have ever felt the need to hold some things constant. The list of things that societies have sought to preserve includes the natural environment and the resources it offers, but covers much more. A moral compass, religious faith, ties to kith and kin, personal and community health, and defensive capacity are all candidates for conservation. The factors that people need to take account of in making conservation decisions about such things are always the same. Whether the problem involves ideas, bricks and mortar, or germplasm is immaterial to how conservation decisions should be made. In all cases, the question to be asked is whether the decision-maker does better by keeping an object in some state, or by allowing its state to change.

This book is first about the generic problem of conservation, and the principles that inform rational conservation choices—whatever the object of conservation. Second, it is about the application of those principles to the management of the natural world. Many intractable environmental conflicts around the world have their origins in the fact that different people make

Conservation. Charles Perrings and Ann Kinzig, Oxford University Press (2021). © Oxford University Press.
DOI: 10.1093/oso/9780190613600.003.0001

different conservation choices. The loss of biodiversity that is the stimulus for all efforts to protect wild living species is the result of historic decisions that individual land owners and land holders have taken about which species to promote and which to suppress, which gene stocks to build, and which to run down. Such decisions may lead to conflict for many reasons. Decision-makers are sometime ignorant of the wider and longer-term effects of their choices, sometimes neglectful of their effects on others, and sometimes deliberately perverse.

In some cases, people have simply misunderstood the consequences of their actions. A pesticide application that solves one problem only to create another is an example. In other cases, people have understood the consequences of their behavior all too well, but have deliberately ignored those consequences. This is often because the consequences are borne by others. The effects of water diversion from the Syr Darya and the Amu Darya rivers on the Aral Sea, or from the Colorado River on the Gulf of California, are examples. In still other cases, people would have made different decisions if they could, but were forced to make strategic choices that left all society worse off. The fertilizer applications that lie behind massive marine pollution events, for example, have many features of the classic prisoners' dilemma. Even though all would benefit from reductions in nutrient runoff, none has an incentive to lower their own fertilizer applications.

We wish to understand how conservation decisions of this sort were made, and with what effects at different spatial and temporal scales. We wish to understand how decisions of one person or one community at one time or place affect people or communities at other times or places. We also wish to understand why. That is, we wish to understand both the anatomy and pathology of conservation.

Our touchstone is a paper of seminal importance for both the economics of natural resources and the economics of conservation. It is Harold Hotelling's study of the economics of exhaustible resources (Hotelling 1931). The immediate goal of the paper was to investigate the conditions in which the owner of a nonrenewable resource, such as a mineral deposit, would be indifferent between extracting the resource and leaving it in place. In answering that question, however, Hotelling provided us with a fully general theory of conservation. For the mining problem, he found that the owner of a mineral resource would be indifferent between extracting it and leaving it in the ground if the value of the resource in place was expected to grow at the same rate as the return on mining proceeds when invested in the best alternative use. It has subsequently been shown that the argument extends naturally to the case of renewable resources—where the growth in value of the resource in place reflects not just a change in its price but also a change in its physical magnitude (Perrings and Halkos 2012). For any asset, it will be optimal to conserve that asset if and only if the value of the asset in the conserved state is expected to grow at a rate at least equal to the rate of return on the asset when converted to an alternative state.

The central insight from Hotelling's work is that conservation decisions depend on the value of resources, and how that value is expected to change over time. For a community to know whether it is worth conserving some resource, it needs to know both the value of the resource to the community today, and how that value is likely to change tomorrow. In cases where resources are being depleted, for example, the expected change in their value can be driven by increasing scarcity. But it can also be driven by changes in demand triggered by changes in preferences, changes in peoples' understanding of the services yielded by the resource, or changes in environmental conditions. Climate change is altering the future value of many natural resources. Changes in temperature and precipitation are changing the value of land for agriculture or other uses. Sea-level rise and the increasing frequency of extreme weather events is changing the value of coastal areas for human habitation.

By putting the expected change in the value of resources front and center, the Hotelling approach requires us to ask why a community confronted by a resource that could be either conserved or converted would want to conserve it. What are the ethical, moral, psychological, and other considerations that determine the value of resources to the community, and how might those change over time? What are the services (or disservices) offered by the resources, and how might those change with changes in technology or environmental conditions? We need to understand what it is that makes resources valuable to different people, and how and why value is expected to change.

The Hotelling approach also requires us to ask whether the use being made of resources by those who have formal or informal rights to them reflects the value of the same resources to the community. The field of environmental economics has grown up around precisely this problem. When resource use involves positive or negative impacts on others that are not taken into account by the resource user, there are said to be externalities. We need to understand the value of those externalities, and whether they are increasing or decreasing over time. We need to understand whether the neglect of externalities means that too little or too much of the resource is being conserved. Many resources and the services they offer are public "goods" (or "bads") and so involve incentives to free-ride on the efforts of others. We need to understand when the public good nature of resources leads them to be undervalued, and so overused.

To approach the anatomy and pathology of conservation the book first explores the principles behind Hotelling's key result, as well as all the reasons why the decisions taken by people in the real world might get things wrong. It then applies these principles to a systematic review of the many dimensions of the problem of environmental conservation. It asks what decision-makers need to know if they are to make rational conservation choices, and what science currently tells us about the opportunity cost of conservation or development decisions. A decision to conserve implies that the expected growth in the value of the conserved resource is above the yield on alternative assets. A decision to convert implies the opposite. It follows that conservation and conversion decisions should both be informed by an understanding of what has to be given up in the process. We consider what is and is not known about the opportunity cost of large-scale environmental changes, and how this knowledge affects assessments about when and what to conserve.

Environmental conservation decisions are not limited to protected areas or remnant wild lands. There are conservation decisions to be made about simplified or modified landscapes, just as there are for natural landscapes. It makes little sense, however, to have the same conservation objectives in agroecosystems, production forests, wild lands, and exclusive (marine) economic zones. This book offers a common way to approach the conservation problem in different systems, while recognizing that the conservation problem itself will vary from ecosystem to ecosystem.

The background against which the book is written is complicated. A series of international assessments of the state of the science over the last three decades has revealed mounting evidence that all the earth's biomes are changing at rates unprecedented in recorded history, and that human agency is implicated in every case. Successive assessments by the Intergovernmental Panel on Climate Change (IPCC) have focused on the role of anthropogenic emissions to air and water, arguing their role in altering the general circulation system in ways that threatens the remarkable climatic stability of the Holocene.

Climate change is both a consequence and a cause of many of the issues addressed in the book. Agriculture and forestry are responsible for around 13% of carbon dioxide emission, 44% of methane emissions, and 82% of nitrous oxide emissions, or roughly 12.0 Gt of CO_2 equivalent per year. At the same time, climate change is leading to declining crop yields and lower animal growth rates in lower latitudes, but increasing crop yields and animal growth rates in higher latitudes. Agricultural pests and pathogens have also increased. Climate change exacerbates the degradation of land in coastal and estuarine areas, in drylands, and in permafrost areas. The area of drylands in drought, for example, has increased on average by around 1% per year over the last 50 years—adversely affecting 380 to 620 million people in South and East Asia, North Africa, and the Middle East. Coastal areas are particularly affected by increased rainfall intensity, flooding, rising sea levels, and stronger wave action (IPCC 2019).

Climate change is also affecting many dimensions of biodiversity. Species distributions, phenology, population dynamics, community structure, and ecosystem function are all affected by changes in temperature and precipitation. Moreover, these effects are increasing in marine, terrestrial, and freshwater ecosystems. The Global Biodiversity Assessment, the Millennium Ecosystem Assessment, and now the assessments of the Intergovernmental Platform on Biodiversity and Ecosystem Services (IPBES) have focused on the anthropogenic stresses on biodiversity and ecosystem functioning— the effect of land-use change, climate change, and species dispersal. Each is argued to have profound, negative consequences for the capacity of the planet to sustain the flow of services people obtain from ecosystems (IPBES 2019).

In much the same period, concern over the sustainability of the use humans make of the natural world has moved from the wings to center stage. Between the Brundtland Commission (World Commission on Environment and Development 1987) and the second of two major international conferences on Sustainable Development (United Nations Conference on Environment and Development 1992, United Nations 2012), sustainability has become a central concern of nearly every segment of every society on the planet. The 17 sustainable development goals adopted by the United Nations in 2015 still include environmental goals: to combat climate change; to conserve and sustainably use the oceans, seas, and marine resources; and to sustainably manage forests, combat desertification, halt and reverse land degradation, and halt biodiversity loss. However, the vast majority of goals relate to other aspects of the human condition: poverty, hunger, health, education, gender inequality, income inequality, and peace and justice among them. They also include the goal to ensure sustainable consumption and production patterns (United Nations 2015).

A papal encyclical in the same year the sustainable development goals were adopted similarly pointed to the importance of the social dimensions of the environmental problem. Aside from climate change and pollution, water scarcity, and biodiversity change, the encyclical identified societal breakdown, global inequality, and the weakness of international responses as the principal challenges to be addressed (Francis 2015). The increasing concentration of wealth in the hands of a few in the Global North and the persistence of widespread poverty in the Global South are seen as much a part of the sustainability problem as the degradation of many ecosystem processes essential for all life. Most recently, a major review of the economics of biodiversity commissioned by the UK Treasury, The Dasgupta Review, has underlined the threat posed by biodiversity change to economic growth (Dasgupta, 2021).

We have come to see the central environmental challenges of our time as symptoms of a wider malaise of the global social-ecological system. Paul Crutzen famously dubbed the late Holocene as the Anthropocene, an epoch in which the dominance of humans on earth is expected to show in the geological record (Crutzen 2002, Steffen et al. 2007). While human dominance has enabled the rapid growth of both the human population and the goods and services produced, it has also stressed the natural systems on which humans depend. Increasingly, that stress is being interpreted as threatening a set of biophysical limits within the system. Echoing the "Limits to Growth" conclusions of the Club of Rome Report (Meadows et al. 1972), the claim has been made that humans have already exceeded planetary boundaries for climate change, biosphere integrity, biogeochemical flows, and land-system change (Rockström et al. 2009, Steffen et al. 2015).

In this view, what is to be conserved at the global level is nothing less than the climatic and other biophysical characteristics of the Holocene. But if such boundaries are more than just lines in the sand—if they represent real tipping points between alternative stable states—then we may already be in a new basin of attraction. History is full of examples where people have exceeded tipping points quite blindly. It is also is full of examples where people have understood the consequences of their actions, but have been locked into behaviors that drive society beyond the point of no return. Jarad Diamond's catalogue of societal collapses includes examples of both kinds (Diamond 2005).

Against this background, the book explores both the central problem in all conservation decisions, and the many reasons why solutions to particular problems at particular spatial or temporal scales may be inconsistent with solutions to the same problems at different spatial or temporal scales. To set the scene for this we first summarize the evidence for large-scale, systematic changes in biodiversity and ecological functioning across biomes and in different social systems. We do this the better to understand, at a very broad level, what elements of the biophysical system have and have not been conserved, how this differs from one society to the next, and what humanity has gained or lost in the process. We then probe, more deeply, the relation between changes in the biological record and the way the conservation problem has been addressed by scientists.

1.2 The biological record

Successive assessments have established the main anthropogenic drivers of biodiversity change:

- direct hunting and harvesting
- habitat loss from the growth of agriculture and silviculture
- the dispersal of species between systems
- the diversion of water use for human needs
- emissions to land, water, and air.

Of these, direct hunting and harvesting is by far the longest standing source of anthropogenic stress on other species. In the 40,000 years before the Holocene, hunting by humans was implicated in the decline of most of the large-bodied vertebrates (megafauna) that went extinct in Europe, Asia, Oceana, Africa, and the Americas (Pereira et al. 2012). From the beginning of the Holocene, however, hunting was displaced as the primary anthropogenic driver of biodiversity change by the loss of habitat due to the growth of agriculture and silviculture.

Starting from a number of different locations—the Vavilov "centers of origin" in Central and South America, the Mediterranean, the Middle East, Ethiopia, Central Asia, South and Southeast Asia, and East Asia (Vavilov 1926)—agriculture has grown to become the dominant land use across much of the world. The Millennium Assessment reported that by the end of the twentieth century, agriculture accounted for between 20% and 75% of the area of eleven of thirteen terrestrial biomes (tundra; boreal forests; temperate coniferous forests; montane grasslands and shrublands; tropical and subtropical moist broadleaf forests; deserts; tropical and subtropical coniferous forests; temperate broadleaf and mixed forests; Mediterranean forests, woodlands, and scrub; tropical and subtropical dry broadleaf forests; tropical and subtropical grasslands, savannas, and shrublands; flooded grasslands and savannas; and temperate forest, steppe, and woodland). Only biomes relatively unsuited to agriculture, such as boreal forests and tundra, had remained relatively intact (Millennium Ecosystem Assessment 2005b). Currently the proportion of national land under crop and livestock production varies between 0% and 82.5% (Figure 1.1).

Since direct harvesting of wild species has remained an important source of protein throughout the Holocene, the advent of agriculture added another layer to the conservation problem confronting most communities. To the problem of which animal and plant species to promote and which to suppress

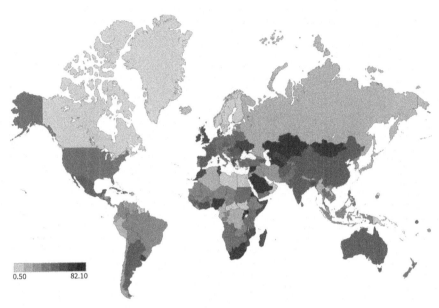

0.50   82.10

Figure 1.1 The proportion of national land under crop and livestock production in 2013.

Agricultural land refers to the share of land area that is arable, under permanent crops, and under permanent pastures. Arable land includes land defined by the FAO as land under temporary crops (double-cropped areas are counted once), temporary meadows for mowing or for pasture, land under market or kitchen gardens, and land temporarily fallow. Land abandoned as a result of shifting cultivation is excluded. Land under permanent crops is land cultivated with crops that occupy the land for long periods and need not be replanted after each harvest, such as cocoa, coffee, and rubber. This category includes land under flowering shrubs, fruit trees, nut trees, and vines, but excludes land under trees grown for wood or timber. Permanent pasture is land used for five or more years for forage, including natural and cultivated crops.

Source: Constructed from data derived from World Bank (2014).

(the problem facing farming communities) was now added to the problem of how to regulate current effort so as to protect future harvests of wild species (the problem facing hunting communities). The domestication of plants was a process that occurred more or less simultaneously in many different environments during the Holocene, and involved quite different species. Domesticated species originating in the Middle East, for example, included einkorn wheat, emmer wheat, barley, rye, lentil, pea, bitter vetch, chickpea, and flax (Lev-Yadun et al. 2000). Species originating in East Asia included rice, soybean, and foxtail millet (Jones and Liu 2009). Those originating in South America included squash, peanut, quinoa, and cotton in South America (Dillehay et al. 2007).

In all cases, the selection of which species to encourage also implied the selection of which species to suppress. Promotion of particular plants or animals implies the suppression of the competitors, predators, and pathogens of those plants or animals. In other words, the domestication of particular plants and animals in different parts of the world saw the decline of other species not as an incidental byproduct of farming but as a necessary concomitant of domestication. Effort to boost abundance of some species simultaneously implied effort to reduce the abundance of others.

The dispersal of species, the third anthropogenic driver of biodiversity change, is a consequence of the decisions people have made to engage with others—whether for commerce or conquest. In many cases people have moved species deliberately from one part of the world to another. A common feature of the early European voyages of discovery for which we have written records, for example, is that they involved more or less systematic efforts to document the characteristics of species encountered along the way, and to take specimens where feasible.[1] The identification of potentially usefully domesticated plants and animals was an important goal of the many voyages of discovery to the America's in the wake of Columbus's first voyage. Indeed, the Columbian Exchange—the movement of species between Europe and the Americas in the sixteenth century—was built around transfer of domesticated plants and animals in both directions. American species introduced to Europe included turkey, maize, manioc, potato, rubber, sunflower, tobacco, and tomato. European species introduced to the Americas included sheep, cattle, horses, goats, and pigs among animals, and bananas, barley, chickpeas, flax, hemp, millet, oats, rice, soybeans, tea, and wheat among plants (Crosby 1972, Crosby 1986).

As the people of Central America discovered to their cost, however, domesticated plants and animals were not the only species exchanged. Along with crops and livestock came pests, pathogens, and harmful commensals, such as cats and rats. American diseases brought to Europe included bejel, Chagas disease, pinta, and syphilis. In exchange, the immunologically naïve populations of the Americas were exposed to bubonic plague, cholera, diphtheria, influenza, leprosy, malaria, measles, smallpox, typhoid, typhus, and yellow fever. It has been estimated that in the century after Columbus first landed in the Caribbean, the population of Central America was reduced by the effects of these diseases by as much as 90% (McNeill 1977, McNeill 2003). Any benefits conferred by the introduction of new crops and livestock strains were dwarfed by the costs of the new diseases.

The net effect of the various stresses on natural ecosystems has been characterized as a mass extinction event—the sixth such event to appear in the geological record. The Millennium Ecosystem Assessment reported that current rates of extinction are up to 1,000 times the rate observed in the fossil record.

[1] Perhaps the best-known example is Darwin's record of the third voyage of the Beagle (Darwin 1839).

It ascribed this primarily to the conversion of natural habitat to a range of productive uses, but noted that the changes recorded in the assessment were the combined effect of multiple stressors. It found that the number of species is declining everywhere, and that the population size and/or the range of the majority of surviving species continue to be reduced. Indeed, up to 30% of remaining mammal, bird, and amphibian species are currently threatened with extinction, with freshwater aquatic species being most at risk. At the same time, it found that the distribution of remaining biodiversity is becoming more homogeneous due to the dispersal of species through trade—whether deliberately or accidentally—while genetic diversity among cultivated species has declined precipitately (Millennium Ecosystem Assessment 2005a). Nor have subsequent attempts to evaluate the state of biodiversity changed the story (Butchart et al. 2010, Secretariat of the Convention on Biological Diversity 2010).

The most recent global assessment of biodiversity (IPBES 2019) identified four main impacts of anthropogenic stress:

- Extinction risks are increasing. Approximately 25% of animals and plants are threatened, implying that around a million species face extinction, often within decades.
- Local varieties and breeds of domesticated plants and animals are disappearing. Over 500 of the roughly 6,000 domesticated breeds of mammals used for food and agriculture have already gone extinct and around 1,000 more are threatened.
- Biological communities are becoming more similar to each other in both managed and unmanaged systems. Anthropogenic dispersal of species and the adoption of common management practices has led to the extirpation of many locally adapted species.
- The rate of biological evolution is increasing. Anthropogenic evolution of species, particularly pests and pathogens, is occurring so rapidly its effects can be seen within months, in some cases.

The sixth mass extinction event continues unabated.

1.3 Implications for conservation

The conservation question raised by the biological record is: When is enough enough? This is not a trivial question. Many of the changes recorded by the Millennium Assessment involved conscious decisions by people to promote some species and to suppress others. The general aim of habitat conversion has been to increase the abundance of domesticated plants and animals, along with the species on which those plants and animals depend, and to reduce the abundance of competitors and predators—pests and pathogens. There have been many unintended consequences to these choices, but it is nonetheless reasonable to say that some level of habitat conversion is warranted by the benefits generated through the production of foods, fuels, fibers, freshwater, and the like. Have we exceeded the optimal level of conversion? To begin to answer this question, we need to know what the costs and benefits of conversion and conservation are.

The Millennium Assessment approached the problem through the classification of the benefits offered by different ecological communities and ecosystems. Termed "ecosystem services," the benefits were argued to fall into four main groups: provisioning services, cultural services, supporting services, and regulating services. The provisioning services include production of foods, fuels, fibers, pharmaceuticals, and other consumable items. The cultural services include benefits such as recreation, amenity, and scientific understanding. These are benefits that do not necessarily deplete the environmental stocks that generate the services. The supporting services include processes such as photosynthesis and nutrient cycling—both essential to the functioning of the underlying ecosystems. The regulating services comprise the buffering functions offered by the diversity of genes, species, and functional groups within those ecosystems (Millennium Ecosystem Assessment 2005b).

The provisioning and cultural services describe environmentally derived goods and services that enter final demand: that is, that directly satisfy peoples wants. The supporting and regulating services describe the ecosystem processes and functions that underpin production of the provisioning and cultural services. The provisioning services can be interpreted as the processes that generate plant and animal products—food and cash crops, livestock products, timber, water, genetic material, and the like. Many are supplied through more or less well-functioning markets. The cultural services describe peoples' nonconsumptive uses of the environment, including recreation, tourism, education, science, and learning. They include more intangible benefits such as the spiritual, religious, aesthetic, and inspirational well-being that people derive from the world about them, and the moral satisfaction generated by the preservation of threatened or endangered species. Some cultural services, like ecotourism, are supplied through well-functioning markets. Most are not served by markets, but are regulated by custom, or by traditional taboos, rights, and obligations.

The supporting and regulating services describe the ecological processes that underpin production of the provisioning and cultural services, and that moderate the impact of environmental variability on production. The supporting services include ecosystem processes and functions such as soil formation, photosynthesis, primary production, and nutrient, carbon, and water cycling. The regulating services depend on the diversity of functional groups of species, and moderate the effects of environmental perturbations on air quality, climate, water quality, erosion, pests and diseases, and natural hazards. They reduce variability in the production of plant and animal products, or other provisioning services. The timing and magnitude of water runoff, flooding, and groundwater recharge, for example, is strongly affected by the composition of plants in watersheds. The value of both supporting and regulating services derives from the value of the provisioning and cultural services they support, and depends on the regime of stresses and shocks experienced. But few are allocated through functioning markets. Many supporting or regulating services are public goods at scales that span national boundaries.

From a conservation perspective, what is important about changes in the combination of goods and services consumed by any community is that they also imply changes in the combination of the assets needed to produce those goods and services—the natural capital needed to generate ecosystem services and the produced capital needed to generate other goods and services. Indeed, this point is critical to all that follows. In the same way that demand for labor stems from demand for the things that labor can produce, so demand for the environmental and nonenvironmental stocks that underpin consumption choices *derives* from demand for final goods and services. The demand for land for the production of food crops, for example, derives from the demand for food. The demand for land as habitat for wild species derives from demand for the conservation of wild species. The demand for watershed protection derives from the demand for water.

It follows that the consumption of goods and services today has potential implications for the consumption of goods and services in the future. Specifically, if consumption of goods and services today reduces the produced or natural capital stocks available in the future, it may force a reduction in consumption of the same goods and services in the future. A pattern of consumption is sustainable only if the implied use of capital stocks is sustainable. The classic conservation problem confronting pre-Holocene hunter-gatherer communities, and every community since, is to determine what can be harvested today without compromising harvests in the future. This is the problem of determining which natural assets to conserve from one time period to the next. In one form or another, it is the problem addressed in much of this book.

The field of conservation biology was developed in the 1970s as a response to the growing anthropogenic pressure on wildlife. One of the architects of the new field, Michael Soulé, described its focus in the following terms: "Conservation biology . . . addresses the biology of species, communities, and ecosystems that are perturbed, either directly or indirectly, by human activities or other agents. Its goal is to provide principles and tools for preserving biological diversity. . . . ethical norms are a genuine part of conservation biology, as they are in all mission- or crisis-oriented disciplines" (Soulé 1985). Although the field is now changing, this description still stands. So, for example, one of the most successful texts in conservation biology describes it as a field developed in response to the challenge of preserving species and ecosystems that aims (a) to document the full range of biodiversity on the planet, (b) to uncover human impacts on species, genes, and ecosystems, and (c) to prevent species extinction, to maintain genetic diversity within species, and to protect and restore ecological communities and associated ecosystem functions (Primack 2014). While (a) and (b) describe objective scientific goals, (c) does not. Conservation biology may have become more human-centric in the intervening years but the normative goals remain: the prevention of extinction, maintenance of genetic diversity, and ecological restoration—the mission of a mission-oriented discipline (Cardinale, Primack, & Murdoch, 2020).

The scientific problem identified by Soulé was to apply the principles of ecology, biogeography, and population genetics to the analysis of the causes and consequences of biodiversity change. Although biodiversity writ large is the diversity of genes, species and ecosystems (Wilson 1988), Soulé's scientific problem pushes the field toward a particular aspect of diversity. Soulé argued that species are the result of coevolutionary processes, are interdependent, and frequently complementary in their functions. Because of this, the extirpation or extinction of one species has the potential to ramify through the system (Soulé 1985). To understand the direct and indirect effects of species extirpation or extinction, conservation biologists have sought to understand the role of diversity in the functioning of ecosystems. The relevant measure of diversity this implies is less a measure of species richness and abundance, or of the taxonomic distinctness or phylogenetic distance between species, and more a measure of the functional traits that enable different species to perform in different ways. It is important to know the effects of a change in the number of species performing some function, and especially whether there exist thresholds of diversity below (or above) which ecosystems lose functionality.

The scientific problem therefore tends to privilege a classification of organisms that puts them into functional groups (such as grasses, C3 plants, C4 plants, and legumes). The number of functional groups in an ecological community then defines its functional diversity, and the number and relative abundance of species bearing the traits of a particular functional group defines the diversity of that group. The consequences of change in the diversity of functional groups can then be measured in terms of the level and stability and the functions performed by the group.

We return to the evidence on the impact of changes in the diversity of different functional groups in later chapters. Here we note only that the scientific agenda of conservation biology maps closely into the methods developed by economists to uncover the value of the biotic and abiotic stocks of ecosystems. Research on the consequences of changes in functional diversity and the diversity of functional groups is effectively research on the production functions that underpin all provisioning and cultural ecosystem services. In coupled social ecological systems, the diversity of functional groups includes the variety of cultivated crops, crop pests, wild crop relatives, and weedy species. It includes the variety of biologically derived fuels and fibers, and the variety of diseases that affect humans, animals, and plants.

At the same time, however, human well-being is also affected by change in the diversity of functional groups that are not directly involved the production of highly valued ecosystem services. The microorganisms that move carbon, nutrients, and water into and out of ecosystems are as important for ecological functions that support the production of valued ecosystem services as they are for the functioning of systems without humans. By understanding the biogeochemical processes involved in ecosystem functioning, and by understanding the linkages between ecosystem functioning and the production of valued ecosystem services, we are able to derive the value of the underlying biotic and abiotic stocks—the atmospheric, lithospheric, and hydrospheric pools of carbon, nutrients, and water, together with the plants, animals, and microorganisms that move carbon, nutrients, and water into and out of the ecosystem.

But what of the normative goals of conservation biology? How do they map into the science of conservation? Soulé's normative statements are clearly not refutable by reference to evidence. They are statements of what should be, based on opinion not fact. They are beliefs, not testable hypotheses. They are also deeply and widely held convictions about the ethical response to the increasing number of species extinctions with long antecedents in American philosophy and ethics, reaching back to Ralph Waldo Emerson and Henry David Thoreau, to John Muir and Aldo Leopold.

To get a sense of what these convictions imply for the science of conservation, consider the statements made by a group of scientists (Mangel et al. 1996) who set out to elucidate the principles of conservation biology originally suggested by (Holt and Talbot 1978). Their starting point was a simple assertion that "The consequences of resource utilization *and the implementation of principles of resource conservation* are the responsibility of the parties having jurisdiction over the resource or, in the absence of clear jurisdiction, with those having jurisdiction over the users of the resource." The principles of resource conservation were then spelled out as a series of normative statements, the gist of which was that any resource utilization should be constrained by an obligation to maintain the state of ecosystems so as to preserve future options, to guard against irreversible change, to embed a safety factor to account for uncertainty and imperfect information, and to avoid unnecessary waste (Mangel et al. 1996).

The protection of future options mirrored the main criterion for sustainability asserted in the Brundtland Report (World Commission on Environment and Development 1987). Indeed, this was used as the primary justification for maintaining biodiversity at genetic, species, population, and ecosystem levels within "natural boundaries of variation" (Mangel et al. 1996). It was also clear, however, that the principles privileged naturalness. The goals of conservation were to avoid fragmentation of natural areas, to maintain natural processes, to avoid disruption of food webs, and so on. The corresponding scientific agenda was to understand the behavior of natural systems, and the response of natural systems to anthropogenic stress. Since many biological processes were recognized to be nonlinear, involving critical thresholds, it was argued that the principles implied the need to identify, understand, and accommodate complex natural ecosystem dynamics (Mangel et al. 1996).

To see what the normative goals of conservation biology imply for the social dimensions of the problem, consider the value that species conservation has for people. Mangel et al. recognized that human resource use decisions are value-driven, implying the need to understand the basis of value and the incentive effects of changes in value. Since conservation is a use much like any other, the goals of conservation biology imply values that favor conservation over other uses. Within the field of conservation biology this is reflected in a two-pronged approach, only one of which has implications for science.

One strategy has been to assert the existence of values that are supposedly independent of the values that drive all other uses of natural resources. Therefore, Soulé argued that biodiversity has intrinsic value independent of any instrumental or utilitarian value it might have: "Species have value in themselves, a value neither conferred nor revocable, but springing from a species' long evolutionary heritage and potential or even from the mere fact of its existence" (Soulé 1985).

We consider the question of the intrinsic value of species in more detail in later chapters. Here we note only that this is a statement of faith rather than fact.

A second strategy has been to identify the conservation value of species through the adoption of criteria that include rareness, endangerment, richness, endemicity, and the like. Examples include the geographical distribution of taxa, and the number of taxa in some location. The more restricted the geographical distribution of a taxon, the greater its conservation value. The larger the number of taxa in some location, the greater the conservation value is of that location. This strategy engages the scientific agenda in ways that are much easier to see. Given a set of criteria, it becomes possible to identify the relative conservation value of both species and geographical areas. Indeed, two of the most widely used instruments for guiding conservation effort—biodiversity hotspots and the International Union for Conservation of Nature (IUCN)'s Red List of endangered species—are a direct result of efforts to identify the relative conservation value of species and habitats.

The biodiversity hotspots, originally introduced by Norman Myers (Myers 1988), reflected a broad-brush attempt to identify the areas of the world of greatest conservation value by two criteria: the number of endemic species they contain, and the extent of habitat loss they experience (Table 1.1).

Since that time the effort to extend the classification of habitats using either the same or different criteria has led to a proliferation of hotspots, and the identification of more areas of high conservation value due to the presence of restricted range species. In 1988 Myers identified just 10 hotspots. By the end of the twentieth century the number had risen to 25 and covered 44% of all vascular plant species, and 35% of all species in four vertebrate groups on 1.4% of the earth's land surface (Myers et al. 2000). By 2015, 35 hotspots covered 17% of the earth's land surface, and maintained 77% of all endemic plant species, 43% of vertebrates (60% of threatened mammals and birds, and 80% of threatened amphibians) (Marchese 2015) (Figure 1.2).

In a parallel development, the IUCN Red List of endangered species classifies individual taxa on the basis of threat (or a mixture of threat and rarity) (Robbirt et al. 2006). As is the case with hotspots, there have been changes in both the criteria by which Red List assessments have been made, and the way that the Red List is used to generate an index of extinction probabilities, the Red list Index (Butchart et al. 2007). Successive lists report

Table 1.1 The growth of biodiversity hotspots.

(Myers 1988)	(Myers 1990)	(Myers 2000)	(Mittermeier et al. 2004)
Uplands of Western Amazonia	Uplands of Western Amazonia	Tropical Andes	Tropical Andes
Western Ecuador	Western Ecuador	Choco/Darien/West Ecuador	
Colombian Choco	Colombian Choco		Tumbes-Choco-Magdalena
Atlantic Coast Brazil	Atlantic Coast Brazil	Atlantic Coast Brazil	Atlantic Forest
		Brazilian Cerrado	Cerrado
	Central Chile	Central Chilea	Chilean Winter Rainfall and Valdivian Forest
		Mesoamerica	Mesoamerica
			Madrean Pine-Oak Woodlands
		Caribbean	Caribbean Islands
	California Floristic Province	California Floristic Province	California Floristic Province
	Ivory Coast	Guinean Forest of West Africa	Guinean Forest of West Africa
	Cape Floristic Region	Cape Floristic Province	Cape Floristic Region
		Succulent Karoo	Succulent Karoo
			Maputaland, Pondoland, Albany
	Tanzania	Eastern Arc and Coastal Forest of Tanzania/Kenya	Eastern Afromontane Coastal Forests
			Horn of Africa
Eastern Madagascar	Eastern Madagascar	Madagascar & Indian Ocean Islands	Madagascar & Indian Ocean Islands
		Mediterranean Basin	Mediterranean Basin
		Caucasus	Caucasus
			Irano-Anatolian
			Mountains of Central Asia
	Western Ghats in India	Western Ghats and Sri Lanka	Western Ghats and Sri Lanka
	Southwestern Sri Lanka	Mountains of South-Central China	Mountains of South-Central China
Eastern Himalayas	Eastern Himalayas	Indo-Burmae	Indo-Burma, Himalaya

Continued

Table 1.1 *Continued*

(Myers 1988)	(Myers 1990)	(Myers 2000)	(Mittermeier et al. 2004)
Peninsular Malaysia	Peninsular Malaysia		
Northern Borneo	Northern Borneo	Sundaland, Wallacea	Sundaland, Wallacea
Philippines	Philippines	Philippines	Philippines
			Japan
	Southwest Australia	Southwest Australia	Southwest Australia
			East Melanesian Islands
		New Zealand	New Zealand
New Caledonia	New Caledonia	New Caledonia	New Caledonia
		Polynesia, Micronesia	Polynesia, Micronesia

Source: (Marchese 2015).

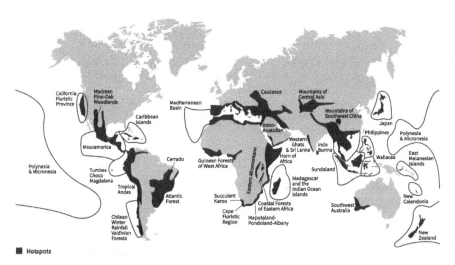

■ Hotspots

Figure 1.2 Terrestrial and marine hotspots.

This often-seen image, originally due to Conservation International, describes the first 34 of the 36 biodiversity hotspots designated to date. For current hotspots see Critical Ecosystem Partnership Fund (2020). A shapefile of hotspots is available from Hoffman et al. (2016).

progressively greater numbers of threatened species (IUCN 2004, IUCN 2014), which reflects both change in the level of effort given to the classification and change in real conditions. As in the case of hotspots, too, the science lies in the identification of species satisfying particular criteria.

The focus on anthropogenic threats to species richness, and particularly the richness of endemic species, is at least partially reflected in two strands of research in the economics of conservation that will be explored later. One is in the analysis of the demand for naturalness (Eichner and Tschirhart 2007), and the other is in the specification of the optimization problem where diversity is measured in terms of the phylogenetic distance between species (Weitzman 1992). Both take the normative goals of conservation biology as given, and ask what economic problem they give rise to.

1.4 Plan of the book

We call the approach adopted in this book the Hotelling approach. This recognizes the fact that the principles were first spelled out in Hotelling's 1931 analysis of the optimal extraction of mineral resources. We are not the first to recognize Hotelling's contribution in this area. In 1981, 50 years after his paper appeared, an article by Deverajan and Fisher had this to say: "There are only a few fields in economics whose antecedents can be traced to a single, seminal article. One such field is natural resource economics . . . its origin is widely recognized as Harold Hotelling's 1931 paper . . . it . . . not only presented the canonical model for modern theorists to build on, but also anticipated the relevant issues—such as the effects of uncertainty and the presence of externalities—by almost a generation" (Deverajan and Fisher 1981).

The same principles now appear in almost every paper on the optimal management of dynamical resource systems. They are frequently thought of as principles governing optimal extraction or harvest, but conservation and extraction or harvest are but two sides of the same coin. A solution to the optimal extraction problem is also a solution to the optimal conservation problem. When resource managers decide how much to extract or harvest in some period, they also decide how much to leave or conserve in the same period. When they decide how much of an ecosystem to convert to human use, they also decide how much to conserve. All we do is draw attention to the fact that all conservation problems have a similar structure, and can benefit from application of the same principles. The challenge is to understand the value of resources—to recognize that the same resource may have value to different people for different reasons, and that values may change at different rates.

The book is divided into four parts. Part I offers an economic theory of conservation that generalizes Hotelling's (1931) results. We show that the Hotelling principle is embodied in all subsequent work on the optimal exploitation of both nonrenewable and renewable natural resources. In fact, we show that every time we find the first order necessary conditions for the optimal management of natural resources, we include a restatement of the

Hotelling principle that resources should be exploited only up to the point where the growth in their value to society is equal to the rate of return on alternative assets. The arguments offered in this part are somewhat mathematical, but for those who are willing to take the formal arguments as read, we include discursive summaries at the end of each chapter.

Part II focuses on the valuation of goods and services, and of the assets underlying the production of goods and services. Given that conservation in the Hotelling approach depends on valuation, this step is critical. Since many natural resources are not bought and sold in the marketplace, however, we cannot rely on market prices. We often need to estimate resource values using a range of nonmarket methods. The chapters in this part explore the options open to us to estimate nonmarket values.

Part III considers the issues involved in aligning the private and social value of environmental assets. Even where resources are exchanged in the market, their price may be a poor approximation of their value. We may need to add in external effects or externalities, particularly where resources are public goods. We show how interventions that confront resources users with the true social opportunity cost of their behavior can be thought of as conservation instruments. Once again, where we make formal arguments, we also include a discursive summary of those arguments.

Part IV then applies the Hotelling approach to a discussion of the main issues in environmental conservation. This includes the classic approach to conservation—protected areas, but also includes conservation in production systems beyond protected areas. We consider the problem of scale, and discuss the impact of changes in both temporal and spatial scale. While we focus on two spatial scales—national and international—we acknowledge that conservation policy and practice play out at multiple spatial scales, and we spell out the principles that apply to conservation that affects people at different scales.

References

Butchart, S. H., H. Resit Akçakaya, J. Chanson, J. E. Baillie, B. Collen, S. Quader, W. R. Turner, R. Amin, S. N. Stuart, and C. Hilton-Taylor. 2007. Improvements to the Red List index. PLoS One 2:e140.

Butchart, S., M. Walpole, B. Collen, A. van Strien, J. P. W. Scharlemann, R. E. A. Almond, J. E. M. Baillie, B. Bomhard, C. Brown, J. Bruno, K. E. Carpenter, G. M. Carr, J. Chanson, A. M. Chenery, J. Csirke, N. C. Davidson, F. Dentener, M. Foster, A. Galli, J. N. Galloway, P. Genovesi, R. D. Gregory, M. Hockings, V. Kapos, J.-F. Lamarque, F. Leverington, J. Loh, M. A. McGeoch, L. McRae, A. Minasyan, M. H.

Morcillo, T. E. E. Oldfield, D. Pauly, S. Quader, C. Revenga, J. R. Sauer, B. Skolnik, D. Spear, D. Stanwell-Smith, S. N. Stuart, A. Symes, M. Tierney, T. D. Tyrrell, J.-C. Vie, and R. Watson. 2010. Global biodiversity: indicators of recent declines. Science 328:1164–1168.

Cardinale, B. J., R. B. Primack, and J. D. Murdoch. 2020. Conservation Biology. Oxford University Press, New York.

Critical Ecosystem Partnership Fund. 2020. Explore the biodiversity hotspots. Conservation International, Arlington, VA.

Crosby, A. W. 1972. The Columbian Exchange: the biological and cultural consequences of 1492. Greenwood Press, Westport, CT.

Crosby, A. W. 1986. Ecological imperialism: the biological expansion of Europe, 900–1900. Cambridge University Press, New York.

Crutzen, P. J. 2002. Geology of mankind: the anthropocene. Nature 415:23.

Darwin, C. 1839. Journal and remarks. 1832–1836 (Voyages of the Adventure and Beagle, Volume III). Henry Colburn, London.

Dasgupta, P. 2021. The Economics of Biodiversity: The Dasgupta Review, H.M. Treasury, London.

Deverajan, S., and A. Fisher. 1981. Hotelling's "economics of exhaustible resources" fifty years later. Journal of Economic Literature XIX:65–73.

Diamond, J. 2005. Collapse. Penguin Books, New York.

Dillehay, T. D., J. Rossen, T. C. Andres, and D. E. Williams. 2007. Preceramic adoption of peanut, squash, and cotton in Northern Peru. Science 316:1890–1893.

Eichner, T., and J. Tschirhart. 2007. Efficient ecosystem services and naturalness in an ecological economic model. Environmental and Resource Economics 37:733–755.

Francis, P. 2015. Laudato si' encyclical letter "on care for our common home." Vatican Publishing House, Vatican City.

Hoffman, M., K. Koenig, G. Bunting, J. Costanza, and K. J. Williams. 2016. Biodiversity hotspots (version 2016.1). Zenodo. http://doi.org/10.5281/zenodo.3261807.

Holt, S. J., and L. M. Talbot. 1978. New principles for the conservation of wild living resources. Wildlife Monographs 59:3–33.

Hotelling, H. 1931. The economics of exhaustible resources. Journal of Political Economy 39:137–175.

IPBES. 2019. Summary for policymakers of the global assessment report on biodiversity and ecosystem services of the Intergovernmental Science-Policy Platform on Biodiversity and Ecosystem Services. Intergovernmental Science-Policy Platform on Biodiversity and Ecosystem Services, Bonn, Germany.

IPCC. 2019. Climate change and land: An IPCC special report on climate change, desertification, land degradation, sustainable land management, food security, and greenhouse gas fluxes in terrestrial ecosystems in 2019. WMO/UNEP, Geneva.

IUCN. 2004. The IUCN Red List of threatened species. IUCN, Gland.

IUCN. 2014. The IUCN Red List of threatened species. IUCN, Gland.

Jones, M. K., and X. Liu. 2009. Origins of agriculture in East Asia. Science 324:730–731.

Lev-Yadun, S., A. Gopher, and S. Abbo. 2000. The cradle of agriculture. Science 288:1602–1603.

Mangel, M., L. M. Talbot, G. K. Meffe, M. T. Agardy, D. L. Alverson, J. Barlow, D. B. Botkin, G. Budowski, T. Clark, J. Cooke, R. H. Crozier, P. K. Dayton, D. L. Elder, C. W. Fowler, S. Funtowicz, J. Giske, R. J. Hofman, S. J. Holt, S. R. Kellert, L. A. Kimball, D. Ludwig, K. Magnusson, B. S. Malayang, C. Mann, E. A. Norse, S. P. Northridge, W. F. Perrin, C. Perrings, R. M. Peterman, G. B. Rabb, H. A. Regier, J. E. Reynolds, K. Sherman, M. P. Sissenwine, T. D. Smith, A. Starfield, R. J. Taylor, M. F. Tillman, C. Toft, J. R. Twiss, J. Wilen, and T. P. Young. 1996. Principles for the conservation of wild living resources. Ecological Applications 6:338–362.

Marchese, C. 2015. Biodiversity hotspots: a shortcut for a more complicated concept. Global Ecology and Conservation 3:297–309.

McNeill, J. R. 2003. Europe's place in the global history of biological exchange. Landscape Research 28:33–39.

McNeill, W. H. 1977. Plagues and people. Anchor Books, New York.

Meadows, D. H., D. L. Meadows, J. Randers, and W. W. Behrens. 1972. The limits to growth. Universe Books, New York.

Millennium Ecosystem Assessment. 2005a. Ecosystems and human well-being: biodiversity synthesis. World Resources Institute, Washington, DC.

Millennium Ecosystem Assessment. 2005b. Ecosystems and human well-being: general synthesis. Island Press, Washington DC.

Mittermeier, R., P. Gil, and M. Hoffman. 2004. Hotspots revisited: earth's biologically richest and most endangered ecoregions. CEMEX/Agrupacion Sierra Madre, Sierra Madre.

Myers, N. 1988. Threatened biotas: "hot spots" in tropical forests. Environmentalist 8:187–208.

Myers, N. 1990. The biodiversity challenge: expanded hot-spots analysis. Environmentalist 10:243–256.

Myers, N., R. A. Mittermeier, C. G. Mittermeier, G. A. B. da Fonseca, and J. Kent. 2000. Biodiversity hotspots for conservation priorities. Nature 403:853–858.

Pereira, H. M., L. M. Navarro, I. S. Martins, R. Dirzo, and P. Raven. 2012. Global biodiversity change: the bad, the good, and the unknown global state of biodiversity and loss. Annual Review of Environment and Resources 37:25–50.

Perrings, C., and G. Halkos. 2012. Who cares about biodiversity? optimal conservation and transboundary biodiversity externalities. Environmental and Resource Economics 52:585–608.

Primack, R. B. 2014. Essentials of conservation biology. Sinauer, Sunderland, MA.

Robbirt, K., D. Roberts, and J. Hawkins. 2006. Comparing IUCN and probabilistic assessments of threat: do IUCN Red List criteria conflate rarity and threat? Biodiversity Conservation 15:1903.

Rockström, J., W. Steffen, K. Noone, Å. Persson, F. S. Chapin, E. F. Lambin, T. M. Lenton, M. Scheffer, C. Folke, and H. J. Schellnhuber. 2009. A safe operating space for humanity. Nature 461:472–475.

Secretariat of the Convention on Biological Diversity. 2010. Global biodiversity outlook 3. Convention on Biological Diversity, Montreal.

Soulé, M. E. 1985. What is conservation biology? Bioscience 35:727–734.

Steffen, W., P. J. Crutzen, and J. R. McNeill. 2007. The Anthropocene: are humans now overwhelming the great forces of nature? AMBIO: A Journal of the Human Environment 36:614–621.

Steffen, W., K. Richardson, J. Rockström, S. E. Cornell, I. Fetzer, E. M. Bennett, R. Biggs, S. R. Carpenter, W. de Vries, and C. A. de Wit. 2015. Planetary boundaries: guiding human development on a changing planet. Science 347:1259855.

United Nations. 2012. United Nations Conference on sustainable development. United Nations, New York.

United Nations. 2015. Sustainable development goals. United Nations, New York.

United Nations Conference on Environment and Development. 1992. Rio Declaration on Environment and Development United Nations Environment Programme, Nairobi.

Vavilov, N. I. 1926. Studies on the origin of cultivated plants. Institute of Applied Botany and Plant Breeding, Leningrad.

Weitzman, M. L. 1992. On diversity. Quarterly Journal of Economics 107:363–405.

Wilson, E. O., ed. 1988. Biodiversity. National Academy Press, Washington DC.

World Bank. 2014. Agricultural land (% of land area). World Bank, Washington, DC.

World Commission on Environment and Development. 1987. Our common future. Island Press, Washington, DC.

PART I

THE ECONOMIC THEORY
OF CONSERVATION

2
The Decision Problem

Without that sense of security which property gives, the land would still be uncultivated.

—François Quesnay, *Tableau Economique*, 1758

2.1 Introduction

When should we maintain some stock in its current state, and when should we convert it to a different state? That is the essence of the conservation problem. The protection of natural habitats or watersheds, the maintenance of the population of an exploited species, the preservation of ex situ collections of germplasm, the curation of art or natural history museum exhibits, the protection of the value of a portfolio of financial assets, and the listing of nationally important buildings or monuments are all examples of conservation problems. To understand the principles at work in deciding what to conserve and what to convert, we exploit the fact that there exists a very powerful unifying theory of conservation in the work of Harold Hotelling. In the next three chapters we show that Hotelling provides a simple and intuitive test of when it is optimal to maintain an object/resource/system in some state, and when it is optimal to convert it to an alternative state (Hotelling 1931).

By focusing on the expected change in the value of resources in different states, Hotelling's approach allows us to see conservation in the current state as one among many alternative future uses. Conservation decisions accordingly reflect the factors that influence the value of resources in these alternative states—relative scarcity, technology, preferences, social norms and mores, legal requirements, international agreements, and the like. We show, for example, that when national parks are created or delisted this reflects changes both in the conservation value of parkland and other park assets, and in the commercial value of adjacent land.

A general theory of conservation should be broad enough to deal with a wide range of assets. It should enable us to understand the decision to hold or sell stocks and bonds as well as the decision to hold or sell natural resources.

Conservation. Charles Perrings and Ann Kinzig, Oxford University Press (2021). © Oxford University Press.
DOI: 10.1093/oso/9780190613600.003.0002

It should make the decision to extract nonrenewables such as minerals, oil, gas, and fossil water as transparent as the decision to harvest or protect wild or domestic populations of fish, mammals, birds, plants, soils, and water. It should also help us determine how to limit the stress placed on forest systems, grasslands, freshwater systems, and marine systems.

The questions posed by Hotelling were twofold. First, he was interested in the problem of how to value a natural asset such as an ore body. Second, he was interested in the question of how best to use the asset. He asked, for example, in what conditions it would be optimal to mine out an ore body within a finite time, and in what conditions it should be left in place indefinitely. Hotelling's approach turns out to provide sufficient information to decide whether to conserve assets of any kind, and for how long. Irrespective of the type of asset, knowledge of its value and how that value is expected to change over time is sufficient to determine whether and when the asset should be conserved or converted.

Note that value does not necessarily imply a money metric. The value of an asset is a measure of what an individual or community is willing to give up to secure the asset in some state. In some cases, it will be possible to assign a monetary value to this. In others, it will not. If a country chooses to conserve a national park, for example, the implication is that it expects the value of the park, when conserved, to increase at a rate at least equal to the rate of return on the best alternative investment. This does not necessarily require that it formally puts a dollar value on the species conserved in the park. It requires only that it can judge whether conservation is a better option than conversion, knowing what is given up in the process.

There are two qualifications to be made. The first is that Hotelling was interested only in assets that are scarce in the sense that their allocation involves an opportunity cost—something has to be given up to get them. Nonscarce resources do not pose an interesting conservation question. Logically, if people are unable to reduce the amount of a resource through their actions, that resource will automatically be conserved. There is no conservation choice to be made. The second qualification is that the answer to the conservation problem is conditioned by available information. The valuation of any asset depends on the information available to the asset holder, and may be expected to change with a change in information. In the late nineteenth century, for example, Thomas Huxley famously observed that there was no meaningful conservation problem involved in the exploitation of marine resources: "The sea which shuts us in, at the same time opens up its supplies of food of almost unlimited extent" (Huxley 1883). Huxley's comment was made, unfortunately, at just the moment that a number of wild capture fisheries were beginning to decline as a result of overfishing. At the moment he made the claim it was consistent with available information, but that information was about to change.

We begin this chapter by reviewing the basics of decision theory as it applies to the management of environmental resources. In so doing, we illustrate principles that apply to all economic problems—not just those involving conservation decisions. These principles guide trade-offs between goods and services consumed by individuals or communities, or between inputs employed by households, firms, or public enterprises. We also identify the elements of conservation and other decision problems. These elements are common to all problems involving purposeful behavior and resource scarcity. For readers willing to take the math for granted, we include a discursive summary at the end of the chapter.

2.2 Elements of the decision problem

The benefits of conversion and conservation alike fall into four main groups: provisioning services, cultural services, supporting services, and regulating services. Recall that the provisioning services are primarily the production of foods, fuels, fibers, pharmaceuticals, and other consumable items. These are "goods" in the common description "goods and services". The cultural services are primarily flows that leave the underlying environmental stocks intact, such as recreation, amenity, and scientific understanding. These are "services" in the common description "goods and services". The supporting services are primarily ecological processes such as photosynthesis and nutrient cycling—both essential to the functioning of the underlying ecosystems. Finally, the regulating services are the buffering functions provided by the diversity of genes, species, and functional groups within ecosystems. They regulate the flow of provisioning and cultural services (Millennium Ecosystem Assessment 2005).

The provisioning and cultural services directly satisfy peoples' wants. Neglecting environmental interactions between groups of people, we can express the preferences of the ith group of individuals for ecosystem services via a social utility or welfare function of the general form:

$$U_i = U_i\big(x_i(K_i), y_i(N_i)\big) \tag{2.1}$$

where y_i denotes the provisioning and cultural services, and x_i denotes all other goods and services consumed by the community. U_i, an index of the well-being of the ith community, depends directly on its arguments, the amount of all goods and services consumed, x_i, y_i. But notice that the welfare of the ith community indirectly depends on two other things. K_i denotes the stock of all nonenvironmental assets used in the production of x_i, referred to as produced capital, and N_i denotes biotic and abiotic environmental stocks used in the production of y_i, referred to as natural capital. The functions $x_i(K_i)$ and $y_i(N_i)$ are production functions. They indicate how output of the goods and services consumed by the community depend on available nonenvironmental and environmental assets. The form of such functions depends on both the technology employed, and on the biogeochemical processes involved. So the form of the function $y_i(N_i)$ reflects ecosystem functions and processes—the regulating and supporting services generated by the biotic and abiotic stocks that make up ecosystems. Of course, this is too simple to capture any real system. Production of x_i frequently involves environmental assets and production of y_i frequently involves nonenvironmental assets. But it enables us to explore the main properties of the decision processes involved in conservation.

As a first approximation we suppose that the well-being of the community is increasing in all goods and services (the first derivatives of the social utility function with respect to its arguments are positive), but that the affect saturates (the second derivatives are negative). That is $U_i' > 0, U_i'' < 0$. So more is preferred to less, but each additional unit of any good or service adds less to welfare than the last. We will consider the case where some things that are consumed are wholly undesirable—involving "bads" or disservices—later. While goods and services add to the well-being of the community, however, they do not necessarily add to well-being equally. Some goods and services may be preferred to others.

We are interested only in the case where communities have limited resources. If resources are unlimited there is no conservation problem, and the community does not have to make choices between alternative goods and services. If acquiring more of one good or service involves a reduction in the amount that can be had of other goods and services, the community faces a choice about the rate at which they would be willing to substitute one for the other. All of the environmental changes recorded by the Millennium Ecosystem Assessment, for example, involve substitutions between goods and services. We ordinarily expect that the rate at which people are willing to substitute different goods and services depends on the relative scarcity of goods and services. Specifically, we ordinarily assume *diminishing marginal rates of substitution*—that a community's willingness to trade off one good or service against others diminishes, the less the community has of that good or service. Note that a diminishing marginal rate of substitution between x_i and y_i also means that all combinations of x_i and y_i that are preferred to some given combination, x_i^*, y_i^*, form a convex set. The implication is that well-balanced combinations of goods and services are preferred to combinations that are skewed toward a single good or service.

People in the ith community will select the combination of goods and services that is best for them, given their preferences over the alternatives. Those preferences will give rise to rational choices if they are both *complete* and *transitive*. Completeness means that if A and B are two different outcomes (two combinations of goods and services for example) people can always specify whether A is preferred to B, B is preferred to A, or A and B are equally preferred. Transitivity means that if A is preferred to B, and B is preferred to another outcome C, then A will be preferred to C. So for our particular case, the ith community will, at a moment in time, solve the following problem:

$$Max_{x_i, y_i} U_i = U_i\left(x_i\left(K_i\right), y_i\left(N_i\right)\right) \tag{2.2}$$

subject to the resources available to the community at that moment:

$$p_x x_i + p_y y_i = R_i \tag{2.3}$$

p_x, p_y denote "prices" of x, y, and R_i denotes the resources available to the ith community at that moment. Note that prices, in this context, are measures of the resources required to secure a unit of x or y. The case where resources take the form of a money income denominated in a particular currency, and where prices are similarly denominated in that currency, is quite special. In many cases, the resources available to communities will take a different form, and prices will not be monetary.

In this problem, $Max_{x_i, y_i} U_i = U_i\left(x_i\left(K_i\right), y_i\left(N_i\right)\right)$ is referred to as the community's objective function, and $p_x x_i + p_y y_i = R_i$ is a constraint. The objective function describes what the community is trying to achieve. The constraint describes the conditions they have to satisfy in the process. A common approach to the solution of such constrained optimization problems is to form a new function out of the objective and constraint functions, called a Lagrangian function after the eighteenth-century French-Italian mathematician, Joseph-Louis Lagrange. The new function sets the constraint function equal to zero, multiplies it by a variable (the Lagrange multiplier), and adds the result to the original objective function. The resulting Lagrangian function

$$L\left(x_i, y_i, \lambda_i\right) = U_i\left(x_i\left(K_i\right), y_i\left(N_i\right)\right) + \lambda_i\left(R_i - p_x x_i + p_y y_i\right) \tag{2.4}$$

is then optimized by finding the values of x_i, y_i at which the constraint is satisfied, and at which U_i is at a maximum. The Lagrange multiplier, λ_i, has an interesting and important interpretation. It is a measure of the marginal impact
of a change in the constraint on social utility—the marginal social utility of
income. More generally, it is referred to as the shadow value of the constraint.
To optimize the Lagrangian function we first identify a set of conditions that
are necessary for the function to be at a maximum. These conditions are that
the partial derivatives of the function with respect to x_i, y_i and λ_i are equal to
zero, implying that any further change in the values of x_i, y_i and λ_i has no impact on well-being. For this problem the first order necessary conditions are
as follows:

$$\frac{\partial L_i}{\partial x_i} = \frac{\partial U_i}{\partial x_i} - \lambda_i P_x = 0$$

$$\frac{\partial L_i}{\partial y_i} = \frac{\partial U_i}{\partial y_i} - \lambda_i P_y = 0 \tag{2.5}$$

$$\frac{\partial L_i}{\partial \lambda_i} = R_i - P_x x_i - P_y y_i = 0$$

Providing that the social utility function exhibits diminishing marginal rates
of substitution, these will also turn out to be sufficient conditions. They can
then be solved for the optimal values of x_i, y_i, and λ_i.

The solution balances expenditures on different goods and services while
respecting the limits imposed by the available resources. More particularly, it
ensures that consumption of all goods and services increases up to the point
where the marginal social utility of each is the same, and all income is spent.
Solving equations 2.5 for λ_i we have:

$$\lambda_i = \frac{\partial U_i / \partial x_i}{P_x} = \frac{\partial U_i / \partial y_i}{P_y} \tag{2.6}$$

This says that at the optimum, the marginal social utility secured by
committing another unit of available resources to acquiring some good or
service should be the same for all goods and services. A graphical representation of the solution is shown in Figure 2.1.

The curve $U_i^*(x_i, y_i)$ is the highest attainable indifference curve, and
describes all combinations of x and y that yield social utility of U_i^*. All combinations of x and y that lie above this curve would be strictly preferred to any
combination on the curve, but are unattainable given the resource constraint

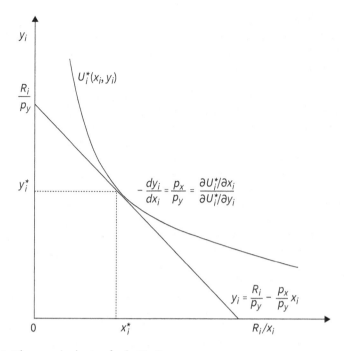

Figure 2.1 The marginal rate of substitution.
The optimal level of consumption of x and y occurs where the decision-maker's marginal rate of substitution of x for y, given by the slope of the indifference curve, is equal to the price ratio, p_x/p_y.

$p_x x_i + p_y y_i = R_i$, and all combinations along the curve will be strictly preferred to any combination lying below the curve. The slope of the curve, $\dfrac{\partial U_i^*/\partial x_i}{\partial U_i^*/\partial y_i}$ defines the marginal rate of substitution between x and y—the rate at which the community is willing to trade one off for the other. The slope of the resource constraint is simply the price ratio, p_x/p_y. At the optimal values of x and y, x^*, and y^* the slope of $U_i^*(x_i, y_i)$ is the same as the slope of the resource, implying that the rate at which the community would be willing to substitute one good or service for the other, should be the same as the ratio of their resource costs or prices:

$$-\frac{dy_i}{dx_i} = \frac{p_x}{p_y} = \frac{\partial U_i^*/\partial x_i}{\partial U_i^*/\partial y_i} \tag{2.7}$$

So at the social optimum, the community resource constraint should be tangent to highest attainable social indifference curve.

The quantity of x_i or y_i demanded by the members of the ith community depends on the both on the relative prices, p_x, p_y and on the resources available to that community, R_i. That is, we can specify demand functions for each:

$$x_i = D_x\left(p_x, p_y, R_i\right)$$
$$y_i = D_y\left(p_x, p_y, R_i\right)$$

(2.8)

These describe how the community responds to changes in the resource cost of goods and services and to changes in the resources available to the community. We expect that demand for any good or service will increase if the available resources increase, if the resource cost of that good falls, or if the resource cost of substitute goods and services rises. If the resource cost of x_i falls relative to y_i as a result of some technological innovation for example, we would expect demand for y_i to change for two different reasons. One is a *substitution effect*—the incentive to substitute goods or services with lower resource costs for goods or services with higher resource costs. The other is an *income effect*—the falling resource cost of x_i increases the total amount of x_i and y_i that can be acquired given R_i. The two effects are shown in Figure 2.2.

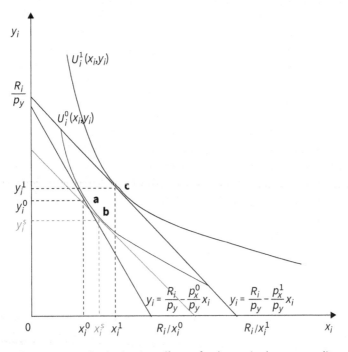

Figure 2.2 The income and substitution effects of a change in the commodity prices.
The change in the quantity of x consumed as a result a reduction in its price involves a substitution effect from a to b, and an income effect from b to c.

Suppose the resource cost of x_i falls from p_x^0 to p_x^1 so that the maximum amount of x_i that could be acquired increases from R_i/x_i^0 to R_i/x_i^1. This will have two effects on the demand for y_i. If the initial equilibrium is at point a and the corresponding combination of goods and services is x_i^0, y_i^0 the first effect, the substitution effect, involves a reduction in the amount of y_i to y_i^s, corresponding to point b. This is due to the fact that the lower relative resource cost of x_i encourages substitution of x_i for y_i. However, since the lower resource cost of x_i also increases the real income of the community—the amount of both x_i and y_i that can be acquired with R_i—there is a second effect, an income effect. This effect allows the community to increase consumption of both x_i for y_i. If the final equilibrium is at point c, this second effect dominates the first, and the quantity demanded of y_i increases to y_i^1. More formally,

$$\frac{\partial y_i}{\partial p_x} = \frac{\partial y_i}{\partial p_x}\bigg|_{U_i^0} - \frac{\partial y_i}{\partial R_i^R} \frac{\partial R_i^R}{\partial p_x} \tag{2.9}$$

This provides important insights into the nature of the trade-offs that communities have made in the past. It tells us that we should expect changes in relative resource costs to lead communities to alter the composition of goods and services in their "consumption bundle." During the early phases of the Holocene, for example, communities progressively substituted one set of foods, fuels, and fibers for another—those secured by arable and pastoral activities for those secured by hunting and gathering. During later phases, they substituted the products of industry and commerce for foods, fuels, and fibers.

If the optimal combination of goods and services consumed by any community changes, then so too does the combination of assets needed to produce those goods and services—the natural capital needed to generate ecosystem services and the produced capital needed to generate other goods and services. Indeed, this point is critical to all that follows. In the same way that demand for labor stems from demand for the things that labor can produce, so demand for the environmental and nonenvironmental stocks that underpin consumption choices *derives* from demand for final goods and services. The demand for land for the production of food crops, for example, derives from the demand for food. The demand for land as habitat for wild species derives from demand for the conservation of wild species. The demand for watershed protection derives from the demand for water. It follows that the consumption of goods and services today has potential implications for the consumption of goods and services in the future. Specifically, if consumption of goods and services today reduces the produced or natural capital stocks available in the future, it may force a reduction in consumption of the same goods and services in the future. A pattern of consumption is sustainable in the sense that it can be repeated over time, which can only happen if the implied use of capital stocks is sustainable.

Consumption choices involving provisioning or cultural ecosystem services have potential implications for the natural capital—the biotic and abiotic environmental stocks—that underpins production of those services. The classic conservation problem confronting pre-Holocene hunter-gatherer communities, and every community since, is to determine what can be harvested today without compromising harvests in the future. This is the problem of determining which natural assets to conserve from one time period to the next. In one form or another it is the problem addressed in much of this book. For now, what is important is that the consumption choices that matter are choices involving consumption over time. If time is discrete, the general form of the function is:

$$U_i\left(x_{it}, y_{it}, t\right) = U_i\left(x_i\left(K_{it}, t\right), y_i\left(N_{it}, t\right)\right) \tag{2.10}$$

where x_{it}, y_{it} are the goods and services generated by the ith community at time t. Assuming that community has a finite time horizon, T, the general consumption problem takes the form

$$Max_{x_{it}, y_{it}} \sum_{t=0}^{T} \rho^t U_i\left(x_i\left(K_{it}, t\right), y_i\left(N_{it}, t\right)\right) \tag{2.11}$$

in which $\rho = 1/(1+\delta)$ is a discount factor, and δ is the discount rate. We explore the discount rate in more detail in later chapters, but for now note that it is the rate at which future consumption of goods and services is weighted relative to consumption of goods and services now. It allows the community to compare the benefits from consuming goods and services at different points along a time path. Equation 2.11 says that the ith community will select the combination of goods and services in each of $T+1$ time periods so as to maximize the present value (the discounted stream) of benefits offered by consumption.

To see what the problem implies for conservation of the underlying stocks of capital, let us focus only on the provisioning services and natural capital stocks, and suppose that the ith community derives well-being both from the flow of goods and service generated during the decision period, and from the stock of resources left at the end of the decision period. If the decision period is the space of a generation, for example, this would imply that community well-being depends both on consumption by the current generation, and on the heritage of the next generation—the assets left to the next generation. The problem takes the form:

$$Max_{y_{it}} \sum_{t=0}^{T-1} \rho^t U_i \left(y_i \left(N_{it}, t \right) \right) + \rho^T V_i \left(N_{iT} \right) \tag{2.12}$$

subject to

$$
\begin{aligned}
N_{it+1} - N_{it} &= f \left(N_{it}, y_{it} \right) \\
N_{i0} &= \bar{N}_i
\end{aligned}
\tag{2.13}
$$

$\sum_{t=0}^{T-1} \rho^t U_i \left(y_i \left(N_{it}, t \right) \right)$ is the present value of the stream of benefits flowing from the provisioning service in the interval $t = 0, ..., T-1$ and $\rho^T V_i \left(N_{iT} \right)$ is the present value of the stocks of N_{iT} left to the next generation. The constraint set includes the initial value of N and a difference equation describing change in the stock of natural capital in some period as a function of the size of the stock and the provisioning service in the previous period. In the simplest case, one could think of N_{it} as a stock of bison at time t, say, and $y_i \left(N_{it}, t \right)$ as the number of bison consumed by the community. More generally, N_{it} describes the stock of environmental assets at time t, and $f \left(N_{it}, y_{it} \right)$ describes the way that production of y_{it} impacts future values of N_{it}.

To solve the problem we can, as before, we construct a Lagrangian function

$$
\begin{aligned}
L \left(y_i, N_{it}, \lambda_{it+1}, t \right) = {} & \sum_{t=0}^{T-1} \rho^t U_i \left(y_i \left(N_{it}, t \right) \right) \\
& + \rho \lambda_{it+1} \left(N_{it} + f \left(N_{it}, y_{it} \right) - N_{it+1} \right) \\
& + \rho^T V_i \left(N_{iT} \right) it
\end{aligned}
\tag{2.14}
$$

that is the sum of the original objective function, and a constraint function set equal to zero and multiplied by the Lagrange multiplier λ_{it+1}. Notice that there are T terms summed together in the Lagrangian function, one for each period from time 0 to time $T-1$. Optimization of the function requires that we identify the necessary conditions that must hold along the time path. Once again, these require that the partial derivatives of the Lagrangian function with respect to y_{it}, N_{it} and λ_{it} are equal to zero.

$$\frac{\partial L}{\partial y_{it}} = \frac{\partial U_i}{\partial y_{it}} + \rho\lambda_{it+1}\left(\frac{\partial f}{\partial y_{it}}\right) = 0, \quad t = 0,...,T-1$$

$$\frac{\partial L}{\partial N_{it}} = \frac{\partial U_i}{\partial y_{it}}\frac{\partial y_{it}}{\partial N_{it}} + \rho\lambda_{it+1}\left(1+\frac{\partial f}{\partial N_{it}}\right) - \lambda_{it} = 0, \quad t = 1,...,T-1$$

$$\frac{\partial L}{\partial N_{iT}} = -\lambda_{iT} + \frac{\partial V_i}{\partial N_{iT}} = 0 \qquad\qquad (2.15)$$

$$\frac{\partial L}{\partial \lambda_{it+1}} = N_{it} + f(N_{it}, y_{it}) - N_{it+1} = 0, \quad t = 0,...,T-1$$

Three sets of conditions need to be satisfied along the time path. A fourth needs to hold only at the terminal time $t = T$. To interpret these conditions, recall that the Lagrange multiplier is the shadow value of the constraint—in this case the change in the stock of natural capital. The first set of T conditions in 2.15 relate to the choice of y_{it}. These conditions require that along an optimal path the marginal social utility of y_{it} should equal the discounted value of future changes in N_{it+1} due to y_{it}:

$$\frac{\partial U_i}{\partial y_{it}} = -\rho\lambda_{it+1}\left(\frac{\partial f}{\partial y_{it}}\right), \quad t = 0,...,T-1 \qquad\qquad (2.16)$$

Think of this as the future cost of current production of y_{it} measured in terms of the loss of well-being associated with a reduction in N_{it+1}. It is often referred to as a *user cost* of y_{it}. Where choice of provisioning services today affects environmental stocks tomorrow, this requires that the discounted shadow value of the changes in future stocks be offset against today's benefits.

The second set of $T-1$ conditions then specify how the shadow value of environmental or natural capital stocks can vary along the optimal path. Notice that we can write these conditions in the form:

$$\rho\lambda_{it+1} - \lambda_{it} = -\frac{\partial U_i}{\partial y_{it}}\frac{\partial y_{it}}{\partial N_{it}} - \rho\lambda_{it+1}\frac{\partial f}{\partial N_{it}}, \quad t = 1,...,T-1 \qquad\qquad (2.17)$$

The left-hand side of 2.17 is the change in the shadow value of natural capital stocks between t and $t+1$ from the perspective of time t. The term $\frac{\partial U_i}{\partial y_{it}}\frac{\partial y_{it}}{\partial N_{it}}$ is the marginal social utility of a change in stocks at time t, measured in terms of the impact stocks have on the provisioning services. The term $\rho\lambda_{it+1}\frac{\partial f}{\partial N_{it}}$ is the discounted shadow value of the density-dependent growth of those stocks. This is the growth induced by variation in the size of the stocks at time t. For abiotic resources $\partial f / \partial N_{it}$ will typically be zero or negative (if stocks degrade naturally). For biotic resources $\partial f / \partial N_{it}$ may be positive, negative, or zero depending on the size of populations relative to the carrying capacity of their environment. Equation 2.17 states that along an optimal time path the shadow value of natural capital stocks will evolve both with changes in the size of those stocks and changes in their marginal social utility. This second set of conditions turns out to be critical to an understanding of the conservation problem.

The third condition requires that the shadow value of natural capital stocks at the terminal time be equal to the marginal social utility of those stocks:

$$\lambda_{iT} = \frac{\partial V_i}{\partial N_{iT}} \tag{2.18}$$

The fourth set of T conditions requires that the first constraint in 2.13 be satisfied, that is, that changes in environmental stocks respect the equations of motion for those stocks:

$$N_{it+1} - N_{it} = f\left(N_{it}, y_{it}\right) \tag{2.19}$$

to which we may add a boundary condition—that the second constraint in 2.13 is also satisfied:

$$N_{i0} = \bar{N}_i \tag{2.20}$$

From a conservation perspective, the solution to the problem described by 2.12 and 2.13 has two important implications.

First, the condition that $\dfrac{\partial U_i}{\partial y_{it}} = -\rho \lambda_{it+1} \left(\dfrac{\partial f}{\partial y_{it}} \right)$ requires that whenever consumption of goods and services affects the environmental assets underpinning their production, the shadow value of resulting changes in assets should be offset against the benefits offered by those goods and services. Many of the changes in environmental stocks recorded in the Millennium Ecosystem Assessment are byproducts of decisions to consume particular bundles of goods and services. The implication is that the shadow value of those environmental changes should inform consumption decisions. If it does not, natural capital stocks will be overexploited. This is one reason why so much attention is paid by environmental and resource economists to the institutional, legal, informational, and other conditions that lead decision-makers to neglect the consequences of their actions. Along an optimal path, the value of natural capital stocks depends on the physical growth or decline in those stocks, and the consequences this has for community well-being. Markets generate reasonable measures of this in some cases, but not in others. While the Millennium Ecosystem Assessment was able to record changes in the physical magnitude of many environmental stocks, for example, it was not able to say much about the value of those changes.

Second, the condition $\rho\lambda_{it+1} - \lambda_{it} = -\dfrac{\partial U_i}{\partial y_{it}}\dfrac{\partial y_{it}}{\partial N_{it}} - \rho\lambda_{it+1}\dfrac{\partial f}{\partial N_{it}}$ requires that along an optimal path, changes in the shadow value of stocks of natural capital should be related to the rate at which future consumption is discounted. Specifically, multiplying 2.17 through by $1+\delta$, substituting for $\partial U_i/\partial y_{it}$ from 2.16 and rearranging yields the expression:

$$\frac{\lambda_{it+1}\left(1 - \dfrac{\partial f}{\partial y_{it}}\dfrac{\partial y_{it}}{\partial N_{it}} + \dfrac{\partial f}{\partial N_{it}}\right) - \lambda_{it}}{\lambda_{it}} = \delta \tag{2.21}$$

This relation is considered in more detail later when we discuss both the concept of the discount rate and the Hotelling principle. For the moment it is enough to note that it is the central idea in the theory of optimal conservation of environmental stocks. Along an optimal time path, this expression implies that the growth in the shadow value of environmental stocks, taking account of both anthropogenic and nonanthropogenic influences on those stocks, should be exactly equal to a term that defines both the rate at which decision-makers discount future consumption and the opportunity cost of holding natural capital.

Notice that we have throughout spoken of the decisions taken by the ith community, where a community is a collection of individuals who share in the decision process. A community may be as small as a nuclear household and as large as a nation-state, or larger—the Global North or the Global South, say. What defines a community is that its members share a common interest in the outcome of particular decisions. Because the world comprises many interacting communities, we need to understand how interactions between communities affects the conservation decisions that each makes. If two communities exploit a common environment, for example, choices that are welfare maximizing for each community separately may not be welfare maximizing for both communities together. Consumption paths by one community that seem to be sustainable if the actions of other communities are ignored, may not be sustainable once the actions of others are taken into account. The interactions between communities will be a recurrent theme of the book.

2.3 A numerical example: the wine storage problem

If a commodity, like wine or cheese, improves with age and therefore appreciates in value over some period, wine or cheese sellers have an incentive to hold on to it before selling it. The decision process involved tells us much about the general conservation problem considered by Hotelling. Indeed, many real-world conservation problems have similar features to the wine storage problem. One example is the problem of whether natural habitats or agricultural lands on the outskirts of a growing city should be conserved, and for how long. In this case, the relative value of land if committed to conservation or development may be expected to change over time as a function of the growth of the city, so altering the calculation of which option is best for society.

To see how the problem is solved, consider a simple numerical example. Suppose that a wine merchant acquires a case of wine for $1,000 (no ordinary wine), and that it improves with age such that its sale value at time t is:

$$V(t) = 1000e^{\sqrt[3]{t}} \tag{2.22}$$

The question is how long should the wine merchant hold the wine before selling it (the answer to how long to hold it before consuming might well be different, as consumption value might rise at a different rate than sale value, though the structure of the problem is the same). It should be obvious that the answer depends on the opportunity cost of the capital tied up while the wine is in storage (which we assume here otherwise has no other costs). Suppose that the wine merchant could have earned interest that would have compounded annually at 7%. The decision problem faced by the wine merchant is to select storage time so as to maximize the present value of the investment in wine—the discounted value

$$P(t) = 1000e^{\sqrt[3]{t}}e^{-0.07t} = 1000e^{\sqrt[3]{t}-0.07t} \tag{2.23}$$

The wine merchant aims to find the value of t that maximizes $P(t)$. Given that the growth in the value of the wine is exponential, we can solve for t by taking the natural log of (1.2), yielding

$$\ln P(t) = \ln 1000 + t^{1/3} - 0.07t \qquad (2.24)$$

A first order necessary condition for some solution, t^*, to be at a maximum is that waiting a little longer will yield no further increase in the present value of the wine. To satisfy this condition we have only to take the time derivative of (2.24), set it equal to zero, and solve for t^*:

$$\frac{d}{dt}\ln P = \frac{d}{dt}\ln 1000 + \frac{d}{dt}t^{1/3} - \frac{d}{dt}0.07t = 0$$

$$\Rightarrow \frac{1}{P}\frac{dP}{dt} = \frac{1}{3}t^{-2/3} - 0.07 = 0$$

$$\Rightarrow \frac{dP}{dt} = P\left[\frac{1}{3}t^{-2/3} - 0.07\right] = 0 \qquad (2.25)$$

$$\Rightarrow \frac{1}{3}t^{-2/3} = 0.07$$

$$\Rightarrow t^* = 0.21^{-3/2} \approx 10.4 \text{ years}$$

To verify that this is indeed a maximum, we may check the second order conditions. These require that any further change in storage time leads to a reduction in the present value of the wine. To check this, take the second derivative of (2.24) with respect to t at the critical value:

$$\frac{d^2P}{dt^2} = P\left(-\frac{2}{9}t^{-5/3}\right) + \frac{dP}{dt}\left(\frac{1}{3}t^{-2/3} - 0.07\right) = -\frac{2P}{9t^{5/3}} < 0 \qquad (2.26)$$

Since this is negative, we have confirmed that P is at a maximum at the critical value.

The core of the wine storage problem is the relation between the two elements that determine the rate of change in the present value of the wine (obtained from 2.25):

$$\frac{dP}{dt} = P\left[\frac{1}{3}t^{-2/3} - 0.07\right] \qquad (2.27)$$

The two terms on the right-hand side of this expression are the marginal rate of growth in the value of the wine, $\frac{1}{3}t^{-2/3}P$, and the opportunity cost—the

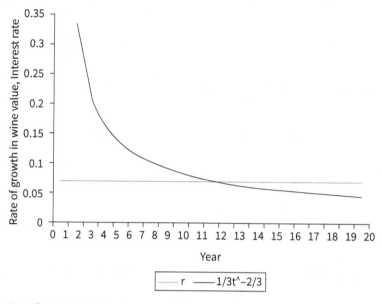

Figure 2.3 The optimal wine storage period.

The opportunity cost of capital (interest rate) is constant, while the rate of increase in the value of the wine starts high and drops. Wine should be stored up to the point where the marginal rate of growth in the value of the wine is equal to the interest that could have been earned on the capital used to acquire the wine.

interest that could have been earned on the capital used to acquire the wine, $0.07P$ (Figure 2.3).

This relation turns out also to be at the core of the Hotelling theory of conservation. We note that it is an efficiency condition that results from the optimization of some index of net benefit, in this case the present value of the wine merchant's investment. But since it is driven by the growth in the value of wine, it is affected by all of the factors that impact the value of wine. A Californian study of the factors influencing wine prices for five varietals in the region found, for example, that while the most important factor in all cases was the "tasting score" of the wine, a number of other factors had a statistically significant association with wine prices, including the grape variety, the grape location (appellation), the label designation (whether estate, vineyard, or reserve grape vintage), and the age of the wine at release. Interestingly, the authors found that an extra year of storage added something like 20% to an average bottle of wine (Bombrun and Sumner 2003).

Many environmental assets lack the kind of firm price indicators that signal the value of wine, and so determining the values and their changes over time is more challenging, but the principle involved is the same, whether the value of the asset is expressed in monetary terms or not. The asset should be conserved if and only if its value when in its conserved state is increasing faster than its value when converted.

2.4 Summary and conclusions

This chapter rehearsed the basics of decision-making. All economic decision problems involve the same four elements: an objective function, a constraint set, a set of boundary conditions, and a set of choice or control variables. The first element, the objective function, defines what it is that the decision-maker is trying to achieve. Economists frequently work with a small number of objectives. Consumers are assumed to maximize utility. Firms are assumed to maximize profits. Governments are assumed to maximize social welfare. In reality, decision-makers have a much wider range of objectives. Households, firms, and public bodies may all try to minimize the cost of meeting a particular target, for example. Individuals may try only to do "well enough" to assure their acceptability to a peer group. Politicians may try to maximize their appeal to voters. Conservationists may try to maximize the number of species they are able to save from extinction. What the objective function does is to summarize the purpose of a decision. It rules out wholly purposeless or random behavior, but is otherwise unrestricted.

The second element, the constraint set, describes the conditions that have to be met by the decision. Once again, economists tend to focus on particular constraints. Consumers are assumed to maximize utility subject to a budget constraint. Firms are assumed to maximize profits subject to a cost constraint or to the production possibilities allowed by existing technology. Once again, though, the constraints on economic decisions are much wider than this. In natural resource management problems, for instance, the constraint set also includes the dynamics of the natural environment. This may be the rate at which particular populations or species reproduce, the rate at which ground or surface water reservoirs recharge, or the rate at which the environment is able to assimilate emissions to land, water, or air. The constraint set also includes the legal or regulatory environment that limits, for example, what actions are permitted where and when.

The third element, the boundary conditions, describes the limitations imposed either by the initial conditions within which the decision has to be made, or by any terminal conditions that might be imposed on the decision. In natural resource management problems, initial conditions include the quantity and quality of stocks of natural resources available—the size and health of some population of animals or plants, for example. Terminal conditions include restrictions on what is to be left at the end of the decision period, in terms of the state either of the natural resource stocks involved, or of the wider environment.

The fourth element, the choice or control variables, describe the instruments available to the decision-maker to achieve their objectives. In the simple consumer choice examples discussed in this chapter, the consumer chooses the quantities of different goods and services to consume. In natural resource management problems, the decision-maker might choose the crops to plant, the effort committed to harvesting fish or wildlife stocks, the volume of water to extract from an aquifer, or the area of land to commit to conservation.

In all cases, the best decision involves a principle that is embedded in almost every economic problem—the equimarginal principle. The principle holds that decision-makers will increase their consumption of a good or employment of an input up to the point where the marginal gain derived from using the good or input is exactly equal to the marginal cost of procuring that good or input, and this gain will be equalized across goods or inputs. In a consumer choice problem, the marginal gain from increasing consumption of one good is the utility that yields. So, the equimarginal principle implies that the consumer will trade one good off against another until the marginal utility of all goods is the same. In a production problem, the decision-maker will increase employment of each input up to the point where the value of the marginal product it yields is exactly equal to its marginal cost. So by the equimarginal principle, costs are minimized where the marginal product per dollar spent on an input is the same for all inputs.

Application of the principle helps us understand the rate at which decision-makers will trade off either goods and services, or inputs in a production process. It also helps us understand how trade-off decisions relate to the relative value of resources. We find that the marginal rate of substitution between goods and services—the rate at which consumers are willing to trade one off for the other—is equal to the ratio of the value of those goods and services. Similarly, the marginal rate of technical substitution between inputs—the rate at which producers are willing to trade one off for the other—is equal to the ratio of the value of those inputs.

For problems involving time, the same principle applies. However, equalizing marginal benefits that occur at different moments in time requires that they be made commensurate. The discount rate plays this very important role. It allows us to compare magnitudes that are separated in time. We can think of the discount rate as fixing the weight attached to future relative to present benefits. If the discount rate is 10% per year, for example, the weight attached to a given benefit in one year, relative to the same benefit today, is $1/(1 + 0.1) = .909$.

We discuss the discount rate in more detail in future chapters. It is sufficient, here, to note that it reflects a combination of impatience, uncertainty, and productivity growth.

The chapter also introduced a concept that plays a critical role going forward. It is called by various names in the literature. Here we referred to it as the shadow value of a resource. It is a measure of value that may differ from the market price of a resource. It can be thought of as the social opportunity cost or true value of the resource. In the decision models discussed in the chapter, the shadow value of a resource whose dynamics constrain the choices to be made is the marginal benefit generated by a small change in the size of the resource. For the particular approach used in the chapter, the Lagrangian approach, it is given by the Lagrange multiplier attaching to the equations of motion for that resource.

To illustrate how the equimarginal principle applies to the optimal use of a resource whose quality changes over time, we constructed a numerical example around the problem of wine storage. Since the quality of some wines improve over time their prices increase, albeit at a decreasing rate, we ask how long a wine seller might choose to hold on to such wines before selling them. We showed that if the rate at which the price of wine is growing is above the rate of return on alternative assets—the interest earned on bank deposits, for example—it will be optimal to hold the wine. If the rate at which the price of wine is growing is below the rate of return on alternative assets it will be optimal to sell the wine. A very similar idea appears, albeit implicitly, in existing studies of the economics of environmental conservation (see, for example, Tisdell, 2005).

References

Bombrun, H., and D. A. Sumner. 2003. What determines the price of wine. AIC Issues Brief 18:1–6.

Hotelling, H. 1931. The economics of exhaustible resources. Journal of Political Economy 39:137–175.

Huxley, T. 1883. Address to the inaugural meeting of the Fishery Congress. William Clowes, London.

Millennium Ecosystem Assessment. 2005. Ecosystems and human well-being: general synthesis. Island Press, Washington, DC.

Tisdell, C. 2005. Economics of Environmental Conservation. Edward Elgar, Cheltenham.

3

Hotelling Conservation

> Contemplation of the world's disappearing supplies of minerals, forests, and other exhaustible assets has led to demands for regulation of their exploitation. The feeling that these products are now too cheap for the good of future generations, that they are being selfishly exploited at too rapid a rate, and that in consequence of their excessive cheapness they are being produced and consumed wastefully has given rise to the conservation movement.
>
> —Harold Hotelling, *The Economics of Exhaustible Resources*, 1931

3.1 Introduction

In this chapter we explore the elements of the general theory of conservation introduced by Harold Hotelling, and connect it to the solution of problems involving the optimal exploitation of natural resources. We show that the Hotelling problem is solved every time a land manager optimizes the use they make of environmental stocks. We also show that the solution is sensitive to the value those stocks have to society, and that value depends on how the stocks support the things that society cares about.

Hotelling saw the emergence of the conservation movement as a response to the perception that natural resources were being undervalued and hence overused. In the light of this, he asked how changes in the value of natural resources affected levels of resource use. Although all natural biotic and abiotic resources can be analyzed in exactly the same way, Hotelling took the simplest case: he asked under what conditions the owner of some mineral right would choose to extract the ore. As in the wine storage problem, Hotelling assumed that the objective of the resource owner was to maximize the present value of the future stream of net benefits to be had from their use of the resource (Hotelling 1931).

The value of an asset reflects not only what it can do for us today, but what it can do for us in the future. To get the net present value of an asset, we simply

Conservation. Charles Perrings and Ann Kinzig, Oxford University Press (2021). © Oxford University Press.
DOI: 10.1093/oso/9780190613600.003.0003

sum (or integrate) all the value it holds for us over time, and subtract all the costs we must expend to maintain it over time. So the present value of a car to its owner is the value of the benefits it yields (being able to drive it until it is sold) plus the final sale price, minus the cost of purchase and maintenance. By comparing this to the opportunity cost of the purchase price, the buyer can decide both whether to buy and when to sell.

3.2 The Hotelling arbitrage condition

Hotelling took the case of mineral resources. Extraction generates a flow of net benefits that, if invested would yield a rate of return, which we can approximate by the interest rate, (δ). This is the opportunity cost of the capital invested in the mine. If the value of net benefits at time t—what Hotelling called the "net price" of the resource—was $p(t)$, then the present value of net benefits at time t would be $p(t)e^{-\delta t}$. It is quite intuitive from this that the maximization of present value should balance δ and the rate of growth in $p(t)$.

At the core of the Hotelling theory of conservation is an arbitrage condition that states how decision-makers would be expected to balance the rate of change in future benefits of the resource $(p(t))$ and the rate of interest (δ). In so doing, the condition explains when and why it will be rational to conserve or convert any resource at any moment in time. Specifically, the arbitrage condition states that a resource owner will be indifferent between conserving and converting a resource at time t if the proportional rate of change in the net price of the conserved resource at that time is equal to the rate of return on the best alternative investment that could be made: that is, if the expected capital gain on the conserved resource is equal to the rate of return on the converted asset. In the discrete-time case the arbitrage condition is that:

$$\frac{p_{t+1} - p_t}{p_t} = \delta \tag{3.1}$$

In the continuous time-case it takes the form:

$$\frac{\dot{p}}{p(t)} = \delta \tag{3.2}$$

where $\dot{p} = dp/dt$. To see how the arbitrage condition relates to the rational use of resources consider a simple model of exhaustible resource extraction (after Conrad 1999). Let the stock of the resource at time t be denoted R_t, and the change in the stock of the resource between t and $t+1$, assuming no new discoveries, be:

$$R_{t+1} = R_t - q_t \qquad (3.3)$$

where q_t is the quantity of the resource extracted at time t. Suppose the benefits society derives from extraction is represented by some function $V(q_t)$, and that these benefits increase in q_t but at a decreasing rate. As an example of this, think of barrels of oil. The United States consumes around 20 million barrels a day. The first million are worth significantly more to consumers than the current sale price. The tenth million still yields a significant "surplus" to consumers at the current sale price, but is less valuable than the first. Beyond the twentieth million, the sale price has to fall to clear the market. Mathematically, $dV/dq_t > 0, d^2V/dq_t^2 < 0$, implying that $V(q_t)$ is a strictly concave function. Concavity simply implies that there is never a decline in total value to society with an additional unit of the resource.

The problem confronting the owner of the resource is to maximize the present value of the stream of net benefits over a finite time horizon, T, by choosing how much of the resource to extract at each moment in time or, conversely, how much to conserve. In the Conrad problem it is assumed that the aim is to exhaust the resource by the end of the planning horizon, so the constrained optimization problem takes the form:

$$\underset{q_t}{Max} \sum_{t=0}^{T} \rho^t V(q_t) \qquad (3.4)$$

subject to

$$R_0 - \sum_{t=0}^{T} q_t = 0 \qquad (3.5)$$

where $\rho = 1/(1+\delta)$, δ being the rate at which future costs and benefits are discounted—an exogenously given interest rate. In words, the decision-maker solves for the best "pattern" of extraction over their time horizon (T), assuming that all of the resource will be extracted by the end of T. Should one extract it all at the beginning and put everything in the bank? Extract it evenly over time? Wait until the very last minute to extract the resource? Some other pattern?

As before, to solve the problem we form the Lagrangian function:

$$L = \sum_{t=0}^{T} \rho^t V(q_t) + \lambda \left(R_0 - \sum_{t=0}^{T} q_t \right) \tag{3.6}$$

in which λ, a Lagrange multiplier, measures the marginal value of a change in the stock of the resource. We then obtain the first order necessary conditions for q_t to be optimized. These include:

$$\rho^t \frac{dV}{dq_t} = \lambda, \quad t = 0, 1, \ldots, T$$
$$R_0 = \sum_{t=0}^{T} q_t \tag{3.7}$$

The first of these conditions, obtained by taking the derivative of the Lagrangian function with respect to q_t and setting it equal to zero, requires that in every period the discounted marginal benefit of extraction is equal to the marginal user cost of extraction—the marginal value of the decline in the available resource due to extraction. The second condition satisfies the constraint that cumulative extraction over the time horizon T is equal to the initial stock of the resource.

To make the link with the Hotelling arbitrage condition transparent, suppose there are just two periods, $T = 1$, and that the value function takes the simple form

$$V(q_t) = p_t q_t \tag{3.8}$$

implying that the marginal benefit of extraction, dV/dq_t, is just the price of the resource in period t, p_t. In this case the first order necessary conditions require that:

$$\frac{dV}{dq_0} = \rho \frac{dV}{dq_1} = \lambda \tag{3.9}$$

implying that

$$(1+\delta) \frac{dV}{dq_0} = \rho \frac{dV}{dq_1} \tag{3.10}$$

and hence that

$$(1+\delta)p_o = p_1 \Rightarrow \frac{p_1 - p_0}{p_0} = \delta \qquad (3.11)$$

Notice that this simply restates the Hotelling arbitrage condition. It implies that if the resource is to be conserved between period 0 and period 1 then it must be growing in value by at least as much as it would if it were converted. That is, conservation of the resource between the two periods implies that $p_1 \geq (1+\delta)p_0$. The higher the rate of return on the resource if converted, the stronger is the incentive to convert it, and the weaker is the incentive to conserve it.

The implication for conversion/conservation of the resource is shown in the two panels of Figure 3.1. The two panels show the same price and demand schedules in the two different time periods, but different interest rates. Those with an interest in the math can refer to the caption. Demand is identical in both time periods, and is decreasing with price. At the price indicated by the intercept on the vertical axes, the quantity demanded is 0. As price falls the quantity demanded (measured on the horizontal axis) increases. The extractor of the resource will only hold some of the resource into the second time period if the price, p_1, increases by at least as much as the opportunity cost of capital, the interest rate δ. So the price in the second period, p_1, must be greater than the price in the first, p_0, by a factor $(1 + \delta)$. Since an increase in price in the second period leads to a decrease in demand in that period, more will be extracted (demanded) in the first period than the second period if $\delta = 0$. As interest rates rise (panel B), this effect becomes more pronounced—the quantity extracted in the first period (q_0) increases, and the quantity extracted in the second period (q_1) decreases. It is intuitive that as the rate of interest goes to infinity, the rate of conservation in the first period goes to zero, and that as the rate of interest goes to zero the rate of conservation in the first period goes to 50%. Negative interest rates would induce higher rates of conservation, but in this story the rate of conservation in the first period would only go to 100% if the rate of interest went to negative infinity. We could solve the same problem for 2, 10, 100, or 1,000 time periods, but the insights would remain the same. The higher the opportunity cost of capital (interest on the money that can be deposited in the bank, or invested in other ways), the greater is the proportion of the resource initially extracted, and the lesser is the proportion of the resource initially conserved.

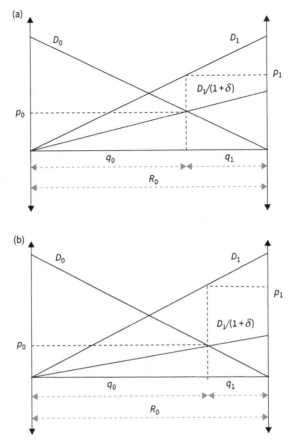

Figure 3.1 The Hotelling arbitrage condition and optimal conservation in a two-period problem.

Price in the first period, p_0, is measured on the left vertical axis. Price in the second period, p_1, is measured on the right vertical axis. Suppose that demand is identical in both periods. Demand in the second period, D_1, measured on the right vertical axis, is flipped and superimposed on demand in the first period, D_0, measured on the left vertical axis. The Hotelling arbitrage condition is satisfied at the point where $D_0 = D_1/(1+\delta)$. Each panel assumes a positive rate of interest, the rate being higher in panel B than in panel A. Applying the arbitrage condition we see that the optimal rate of extraction in the first period is increasing in the rate of interest, and conversely that the optimal rate of conservation in the first period is decreasing in the rate of interest. Specifically, for any given $\delta > 0$ it means that $q_0 > q_1, p_0 < p_1$. And for different levels of $\delta > 0$ it means that $q_0(\delta_0) < q_0(\delta_1)$ if $\delta_0 > \delta_1$ and that $q_0(\delta_0) > q_0(\delta_1)$ if $\delta_0 < \delta_1$.

In this particular example, mineral resources deliver no benefits to society while still in the ground—there is no "stream of benefits" such as recreation, education, or water purification from minerals in situ. They are of value only if converted and used, either now or in the future. In many conservation decisions, of course, there is a value independent of its present or future converted value. Conserved land, for instance, doesn't have value only because its future sale price might rise, but because it provides habitat for biodiversity, purifies water, gives us cultural identity, and offers us recreational opportunities, among other things. This complicates calculation of the value of when conserved, but the general insight remains the same. One must compare the full sweep of the value delivered to society in the conserved state versus the converted state over time, to determine which conservation or conversion pathway delivers the most value.

3.3 Hotelling prices and quantities

The arbitrage condition is Hotelling's major contribution to the theory of conservation, and we will see it in operation throughout this book. However, Hotelling went further, arguing that the arbitrage condition would ensure that the net price of the unexploited resource at any point in the future would, in certain conditions, rise at exactly the rate of interest. Figure 3.1 explains this observation—the optimum extraction pathway removes just enough of the resource in the first period so that the increased scarcity of the resource triggers a price increase equivalent to the interest rate, even with constant demand.

Consider a discrete-time case. If the initial net price of the resource were p_0, then the resource owner would be indifferent between receiving p_0 now and $p_0(1+\delta)^t$ at time t since that is exactly what an investment of p_0 would yield. Similarly, in continuous time, the resource owner would be indifferent between receiving $p(0)$ now and $p(0)e^{rt}$ at time t since that is what an investment of $p(0)$ now would be worth at that time. The resource owner would be indifferent between extracting the resource now and leaving it in the ground at each moment only if its net price while in the ground were expected to rise at the rate of interest.

This led Hotelling to propose that, in perfect competition, the net price of in situ natural resources *should* rise at the rate of interest. That is, given an initial net price of $p(0)$, the net price at time t in continuous time should be $p(t) = p(0)e^{\delta t}$ (see Figure 3.2).

The appeal of the Hotelling price path was that it simultaneously determined both the change in the value of natural resources and the rate at which those resources would be converted or conserved. Suppose, for example, that the owner of a natural resource faces an inverse demand curve for the resource of:

$$p_t = p_c - bq_t \tag{3.12}$$

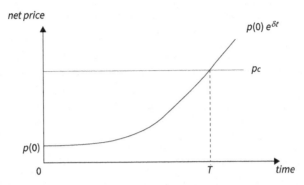

Figure 3.2 The Hotelling price path.

The price of the natural resource will increase at the rate of interest up to the point at which it is equal to the choke price.

in which p_c is defined as the choke price of the resource. The choke price might be determined by the marginal cost of producing a substitute for the resource. As long as the resource is priced below the choke price, the substitute is unused, but as soon as the price of the resource rises to the choke price or above demand shifts to the substitute, and the resource is no longer exploited. That is, along the Hotelling price path, the price of the resource would rise at the rate of interest up to the point where $p_t = p_c$.

To see how this determines extraction, suppose the owner of the resource aimed to exhaust it by the time the price reached the choke price, and call this time T. The Hotelling price path requires that

$$p_c = p_T = \left(1+\delta\right)^T p_0 \tag{3.13}$$

from which it follows directly that

$$p_0 = p_c\left(1+\delta\right)^{-T} \tag{3.14}$$

Using the inverse demand curve, we can then use the Hotelling price path solve for the extraction path, q_t. That is, since:

$$p_c - bq_t = p_c\left(1+\delta\right)^{t-T} \tag{3.15}$$

it follows that:

$$q_t = \frac{p_c}{b}\left[1-\left(1+\delta\right)^{t-T}\right] \tag{3.16}$$

If extraction costs do not depend on the size of the remaining reserve, and if there are no new discoveries, the extraction path over the period $0,...,T$ will exhaust the resource. That is:

$$\sum_{t=0}^{T} q_t = \sum_{t=0}^{T} \frac{p_c}{b} \left[1 - \left(1 + \delta \right)^{t-T} \right] = R_0 \qquad (3.17)$$

This is the implied extraction path (Figure 3.3).

It is easy to imagine reasons why the price of particular natural resources should not follow a Hotelling path exactly. Substitutes for the resource can be discovered or invented. Producers can create cartels to artificially inflate prices. Consumers can create coalitions to put downward pressure on prices. Of greatest interest for this book are cases where changes in the perceived value of natural resources can cause the prices of resources to deviate from the Hotelling price path. The Millennium Ecosystem Assessment, for example, has had a far-reaching impact on peoples' understanding of the many ways in which ecosystems support human well-being. This in turn has changed perceptions of the value of, in particular, renewable natural resources.

Considerable effort has gone into empirical tests of Hotelling's proposition that in perfect competition the net price of natural resources should rise at the rate of interest, other things being equal. Part of the difficulty is that controlling for other impacts on natural resource prices is notoriously difficult. On the supply side, there are the effects of producer organizations, such as the Organization of Petroleum Exporting Countries (OPEC), together with technological progress in production, exploration, and development, quality differentials, the effect of capacity constraints, and the like (Deverajan and Fisher 1981, Lin et al. 2009). Even where these supply side

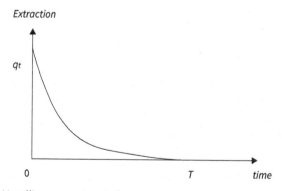

Figure 3.3 The Hotelling extraction path.

effects are controlled for, however, evidence in support of the Hotelling price path is weak (Lin 2009).

There are also demand side effects stemming from changes in the way that natural resources enter the production of other commodities, or affect the supply of nonmarketed ecosystem services. The choke price is always sensitive to the cost of producing substitutes for the resource in question. As we saw in the case of sperm whales, for example, demand for spermaceti collapsed when the cost of producing lamp oil from other sources fell rapidly. In the same way, the value of rubber changed forever with the invention of the automobile. In the case of oil, as Lin showed, geopolitical interventions on both sides of the market that have had major effects on oil prices. Cartels of producer nations have put upward pressure on prices. Military interventions by consumer nations have had the opposite effect. The net result is that the price of few, if any, marketed resources actually follow a Hotelling path. In a rapidly evolving global economic system, too many factors with the capacity to alter the value of resources are changing. Nevertheless, the concept of the Hotelling price path helps us intuitively understand how the conservation of stocks is related to the evolution of value through time.

3.4 Renewable natural resources and the Hotelling arbitrage condition

Recall that the decision-maker will be indifferent between conservation and conversion of environmental resources only if the expected capital gain of holding on to the natural resource is the same as the rate of return on the alternative asset. In the simplest case, this occurs when the proportional rate of change in the value of the resource is the same as the rate of interest (strictly the rate of return on the best alternative investment). The difference between renewable and nonrenewable resources is that value of renewable resources can change for two reasons. As with nonrenewable resources, the value of the resource can change for any of the supply side or demand side reasons discussed in Section 3.2. Unlike nonrenewable resources, however, the value of renewables can change because of changes in the size of the resource itself.

Suppose that a renewable natural resource, the population of a particular species N, grows according to the general relation

$$N_{t+1} - N_t = f\left(N_t, h_t\right) \tag{3.18}$$

in discrete time or

$$\dot{N} = f\big(N(t),h(t)\big) \tag{3.19}$$

in continuous time. This implies that growth is dependent both on the size of the stock and some control factor h, which captures the influence of culling and/or management that encourages growth. Growth is density dependent— it depends on the size of the stock at the beginning of that period or at that moment. We will encounter cases where growth depends positively or negatively on the size of the resource stock, depending on the relation between stock size and some measure of the carrying capacity of the ecosystem in which the resource is embedded. That is, growth may be both increasing in X, $df(N)/dN \geq 0$, and decreasing in N, $df(N)/dN \leq 0$. h can be thought of as a control action. It might be an action that directly or indirectly reduces the size of the resource such as harvest, culling, or the use of pesticides or herbicides, in which case $df(h)/dh < 0$. It might also be an action that directly or indirectly increases the size of the resource by increasing the flow of nutrients, water, access to sunlight, or by the promotion of symbionts or the suppression of competitors, in which case $df(h)/dh > 0$. Neglecting the effect of any controls for the moment, if growth is density dependent the Hotelling arbitrage condition takes the form:

$$\frac{p_{t+1} - p_t}{p_t} + \frac{f(N_t)}{N_t} = \delta \tag{3.20}$$

or

$$\frac{\dot{p}}{p(t)} + \frac{\dot{N}}{N(t)} = \delta \tag{3.21}$$

implying that the pure capital gain element might be either more or less than it would in the case of nonrenewable resources. In the more general case, where growth is increasing in the size of the stock, this means that conservation of the stock in situ is warranted by a smaller capital gain than would otherwise be needed.

There are many examples of single species density-dependent population growth models, the earliest of which, the logistic growth model, is due to the Belgian mathematician Pierre François Verhulst (Verhulst 1845). For any single population growth model to make sense, the limiting role of the environment within which that population exists needs to be included (otherwise the population would just grow to infinity). Verhulst proposed that the limiting role of the environment be captured in a measure of its carrying capacity in terms of the target species. In particular he proposed that the dynamics of species N be described by the differential equation:

$$\frac{dN}{dt} = rN\left(1 - \frac{N}{K}\right)$$

(3.22)

in which r is the intrinsic growth rate of species, and K is the carrying capacity of the system in terms of N. It is clear that whether growth is positive or negative depends on whether N is less than or greater than K—whether the population is below or above the carrying capacity of the environment in terms of N. It is equally clear that system has two equilibria (population sizes where there is 0 population growth): one where $N = 0$, the other where $N = K$. The first of these is unstable. Any small positive perturbation of N will lead to exponential growth of the population at the rate r. The second is stable. Any positive or negative perturbation of N will lead to counteracting contraction or expansion of the population. The model describes a form of compensatory growth, in which the long run stable equilibrium is the carrying capacity of the system.

A common extension of the logistic model adds an additional equilibrium, L, to represent the critical minimum size of the population, below which it will go extinct.

$$\frac{dN}{dt} = rN\left(1 - \frac{N}{K}\right)\left(\frac{N}{L} - 1\right)$$

(3.23)

Any positive perturbation of N from L will lead to growth of the population, initially at rate r. Any negative perturbation will cause the population to collapse to zero. This form of the model describes a critically depensatory growth path. The relation between growth and the size of the stock in both cases, along with the equilibria of the system are shown in Figure 3.4.

Neither should be taken as a perfect representation of any real growth process, any more than the Hotelling extraction path should be taken as a perfect representation of any real extraction process. But they do illustrate an important property of all renewable resources: that the environment within which those resources exist constrains their dynamics. In most natural systems, the carrying capacity of the system for any one species will be determined by the other species in the same system. Another archetypal density

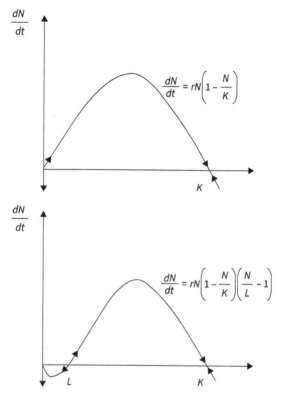

Figure 3.4 Compensatory and critically depensatory density dependent population growth.

dependent growth model, discovered independently by mathematicians Alfred Lotka and Vito Volterra, embeds interactions between species within a logistic model (Lotka 1925). The Lotka-Volterra predator prey model has the general form:

$$\frac{dN_1}{dt} = \alpha N_1 - \beta N_1 N_2$$
$$\frac{dN_2}{dt} = \varphi N_1 N_2 - \gamma N_2$$

(3.24)

in which N_1 is a prey species, N_2 is a predator species, and $\alpha, \beta, \varphi, \gamma$ are parameters describing the interaction between the two. Note that the prey species is negatively affected by predators ($-\beta N_1 N_2$ implies that the more predators there are, N_2, the higher the death rate of prey), and that predators are positively affected by prey ($\varphi N_1 N_2$ implies that the more prey there is, N_1, the higher the growth rate of predators). This model typically generates predator prey cycles, in which the population changes of the predator species lags that of the prey species, but both cycle between high population sizes and population "crashes" (declines in population size).

The human harvest of a density dependent population involves a predator prey relationship of a different kind. In this case predation is often regulated so as to optimize an index of well-being. Well-being might be optimized, for instance, by permitting the same harvesting rate in each period in contrast to the "natural" predator-prey cycles described earlier, where predation rates rise and fall, or by allowing a period of growth of the stock followed by harvest. To see how the Hotelling arbitrage condition determines the rate at which a density dependent species is harvested or, conversely, the rate at which the stock of the species is conserved, consider the following general problem:

$$Max_{h(t)} \int_0^T e^{-\delta t} U\big(N(t),h(t),t\big)dt + e^{-\delta T} F\big(N(T)\big) \tag{3.25}$$

subject to

$$\dot{N} = f\big(N(t),h(t)\big)$$
$$N(0) = N_0 \tag{3.26}$$

A manager chooses the level of harvest of species N so as to maximize an index of well-being (measured by the function U), the utility gained from the stream of benefits from both the abundance of the species and harvest during the interval $0,T$, and from the size of the stock remaining at T (the utility or value of which is represented by $F\big(N(T)\big)$ in equation 3.26). All benefits are discounted at the rate δ, which we take to be equal to the rate of interest on alternative investments. The manager's actions are constrained by the initial size of the stock, N_0, and its rate of growth, $\dot{N}$. We shall later consider specific forms for the functions $U\big(N(t),h(t),t\big)$ and $f\big(N(t)\big)$, but for the moment we use these general forms to explore the role of the Hotelling arbitrage condition.

To solve a problem of this type we first form the Lagrangian function introduced in Chapter 2.

$$L\big(N(t),h(t),\lambda(t),t\big) =$$
$$\int_0^T \Big[e^{-\delta t} U\big(N(t),h(t),t\big) + \lambda(t)\big(f\big(N(t),h(t)\big) - \dot{N}\big)\Big]dt - e^{-\delta T} F\big(N(T)\big) \tag{3.27}$$

As before, this function adds the constraint, multiplied by $\lambda(t)$ and set equal to zero, to the objective function. Integrating the term $-\lambda(t)\dot{N}$ by parts, and substituting the result into (3.27) yields:

$$
\begin{aligned}
L(\cdot) = \int_0^T & \left[e^{-\delta t} U(\cdot) + \lambda(t)\big(f(\cdot)\big) + \dot{\lambda} N(t) \right] dt \\
& + e^{-\delta T} F(\cdot) - \left[\lambda(T)N(T) - \lambda(0)N(0) \right]
\end{aligned}
\tag{3.28}
$$

While (3.28) could be used directly to obtain the first order necessary conditions for harvest to be optimal, it is helpful to introduce one other function—due to the Irish mathematician William Hamilton. The Hamiltonian combines the decision-maker's objective function and the constraint dynamics at a moment in time. For this particular problem the Hamiltonian takes one of two forms:

$$
H\big(N(t),h(t),\mu(t),t\big) = e^{-\delta t} U(\cdot) + \lambda(t) f(\cdot)
\tag{3.29}
$$

or

$$
\tilde{H}\big(N(t),h(t),\mu(t),t\big) = U(\cdot) + \mu(t) f(\cdot)
\tag{3.30}
$$

In both (3.29) and (3.30) the Hamiltonian is the sum of the value of the net benefits from use of the resource at time t (a flow value) and the value of the future net benefits associated with the size of the resource left at time t (a stock value). The difference between them is that the value in (3.29) is from the perspective of the present. It is a discounted or *present value*. The value in (3.30) is from the perspective of time t. It is an undiscounted or *current value*. It follows that $\mu(t) = e^{\delta t} \lambda(t)$. Using (3.29) we can rewrite the Lagrangian function in terms of the Hamiltonian.

$$
L(\cdot) = \int_0^T \left[H(\cdot) + \dot{\lambda} N(t) \right] dt + e^{-\delta T} F(\cdot) - \left[\lambda(T)N(T) - \lambda(0)N(0) \right]
\tag{3.31}
$$

As before the first of the first order necessary conditions requires that the control, $h(t)$, be increased up to the point at which the marginal benefits are just offset by the marginal costs of control. This is the condition that:

$$
\begin{aligned}
\frac{dL}{dh(t)} = \frac{dH}{dh(t)} &= e^{-\delta t} \frac{dU}{dh(t)} + \lambda(t)\frac{df(\cdot)}{dh(t)} = 0 \\
\Rightarrow e^{-\delta t} \frac{dU}{dh(t)} &= -\lambda(t)\frac{df(\cdot)}{dh(t)}
\end{aligned}
\tag{3.32}
$$

The second condition concerns the state variable $N(t)$. It requires that, along an optimal trajectory, the marginal net benefits of a change in stock size are zero, implying that the user cost of a change in $N(t)$—the value of the stream of future services forgone or gained by changing $N(t)$—just offsets the current marginal benefits of that change:

$$\frac{dL}{dN(t)} = \frac{dH}{dN(t)} + \dot{\lambda} = e^{-\delta t}\frac{dU}{dN(t)} + \lambda(t)\frac{df(\cdot)}{dN(t)} + \dot{\lambda} = 0$$
$$\Rightarrow \dot{\lambda} = -\frac{dH}{dN(t)} = -e^{-\delta t}\frac{dU}{dN(t)} - \lambda(t)\frac{df(\cdot)}{dN(t)} \tag{3.33}$$

and

$$\frac{dL}{dN(T)} = e^{-\delta T}\frac{dF(\cdot)}{dN(T)} - \lambda(T) = 0$$
$$\Rightarrow e^{-\delta T}\frac{dF(\cdot)}{dN(T)} = \lambda(T) \tag{3.34}$$

The remaining conditions are that:

$$\frac{dL}{d\lambda(t)} = \frac{dH}{d\lambda(t)} - \dot{N} = 0$$
$$\Rightarrow \dot{N} = f(\cdot) \tag{3.35}$$
$$N(0) = N_0$$

Consider condition (3.33). This condition determines the change in the user cost or shadow value of the resource along an optimal trajectory. Using the expression for $\lambda(t)$ from (3.32), condition (3.33) implies that

$$\frac{\dot{\lambda}}{\lambda(t)} + \frac{df(\cdot)}{dN(t)} = \frac{dU/dN(t)}{dU/dh(t)}\frac{df(\cdot)}{dh(t)} \tag{3.36}$$

Along an optimal trajectory, the proportional rate of change in the shadow value of the resource plus the marginal growth impact of a change in the size of the stock at time t should be equal to the marginal rate of substitution between the stock, $N(t)$, and the flow, $h(t)$, $\dfrac{dU/dN(t)}{dU/dh(t)}$, multiplied by the marginal growth impact of a change in level of harvest, $\dfrac{df(\cdot)}{dh(t)}$. Recall that the marginal rate of substitution measures the rate at which the decision-maker is willing to trade off the benefits of the stock and the benefits of the flow. In some cases, livestock on commercial farms, for example, the stock itself may have no value other than the capacity it has to yield future flows. In others, wildlife stocks in game parks, for example, the benefits to park visitors from stocks may dominate the value of any culling or sale program.

If the marginal rate of substitution between the stock and flow benefits from $N(t)$ and $h(t)$, respectively, is zero it says that the proportional rate of change in the shadow value of the resource is $-\dfrac{df(\cdot)}{dN(t)}$, the negative of the marginal impact of stock size on growth. So if the stock itself has no current value, the proportional growth rate in its user cost will decline more rapidly the higher its rate of growth. The value of small, fast-growing stocks will fall faster than the value of large slow-growing stocks. If the marginal rate of substitution between $N(t)$ and $h(t)$ is not zero it says that the proportional rate of change in the shadow value of the resource depends on the marginal impact on the physical growth of the resource of changes in both stock, $N(t)$, and the harvest, $h(t)$.

To connect condition (3.33) to the Hotelling arbitrage condition, note that the Hotelling arbitrage condition for this problem implies that

$$f(N(t),h(t)) = N(t)\left[\delta - \frac{\dot{p}}{p(t)}\right]$$

from which it follows that at the point where the resource owner is indifferent between holding and conserving the resource the slope of the growth function, $\dfrac{df(N(t),h(t))}{dN(t)}$, will be equal to the difference between the opportunity cost of capital and the expected capital gain on the stock, $\delta - \dfrac{\dot{p}}{p(t)}$. Now consider the following problem:

$$Max_{h(t)} \int_0^T e^{-\delta t} p(t) h(t) dt + e^{-\delta T} F(N(T)) \qquad (3.37)$$

subject to

$$\dot{N} = rN(t)\left(1 - \frac{N(t)}{K}\right) - h(t) \qquad (3.38)$$

$$N(0) = N_0$$

The manager chooses harvest so as to maximize the discounted stream of benefits from harvest, the marginal benefit at time t being the "price" of harvest at that time, and the value of the stock left at time T. This is a classic problem in natural resource economics, but at the same time it nicely illustrates the role of the Hotelling arbitrage condition in determining how much of the stock of $N(t)$ should be conserved along an optimal path. From (3.38) growth depends on three things: harvest, the intrinsic growth rate of the species, and the size of the stock relative to the carrying capacity of the environment. Trivially, it is not possible to harvest more than the available stock, $h(t) \le N(t)$. It is also not possible to maintain the size of the stock unless harvest is less than the growth in the stock,

$$\dot{N} \ge 0 \Rightarrow h(t) \le rN(t)\left(1 - \frac{N(t)}{K}\right)$$

The Lagrangian function for this problem takes the same general form as equation (3.31)

$$L(\cdot) = \int_0^T \left[H(\cdot) + \dot{\lambda}N(t)\right]dt + F(\cdot) - \left[\lambda(T)N(T) - \lambda(0)N(0)\right] \qquad (3.39)$$

which we can use to find the first order necessary conditions for choice of $h(t)$ to maximize (3.37). Since the present value Hamiltonian for this problem has the form:

$$H(N(t), h(t), \mu(t), t) = e^{-\delta t} p(t)h(t) + \lambda(t)\left(rN(t)\left(1 - \frac{N(t)}{K}\right) - h(t)\right)$$

following the same approach as before yields these conditions:

$$e^{-\delta t} p(t) = \lambda(t) \qquad (3.40)$$

$$\dot{\lambda} = -\lambda(t)r\left(1 - \frac{2N(t)}{K}\right) \qquad (3.41)$$

$$\lambda(T) = \frac{dF(N(T))}{dN(T)} \qquad (3.42)$$

$$\dot{N} = rN(t)\left(1 - \frac{N(t)}{K}\right) - h(t)$$

$$N(0) = N_0 \tag{3.43}$$

Multiplying (3.40) to (3.42) through by $e^{\delta t}$ transforms the costate variable, the shadow value of $N(t)$, from a present to a current value. We denote the current value multiplier $\mu(t)$. The maximum principle now requires that

$$p(t) = \mu(t) \tag{3.44}$$

Further, since $\lambda(t) = e^{-\delta t}\mu(t)$, $\dot{\lambda} = -\delta\mu e^{-\delta t} + \dot{\mu}e^{-dt}$, the adjoint equation takes the form

$$\dot{\mu} - \delta\mu(t) = -\mu(t)r\left(1 - \frac{2N(t)}{K}\right) \tag{3.45}$$

This is just the marginal condition on $N(t)$ that needs to be satisfied at the point where the resource owner is indifferent between conserving and converting the resource—the derivative of the Hotelling arbitrage condition with respect to $N(t)$. Specifically:

$$\frac{\dot{\mu}}{\mu(t)} + r\left(1 - \frac{2N(t)}{K}\right) = \delta = \frac{\dot{p}}{p(t)} + r\left(1 - \frac{2N(t)}{K}\right) \tag{3.46}$$

It says that the growth in the value of the asset as a result of changes in both the shadow price/price and the growth in physical stock should be equal to the rate of interest (the rate of growth in the value of alternative capital stocks). In fact, the adjoint equations always restate the Hotelling principle for renewable resources in terms of the shadow value of the stock or state variable.

The same expression also gives us some insight into the relation between the size of the stock to be conserved and the critical parameters of the growth problem along the optimal trajectory. Since $N(t) = \frac{K}{2}\left(\frac{\dot{p}/p(t) + r - \delta}{r}\right)$ we should expect stocks to be increasing in $\dot{p}/p(t)$ and decreasing in δ. Whether stocks are increasing or decreasing in r depends on the difference between $\dot{p}/p(t)$ and δ. $N(t)$ will be increasing/decreasing in r as $\dot{p}/p(t)$ is less than/greater than δ. It is also immediate that if $\dot{p}/p(t)$ and δ are both zero, $N(t)$ will be at $K/2$, which corresponds to the maximum sustainable yield of a logistic growth function.

Note that if $U(h(t),t)$ is twice differentiable in $h(t)$, we may use the first order necessary conditions to obtain a set of differential equations with which to solve for the steady state values of $h(t)$ and $N(t)$. The first order necessary conditions expressed in terms of the current value Hamiltonian include the requirements that:

$$\frac{d\tilde{H}}{dh(t)} = 0 \Rightarrow \frac{dU(\cdot)}{dh(t)} = \mu(t) \tag{3.47}$$

$$-\frac{d\tilde{H}}{dN(t)} = \dot{\mu} - \delta\mu(t) = -\mu(t)\frac{df(\cdot)}{dN(t)} \tag{3.48}$$

Taking the time derivative of (3.47), $\dfrac{d^2U(\cdot)}{dh(t)^2}\dot{h} = \dot{\mu}$, and substituting it in (3.48) we obtain:

$$\dot{h} = \frac{dU(\cdot)/dh(t)}{d^2U(\cdot)/dh(t)^2}\left(\delta - r\left(1 - \frac{2N(t)}{K}\right)\right) \tag{3.49}$$

Along with (3.38) this provides a system of differential equations that may be solved for the optimal (steady state) harvest, h^*, and the optimal (steady state) stock, N^*. These occur where $\delta = r\left(1 - \dfrac{2N^*}{K}\right)$ and where $rN^*\left(1 - \dfrac{N^*}{K}\right) = h^*$ (Figure 3.5). Notice that the higher the interest rate, the steeper is the slope

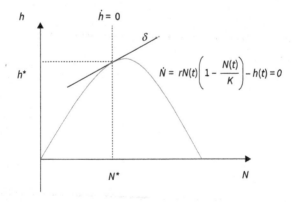

Figure 3.5 Harvest and stock size in the steady state.

The steady state harvest, h^*, occurs when the natural rate of growth of the resource stock, N^*, is equal to the interest rate, δ.

of the line, δ, and the smaller is the steady state harvest, h^*, and the steady state stock, N^*. In other words, the larger is the rate of growth in the value of the stock if converted, the smaller is the size of the stock that will be conserved. Notice also that if the rate of growth in the value of the stock if converted were larger than the intrinsic growth rate of the resource, none of the stock would be conserved.

3.5 Connecting Hotelling conservation and conservation biology

How does the Hotelling approach connect to the propositions inherent in conservation biology? Recall that Hotelling himself saw the origins of the conservation movement in the perception that the natural environment was both undervalued and overexploited. He sought to understand the basis of the value of natural resources, why that value might change over time, and how change in the value of natural resources might influence their conservation. The critical element in Hotelling's approach is the arbitrage condition, since that fixes the circumstances under which asset holders will choose to conserve or convert their assets. The arbitrage condition tells us that conservation depends on the expected growth in the value of assets if conserved relative to the expected growth in their value if converted.

The central tenet of conservation biology as it originally developed was that the value attached by the majority of landowners and landholders to wild species is strictly less than its true value to society—that there is a wedge between the value assigned by individuals to wild species and the value of those species to society. Several reasons were advanced as to why this has occurred. The most important of these was landowner/landholder ignorance about the role played by particular species, and communities of species, and the relation between ecological functioning and the ecosystem services that benefit humans. Ignorance about the effects of reduced diversity of food webs on decomposition, nutrient retention, plant productivity, and water retention, for example, was argued to threaten a number of ecological functions of direct or indirect benefit to humans (Naeem et al. 1996). Ignorance about source and sink dynamics was cited as a major reason for the extirpation of many protected sink populations. Failure to protect disproportionately valuable source populations necessarily put associated sink populations at risk, even if those populations were otherwise protected (Mangel et al. 1996). More generally, by focusing on single species, populations, or biotopes, in isolation from the system that support them, landowners paid insufficient attention to critical elements of the wider system (Myers 1996).

A related concern was that decisions that reduced biodiversity tended to be focused on short-term gain, and to pay insufficient attention to the longer-term costs in terms of reduced capacity to protect future options against fundamental change (Mangel et al. 1996). Since the neglect of longer-term costs stems either from ignorance or from the application of high discount rates, and since there is an ethical component to discounting, the undervaluation of species and whole ecosystems was taken to reflect—at least in part—an ethic of myopic greed. By contrast, conservation biology was argued to be concerned about the maintenance of whole ecosystems over the long term. It was claimed that the difference in the values attached by conservation biologists to species reflected a fundamental difference in ethics. At the core of the conservation ethic was the proposition that biodiversity has intrinsic value, irrespective of its instrumental or utilitarian value, and that value is "neither conferred nor revocable," but springs from the fact of the species existence (Soulé 1985).

There are obvious practical difficulties with a concept of value that is independent of human preferences and yet is expected to guide human action. But if we think of the argument as a statement that there is value attaching to species that stems from their place in the natural system, rather than their incorporation in a managed production process, then it is quite consistent with the general proposition that nature is undervalued when measured by the market price of harvested species. It is also consistent with the key proposition implicit in the Hotelling arbitrage condition for renewable natural resources: that the expected growth in value of natural resources comprises the sum of the expected capital gain in holding those resources in situ, and the value added through their role in the functioning of the natural system.

As we saw in Chapter 1, many of the original propositions of conservation biology have evolved with efforts to uncover the value attaching to the many and varied roles played by genes, species, landscapes, and ecosystems. There is now a more systematic attempt to ask what benefits are lost when there is a change in either species richness or abundance. The notion of intrinsic value still has a place in the language of conservation biologists, but it is increasingly linked to the value deriving from the place of species in the ecosystem rather than their mere existence. We explore the determination of conservation and other values in greater detail in later chapters. What is important here is the fact that the decision to conserve a natural system in some state depends on the expected growth in the value of the system in that state, taking account both of the value reflected in market prices and of the value stemming from the wider functioning of the system.

3.6 Summary and conclusions

This chapter reviewed the Hotelling approach to conservation. It made five main points. First, the Hotelling arbitrage condition, an application of the equimarginal principle, holds that a decision-maker will be indifferent between conserving and converting a resource if the proportional rate of change in the value of the conserved resource is equal to the rate of return on the best alternative investment that could be made if the resource was converted. From a social perspective, the rate of change in the value of natural resources committed to some use reflects the full range of impacts of resource use associated with that use. In later chapters we explore the reasons why there may be a wedge between the value of resources to an individual and their value to wider society. Here, it is enough to say that conservation decisions should rest on expected changes in the value of natural resources to all stakeholders (which could include future generations). It follows immediately that the incentive to conserve a natural resource in some state will be increasing in the expected growth in its social value in that state, and will be decreasing in the rate of return on the alternative assets.

Second, Hotelling concluded that in certain conditions—perfect information, perfect competition, no new discoveries, no technical change—one would expect the price of an exhaustible resource to rise at the same rate as the rate of return on alternative assets. Much effort has gone into testing this result for particular exhaustible resources in the real world (where none of Hotelling's conditions apply). Not surprisingly, there is no evidence for a classic Hotelling price path. There is, however, evidence for the more general proposition that if natural resources are conserved their expected future value is increasing.

Third, we showed that the Hotelling arbitrage condition extends naturally to the case of renewable natural resources that may be growing over time. The conditions are the same as that for a nonrenewable resource—decision-makers will be indifferent between conserving and converting a resource if the proportional rate of growth in the value of the resource is equal to the rate of return on the best alternative investment that could be made if the resource was converted. The difference is that for renewable resources, there are two ways the value of the resource, if conserved, can grow. One is through the same mechanism affecting the value of nonrenewable resources, namely a change in its price (a capital gain). The other way the value of a renewable resource can grow is through a change in the size of the stock (its growth or depletion). It follows that if a natural resource stock is growing physically, it may be worth conserving that stock even if its price is not increasing as fast as the rate of return on alternative assets. Conversely, if a natural resource stock is declining, it will be worth conserving the stock only if its price is increasing faster than the rate of return on alternative assets.

Fourth, we showed that the Hotelling principle is among the conditions for a natural resource stock to be managed optimally. More particularly, we showed that the first order necessary conditions for the optimal management of a renewable resource stock is a requirement that the shadow value of the stock (its real value to society, as opposed to a market value) is increasing at a rate equal to the difference between the rate of return on alternative assets (the discount rate), and the proportional rate of growth of the resource stock.

Finally, we observed that while conservation biologists tend to focus on different traits and different measures than those motivating other resource users, their insistence that these traits and measures are important in conservation decisions is consistent with the Hotelling approach. The value that resource users should take into account in making decisions to conserve or convert resources ought to be inclusive of the impacts of those decisions on all members of society. There are many reasons why resource users might not take all impacts into account, and the values identified by conservation biologists have frequently been among those neglected by decision-makers. In later chapters we draw attention to the particular problems posed by externalities and the public good nature of resources. The Hotelling approach assumes that these problems have been addressed, but as we shall see, this frequently requires active policy interventions to change the signals to resource users.

References

Conrad, J. M. 1999. Resource economics. Cambridge University Press, Cambridge.

Deverajan, S., and A. Fisher. 1981. Hotelling's "Economics of Exhaustible Resources" fifty years later. Journal of Economic Literature XIX:65–73.

Hotelling, H. 1931. The economics of exhaustible resources. Journal of Political Economy 39:137–175.

Lin, C. Y. 2009. Insights from a simple Hotelling model of the world oil market. Natural Resources Research 18:19–28.

Lin, C. Y., H. Meng, T. Ngai, V. Oscherov, and Y. Zhu. 2009. Hotelling revisited: oil prices and endogenous technological progress. Natural Resources Research 18:29–38.

Lotka, A. J. 1925. Elements of physical biology. Williams & Wilkins Co, Baltimore.

Mangel, M., L. M. Talbot, G. K. Meffe, M. T. Agardy, D. L. Alverson, J. Barlow, D. B. Botkin, G. Budowski, T. Clark, J. Cooke, R. H. Crozier, P. K. Dayton, D. L. Elder,

C. W. Fowler, S. Funtowicz, J. Giske, R. J. Hofman, S. J. Holt, S. R. Kellert, L. A. Kimball, D. Ludwig, K. Magnusson, B. S. Malayang, C. Mann, E. A. Norse, S. P. Northridge, W. F. Perrin, C. Perrings, R. M. Peterman, G. B. Rabb, H. A. Regier, J. E. Reynolds, K. Sherman, M. P. Sissenwine, T. D. Smith, A. Starfield, R. J. Taylor, M. F. Tillman, C. Toft, J. R. Twiss, J. Wilen, and T. P. Young. 1996. Principles for the conservation of wild living resources. Ecological Applications 6:338–362.

Myers, N. 1996. Environmental services of biodiversity. Proceedings of the National Academy of Sciences of the United States of America 93:2764–2769.

Naeem, S., K. Haakenson, L. J. Thompson, J. H. Lawton, and M. J. Crawley. 1996. Biodiversity and plant productivity in a model assemblage of plant species. Oikos 76:259–264.

Soulé, M. E. 1985. What is conservation biology? Bioscience 35:727–734.

Verhulst, P. F. 1845. Recherches mathématiques sur la loi d'accroissement de la population. Nouveaux Mémoires de l'Académie Royale des Sciences et Belles-Lettres de Bruxelles 18:14–54.

4

The Conservation of Renewable Resources

> In colonial and pioneer days the forest was a foe and an obstacle to the settler. It had to be cleared away . . . But [now] as a nation we have not yet come to have a proper respect for the forest and to regard it as an indispensable part of our resources—one which is easily destroyed but difficult to replace; one which confers great benefits while it endures, but whose disappearance is accompanied by a train of evil consequences not readily foreseen and positively irreparable.
>
> —Eliot Blackwelder, "A Country that has Used up its Trees," 1906

4.1 Introduction

We have seen that the Hotelling theory of conservation requires the decision-maker to balance the expected growth in the value of stocks of assets in alternative uses. If the expected growth in the value of a stock when conserved is greater than the expected growth in the value of a stock when converted, it will be optimal to conserve the stock. It follows that conservation decisions presuppose both the capacity to value stocks and the capacity to form expectations about future changes in the value of stocks. We consider the valuation problem in Chapters 5 and 6. In this chapter we address another implication of the Hotelling principle: that it offers a theory both of what to keep, and what not to keep.

Ever since the publication of the Brundtland Commission's report "Our Common Future" (World Commission on Environment and Development 1987), concern has been expressed about the sustainability of the various uses made of environmental resources. The central question is how much of a resource to conserve at any moment in time. In what follows we explore this question for a selection of environmental stocks now argued to be overexploited, and show how the rate at which those stocks are being run down is influenced by changes in their relative value. More particularly, we

Conservation. Charles Perrings and Ann Kinzig, Oxford University Press (2021). © Oxford University Press.
DOI: 10.1093/oso/9780190613600.003.0004

explore the conservation problem embedded in the exploitation of marine capture fisheries, the management of forest systems, and the harvesting of wildlife. In each case we set up and solve a canonical version of the problem. We show how the solution reflects the Hotelling principle, and we test the sensitivity of the conservation trajectory to the value of the resource.

Any asset management problem can be cast as an optimal control problem. The assets or stocks in such a problem are the state variables of the problem— their quantity or value at any given time is a measure of the state of the system. Those stocks are then managed through a set of control variables. The controls used to manage environmental assets cover a very wide range of actions. In the simplest systems they might include harvest, culling, restocking, reseeding, and replanting. In more complicated problems the controls can include a range of land management interventions affecting, for example, the fire regime, hydrological flows, the structure of habitats, the functioning of the system, and the ecosystem processes involved.

In a simple wildlife management problem, for example, the wildlife stocks are the state variables of the problem, and the offtake from each stock is the control variable. Any offtake policy directly implies a stock conservation policy, since offtake today determines the size of the stock tomorrow. As we saw in Chapter 3, the optimal conservation policy in such a case depends on the growth in value of future stocks relative to the return that could be had from investing the proceeds of the sale of harvested animals today. The size of the optimal stock may be less than if there were no harvest, but as long as the expected growth in the value of stocks at some level is greater than the expected growth in value of alternative assets, stocks will be conserved at least at that level.

In this chapter we show how the optimal control of environmental resources solves for the optimal level of conservation in terms of the Hotelling principle. We also show how the solution to an optimal control problem generates a time path for the conservation of resource stocks just as it generates a time path for the active controls. In fact, we can identify conservation phases in an optimal control policy in a very straightforward way. For example, where the optimal control problem is such that the Hamiltonian function (introduced in Chapter 3) is linear in the control, we can show that if initial stocks are below the optimal level, the optimal policy will include a pure conservation phase until stocks have built up to the optimal level. We can also show that in the long-term management of some systems the optimal control of the system may generate alternating exploitation and conservation phases.

In terms of the economics of natural resources we are interested in problems that involve renewable resources only. Implicitly, models of renewable natural resource extraction assume that the decision-maker operates over a time horizon that is longer than the renewal period of the renewable resource. If this is not the case, the resource is assumed to be exhaustible, and its dynamics irrelevant to the problem. Stocks of coal, minerals, oil, or fossil water all fall into this category. The Hotelling approach to conservation still applies to such resources, but they are not the resources that interest conservationists.

The chapter is organized in five sections. Section 4.2 considers the problem of marine resources. 4.3 addresses forests, and 4.4 takes the case of rangelands. In each case we show how the optimal use of the environmental stocks involved implies a decision about how much of the stock to conserve, and illustrate the link between that decision and the expected growth in the value of those stocks relative to the discount rate. Each case has been selected to reflect a different kind of conservation challenge: the problem of open access in 4.2, the existence of ancillary benefits in 4.3, and the importance of differences in the rate at which distinct environmental stocks grow or regenerate in 4.4. A final section provides a summary and conclusions.

4.2 Marine capture fisheries

We begin with one of the most widespread and intractable conservation problems: the depletion of marine fish stocks in sea areas beyond national jurisdiction (Figure 4.1). This is a problem that has many causes,

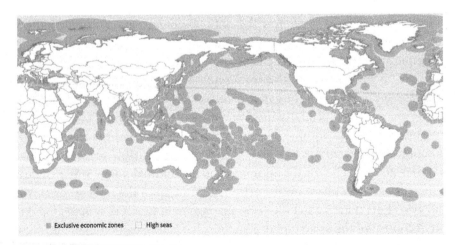

Figure 4.1 The high seas or sea areas beyond national jurisdiction (light gray).
The high seas cover 64% of the ocean's surface, or 43% of the earth's surface.
Source: Rogers et al. (2014).

the most important of which is that high seas fisheries are essentially open access, meaning that no one can be excluded from accessing any fisheries in the area (Berkes et al. 2005, Worm et al. 2006, Costello et al. 2008). What makes this problematic is that open access is the source of the "tragedy" in the "tragedy of the commons" (Hardin 1968). It is the driver behind the overexploitation of common pool environmental resources in both marine and terrestrial systems (Feeny et al. 1990, Ostrom 1990, Dasgupta 2001, Ostrom et al. 2002, Libecap 2009, McWhinnie 2009, Perrings 2014).

Since the turn of the century, marine biologists have raised the alarm about the number of open access marine fish stocks still being exploited at or beyond maximum sustainable yield, and the number of coastal mangrove and coral reef fish nurseries threatened by coastal habitat conversion and land-based emissions (Jackson et al. 2001, Hughes et al. 2003, Worm et al. 2006, Worm et al. 2007, Jackson 2008). The maximum sustainable yield from traditional fish stocks was reached in the mid-1980s (Food and Agriculture Organization 2004). Since then, increases in catches have involved the depletion of traditional stocks and development of new, nontraditional fisheries. The net result is that while the level of effort in wild capture fisheries in the high seas continues to increase, global catches have been declining since the 1990s (Figure 4.2).

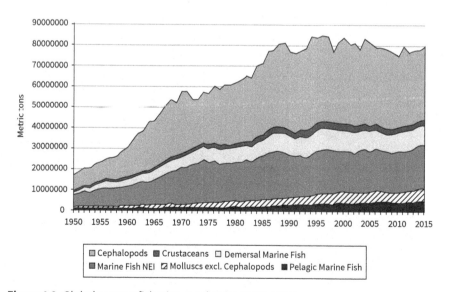

Figure 4.2 Global capture fisheries, production 1950–2015.
Source: Constructed from data at Food and Agriculture Organization (2017).

Marine mammals have similarly been systematically overexploited in sea areas beyond national jurisdiction. Indeed, the pattern of whaling in which overharvesting of any one species triggers the exploitation of others was established in the nineteenth century. Several whale species were severely depleted before 1900, including a number of baleen whales hunted for blubber (the bowhead, grey, humpback, and right whales), and the sperm whale hunted for spermaceti (at least until the discovery of kerosene in the 1840s).

In the twentieth century the range of whales exploited widened, the number of firms accessing whale fisheries increased, and the rate at which whale populations were harvested rose dramatically. Many stocks were driven to commercial extinction, including the blue, fin, sei, and beluga whales. Between 1900 and 1986, when the International Whaling Commission (IWC) approved a moratorium on commercial whaling, it is estimated that some three million whales were harvested (Rocha et al. 2014). Nor did the moratorium change the pattern. Whalers either continued whaling under objection to the moratorium (Norway and Iceland), under special permit (Japan, Korea), or as nonmembers of the IWC. Given the impact of mid-century whaling on traditional stocks, however, whalers switched to a number of lesser known toothed whales and porpoises—particularly Dall's porpoise and the harbour porpoise. In fact a substantially greater number of animals was harvested in the 20 years after the moratorium than in the 20 years before the moratorium (Figure 4.3).

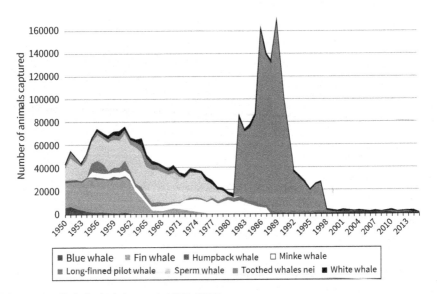

Figure 4.3 Global whale harvest, 1950–2015.

Source: Constructed from data at Food and Agriculture Organization (2017).

To understand the conservation problem reflected in these data, consider the canonical fishery model developed by Clark (Clark 1973, Clark 1976, Clark 1979, Clark 2010). The formal problem addressed is to choose the level of harvest so as maximize the net benefits of fishing activity, subject to the dynamics of the harvested species. Harvest is thus the control variable, and the fish stock the state variable of the problem. The Hotelling problem concerns the rate at which the state variable changes.

The dynamics of the fish population are assumed to follow the same logistic growth path introduced in Chapter 3, in which the critical parameters are the intrinsic rate of growth, r, the carrying capacity of the environment, K, and initial size of the stock, N_0:

$$\dot{N} = rN(t)\left(1 - \frac{N(t)}{K}\right) \tag{4.1}$$

Recall that this generates compensatory growth. If the size of the stock is low relative to the carrying capacity of the environment growth, rates will be close to the intrinsic or maximum potential rate, and when the size of the stock is high relative to the carrying capacity of the environment growth, rates will tend to zero (Rose et al. 2001). The relationship between growth and stock size for models of this kind is illustrated in Figure 4.4, which shows that growth is at a maximum at exactly $\frac{1}{2}K$.

An implicit assumption is that the stock is small enough that it has no impact on the wider environment. This means carrying capacity is treated as fixed and exogenously determined. This is seldom realistic from an ecological perspective, but it does make it possible to focus on conservation of the fish stock itself, without having to be concerned with the wider environment. We

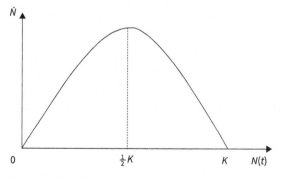

Figure 4.4 Logistic growth function.
The rate of population growth first increases and then decreases with population size, falling to zero when population size is equal to the carrying capacity of the resource.

later consider the more general problem in which conservation of some population implies conservation of the supporting environment.

We suppose that the fishery is harvested at a cost that is a function of time, $c(t)$, and that the harvest is sold at a price that is a function of time, $p(t)$. Any level of harvest that is less than or equal to the growth rate of the fish stock is sustainable. We therefore describe sustainable harvests as all those for which:

$$h_s \le rN(t)\left(1 - \frac{N(t)}{K}\right) \tag{4.2}$$

Potential harvest reaches a maximum when $N(t) = \frac{1}{2}K$ but, for compensatory growth functions of this kind, it is important to note that there are sustainable harvest rates corresponding to any stock size between zero and K.

Fishers are assumed to maximize the net benefits of harvest: $p(t) - c(t) = p_n(t)$. We refer to $p_n(t)$ as the net price of harvest (or net profit). The economic problem to be solved by a forward-looking fisher can then be written as:

$$Max_{h(t)} \int_0^\infty e^{-\delta t} p_n(t) h(t) dt \tag{4.3}$$

subject to

$$0 \le h(t) \le h_{max}$$
$$\dot{N} = rN(t)\left(1 - \frac{N(t)}{K}\right) - h(t) \tag{4.4}$$
$$N(0) = N_0$$

The constraint set includes the equations of motion for the fish stock and the initial size of that stock. In addition, it includes the harvest capacity of the fisher, h_{max}. This is taken as given, implying that investment in new vessels or gear is beyond the scope of the model. The choice being made is only how much effort to commit to harvest, given available vessels and gear, and given the carrying capacity of the environment.

The solution to a problem of this type requires that we form the (current value) Hamiltonian function,

$$\tilde{H}(N(t), h(t), \mu(t), t) = p_n(t) h(t) + \mu(t)\left[rN(t)\left(1 - \frac{N(t)}{K}\right) - h(t)\right] \tag{4.5}$$

in which the multiplier or costate variable, $\mu(t)$, is a measure of the impact of a marginal change in the state variable on the objective function—in this case the marginal effect of a change in fish stocks on the net benefits of fishing. $\mu(t)$ is therefore the future net benefits forgone by reducing the size of the fish stock through harvest today. It is the social opportunity cost of converting a unit of stock through harvest.

The first order necessary conditions for the net benefits of fishing to be maximized are obtained by taking the partial derivatives of the Hamiltonian with respect to the state, costate, and control variables. These conditions include the requirement that harvest be increased up to the point where the marginal net benefit of harvest is exactly equal to its social opportunity cost

$$\tilde{H}_{h(t)} = p_n(t) - \mu(t) = p(t) - c(t) - \mu(t) = 0 \tag{4.6}$$

They also include requirements for the costate and state variables

$$\dot{\mu} - \delta\mu(t) = -\tilde{H}_{N(t)} = -\mu(t) r \left(1 - \frac{2N(t)}{K} \right) \tag{4.7}$$

$$\tilde{H}_{\mu(t)} = rN(t) \left(1 - \frac{N(t)}{K} \right) - h(t) - \dot{N} = 0 \tag{4.8}$$

Because the Hamiltonian is linear in the control (harvest) these conditions imply a "most rapid approach" to the optimal stock size. That is, harvest is determined as follows:

$$h(t) = \begin{cases} 0 \text{ if } p_n(t) < \mu(t) \\ h^* \text{ if } p_n(t) = \mu(t) \\ h_{max} \text{ if } p_n(t) > \mu(t) \end{cases} \tag{4.9}$$

From conditions (4.7) and (4.8) we can calculate the size of the natural resource stock that satisfies the optimality conditions. Notice that the time derivative of (4.6) is $\dot{\mu} = \dot{p}_n = \dot{p} - \dot{c}$. Substituting this in returns the condition for renewable resources:

$$\frac{\dot{p}_n}{p_n} + r \left(1 - \frac{2N(t)}{K} \right) = \delta \tag{4.10}$$

If there is no change in the net price of the fish, then this expression collapses to the canonical steady state solution for fisheries at which $\delta = r\left(1 - \dfrac{2N(t)}{K}\right)$.

The solution to (4.10) is the economically efficient stock size (Figure 4.4)—given by the point at which the marginal benefit of a change in the fish stock, $r\left(1 - \dfrac{2N(t)}{K}\right)$, is the same as the marginal opportunity cost of a change. The opportunity cost, in this case, is the sum of the interest rate that could be earned if the stock were converted and the forgone capital gain from converting the fish stock, $\delta - \dfrac{\dot{p}_n}{p_n(t)}$. Note that if the net price of fish stocks is increasing, then the slope of the line describing the opportunity cost of is flatter than it would otherwise be. If the net price of fish stocks is falling, the slope of the line is steeper than it would otherwise be. The flatter the slope the larger the stock size it is optimal to conserve. The steeper the slope, the smaller the stock size it is optimal to conserve (Figure 4.5).

If the net price of fish stocks is increasing at a rate greater than the interest rate, then the slope of the line $\delta - \dfrac{\dot{p}_n}{p_n(t)}$ is negative, and the point of tangency between that line and the fish stock growth curve is to the right of the maximum sustainable yield stock size. In other words, it will be optimal to

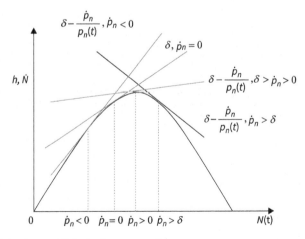

Figure 4.5 Net price and fish stock conservation.

Showing the effect of the rate of change in the net price of a fishery on the size of the stock to be conserved.

conserve a larger fish stock than that corresponding to maximum sustainable yield, and to harvest at a lower rate.

Since the net price is just the difference between the price of the harvested fish and the cost of harvest, it can change with both things. Other things being equal, an increase in the cost of harvest will cause the net price to fall, thereby increasing the slope of the line $\delta - \dfrac{\dot{p}_n}{p_n(t)}$, reducing both the optimal harvest and the size of the stock conserved. A decrease in the cost of harvest will have the opposite effect. The net price will rise, so decreasing the slope of the line $\delta - \dfrac{\dot{p}_n}{p_n(t)}$, and increasing both the optimal harvest—at least up to the maximum sustainable yield—and the size of the stock conserved. Symmetrically, a reduction in the price of fish will reduce both the optimal harvest and the size of the stock conserved, while an increase in the price of fish will have the opposite effect.

The implication of papers such as (Worm et al. 2006) is that many marine capture fisheries have been consistently exploited at rates above maximum sustainable yield, and hence that stocks have been declining. To understand why overharvesting may occur we need to consider not just the harvest decisions of a single fisher or fishing firm, but the entry decisions of all fishers or fishing firms. That is what determines the aggregate level of fishing effort, or the size of the fishing fleet. To do this, let us denote the size of the whole fishing fleet at time t to be $Z(t)$, and the size of the fishing fleet of the ith firm to be $z_i(t)$. The size of the resource, as before, is denoted $N(t)$. Suppose that there is no restriction on entry. This is the classic case considered by (Hardin 1968). In this case the profits earned by each fishing firm depend both on the harvest decisions of that firm, and the entry decisions of all other firms seeking to access the fishery.

If we denote the profits accruing to the jth firm by π_j, this implies that:

$$\pi_j = \frac{z_j}{\sum\limits_i z_i} f\left(\sum_i z_i\right) - cz_j \tag{4.11}$$

in which c is the fixed cost of a vessel to the individual firm, z_j is the size of the fleet of the jth firm, and $\sum\limits_i z_i = Z$ is the size of the aggregate fleet.

Consider, first, the effect of a change in the size of any one fleet on the net benefit of harvest by other fleets. It follows from (4.11) that the marginal impact of a change in the size of the ith fleet on profits accruing to the owner of the jth fleet is:

$$\frac{d\pi_j}{dz_i} = \frac{z_j}{\sum_i z_i} f'(Z) - z_j \frac{f(Z)}{Z^2} = \frac{z_j}{Z}\left(f'(Z) - \frac{f(Z)}{Z}\right) \tag{4.12}$$

Note that this is positive only if the marginal physical product of a vessel added in the ith fleet, $f'(Z)$, is greater than the average physical product of the aggregate fleet, $\frac{f(Z)}{Z}$, if the last vessel added is more productive than the average vessel. Otherwise each vessel added reduces profits to all other fishers (see Figure 4.6).

In most cases, the jth fishing firm would not be expected to take account of the impact of their activities on the profitability of other fishing firms. The level of fishing effort/fleet size that adopted by the jth fishing firm would be the solution to the problem:

$$Max_{z_j}\,\pi_j = \frac{z_j}{\sum_i z_i} f\left(\sum_i z_i\right) - cz_j \tag{4.13}$$

The first order necessary conditions for z_j to be optimal by these criteria include the requirement that:

$$\frac{d\pi_j}{dz_j} = \frac{z_j}{Z}\left(f'(Z) - \frac{f(Z)}{Z}\right) + \frac{f(Z)}{Z} - c = 0 \tag{4.14}$$

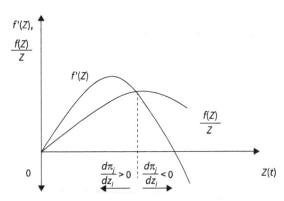

Figure 4.6 Fleet size and fishery profits.

Showing the impact of a change in individual fleet size on the net benefits of fishing in other fishing firms.

implying that the size of the jth fleet would be

$$z_j = Z\left(c - \frac{f(Z)}{Z}\right) \Big/ \left(f'(Z) - \frac{f(Z)}{Z}\right) \tag{4.15}$$

Compare this to the fleet size that would occur if all fishers were selecting z_j to maximize not the net benefit to themselves, but the net benefit to all. From a social perspective, maximization of aggregate profit through choice of the aggregate fleet size

$$Max_Z \sum_j \pi_j = \frac{\sum_j z_j}{Z} f(Z) - c \sum_j z_j \tag{4.16}$$

requires that the marginal net benefit of a change in the size of the aggregate fleet, Z, should be equal to the marginal cost:

$$f'(Z^*) - c = 0 \tag{4.17}$$

What matters here is that effort is being chosen to maximize the net benefit of aggregate effort. Indeed, if each fishing firm were to select their own fleet size to maximize the net benefits to all fishing firms, that is, to solve the problem:

$$Max_{z_j} \sum_j \pi_j = \frac{\sum_j z_j}{Z} f(Z) - c \sum_j z_j \tag{4.18}$$

the requirement would be exactly the same: that the marginal net benefit of increasing aggregate fleet size would be equal to average cost.

To see how this contrasts with the open access case, suppose that there are no restrictions on entry to the fishery, and that the number of firms in the industry is n. Suppose, further, that the jth firm is representative of all fishing firms (i.e., all firms are the same). It then follows that that the share of each fishing firm in the aggregate fleet is just $\frac{z_j}{Z} = \frac{1}{n}$ and, from (4.14), that the size of the representative fleet is the solution to:

$$\frac{z_j}{Z}\left(f'(\cdot) - \frac{f(\cdot)}{Z}\right) + \frac{f(\cdot)}{Z} = c \tag{4.19}$$

That is, z_j depends on the size of the aggregate fleet, fleet productivity, and the cost of vessels. If the open access aggregate fleet size is denoted $\hat{Z}$ we can show that this number is strictly greater than the number that maximizes aggregate profit, Z^*. Adding $\frac{n}{n}\left(f'(\hat{Z}) - \frac{f(\hat{Z})}{\hat{Z}}\right)$ to both sides of (4.19) and rearranging yields:

$$\frac{n-1}{n}\left(f'(\hat{Z}) - \frac{f(\hat{Z})}{\hat{Z}}\right) = f'(\hat{Z}) - c \tag{4.20}$$

Recall that maximizing social profit by choice of Z^* requires that $f'(Z^*) - c = 0$. If $f'(\hat{Z}) - \frac{f(\hat{Z})}{\hat{Z}} < 0$, and if the marginal revenue product of vessels is declining, $f'(\hat{Z}) < 0$, it follows that $\hat{Z} > Z^*$. That is, the equilibrium fleet size in an open access regime is greater than the profit maximising fleet size. Note also from equation (4.19) that as N becomes very large, the fleet size will be selected to equate the rental on fishing vessels with the average productivity of those vessels. That is, the fleet size will be set to satisfy $\frac{F(\hat{Z})}{Z} = c$, and not $F'(Z^*) = c$ (Figure 4.7).

Access rules vary widely across the oceans, but for purposes of this discussion they can be grouped into two sets. Within territorial waters and the exclusive economic zones, nation-states have the authority to assign and police property rights in marine resources. In sea areas beyond national jurisdiction there is no sovereign authority with such power. Access to fish stocks in territorial waters and the exclusive economic zones is at least potentially regulated, while access in sea areas beyond national jurisdiction is open. In reality, many

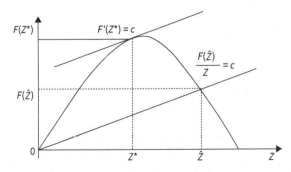

Figure 4.7 Aggregate fleet size and profitability under open access conditions.

stocks in both territorial waters and the exclusive economic zones are only weakly regulated. Individual users of coastal resources in many countries are able to ignore the effect of their actions on others. In some instances there is near-open access to coastal resources within the nation-state. This is the case with many mangrove and melaleuca forests, for example. Similarly, land-based industries frequently have a de facto right to discharge untreated waste directly into rivers or the sea. Indeed, overfishing is directly implicated in the decline of stocks in many large marine ecosystems that lie within the exclusive economic zones. These include the US Northeast Shelf, the Yellow Sea, and the East China Sea (Hoagland and Jin 2006).

The 2006 study by Worm et al., referred to earlier, had argued that globally the rate of fisheries collapses had been accelerating since 1950, with 29% of species considered collapsed (catch <10% of the recorded maximum catch) by 2003. They also noted that despite a significant increase in global fishing effort, cumulative yields across all species and all large marine ecosystems had declined by 13% in the period since the global catch had peaked in 1994 (Worm et al. 2006). The same data have, however, been interpreted rather differently by others. Costello et al. analyzed the relationship between catches and the implementation of schemes to regulate access during the same period, focusing on schemes that allocated rights to a share of variable total allowable catch. They concluded that the implementation of catch share schemes had reversed the trend toward fishery collapses in many cases (Costello et al. 2008).

What is clear is that there are wide differences in the performance of fisheries around the world. The 2012 FAO report on the status of world fisheries reported that the proportion of "non-fully exploited stocks" had fallen since 1974 (the date of the first FAO assessment) to around 13%, while the proportion of overexploited stocks had increased, and then stood at around 30%. The proportion of "fully exploited stocks" in which catches were close to the maximum sustainable yield was relatively stable at around 57 (Food and Agriculture Organization 2012). The report concluded that "the declining global marine catch over the last few years together with the increased percentage of overexploited fish stocks and the decreased proportion of nonfully exploited species around the world convey the strong message that the state of world marine fisheries is worsening and has had a negative impact on fishery production . . . The situation seems more critical for some highly migratory, straddling and other fishery resources that are exploited solely or partially in the High Seas" (Food and Agriculture Organization 2012, pp 12–13).

While a number of studies have emphasized the role of access management regimes in rebuilding stocks in the exclusive economic zones (Worm et al. 2009, Costello et al. 2012), it is clear that the story is quite different in areas where access remains open—either because there is no national jurisdiction, or because national jurisdiction has not translated into effective fishery management. Fleet sizes and fishing effort in the high seas reflects the open access incentives described earlier. The tightening of regulations within national jurisdictions has displaced fishing effort to the high seas where international law and management mechanisms are unable to operate effectively. Access to deep-water fisheries is open, and the absence of any supranational authority means that no one has a mandate to enforce compliance with management measures. The result is that fishing effort committed to oceanic species, and to deep-water species in particular, has increased relative to effort in other capture fisheries.

This has led to increasing pressure on epipelagic and deep-water species[1] characterized by slow growth rates and late age at first maturity, which implies low sustainable yields (Garibaldi and Limongelli 2002). Deep-water fisheries have developed largely in the Pacific and the Atlantic, most of the growth occurring in the Atlantic. The use of bottom trawls has had additional impacts on marine habitats, especially seamounts and cold-water and deep-water corals. A second manifestation of open access in the high seas is the sequential fishing of spatially separate stocks (the "roving bandit" problem), which has significantly increased pressure on affected fisheries (Berkes et al. 2005). Small or localized stocks may be fished out before fisheries managers are even aware that there is a problem.

4.3 Forests and forestry

From a conservation perspective, the dominant concerns in forest ecosystems are conversion to alternative uses—primarily crop or livestock production—and fragmentation. Habitat conversion and habitat fragmentation are widely recognized as the two most important threats to biodiversity, particularly in tropical regions. Changes in forest cover are illustrated in Figure 4.8.

---

[1] These include hairtail, orange roughy, oreos, alfonsinos, cusk eels and brotulas, Patagonian toothfish, Pacific armourhead, sablefish, Greenland halibut, morid cods, and various species of Scorpaenidae. Away from seamounts, Gadiformes are the most commonly exploited deep-water species. A number of deep-water species, such as blue whiting—which accounts for around half of all deep-water catches—are caught for reduction into fishmeal.

(a) Forest cover 2000

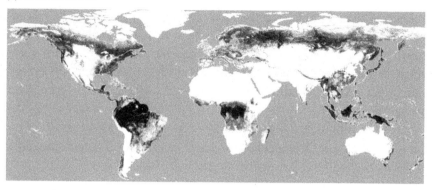

(b) Forest cover 2010

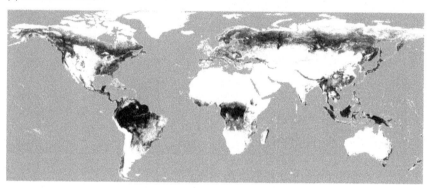

Figure 4.8 Tree canopy cover 2000–2010.
Source: Reprinted in grayscale from Hansen et al. (2013).

We discuss these concerns in Chapter 12. Here we consider the use made of forests, as forests, for the production of a range of ecosystem services. This includes the production of wood and wood products from both managed and natural forests—a set of provisioning services. But it also includes the production of nonconsumptive cultural services such as recreation and amenity, the provision of habitat for pollinators, pest controllers, or endangered wild species, and regulating services such as water quality maintenance, the management of soil nutrients, or fire control. That is, we consider activities that extend all the way from industrial forestry to swidden agriculture. We are especially interested in multiuse forests, though we begin with the industrial forestry case. We ask how the Hotelling principle helps identify the optimal extent and frequency of forest disturbance—how much and how often to cut down trees

Our starting point is the canonical forestry model inspired by the German forester, Martin Faustmann, in the mid-nineteenth century. This established the conditions for the optimal rotation of forests managed exclusively for timber production. What Faustmann aimed to do was to advise forest managers when to cut a forest stand and when to replant, taking account of the growth in value of the stand, the cost of regeneration, the opportunity cost of capital, and the opportunity cost of land. His formula assumed a silvicultural regime that involved both rotational clear-cuts, and artificial regeneration through replanting.

The canonical model assumes that foresters seek to maximize the net present value of a forest through choice of the rotation time. If we consider only a single rotation, this implies assumes a problem of the form:

$$Max_t \, \Pi = \left(\left(p-h\right)V(t)-c\right)e^{-\delta t} \tag{4.21}$$

where
Π = the net present value of the forest
$V(t)$ = the stand size at rotation length t
p = the market price per unit of timber
h = the cost of harvest per unit of timber
c = the fixed cost of replanting
δ = the discount rate/rate of interest
t = the rotation time or length of rotation

The first order necessary conditions for the net present value of the stand to be at a maximum requirement that the rotation time be extended up to the point where the additional value of the stand net of the marginal cost of harvest and replanting is just offset by the opportunity cost of capital:

$$\frac{d\Pi}{dt} = \left(p-h\right)\frac{dV(t)}{dt}e^{-\delta t} - \delta e^{-\delta t}\left(\left(p-h\right)V(t)-c\right)=0 \tag{4.22}$$

Dividing through by $e^{-\delta t}$ and rearranging terms yields the Faustmann formula for a single clear-cut rotation:

$$\frac{\left(p-h\right)dV(t)/dt}{\left(p-h\right)V(t)-c} = \delta \tag{4.23}$$

This requires that the growth in the value of the stand should be equal to the discount rate at the point of harvest. Comparing the Faustmann formula for a single rotation to the Hotelling principle, $\dfrac{dp(t)/dt}{p(t)} = \delta$, we can see the equivalence between the two. The Faustmann formula leads to a decision to cut the forest when the time rate of change in its value is equal to the interest on the value of the forest and the land on which it stands.

If there are multiple rotations, the problem is to choose a rotation length that will be repeated into the indefinite future:

$$Max_T \Pi = \sum_{T=1}^{\infty} ((p-h)V(T)-c)e^{-\delta t}$$

By expanding the terms in the summation, we can write this as:

$$Max_T \Pi = (1+e^{-\delta t}+e^{-2\delta t}+e^{-3\delta t}+...)((p-h)V(T)-c)e^{-\delta t}$$

and since $(1+e^{-\delta t}+e^{-2\delta t}+e^{-3\delta t}+...)$ converges to $\left(\dfrac{1}{1-e^{-\delta t}}\right)$ this implies that

$$Max_T \Pi = \left(\frac{1}{1-e^{-\delta T}}\right)((p-h)V(T)-c)e^{-\delta t} \qquad (4.24)$$

The first order necessary conditions for the net present value of forestland to be maximized over an infinite number of rotations now require that:

$$\frac{d\Pi}{dT} = \frac{(1-e^{-\delta t})(p-h)dV(T)/dt - ((p-h)V(T)-c)\delta e^{-\delta t}}{(1-e^{-\delta t})^2} = 0$$

$$\Rightarrow (1-e^{-\delta t})(p-h)dV(T)/dt = ((p-h)V(T)-c)\delta e^{-\delta t} \qquad (4.25)$$

$$\Rightarrow \frac{(p-h)dV(T)/dt}{((p-h)V(T)-c)} = \frac{\delta e^{-\delta t}}{(1-e^{-\delta t})} = \frac{\delta}{(e^{\delta t}-1)}$$

This gives us the Faustmann formula for multiple rotations. It implies that

$$(p-h)dV(T)/dt = \delta((p-h)V(T)-c)/(e^{\delta t}-1) \qquad (4.26)$$

The left-hand side of this equation is the net increase in the value of the forest. The formula requires that it be exactly equal to the opportunity cost of the current and future stands on the same footprint. An increase in the length of rotation involves a future cost caused by the delay in all future stands. It follows that the rotation length where there are multiple rotations would be expected to be shorter than the rotation length where there is only a single rotation.

So even for this restrictive sylvicultural regime—clear-cut rotation and artificial regeneration—the Hotelling principle is what determines the rotation length. For other regimes such as selective felling; polycyclic harvest; mixed-use agroforestry, forestry, and recreation; forestry and gathering of nontimber forest products; forestry and watershed management; and so on, the canonical model requires adjustment, but is still driven by the Hotelling principle.

The problem of rotation length in multiple use forests was first introduced by Hartman (1976). He took the case where a forest was managed both for the production of timber (a flow benefit) and for the provision of habitat, for recreation, amenity, or the regulation of water flows or soil erosion (a stock benefit). Taking the single rotation case, the forester was assumed to choose the rotation period, T, to maximize

$$\underset{T}{Max}V(T) = \int_{t=0}^{T} e^{-\delta t}F(t)dt + e^{-\delta T}G(T) \qquad (4.27)$$

where

$G(T)=$ a flow benefit (timber production)

$F(t)=$ a stock benefit (habitat provision, recreation, watershed management etc)

For a single rotation the first order necessary conditions include the requirement that:

$$V'(T) = e^{-\delta T}\left(F(T) + G'(T) - \delta G(T)\right) = 0$$
$$\Rightarrow$$
$$F(T) + G'(T) = \delta G(T)$$

in which the left-hand side describes the habitat and growth gains from postponing harvest, and the right-hand side describes the opportunity cost (interest forgone in this case) in the process. Note that if there are no stock benefits, then this implies that forests should be harvested at the point where the growth (in the value) of the forest is equal to the discount rate (Figure 4.9).

The second order conditions are as follows

$$V''(T) = -\delta e^{-\delta T}\left(F(T) + G'(T) - \delta G(T)\right) +$$
$$e^{-\delta T}\left(F'(T) + G''(T) - \delta G'(T)\right) = 0$$
$$\Rightarrow$$
$$F'(T) + G''(T) < \delta G(T)$$

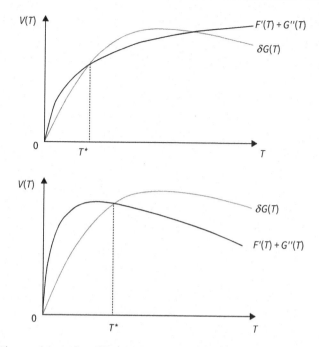

Figure 4.9 The stock benefits of forests and optimal rotation lengths.
Taking the single rotation case, the figure shows that the stronger the stock benefits of forestry, the longer is the rotation length. The upper panel indicates weaker stock benefits than the lower panel.

The implication of this condition is that the $F'(T) + G''(T)$ curve intersects the $\delta G(T)$ curve from above.

For the multiple rotation case the problem is of the form

$$
\underset{T}{Max}\, V(T) = \int_{t=0}^{T} \frac{e^{-\delta t}}{\left(1-e^{-\delta T}\right)} F(t)\,dt + \frac{e^{-\delta T}}{\left(1-e^{-\delta T}\right)} G(T)
$$

$$
\Rightarrow V'(T) = -\frac{\delta G(T)e^{-\delta T} + e^{-\delta T}G'(T) + e^{-\delta T}F(T)}{\left(1-e^{-\delta T}\right)}
$$

$$
+ \frac{\int_{t=0}^{T} e^{-\delta t}F(t)\,dt\,\delta e^{-\delta T} - G(T)e^{-\delta T}}{\left(1-e^{-\delta T}\right)^{2}} = 0
$$

implying that

$$
\frac{G'(T)}{G(T)} = \delta \left[\frac{\int_{t=0}^{T} e^{-\delta t}F(t)\,dt}{G(T)\left(1-e^{-\delta T}\right)} + \frac{1}{\left(1-e^{-\delta T}\right)} \right] - \frac{F(T)}{G(T)} \tag{4.28}
$$

This differs from the condition in the single rotation case by the term in square brackets. As in the industrial forestry case, since that term is positive the optimal rotation will be shorter in the multiple rotation case than in the single rotation case.

The trade-offs between stock and flow benefits in forest systems have been explored in a number of papers since. In many cases these depend on the impact of each activity on basic forest processes, or on the fire regime. To illustrate we consider an examination of the trade-offs between timber production and recreation when recreational activities have implications for fire risk (Englin et al. 2000). The application involves a jack pine forest in the Canadian Shield region. The forester's problem is to maximize the present value of a discounted stream of net flow and stock benefits from the forest by choice of the optimal rotation period. The forester's problem with fire risk takes the form:

$$\underset{T}{Max}\, V(X,T) = \sum_{n=1}^{\infty}\left[\prod_{i=1}^{n-1}E\left(e^{-\delta X_i}\right)\left[e^{-\delta X}Y(X,T)\right]\right] = E\left[\frac{e^{-\delta X}V(X,T)}{1-E\left(e^{-\delta X}\right)}\right] \quad (4.29)$$

where
V = the present value of the discounted stream of benefits of the forest
Y = benefits from harvest at rotation T
T = the rotation period
X = a random variable describing the time between harvest or fire events,
E = the expectation operator
δ = the discount rate/rate of interest

It is supposed that forest fires occur according to a Poisson process. Named after the French mathematician, Siméon Denis Poisson, a Poisson process implies that fires arrive randomly, but at a known rate. More particularly, the time between forest fires is assumed to have an exponential distribution, $1-e^{-X\lambda}$, the probability density function of which is given by $\lambda e^{-X\lambda}$. So if the mean time between forest fires is 60 years ($X = 60$), the mean number of fires per year across the landscape is 1/60. Fire events are independent of each other, and do not occur simultaneously.

The expected discounted value of a single rotation is:

$$E\left[e^{-\delta X}Y(X,T)\right] = \int_0^T e^{-\delta X}\left(-c_p e^{\delta X} - c_b + e^{\delta X}\int_0^X F(Z)e^{-\delta Z}dZ\right)\lambda e^{-\lambda X}dX$$
$$+ e^{-\lambda T}\left(-c_p e^{\delta T} + e^{\delta T}\int_0^T F(X)e^{-\delta X}dX + V(T)\right)e^{-\delta T}$$

$$\int_0^T e^{-\delta X}\left(-c_p e^{\delta X} - c_b + e^{\delta X}\int_0^X F(Z)e^{-\delta Z}dZ\right)\lambda e^{-\lambda X}dX,$$ the first term on the right-hand side, is the discounted value of the recreational or stock benefits, weighted by probability of fire, for forest age less than T. The second term,

$$e^{-\lambda T}\left(-c_p e^{\delta T} + e^{\delta T}\int_0^T F(X)e^{-\delta X}dX + V(T)\right)e^{-\delta T},$$ is the discounted value of timber or flow benefits, weighted by the probability of the forest stand reaching harvest age T. c_p and c_b are planting and postfire site remediation costs respectively. Using this model (Englin et al. 2000), then simulate the trade-off between rotation length and visitor numbers for different levels of fire risk. Their results are shown in Figure 4.10.

The two main results reported here are that higher fire risk shortens the optimal rotation time, and that higher stock versus flow benefits of forests lengthens the optimal rotation time. The more that people use forests for recreation (or for any other stock benefit), the longer will be the optimal rotation time. There is also an interaction between these two results. If there is no value attached to stock benefits, fire risk will reduce the optimal rotation time, but not by much. As the value of stock benefits increases, however, the gap between the optimal rotation length with and without fire risk increases. If stock benefits increase enough, it will be optimal never to cut the forest, and this is independent of the level of fire risk. Once again, the decision depends

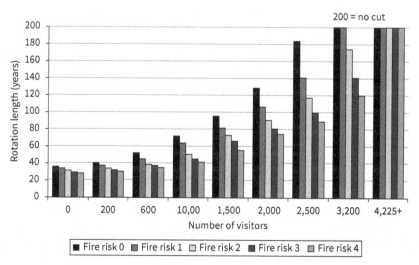

Figure 4.10 Effect of amenity value and fire risk on rotation length.
Source: Figure constructed from data in Englin et al. (2000).

on balancing the expected growth in the value of the forest under each harvest/conservation regime against the opportunity cost of the capital associated with that regime.

Calls for the preservation of tropical moist forests in particular hinge on the value of the stock benefits they offer relative to their value if converted to alternative uses, or disrupted through harvest. In recent years, the stock benefit that has attracted most attention is carbon sequestration, but there are many others including the regulation of water quality and quantity, microclimatic regulation, soil stabilization, and habitat provision for a range of species valued for different reasons (Cardinale et al. 2012). Most important of these is the provision of habitat for endemic species, many of which are currently threatened with extinction. The latitudinal gradiant in species richness, by which richness decreases with distance from the equator (Willig et al. 2003), has meant that those focused on preservation of species richness have targeted tropical forests above all other ecosystems. Fifteen of twenty-five biodiversity hotspots (areas exceptionally rich in endemic species and experiencing exceptional loss of habitat) identified by Myers (2000) were located in tropical moist forests. This focus has been reinforced by the fact that a number of ecosystem services, particularly the regulating services, are increasing in species richness (Gamfeldt et al. 2013).

4.4 Rangelands

Rangelands account for something like 40% of the terrestrial surface of the world. They comprise a set of ecosystems dominated by grasses, forbs, and shrubs, and are important primarily for the domesticated and wild animals they support (Figure 4.11). Aside from animal foods and fibers, rangelands

Figure 4.11 Rangelands of the world.
Source: Launchbaugh and Strand (2015).

are also sources of other ecosystem services, including carbon sequestration, the regulation of water quality and quantity, soil erosion control, and habitat provision for many of the world's most charismatic megafauna (Havstad et al. 2007).

As in other exploited ecosystems, there are trade-offs between the production of animal foods and fibers and the provision of other ecosystem services. It has, for example, been shown that a number of the ancillary ecosystem services generated by rangelands are negatively affected by grazing pressure (Petz et al. 2014). In many cases, the mechanisms involved lie in the effect that grazing pressure by one species has on other species in the system. The impact of grazing pressure by livestock on wildlife, for instance, includes the direct effects of competition for graze or browse. But it also includes the transmission of epizootic diseases (Prins 2000). Grazing pressure also affects the composition of rangeland plants. In savannas, for example, this includes the effect of interactions between browsers and grazers, and the effect of both grazing and browsing pressure on the fire regime (Scholes and Archer 1997).

In this section we consider the conservation problem generated by interactions between ungulates, trees, and grasses in a semiarid savanna typical of Central or Southern Africa. A canonical harvest model of the type that has dominated fisheries science, for example, typically treats the environment within which animal management takes place as fixed, or at least as independent of animal management decisions. Take the problem described in equations (4.3) and (4.4):

$$Max_{h(t)} \int_0^\infty e^{-\delta t} p_n(t) h(t) dt$$

subject to

$$0 \le h(t) \le h_{max}$$
$$\dot{N} = rN(t)\left(1 - \frac{N(t)}{K}\right) - h(t)$$
$$N(0) = N_0$$

The environment in this model is captured by the constant carrying capacity, K, which is a measure of the net effect of all environmental conditions on the size of the population, $N(t)$, that can be sustained. For $N(t)$ less than K the population growth rate is positive and the population is increasing. For $N(t)$ greater than K the population growth rate is negative and the population is decreasing. The steady state equilibrium population occurs at $N(t) = K$. Since K is unaffected by $h(t)$, population management has no effect on the carrying capacity of the environment. It follows that K summarizes a lot of ecology. It captures both biotic and abiotic processes, and the interactions between them. It captures the effects of competition and predation, the relation between the distribution and abundance of organisms, and the functioning of ecosystems. In many cases it is simply too restrictive to treat the environment this way. If the size of the population affects carrying capacity, for example, the model needs to be able to capture the feedbacks involved.

In the case of rangelands, it turns out that the population of some species that can be sustained depends on a set of trophic interactions between species, and on a set of abiotic processes. Specifically, the size of any ungulate populations that can be sustained depends on the populations of other species in the community, but also on the balance between grass and woody vegetation. This in turn depends on soils and rainfall, but also on the fire regime (Scholes and Walker 1993). Fire keeps the vegetation in such systems in a relatively open state. If fire is excluded, woody plants become established in wet years and develop into thickets that exclude grass.

To illustrate the interaction between grazing pressure, woody vegetation, grass and fire we use a simplified three state variable model (Perrings and Walker 2004), in which production of grass and wood depends on competition between plants, grazing pressure by wildlife, and the effects of fire. Grazing pressure is assumed to affect grass and woody biomass in different ways. Specifically, herbivores are assumed to consume grass more than woody biomass. Fire occurs if there is a sufficient fuel load.

The decision-maker is assumed to choose a level of offtake, $0 \leq k(t) \leq k_{max}$, so as to maximize the difference between the revenues from harvest, $p(t)k(t)$, and the costs of maintaining the system, $c(x(t), y(t), z(t))$:

To illustrate we take a discrete time version of the problem:

$$Max_k \sum_{t=0}^{T} \rho^t \left(p_t k_t - c(x_t, y_t, z_t) \right) \tag{4.30}$$

subject to:

$$x_{t+1} = x_t \left(1 + \alpha \left(1 - \frac{\psi x_t}{y_t} \right) \right) - k_t$$

$$y_{t+1} = y_t + \beta y_t \left(1 - c_{yy} \frac{y_t}{y_{max}} - c_{zy} \frac{z_t}{z_{max}} \right) - \sigma_y \varphi (y_t - y_{min}) - \psi x_t \tag{4.31}$$

$$z_{t+1} = z_t + \gamma z_t \left(1 - c_{zz} \frac{z_t}{z_{max}} - c_{yz} \frac{y_t}{y_{max}} \right) - \sigma_z \theta (z_t, y_t - y_{min})$$

x_0, y_0, z_0 given, and

p_t = the extracted value of wildlife

u_t = harvest of wildlife

$c(x_t, y_t, z_t)$ = the cost of ecosystem maintenance

α = wildlife growth rate

β = grass growth rate

γ = woody biomass growth rate

ρ = discount factor

ψ = wildlife consumption of grass

c_{yy} = competition coefficient: grass/grass

c_{yz} = competition coefficient: grass/wood

c_{zz} = competition coefficient: wood/wood

c_{zy} = competition coefficient: wood/grass

y_{max} = maximum potential grass biomass

z_{max} = maximum potential wood biomass

y_{min} = the minimum fuel load required to sustain a fire

σ_y = proportion of grassy biomass removed by fire

σ_z = proportion of woody biomass removed by fire

The growth function for wildlife is logistic, and is positive only if the grazing requirements of the herd do not exceed the available fodder. The growth functions for grass and woody biomass reflect the effects of (a) consumption by wildlife, (b) competition, and (c) fire. It is assumed that fire occurs with probability one providing that the fuel load exceeds a critical threshold, and that if fire does occur it induces a constant rate of loss in both grass and woody plants. The ecological parameters are drawn from the CSIRO SEESAW rangeland production model. It is assumed that $\beta > \alpha > \gamma$: that is, that the rate of growth of grassy biomass is greater than the rate of growth of wild herbivore biomass which is greater than the rate of growth of woody biomass. All three state variables are also interdependent. In the absence of herbivores, grasses dominate and the system is regulated by fire. In the presence of herbivores, woody plants dominate, although this depends on the level of grazing pressure. Importantly, fire is excluded from the system when woody plants dominate.

The maximum principle requires that $p(t) = \lambda(t)$. Given that the Hamiltonian is linear in the control, the approach to the optimum is "most rapid," implying that if the initial level of the state variables is less than the optimum, then there will be a conservation phase during which $k(t) = 0$. That is, the optimal control is such that:

$$k(t) = \begin{cases} 0 & \text{if } p(t) < \lambda(t) \\ k_{max} & \text{if } p(t) > \lambda(t) \\ k* & \text{if } p(t) = \lambda(t) \end{cases} \qquad (4.32)$$

So long as the market price of the harvested resource is less than its social opportunity cost—its value to society—the stock of the resource should be allowed to build up naturally. The important element here is the rate of growth in the value of the natural asset relative to that of produced capital. The Hotelling rule for renewable resources implies that conservation is efficient so long as the growth in value of a natural resource inclusive of its regeneration rate is greater than or equal to the growth in value of produced capital. It follows that if the price of a renewable resource is constant over time, and it's in situ rate of growth is greater than the rate of return on produced capital, then it will be optimal to conserve the resource.

Simulations of the optimal time path of the system as the opportunity cost of capital varies are shown in Figure 4.12. This offers a straightforward way to see the conservation implications of variations in the opportunity cost of rangeland use. The figure reports values for the three state variables—woody plants, grasses, and wild herbivores—for three rates of discount: 17.5% (panel A), 1% (panel B), and 7.5% (panel C). Costs are assumed to be increasing in the stock of herbivores.

In Panel A, the selected discount rate is close to the maximum natural rate of growth of wild herbivores. If the discount rate were equal to the maximum natural rate of growth of wild herbivores it would be optimal to treat them as a nonrenewable resource—and hence to remove them from the system in the first period. In this case the stock of wild herbivores is run down over time. Note that the high frequency of fire is a function of the structure of the model.

The panel also shows the effect of herbivores on the balance between woody vegetation and grasses. In the absence of herbivores, woody vegetation is excluded, and the system converges on a state at which it has the characteristics of a fire-regulated grassland.

In Panel B, the discount rate is very low, and leads to a regime based on sustainable long-term use or exploitation. The initial phase—the conservation phase—involves a fire regulated regime. During this phase herd sizes are built up to the point where grazing pressure begins to dominate fire as the regulating mechanism. The second phase—the exploitation phase—is one in which the system moves through damped oscillations toward a steady state at which woody plants are dominant, and grasses are controlled through grazing pressure. Fire is absent from the system.

Panel C shows that just as fallow can be an integral part of a cropping system, an optimally managed rangeland can exist as a fire-regulated grassland and as a grazing-regulated savanna sequentially. When a fire-regulated

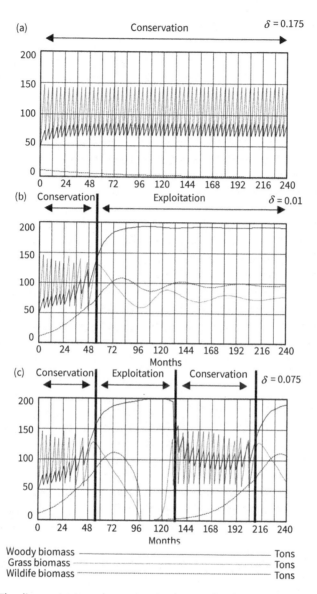

Figure 4.12 The discount rate and conservation in rangelands.

Simulations of the control of rangelands where there are interactions between grazing pressure, grasses, woody vegetation, and fire, over a range of discount rates.

Source: Perrings and Walker (2004).

grassland, it is said to be in a conservation phase. When a grazing-regulated savanna, it is said to be in an exploitation phase. Conservation in this sense is frequently integral to the theory of optimal renewable natural resource management.

4.5 Summary and conclusions

In Chapter 3 we showed how the first order necessary conditions for the optimal management of renewable resource embed the Hotelling arbitrage condition. More particularly, the condition for use made of stocks or state variables to be optimal is that the proportional rate of growth in the shadow value of the resource should be equal to the difference between the discount rate or rate of return on alternative assets and the marginal impact of a change in stock size on the growth of the stock (see equation 4.51). In Chapter 4 we used three different natural resources to show how the optimization of harvest rates simultaneously optimizes conservation. We took, as our examples, resources that are especially vulnerable to overexploitation: marine stocks in sea areas beyond national jurisdiction, forests that provide benefits over and above the benefits offered by timber, and rangelands providing habitat for wildlife.

The case of marine resources in the high seas nicely illustrates the conservation challenges associated with open access resources. For open access resources, decision-makers will increase harvest effort up to the point where total revenue is equal to total cost—where net benefits are zero. This is in contrast to the case where the resource is subject to well-defined property rights, and access is regulated. In such a case, decision-makers will increase harvest effort up to the point where marginal revenue and costs are equal—where net benefits are at a maximum. We showed how changes in the value of stocks (changes in the net price of the resource) might be expected to affect the optimal level of harvest/conservation.

Open access involves higher levels of effort, and lower resource stocks. Indeed, most examples of species that have been driven to extinction by overharvesting have involved open access. The whale species driven close to extinction in the nineteenth and twentieth centuries were all victims of open access as were, for example, the dodo and carrier pigeon. Applying the Hotelling principle, it is easy to see why this might happen. The Hotelling principle holds that it is optimal to conserve a stock if the expected rate of growth in the value of that stock is greater than the rate of return on alternative investments. But if there is open access each decision-maker has no guaranteed future claim on the resource. While they are able to access the resource today, this confers no future rights. Therefore, a decision to refrain from exploiting the resource confers no future benefits. Since the expected gain from waiting to harvest is zero, the incentive to conserve the resource is also zero. The incentive is to extract as much of an open access resource as possible, and to convert it to an asset to which the decision-maker has future rights. It follows that a key element in the conservation of species is the establishment of well-defined rights and the regulation of access.

The case of forests offering multiple benefits illustrates a different sort of conservation challenge. While a high proportion of forest loss is due to similar open access problems, in this chapter we assumed well-defined property rights to forest resources, but allowed forests to offer multiple benefits beyond the supply of timber. We showed that the canonical Faustmann model of forest harvest embeds the Hotelling principle, and illustrated the effect on forest rotations of both the value of harvest and the rate of return on alternative investments. We saw that by the Faustmann formula, forest resources should be harvested until the growth in the value of a forest stand is equal to the discount rate. We then discussed implications of including not just the flow of timber as a benefit, but also benefits that might depend on the forest stock. Such benefits might include recreation, habitat provision, flood and erosion control, and the regulation of climate locally and globally. We showed that the greater the stock benefits the longer the optimal rotation length—and so the greater the incentive to conserve stocks.

The third case discussed in the chapter, rangelands, was included to illustrate another dimension of the conservation problem in renewable natural resource management. In an ecological system involving multiple species, each with distinct but interdependent growth paths, the optimal exploitation/conservation of one species likely depends on the dynamics of the other species with which it interacts. The dynamics of wild ungulates, for example, likely depend on the dynamics of the plant species that comprise their habitat, and the fire regime that regulates the balance between grassy and woody plants. While the optimal conservation of the targeted species can be analyzed using the same principles that we applied to marine stocks, or forests, the solution depends on the interaction between species.

Although the economic theory of conservation is relatively poorly developed, we showed that it is latent in the theory of renewable resource extraction. We also showed that optimal conservation does not necessarily imply a once and for all commitment to preservation. For most resources, conservation is part of a strategy of optimal use—sustainable over some given planning horizon. An optimal strategy may imply a greater or lesser commitment to conservation at different times, and this will reflect changes in both the value of the resources to be conserved at particular times, the objectives of the decision-maker, and the status of assets that are either substitutes or complements for the target resource.

References

Berkes, F., T. P. Hughes, R. S. Steneck, J. A. Wilson, D. R. Bellwood, B. Crona, C. Folke, L. H. Gunderson, H. M. Leslie, J. Norberg, M. Nyström, P. Olsson, H. Österblom, M. Scheffer, and B. Worm. 2005. Globalization, roving bandits, and marine resources. Science 311:1557–1558.

Cardinale, B. J., J. E. Duffy, A. Gonzalez, D. U. Hooper, C. Perrings, P. Venail, A. Narwani, G. M. Mace, D. Tilman, D. A. Wardle, A. P. Kinzig, G. C. Daily, M. Loreau, J. B. Grace, A. Larigauderie, D. S. Srivastava, and S. Naeem. 2012. Biodiversity loss and its impact on humanity. Nature 486:59–67.

Clark, C. W. 1973. The economics of overexploitation. Science 181:630–634.

Clark, C. W. 1976. Mathematical bioeconomics: the optimal management of renewable resources. John Wiley, New York.

Clark, C. W. 1979. Mathematical models in the economics of renewable resources. SIAM Review 21:81–99.

Clark, C. W. 2010. Mathematical bioeconomics: the mathematics of conservation. John Wiley, Hoboken, NJ.

Costello, C., S. D. Gaines, and J. Lynham. 2008. Can catch shares prevent fisheries collapse? Science 321:1678–1681.

Costello, C., D. Ovando, R. Hilborn, S. D. Gaines, O. Deschenes, and S. E. Lester. 2012. Status and solutions for the world's unassessed fisheries. Science 338:517–520.

Dasgupta, P. 2001. Human well-being and the natural environment. Oxford University Press, Oxford.

Englin, J., P. Boxall, and G. Hauer. 2000. An empirical examination of optimal rotations in a multiple-use forest in the presence of fire risk. Journal of Agricultural and Resource Economics 25:14–27.

Feeny, D., F. Berkes, B. J. McCay, and J. M. Acheson. 1990. The tragedy of the commons: twenty-two years later. Human Ecology 18:1–19.

Food and Agriculture Organization. 2004. The state of world fisheries and agriculture. FAO, Rome.

Food and Agriculture Organization. 2012. The state of world fisheries and aquaculture 2012. FAO, Rome.

Food and Agriculture Organization. 2017. Fisheries and Aquaculture Statistics. FAO, Rome.

Gamfeldt, L., T. Snäll, R. Bagchi, M. Jonsson, L. Gustafsson, P. Kjellander, M. C. Ruiz-Jaen, M. Fröberg, J. Stendahl, C. D. Philipson, G. Mikusiński, E. Andersson, B. Westerlund, H. Andrén, F. Moberg, J. Moen, and J. Bengtsson. 2013. Higher levels of multiple ecosystem services are found in forests with more tree species. Nature Communications 4:1340.

Garibaldi, L., and L. Limongelli. 2002. Trends in oceanic captures and clustering of large marine ecosystems: two studies based on the FAO capture database, FAO Fisheries Technical Paper. No. 435. FAO, Rome.

Hansen, M. C., P. V. Potapov, R. Moore, M. Hancher, S. A. Turubanova, A. Tyukavina, D. Thau, S. V. Stehman, S. J. Goetz, T. R. Loveland, A. Kommareddy, A. Egorov, L. Chini, C. O. Justice, and J. R. G. Townshend. 2013. High-resolution global maps of 21st-century forest cover change. Science 342:850–853.

Hardin, G. 1968. The tragedy of the commons. Science 162:1243–1248.

Hartman, R. 1976. The harvesting decision when a standing forest has value. Economic Inquiry 14:52–58.

Havstad, K. M., D. P. C. Peters, R. Skaggs, J. Brown, B. Bestelmeyer, E. Fredrickson, J. Herrick, and J. Wright. 2007. Ecological services to and from rangelands of the United States. Ecological Economics 64:261–268.

Hoagland, P., and D. Jin. 2006. Accounting for economic activities in large marine ecosystems and regional seas. UNEP, Nairobi.

Hughes, T. P., A. H. Baird, D. R. Bellwood, M. Card, S. R. Connolly, C. Folke, R. Grosberg, O. Hoegh-Guldberg, J. B. C. Jackson, J. Kleypas, J. M. Lough, P. Marshall, M. Nystrom, S. R. Palumbi, J. M. Pandolfi, B. Rosen, and J. Roughgarden. 2003. Climate change, human impacts, and the resilience of coral reefs. Science 301:929–933.

Jackson, J. B. C. 2008. Ecological extinction and evolution in the brave new ocean. Proceedings of the National Academy of Sciences 105:11458–11465.

Jackson, J. B. C., M. X. Kirby, W. H. Berger, K. A. Bjorndal, L. W. Botsford, B. J. Bourque, R. H. Bradbury, R. Cooke, J. Erlandson, J. A. Estes, T. P. Hughes, S. Kidwell, C. B. Lange, H. S. Lenihan, J. M. Pandolfi, C. H. Peterson, R. S. Steneck, M. J. Tegner, and R. R. Warner. 2001. Historical overfishing and the recent collapse of coastal ecosystems. Science 293:629–638.

Launchbaugh, K., and E. Strand. 2015. Rangelands of the world. Society for Range Management, Moscow, ID.

Libecap, G. D. 2009. The tragedy of the commons: property rights and markets as solutions to resource and environmental problems. Australian Journal of Agricultural and Resource Economics 53:129–144.

McWhinnie, S. F. 2009. The tragedy of the commons in international fisheries: an empirical examination. Journal of Environmental Economics and Management 57:321–333.

Myers, N., R. A. Mittermeier, C. G. Mittermeier, G. A. B. da Fonseca, and J. Kent. 2000. Biodiversity hotspots for conservation priorities. Nature 403:853–858.

Ostrom, E. 1990. Governing the commons: the evolution of institutions for collective action. Cambridge University Press, Cambridge.

Ostrom, E. E., T. E. Dietz, N. E. Dolšak, P. C. Stern, S. E. Stonich, and E. U. Weber. 2002. The drama of the commons. National Academy Press, Washington, DC.

Perrings, C. 2014. Our uncommon heritage: biodiversity, ecosystem services and human wellbeing. Cambridge University Press, Cambridge.

Perrings, C., and B. H. Walker. 2004. Conservation in the optimal use of rangelands. Ecological Economics 49:119–128.

Petz, K., R. Alkemade, M. Bakkenes, C. J. E. Schulp, M. van der Velde, and R. Leemans. 2014. Mapping and modelling trade-offs and synergies between grazing intensity and ecosystem services in rangelands using global-scale datasets and models. Global Environmental Change 29:223–234.

Prins, H. H. T. 2000. Competition between wildlife and livestock in Africa. Pages 51–80 in H. H. T. Prins, J. G. Grootenhuis, and T. T. Dolan, editors. Wildlife conservation by sustainable use. Springer Netherlands, Dordrecht.

Rocha, R. C., P. J. Clapham, and Y. V. Ivashchenko. 2014. Emptying the oceans: a summary of industrial whaling catches in the 20th century. Marine Fisheries Review 76:37–48.

Rogers, A., U. Sumaila, S. Hussain, and C. Baulcomb. 2014. The high seas and us: understanding the value of high-seas ecosystems. Global Ocean Commission, Oxford.

Rose, K. A., J. H. Cowan, K. O. Winemiller, R. A. Myers, and R. Hilborn. 2001. Compensatory density dependence in fish populations: importance, controversy, understanding and prognosis. Fish and Fisheries 2:293–327.

Scholes, R., and S. Archer. 1997. Tree-grass interactions in savannas 1. Annual Review of Ecology and Systematics 28:517–544.

Scholes, R., and B. Walker. 1993. Nylsvley: the study of an African savanna. Cambridge University Press, Cambridge.

Willig, M. R., D. Kaufman, and R. Stevens. 2003. Latitudinal gradients of biodiversity: pattern, process, scale, and synthesis. Annual Review of Ecology, Evolution, and Systematics 34:273–309.

World Commission on Environment and Development. 1987. Our common future. Island Press, Washington, DC.

Worm, B., E. B. Barbier, N. Beaumont, J. E. Duffy, C. Folke, B. S. Halpern, J. B. C. Jackson, H. K. Lotzke, F. Micehli, S. R. Palumbi, E. Sala, K. A. Selkoe, J. J. Stachowicz, and R. Watson. 2006. Impacts of biodiversity loss on ocean ecosystem services. Science 314:787–790.

Worm, B., E. B. Barbier, N. Beaumont, J. E. Duffy, C. Folke, B. S. Halpern, J. B. C. Jackson, H. K. Lotze, F. Micheli, S. R. Palumbi, E. Sala, K. A. Selkoe, J. J. Stachowicz, and R. Watson. 2007. Biodiversity loss in the ocean: how bad is it? Response. Science 316:1282–1284.Worm, B., R. Hilborn, J. K. Baum, T. A. Branch, J. S. Collie, C. Costello, M. J. Fogarty, E. A. Fulton, J. A. Hutchings, S. Jennings, O. P. Jensen, H. K. Lotze, P. A. Mace, T. R. McClanahan, C. Minto, S. R. Palumbi, A. M. Parma, D. Ricard, R. A.A., R. Watson, and D. Zeller. 2009. Rebuilding global fisheries. Science 325:578–585.

PART II

VALUATION

5

The Valuation of Environmental Goods and Services

It is not good for man to be kept perforce at all times in the presence of his species . . . Nor is there much satisfaction in contemplating the world with nothing left to the spontaneous activity of nature; with every rood of land brought into cultivation, which is capable of growing food for human beings; every flowery waste or natural pasture ploughed up, all quadrupeds or birds which are not domesticated for man's use exterminated as his rivals for food, every hedgerow or superfluous tree rooted out, and scarcely a place left where a wild shrub or flower could grow without being eradicated as a weed in the name of improved agriculture.

—John Stuart Mill, *Principles of Political Economy*, 1848

5.1 Introduction

At the core of the Hotelling approach to the conservation of natural assets is the relationship between use and value—the discounted stream of services the asset yields. In some cases, measuring the value of environmental assets is a relatively simple exercise. If we have complete information about all alternatives, and if markets exist for all the services provided by an asset, then the price of services can then be used to determine the value of the underlying assets. If information is not complete, however, or if there are missing markets, then the price of services may not be good measures of social opportunity cost. We then need a different approach to the estimation of value.

Many environmental assets are in this category. Common lands that provide a range of services to individuals, households, or communities are never priced in this way. Water resources that are accessed by many but owned by none are frequently in the same category. In a few well-known cases, such as the Catskills, the value of watersheds in regulating water quantity and quality is recognized. In most cases, however, we do not have good measures of the value of watersheds. Forests that sequester carbon from

Conservation. Charles Perrings and Ann Kinzig, Oxford University Press (2021). © Oxford University Press.
DOI: 10.1093/oso/9780190613600.003.0005

the atmosphere can be either privately or publicly owned. Where publicly owned they are generally unpriced. Where privately owned they will have a price, usually based on the timber harvest they yield. But that price will seldom reflect the value of carbon sequestration. Landscapes that are home to wild species may offer benefits to the wider community if those species have high conservation value, or provide beneficial services such as pollination. They may also or impose costs if wild species are pests or pathogens. In neither case, however, are the benefits or costs associated with wild species reflected in the price of land.

This chapter addresses the ways in which economists go about the valuation of environmental goods and services that are unpriced in the marketplace. We first consider the basis of value in human societies—peoples' wants and needs. We show how the value of a marginal change in any good or service is defined in terms of the goods or services given up to get it. We then discuss the various methods used to estimate the value of the provisioning and cultural services—environmental goods and services. Following that we consider the valuation of the regulating services, and the treatment of uncertainty. The chapter concludes with a summary of remaining challenges in the valuation of environmental goods and services.

5.2 The basis of value

The basis of value in human societies is the set of principles, ethics, wants, and needs that inform human behavior. These are generally summarized by a preference or utility function that describes how individuals or societies rank the options available to them. We have seen that all economic choices involve the achievement of some objective, subject to a set of constraints, and the preference function defines the decision-maker's objectives or priorities. There are many different forms of the preference function. Commercial enterprises, for example, are frequently assumed to be interested only in profit. The archetypal model of the firm accordingly assumes that the firm maximizes profit, subject to a set of resource, technology, and information constraints. Other common objectives include cost minimization, satisficing (doing well enough), avoiding worst case damages, and risk minimization.

The approach taken here assumes that peoples' preferences have certain characteristics: that they are both complete and transitive. Completeness implies that if A and B are two combinations of goods and services, decision-makers can always determine whether they prefer A to B, B to A, or are indifferent between A and B. All options can be ranked. Transitivity implies that if a decision-maker prefers A to B and B to C, then they must also prefer A to C. Choices are consistent.

The motivation behind the ranking that people make over choices may be complex. It may be driven by self-advantage, as is often assumed, but it may also be driven by impulse, whimsy, bigotry, an altruistic concern for others, or a sense of stewardship for the other species with whom we share the planet. For people to make trade-offs in a rational way, all that matters is that they are able to rank options. The notion that preferences allow a complete ordering of choices, and that choices are made rationally and consistently, is also compatible with the idea that if the costs of acquiring sufficient knowledge about alternatives to rank them is too high, people will adopt rules of thumb or rely on the rankings of others (Simon 1957).

Many of the choices people make reflect social or cultural conditions, peer group pressures, or social norms. Fads and fashions affect choices as much as reasoned evaluation of the private net benefits of alternative actions. This is especially true of public goods whose benefits may depend on the number of people committing to them, but also applies to many private goods. Put another way, the ranking people make over alternative bundles of goods and services is conditional. It depends on environmental conditions writ large. These may include biophysical conditions such as temperature, precipitation, the disease environment and so on, but also include socioeconomic conditions such as the regulatory environment, or social and cultural pressures to conform.

Preferences over consumption options are assumed captured by a utility function of the general form:

$$U = U\left(x_1, \ldots, x_n\right) \tag{5.1}$$

where $x_1, \ldots, x_n$ is a vector of the quantities of goods and services consumed, or of bads avoided. The combinations of two goods/services that yield the same level of satisfaction or utility—say x_i and x_j—can be described by an indifference curve, the slope of which defines the marginal rate of substitution between the goods (Figure 5.1). The marginal rate of substitution is diminishing in x_j. At low levels of x_j the decision-maker is willing to give up large quantities of x_i to get an additional unit of x_j. At high levels of x_j the decision-maker is willing to give up very little of x_i to get an additional unit of x_j. Note that by the assumption of transitivity of preferences, indifference curves describing combinations of goods that yield higher levels of utility than U_0, such as U_1, cannot intersect U_0.

The marginal rate of substitution between x_i and x_j depends on the contribution each makes to the utility of the decision-maker. To see this, take the

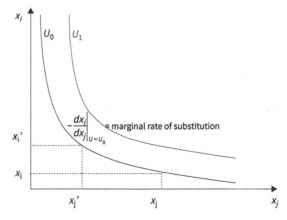

Figure 5.1 Trade-offs between different goods and services.
The indifference curve describes the combinations of x_i and x_j yielding utility level U_0. The slope of the curve describes the rate at which the decision-maker is willing to trade off x_i against x_j.

total differential of the utility function at a particular level of utility (so the change in utility is zero)

$$dU = \frac{\partial U}{\partial x_1}dx_1 + ... + \frac{\partial U}{\partial x_i}dx_i + ... + \frac{\partial U}{\partial x_j}dx_j + ... + \frac{\partial U}{\partial x_n}dx_n = 0 \qquad (5.2)$$

and allow only x_i and x_j to change ($dx_k = 0, k \neq i, j$). It follows that

$$-\frac{dx_i}{dx_j} = \frac{\partial U/\partial x_j}{\partial U/\partial x_i} \qquad (5.3)$$

The rate at which the decision-maker is willing to trade off x_i against x_j is equal to the ratio of the marginal contributions to utility of x_j and x_i. That is, people will be willing to trade one good or service off against another if the marginal utility gained from the second at least compensates for the marginal utility lost from the first. What combination of goods the decision-maker actually chooses depends on the opportunity cost—what has to be given up—of each. In Chapter 2 we considered the case where a decision-maker seeks to maximize utility from consumption of two goods, x and y, subject to a resource constraint

$$Max_{x,y} U = U(x, y)$$
$$s.t. \qquad (5.4)$$
$$p_x x + p_y y = R$$

in which p_x, p_y denote the prices of x, y, and R denotes the resources available to the decision-maker. We showed that utility would be maximized where

$$-\frac{dy}{dx} = \frac{p_x}{p_y} = \frac{\partial U/\partial x}{\partial U/\partial y} \tag{5.5}$$

That is, utility would be maximized where the marginal rate of substitution was equal to the ratio of prices of the two goods. The optimal combination of x and y will be given by the point at which the highest attainable indifference curve is tangent to the budget line. In Figure 5.2 this will be at point a for prices p_y, p_x^0 and point c for prices p_y, p_x^1.

We can use a consumer's response to a change in prices to uncover the value of x in terms of y. In Figure 5.2 a reduction in the price of x from p_x^0 to p_x^1 relaxes the budget constraint, allowing the decision-maker to move to a higher (more preferred) indifference curve and a new combination of goods at point c. We have already seen in Chapter 2 that this move involves both a *substitution effect* (the incentive to substitute goods or services with lower costs for goods or services with higher costs) and an *income effect* (due to the falling cost of one or more goods and services). It also allows us to identify two measures of the value of x in terms of y. The first, the equivalent variation (*ev*) or "willingness to accept", is a measure of the amount of y that yields the same

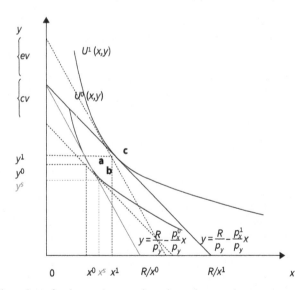

Figure 5.2 The value of a change in a marketed good or service.

Two measures of the value of change in the level of consumption of x are shown: the equivalent and compensating variation in y, *ev* and *cv*.

increase in utility as the change in x. The second, the compensating variation (cv) or "willingness to pay'" is the amount of y that, if given up to acquire the increase in x, leaves utility unchanged.

Note that although we have illustrated willingness to pay and willingness to accept by assuming a change in the price of x, the same measures of value can be identified even if x is a nonmarketed environmental good. This is illustrated in Figure 5.3 in which an initial combination of x^0, a nonmarketed environmental good, and y^0, all other goods and services, yields utility $U^0(x, y)$.

If there is an increase in the supply of x from x^0 to x^1, resulting in an increase in utility to $U^1(x, y)$, we can identify both the equivalent variation in y or willingness to accept ($y^1 - y^0$) and the compensating variation in y or willingness to pay $(y^0 - y^{0*})$ associated with the change.

Willingness to accept is the amount of all other goods and services that yields the same increase in utility as the change in the nonmarketed environmental good. Willingness to pay is the amount of all other goods and services that, if given up to acquire the increase in the nonmarketed environmental good, leaves utility unchanged.

Recall that indifference curves of this form reflect the assumption of diminishing marginal utility. The less of x that the decision-maker initially has, the more y they would require to compensate for a in x. Conversely, the more of x that the decision-maker initially has, the less y they would require to compensate for a in x. The value placed by the decision-maker on an extra unit of x is decreasing in the amount they already have. In fact this was the solution offered by the economist Alfred Marshall to the age-old paradox of diamonds and water—that while water is not just useful but is essential

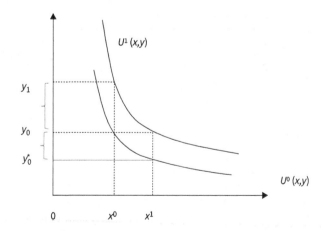

Figure 5.3 The value of a change in a nonmarketed good or service.
This shows the equivalent variation $(y^1 - y^0)$ and compensating variation $(y^0 - y^{0*})$ in y associated with an increase in the nonmarketed good x from x^0 to x^0.

to life, it is nonetheless valued well below diamonds. It was later shown that diminishing marginal utility also implies diminishing marginal rates of substitution (at least if a marginal increase in x does not imply a reduction in the marginal utility of y). That is, if x becomes less valuable at the margin the more plentiful it is, then the rate at which the decision-maker is willing to give up y to obtain an additional unit of x declines as the quantity of x increases.

In extreme cases decision-makers may be absolutely unwilling to trade off the nonmarketed environmental good against all other goods (Figure 5.4 Panel A), or may be completely indifferent between them (Figure 5.4 Panel B). If x and y are perfect complements (panel A), then the nonmarketed environmental good and all other goods and services are required in fixed proportions, and more of one that is not accompanied by an increase in the other adds no value. If x and y are perfect substitutes (panel B), then the nonmarketed environmental good and all other goods and services are completely interchangeable. Most real-world cases lie somewhere in between. In fact, much of the discussion about the value of nonmarketed environmental resources, such as public lands committed to wildlife conservation, centers on the degree to which they complement or substitute for other goods and services, as we'll see in later chapters.

The central point here is that the value of particular goods and services depends on decision-makers' preferences over goods and services and their relative scarcity. The measures of value most frequently used—the equivalent and compensating variation in other goods and services—denote the opportunity cost of acquiring goods or services in a world of diminishing marginal utility, and diminishing marginal rates of substitution. So long as there is an

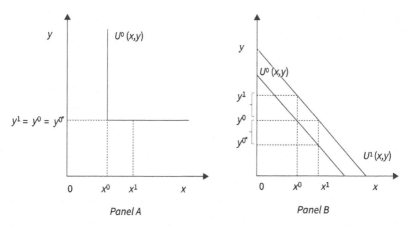

Panel A   *Panel B*

Figure 5.4 Perfect complements and substitutes.

The panels describe polar cases where the decision-maker is unwilling to trade any y for x whatever the level of x (panel A), or treats the two as perfect substitutes whatever the level of x (panel B).

opportunity cost to the acquisition of an additional unit of some good or service it is possible to compute its value, and this is true whether or not markets exist for that good or service, and whether or not markets are complete. This point is particularly important for environmental goods and services, many of which are not transacted in the marketplace, but do cost society if they are reduced or degraded.

5.3 Ecosystem services and the value of nonmarketed environmental resources

The characteristics of nonmarketed environmental resources that are valued by people are those that deliver one or more recognized benefits, generally referred to as ecosystem services. Since publication of the Millennium Ecosystem Assessment (Millennium Ecosystem Assessment 2005) we have seen that people distinguish four main benefit streams: provisioning services, cultural services, regulating services, and supporting services. Provisioning services cover foods, fibers, fuels, water, biochemicals, medicines, pharmaceuticals and genetic material, and so on. They are the most familiar of all ecosystem services, and are frequently subject to well-defined property rights. That is, the legal rights and responsibilities of those who produce such services are often well defined. They are often bought and sold in markets, and so carry a price that balances supply and demand. While the prices of many provisioning services may leave out externalities of either production or consumption, they rise or fall depending on the scarcity of resources. In many cases, too, the prices of provisioning services reflect expectations about future supplies. Corn futures, for example, are traded at the Chicago Board of Trade, NYSE, Euronext, and the Tokyo Grain Exchange, and are priced to reflect buyers' expectations of how future conditions will affect the relative scarcity of corn.

The cultural services include the spiritual, religious, aesthetic, and inspirational benefits that people obtain from the environment. They include some services that are bought and sold in the marketplace, and others that are not. Examples of cultural services that carry market prices include recreation and tourism, the fastest growing sector in many economies. Tourism services are supplied by tour operators and consumed by tourists at well-established prices. As with the provisioning services tourism prices may leave out a number of external effects, but they do typically vary with changes in the relative scarcity of tourism services. Examples of cultural services that are unpriced include the sense of "place" that people have for particular locations, the totemic importance of certain species, or the aesthetic or spiritual value of particular landscapes. These are frequently public goods that are nonrival and nonexclusive. They are either collectively owned or owned by none. They are frequently regulated by custom and usage rather than by market prices but, because they are used by people, they are also amenable to valuation by methods designed to reveal people's preferences. Cultural services of both kinds are offered by national parks, national monuments, and wilderness areas, and are frequently a major part of the value of those landscapes.

The regulating services comprise the buffering functions of nature. Examples include the role of trees in regulating air quality, in sequestering carbon, or in reducing soil erosion the role of wetlands in water purification and waste treatment, or in reducing flood damage and the role of mangroves in mitigating the risk of coastal damage due to hurricanes, cyclones, or typhoons. The regulating services affect the impact of stresses and shocks to the system. As with many of the cultural services, regulating services are often public goods that are not directly priced in the market, although it turns out that the benefits they offer may be capitalized into the value of private land, housing, or other assets.

Some regulating services are public goods at the global scale. Macroclimatic regulation and the mitigation of the risks of emerging zoonotic diseases, for example, are both global public goods that are the outcome of local actions. The carbon sequestered by a local forest provides benefits to all humankind—indeed to all living organisms. Other regulating services are public goods at the local scale, offering nonexclusive and nonrival benefits to particular communities. The regulation of water flows within a particular catchment, for example, benefits only those who consume water from that catchment. The rest of the world may have minimal interest in such benefits.

The last set of ecosystem services, the supporting services, includes the ecosystem processes that underpin all other services. Examples are photosynthesis, primary production, soil formation, and nutrient cycling. The benefits offered by these services occur at very different spatial and temporal scales. Nutrient cycling, for example, maintains the nutrients essential for life in a quite localized way, and so may be captured in the price of the land on which it takes place. Carbon cycling, on the other hand, operates at a global scale and, despite the development of carbon markets in the last two decades, is still poorly reflected in land prices. Since many supporting services are necessary to the production of other ecosystem services, they are captured in the valuation of those services.

The ecosystem services identified by the Millennium Ecosystem Assessment in turn map into a typology of values that focuses on where they fall relative to the goods and services that enter final demand—that are directly consumed individuals and households. Figure 5.5 offers a sketch of this typology. It distinguishes between goods and services that are directly consumed by the decision-maker, those that are directly consumed by others, and those that are intermediate inputs into the goods and services that enter final demand. The value of goods and services that directly satisfy final demand derive from the decision-makers' preferences for those goods and services. The value of goods and services that are directly consumed by others derives from the weight decision-makers' place on the preferences of those others. And the value of intermediate inputs that are used to produce directly valued goods or services derives from the value of the directly produced goods and services (Turner 1999).

In this typology "use value" refers to benefits deriving from consumptive or nonconsumptive use by the decision-maker, while "nonuse value" refers to benefits from consumptive or nonconsumptive use by others (Weisbrod 1964, Krutilla 1967). Direct use value comprises the value of goods and services entering final demand, whether consumptive (as in the provisioning services) or nonconsumptive (as in the cultural services). Indirect use value refers to the derived demand for ecosystem services that are intermediate inputs, such as the various regulating services (Barbier 2007). If a particular good or service is not currently in use, but the decision-maker would like to be able to use it in the future, it is said to have an option value (Heal et al. 2005).

Nonuse values include three main categories: vicarious use, bequest value, and existence value. Vicarious use and bequest value both imply an altruistic willingness to pay for the benefits that other members of the present generation or future generations get from ecosystem services. Existence value can be thought of as an altruistic willingness to pay for the benefits that other species

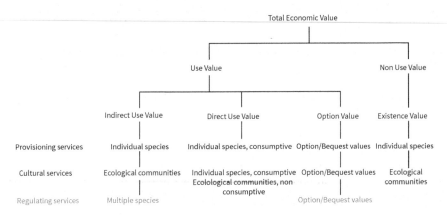

Figure 5.5 Direct and indirect use and nonuse value typology.

get from ecosystem services, and is frequently driven by ethical or religious concerns.

The value of environmental goods and services, whether marketed or not, is not an inherent property of the underlying environmental assets, but is attributed by people through their willingness to pay/accept compensation for the services that flow from those assets. It does partly depend on the characteristics of the asset, but it is more a function of the socioeconomic context in which valuation occurs. The context includes human preferences, institutions, and culture. It includes the distribution of income and wealth, production and consumption technologies, and expectations about the future. Put another way, the value of environmental goods and services is anthropocentric, instrumental, and state-dependent (Heal et al. 2005, Barbier et al. 2009). If B_{it} denotes the benefits to all people from the ith service offered by some environmental resource at time t, then today's value of that resource is simply: $V_0 = \sum_{t=0}^{T} \sum_{i=1}^{n} \rho^t B_{it}$ where ρ is a discount factor. This will be positive only if the resource is scarce in the sense that it has an opportunity cost— something has to be given up to get an additional unit. If B_{it} is not revealed through market prices, then it has to be estimated using the one or more of the methods described in the next section.

5.4 The valuation of provisioning and cultural services

The main methods used estimate the value of nonmarketed environmental goods and services are summarized in Table 5.1. They fall into two broad categories: revealed and stated preference. Revealed preference methods use observations on peoples' behavior to infer the value they place on nonmarketed environmental goods and services that affect well-being in some way.

Since people will typically pay to access the benefits offered or to avoid the costs imposed by the environment around them, observations on such payments provides information on at least the lower bound on the value of the unpriced environmental benefits and costs. More particularly, if a relationship between some action and the flow of environmental goods or services can be estimated, and if the cost of the action is known, it is possible to infer the value of the environmental goods and services. There are many revealed preference methods used to estimate the valued of nonmarketed environmental resources, of which the travel cost, averting behavior, replacement

Table 5.1 Valuation methods applied to ecosystem services.

	Valuation method	Types of value estimated[b]	Common types of applications	Ecosystem services valued
Revealed Preference Methods	Travel cost	Direct use	Recreation and tourism	Aesthetic, recreational, spiritual, religious, and inspirational benefits of landscapes
	Averting behavior	Direct use	Environmental impacts on human health	Pollution control and detoxification
	Hedonic price	Direct and indirect use	Environmental impacts on residential property and human morbidity and mortality	Storm protection; flood mitigation; maintenance of air quality
	Production function	Indirect use	Commercial and recreational fishing; agricultural systems; control of invasive species; watershed protection; damage costs avoided	Maintenance of beneficial species; maintenance of arable land and agricultural productivity; prevention of damage from erosion and siltation; groundwater recharge; drainage and natural irrigation; storm protection; flood mitigation
	Replacement cost	Indirect use	Damage costs avoided; freshwater supply	Drainage and natural irrigation; storm protection; flood mitigation
Stated Preference Methods	Contingent valuation	Use and nonuse	Projects or policies expected to deliver environmental benefits at some cost	All services but most studies focus on provisioning and cultural services
	Contingent behavior	Use and nonuse	Recreation, cultural heritage, environmental changes impacting human behavior	Aesthetic, recreational, spiritual, religious, and inspirational benefits of landscapes
	Choice modeling	Use and nonuse	Environmental effects of policy options	All services but most studies focus on provisioning and cultural services

Source: Adapted from Barbier (2007) and Hanley et al. (2001).

cost, and production function methods are most common. We describe these methods and their relation to the conservation of the natural environment in more detail later.

Stated preference methods, as the name implies, are designed to elicit statements from respondents about their preferences over states or actions that can then be used to infer the value of nonmarketed environmental resources. All are implemented through surveys of a sample of the population affected by those resources. There are currently three main methods applied: dichotomous choice referenda, contingent behavior, and choice experiments. Dichotomous choice referenda ask people to respond yes or no to questions about peoples' willingness to support actions that achieve defined environmental outcomes at known costs. By varying the questions put across the sample it is possible to infer the population's willingness to pay function. Contingent behavior methods pose questions about the change in activity levels that would be triggered by a change in environmental conditions, and choice experiments ash people to rank alternative environmental states/action combinations. We describe these methods in more detail next.

While stated preference methods are clearly more flexible than revealed preference methods—they can be used to estimate the value of any combination of actions and states, and so any of the sources of value referred to earlier— they are also more information-constrained. Whereas revealed preference methods use observed behavior in real situations to infer the value placed on nonmarketed environmental goods and services, stated preference methods infer value from peoples' responses to hypothetical situations. Peoples' behavior in real situations is constrained by their understanding of the structure of the natural system, and the processes at work, but they at least have access to multiple sources of information and time to consider their options. Peoples' responses to survey instruments, on the other hand, are constrained by the information presented in the survey instrument, and the time they are willing to commit to the survey.

5.5 Revealed preference methods

Travel cost method: The oldest of the revealed preference methods relevant to the conservation of environmental assets is the travel cost method first used by Trice and Wood (Trice and Wood 1958). The method uses travel costs as a proxy for the price of visiting recreational sites such as national parks or monuments. An observed relationship between site visits and the cost of visiting is used to derive a demand curve from which consumer surplus may be calculated. The approach assumes that recreational sites and site access expenditures are weakly complementary, implying that if access expenditures are zero, then the marginal utility of the site is also zero. That is, the marginal social cost of a change in the quality of a site is assumed to be positive only if site access expenditures are positive.

In the simplest case, visits to the ith site, v_i, are assumed to depend on travel costs to that site, c_i, and to all other potential sites, $c_{-i} = c_1,...,c_{i-1},c_{i+1},...,c_n$, on the socioeconomics characteristics of the population, S, including income, demographic and cultural factors, and on site qualities in the ith site, q_i and all other potential sites, $q_{-i} = q_1,...,q_{i-1},q_{i+1},...,q_n$. By estimating how visits fall as travel costs rise, it is possible to obtain a demand curve for that site. The estimated model in this case takes the general form:

$$v_i = f\left(c_i, c_{-i}, q_i, q_{-i}, S, \beta_i\right) + \varepsilon_i \qquad (5.6)$$

where $f(.)$ is the functional form selected, β_i is the set of parameters to be estimated, and ε_i is an error term. The approach has been widely used to estimate demand for ecotourism based on protected areas, and so uncovers at least one element in the social value of such areas. Importantly it can be used to show how changes in the attributes of a site—including changes in species richness or abundance at the site—affect demand.

Of the remaining revealed preference methods, averting behavior, defensive or preventive expenditures methods mirror the travel cost approach. However, instead of using observed expenditures on travel to measure willingness to pay to access a site, they use observed defensive or averting expenditures to measure willingness to pay to avoid the potential harms imposed by environmental conditions. Expenditures on water purification, vaccination, protection against disease vectors, heating, air conditioning, and so on are all examples of defensive or averting expenditures. In the same way that travel cost expenditures are expected to increase up to the point where the marginal benefits from travel just offset the marginal costs, so defensive or averting expenditures are expected to increase up to the point where the marginal damage avoided just offsets the marginal cost.

Note that in extreme cases averting or defensive behaviors include the abandonment of environmentally harmful sites. The phenomenon of environmental refugees—people moving away from degraded, polluted, or hazardous landscapes—is an extreme example of defensive or averting behavior. There are, however, many fewer studies of this phenomenon than there are of recreational demand.

Hedonic pricing: Like the travel cost method, the hedonic approach uses observed expenditures to infer the value of environmental attributes that are not directly priced. The underlying assumption behind the approach is that the observed price paid for an asset, such as a house, reflects the bundle of attributes that characterize that asset. Any residential property, for example, may be characterized by the size of the house and the lot; the house age, style, and method of construction; the composition of rooms; as well as a number of location variables. Location variables include the position of the relative to public services such as hospitals and schools, or to public and private transport options. They also include neighborhood characteristics such as public safety.

To calculate the MWTP for reliability through house purchase decisions we specify and estimate a hedonic price function of the form:

$$p_i = f\left(\mathbf{h}_i, \mathbf{a}_i, \mathbf{s}_i, \beta, \mu, \lambda\right) + \varepsilon \tag{5.7}$$

where p_i is the price of the ith property sold during the reference period, $\mathbf{h}_i$ is a vector of house characteristics, $\mathbf{a}_i$ is a vector of environmental or ambient conditions, $\mathbf{s}_i$ is a vector of power infrastructural conditions, and ε is an error term. The remaining terms are vectors of estimated coefficients on house characteristics, ambient conditions and infrastructure conditions. This implies an underlying household utility function of the form:

$$U_j = U\left(\mathbf{x}_j, \mathbf{h}_j, \mathbf{a}_j, \mathbf{s}_j\right) \tag{5.8}$$

where x_j is a vector of all other commodities consumed by the jth household. Household preferences are assumed to be weakly separable in the set of housing and housing-related services and all other commodities (implying that preferences over housing and housing-related services are independent of the quantities of other commodities). The assumption allows us to estimate demand for housing services independent of the prices of other commodities, since demand for housing services depends only on service "prices" and total expenditure.

Production function approaches: The second widely used revealed preference method focuses on the environment as an input in the production of marketed goods and services. In the simplest case, changes in environmental conditions are related to changes in either productivity or earnings. The measure of value this yields is either the net value of lost production, or the net loss in earnings due to environmental change. Closely related to this is the cost of offsetting the environmental change. The measure of value in this case is the replacement cost of cost of inputs used to replace or restore productivity or earnings lost by environmental change. This might include, for example, fertilizers used to counter the loss of soil nutrients, or the construction of dams, wells, and canals to counter the depletion of surface or groundwater reserves.

One frequently cited example of the approach relates to the provision of clean drinking water for New York City from watersheds in the Catskills. In this case the problem addressed was not driven by a decline in environmental quality, but by an increase in the demand for water purification. New York City faced the option of building a new water filtration plant or enhancing the quality of the water obtained from the watershed. The present value cost of building and operating the water filtration plant was estimated to be $6 to $8 billion (Chichilnisky and Heal 1998). The cost of enhancing the water quality regulatory functions of the Catskills watersheds was $1 to $1.5 billion. The value of the ecosystem service provided is the avoided cost of replacing the ecosystem service with some engineered alternative.

The production function method has been widely used to uncover the value of specific attributes of the environment, or of particular ecological functions and processes. The approach follows the method generally used to determine the value of any input in a production process. The demand for any input in the production of some output, whether the input is marketed or not, derives from demand for the output. How much labor or capital is required for the production of housing in some location, for example, derives from the demand for housing. In this respect, environmental resources are no different from any other input. Decision-makers will increase employment of environmental resources up to the point where the value they add to the process just offsets their cost. The value added by an environmental input, like the value added by any other input, is equal to the price of the output multiplied by the marginal physical product of the input. There are two steps involved. First, the marginal physical effects of environmental changes on the production of some marketed good or service are determined. Second, the impact of these changes is valued in terms of the change in the marketed output.

Suppose that q is the marketed output of an economic activity that depends on a range of inputs, including environmental resources:

$$q = f(k, l, r) \tag{5.9}$$

where k and l denote capital and labor and r denotes an environmental resource. One example is the role of mangroves in supporting offshore fisheries. Mangroves serve both as a spawning ground and a nursery for fish fry. In this, and many other cases, ecosystem function is proxied by ecosystem area (Barbier 2007, Freeman et al. 2014). If r denotes the area of mangroves in a coastal region, and if $dq/dr > 0$, a decrease in r reduces the catch of mangrove-dependent species in ways that are independent from the capital and labor employed in the industry. The derivative of q with respect to r characterizes the primary impact of a set of ecological support functions Whether the impact accelerates or attenuates with increases in the mangrove area depends on the sign on the second derivative d^2q/dr^2. If the market price of fish is p the value added by adding a small amount of mangrove, value of the marginal physical product of mangroves, is pdq/dr. Estimation of the function

$$q = f(k,l,r,\beta) + \varepsilon \tag{5.10}$$

thus makes it possible to calculate the marginal physical product of the environmental resource and hence the value implications of a change in its supply (Barbier 2007, Barbier 2011). Another frequently cited example of the production function approach is the role of pollinators in supporting coffee production in Costa Rica. Ricketts and colleagues found that pollination services contributed 7% of total farm income to coffee producers in Costa Rica (in 2002–2003 when coffee prices were depressed) (Ricketts et al. 2004).

Note that it is not necessary for the environmental resource (or resources) of interest to enter directly into the production of a marketed output for this method to apply. All that is required is that there is some functional relationship between an environmental resource and the production of a good or service that is directly valued. So, for example, Allen and Loomis used a production function approach to derive the value of species at lower trophic levels from the value of species at higher trophic levels (Allen and Loomis 2006). Specifically, they derived the implicit willingness to pay for the conservation of prey species from direct estimates of willingness to pay for top predators. Nor was it necessary, in this case, for people to understand the trophic structure of the ecosystem, since their willingness to pay for top predators effectively captured their willingness to pay for the whole system. As long as the science exists to connect trophic levels in the system, it is possible to estimate the derived value of all trophic levels.

The same idea can be extended to deal the case where the productivity of one species is conditional on either the abundance of other species or on state of the environment more generally. So, for example, the derived value of members of a functional group of species, each of which performs differently in different environmental conditions, will vary with those conditions. The value of species that are "productive" in some conditions but not in others depends on the likelihood that the conditions in which they do have value will occur (Loreau et al. 2002). We come back to this in our discussion of the value of biodiversity as species "portfolios" later in this chapter.

5.6 Stated preference methods

The most widely used class of methods for estimating willingness to pay for many ecosystem services, and especially for the cultural services, is the class of "stated preference methods." These include contingent valuation, contingent behavior, and choice experiments. These valuation methods share a common approach with market research in that they use surveys to elicit peoples' willingness to pay for goods and services. The main advantage of stated preference methods is they are flexible enough to include nonconsumptive uses (Freeman et al. 2014). Their main weakness, as has already been noted, is that they are highly sensitive to the information provided to respondents. The survey instrument has to describe environmental change in a manner that people will understand, and the impact of environmental changes in terms of familiar goods and services (Heal et al. 2005). In practice, it has been difficult to use the hypothetical scenarios required by stated-preference surveys to explain the effect of changes in ecosystem processes on the regulatory functions of ecosystems. This is partly because there is still scientific uncertainty about these things. There is a by now a very large literature on stated preference methods. Overviews by Bateman et al. (2002), Carson and Hanemann (2005), and Carson (2012) provide details on both methods and the literature.

Contingent valuation: Taking the first of these methods, contingent valuation, the approach has three elements: background information about the environmental good or service to be valued, a specified payment instrument, and a method of elicitation. The background information conditions respondents' answers to the questions posed. In some cases surveys will include questions about the respondent's prior knowledge of the problem addressed. In many cases, it is assumed that the information provided in the survey is all that the respondent knows. Contingent valuation studies, whatever the elicitation method, all include a payment vehicle. For the responses to be meaningful the payment vehicle should not itself bias the response unduly. Payment vehicles that involve taxes or special purpose public funds, for example, frequently induce a strongly negative response.

Elicitation methods have changed from open-ended questions to single and double bounded dichotomous choice questions. Open-ended questions that simply ask respondents what they would be willing to pay generate direct measures of value for the population at hand, but tend to encourage false statements—either higher than the respondent's true willingness to pay or zero. For this reason economists consider open-ended questions to be incentive incompatible, in the sense that they fail to induce respondents to declare their real willingness to pay (Freeman et al. 2014).

By contrast, dichotomous choice questions ask for "yes" or "no" answers to questions about the respondent's willingness to pay specific amounts for some environmental good or service. In the simplest case, respondent, are asked if they are willing to pay X dollars to bring about or avoid some environmental change, the value of X being then being systematically varied across the sample population. In other cases, respondents are asked a series of "yes" or "no" questions to iterate toward their maximum willingness to pay. If they respond "yes" to the first value, they are then asked to respond to a higher value. If they answer "no" to the first value, they are offered a lower value.

The "yes" or "no" answers then need to be converted into a value. A common method for doing this is to exploit the bid function for the compensating or equivalent surplus associated with some environmental change. Taking the problem to be one in which we are interested in the compensating surplus, the bid function has the form:

$$B(q_0,q_1,u_0,S) = e(q_1,u_0,S) - e(q_0,u_0,S) \tag{5.11}$$

where q_0,q_1,u_0,S are, respectively, the state of the environment without and with the change, the respondent's utility without the change, and a set of socioeconomic conditions, and where $e(q_1,u_0,S) - e(q_0,u_0,S)$ is the difference in the respondents' expenditures in the two states. If the amount specified in the questionnaire was X the respondent would answer "yes" if $B(q_0,q_1,u_0,S) \geq X$ and "no" otherwise, implying that the probability that the respondent would accept q_1 at X is $\Pr\left(B^o(q_0,q_1,u_0,S) \mid \eta \geq X\right)$, where B^o is the observable part of the bid function, and η is the unobserved random part. If η is normally distributed with zero mean and standard deviation σ, the result is a probit model of the form

$$\Pr Y = \Phi\left(B(q_0,q_1,u_0,S,\beta/\sigma) - X/\sigma\right) \tag{5.12}$$

Φ being a standard normal cumulative density. The estimated bid function then takes the form:

$$B = B(q_0,q_1,u_0,S,\beta) + \sigma\eta_s \tag{5.13}$$

in which η_s is a standard normal random variable. This can then be used to recover total and marginal willingness to pay (Freeman et al. 2014).

Contingent behavior: The second commonly applied stated preference approach is the contingent behavior approach. This differs from contingent valuation in that instead of asking respondents what they would be willing to pay for some environmental change, it asks respondents how that environmental change would alter their behavior. So, for example, visitors to a protected area might be asked how a change in some attribute of the protected area might alter the likelihood that they would visit it in the future. The approach is especially useful when the intent is to measure the value of environmental changes outside the range currently observed. For example, Hanley et al. (2003) investigated the effect of changes in bathing water quality standards in Europe on visitation to beaches. Using a negative binomial model they estimated the expected number of visits to affected beaches by the ith individual, v_i, as a function of a set of general explanatory variables including the change in water quality standards, Z, and travel cost, c_i:

$$v_i = \exp\left(Z_i\delta - c_i\alpha\right) \tag{5.14}$$

The consumer surplus obtained from this semilog demand function is

$$CS_i = \int_{c_i}^{\infty} \exp\left(Z_i\delta - c_i\alpha\right)dc_i = \exp\left(Z_i\delta - c_i\alpha\right)/\alpha = v_i/\alpha$$

where δ and α are parameters, so the change in consumer surplus associated with a change in water bathing standards is just

$$\Delta CS_i = \frac{\exp\left(Z_i^*\delta - c_i\alpha\right)}{\alpha} - \frac{\exp\left(Z_i\delta - c_i\alpha\right)}{\alpha} = \frac{v_i^* - v_i}{\alpha} \tag{5.15}$$

Choice modeling: The third commonly applied stated preference method is choice modeling. This approach builds on Lancaster's approach to the valuation of goods in terms of their various characteristics. When applied to environmental goods and services, the approach decomposes distinct goods and services into a number of constituent attributes, including price. Respondents are then asked to rank the goods or services in order of preference, or to score them on a scale of 1 to 10. The different approaches to measurement correspond to different variants of choice modeling: choice experiments, contingent ranking, contingent rating or paired comparisons (Hanley et al. 2001).

Choice experiments involve a comparison between the status quo and one or more alternatives. Contingent ranking involves the ranking of a set of alternatives. Contingent rating and paired comparisons both involve scoring a set of alternatives. Since price is included as an attribute, respondents' preferences over prices can, in principle, be used to infer their willingness to pay under all choice modeling variants.

Choice experiments suppose that a respondent's utility can be decomposed into a deterministic element (a function of the attributes of the good or service) and a stochastic element (capturing unobservable influences on their choice). That is, the ith individual's utility from the jth option is assumed to be $U_{ij} = V_{ij}(X_{ij}) + e_{ij}$, where e_{ij} is a random error term. If the deterministic element is taken to be a linear function of the attributes, this takes the form:

$$U_{ij} = \beta_j X_{ij} + e_{ij} \tag{5.16}$$

and the probability that a respondent prefers the jth option to any other option is just the probability that the utility offered by the jth option is greater than the utility offered by any other option. If the errors are assumed to be independent and identically distributed (IID), this probability is given by the conditional logit:

$$\Pr\left(U_{ij} > U_{ih}\right) = \frac{e^{\mu V_{ij}}}{\sum_h e^{\mu V_{ih}}} \tag{5.17}$$

where $h \neq j$. Estimation of this model can then be used to obtain a measure of willingness to pay

$$WTP = \frac{1}{\beta_y} \frac{\sum_i e^{\mu V_{ij}}}{\sum_i e^{\mu V_{i0}}} \tag{5.18}$$

where V_{i0} is the utility of the status quo to the ith respondent, and β_y is the coefficient on the price or cost of the status quo—interpreted as the marginal utility of income. For the linear function assumed in 5.18 willingness to pay for the jth alternative is simply $-\beta_j/\beta_y$.

Contingent ranking requires respondents to rank a set of alternatives. This implies a sequence of choice experiments in which respondents first find the most preferred option among all available alternatives. They then delete that option, and find the most preferred option among all remaining alternatives.

The process continues until only one option remains. It follows that the method for estimating willingness to pay should be similar to that used in choice experiments. The probability that the ith respondent will have particular ranking is similar to (5.17):

$$\Pr\left(U_{i1} > U_{i2} > ... > U_{ih}\right) = \prod_j \left[\frac{e^{\mu V_{ij}}}{\sum_h e^{\mu V_{ih}}}\right] \tag{5.19}$$

As with choice experiments, estimation of this model can then be used to obtain measures of willingness to pay similar to 5.18. Assuming that the status quo is among the set of alternatives being ranked, once it is chosen remaining rankings should be dropped from the estimation. This is because any subsequent options do not convey information on the respondent's real demand—but on demand conditional on the remaining options.

Contingent rating, whether based on multiple options or paired comparisons, uses a scoring system to distinguish between alternatives. To make the approach consistent with the theory of demand, economists convert the resulting ratings to utility via a transformation function, $\phi\left(V_{ij}\left(X_{ij}\right)\right)$. That is, a particular rating is assumed to map into a particular level of utility:

$$R_{ij}\left(X_{ij}\right) = \phi\left(V_{ij}\left(X_{ij}\right)\right) \tag{5.20}$$

where R_{ij} is the ith individual's rating of the jth option. One method for converting rating information to a measure of willingness to pay is to subtract a monetary amount from each alternative up to the point where the difference in ratings disappears:

$$R_{ij}\left(X_{ij}, M_i - WTP_{ij}\right) - R_{ih}\left(X_{ih}, M_i\right) = 0 \tag{5.21}$$

where M_i, WTP_{ij} are income and implicit willingness to pay for the semi log j^{th} alternative respectively. In the paired choice variant of the approach only two options are considered at any moment in time.

Benefit transfer: One other approach to the valuation of nonmarketed environmental goods and services is value or benefit transfer. This method uses estimates of the value of environmental goods and services at one location to infer the value of the same ecosystem goods and services at another location, the "policy site." In some cases, this approach works well. Because the atmosphere is well mixed, for example, carbon sequestration makes the same contribution to the general circulation system, and hence to global well-being wherever it occurs. Sequestering a ton of carbon accordingly has the same value wherever it occurs. However, if the value of ecosystem services depends on local environmental conditions, or on the characteristics of the societies who benefit from those services, then benefit transfer is less reliable. Given the cost of original valuation studies, however, the use of benefit transfer is growing rapidly, and economists have invested considerable effort in the refinement of benefit transfer procedures.

Meta-regression models—regression models based on a range of estimates of the value of a given resource at different sites—are the most frequently used method for approximating the value of particular resources at some policy site (Rosenberger and Loomis 2000, Shrestha and Loomis 2001). These methods are most often used as an alternative to a stated preference approaches, such as contingent valuation, contingent behavior, or choice experiments, where the cost of original research is high. The approach has, for example, been used to estimate the value of recreational fisheries (Johnston et al. 2005, Johnston et al. 2006). Meta-regression methods have also, however, been used to estimate values based on hedonic valuation methods (Smith and Pattanayak 2002, Moeltner et al. 2007). In all cases, the models take information from a set of existing studies, allowing each study to carry some weight in the estimation of willingness to pay, and making it possible to isolate the effects of user characteristics and the features of the different sites investigated, as well as differences in the valuation methodology applied. The adoption of Bayesian methods has improved the capacity to use all the results of the underlying studies, irrespective of the method used to obtain those results (Brunsdon and Willis 2002, Smith et al. 2006). Specifically, it makes it possible to find the posterior distribution of willingness to pay estimates conditional only on user and site characteristics, by averaging predictions associated with different methodologies. If the estimated willingness to pay is denoted by $\hat{y}$, the policy site characteristics by $\hat{X}_p$, and the policy population characteristics by $\mathbf{q}_p$, then the marginal posterior distribution of $\hat{y}$ is given by:

$$p\left(\hat{y} \mid \hat{X}_p, \mathbf{q}_p \right) = \int_\theta \left(\sum_{i=1}^{n} p\left(\hat{y} \mid \theta, \hat{X}_p, \mathbf{q}_p, m_i \right) \pi_i \right) p\left(\theta \mid y, X \right) d\theta \qquad (5.22)$$

where θ is the set of Bayesian model parameters, $m_i, i = 1,...,n$ is the set of methodologies applied in the reference studies, $\pi_i, i = 1,...,n$ are the probabilities assigned to each methodology outcome (summing to 1), and y and X are willingness to pay and site characteristics in the reference studies.

5.7 The valuation of regulating services

The Millennium Ecosystem Assessment drew attention to the importance of services that regulate the earth's capacity to respond to environmental shocks and stresses—the regulating services, but was unable to report the value of these services. This is partly because there were then (and still are) few estimates of the value of regulating services. There is still uncertainty about the science, but there is also agreement that many regulating services depend on functional diversity. Greater functional diversity allows ecosystems to respond to short-run shocks and stresses in constructive and creative ways, with implications for the value of the underlying assets. This has been investigated both theoretically (Brock and Xepapadeas, 2003) and empirically (Smale et al. 1998, Schläpfer et al. 2002, di Falco and Perrings 2005, di Falco and Chavas 2007). Crop diversity has been shown to affect the mean and variance of both agricultural yields and farm income. While the homogenization of agroecosystems can increase yields in the short run, it is often at the cost of increasing longer run vulnerability to pests and pathogens. The value of the regulating services provided by agrobiodiversity in this case depends on peoples' willingness to pay for a reduction in pest and pathogen risks.

Within ecology, the best-known experimental results on the same phenomenon stem from the grassland experiments conducted by Tilman (Tilman et al. 1996, Tilman et al. 2001). Similar controlled experiments by Naeem and others found that increasing the number of species in the system tended to increase system productivity (Naeem et al. 1995, Naeem and Li 1997, Hector and Bagchi 2007, Hector et al. 2010, Hector 2011). In heterogeneous environments, having more species will generally allow the collection of species to better utilize all ecological niches and so be more productive through a niche differentiation effect. Coverage increases, either in niche space or genetic space, when more species are added. The conclusion is that an increase in the diversity of functional groups of species increases both ecological stability (Tilman et al. 2005) and resilience (Carpenter and Gunderson 2001). The mechanisms involved fall into three categories: overyielding, statistical averaging, and compensatory dynamics. Overyielding exists when mean biomass production increases with diversity more rapidly than does its standard deviation. Statistical averaging implies that random variation in the abundance of different species reduces variability in aggregate ecosystem variables, and compensatory dynamics occur when environmental responses are asynchronous (Hooper et al. 2005, Cardinale et al. 2012).

A summary of what was known about the value of the regulating services at the end of the first decade of this century was able to point to only a handful of studies, but also suggested that the regulating services were likely to be the most valuable services offered by most ecosystems (Kumar 2010). To estimate the value of the regulating services we need to understand, first, how the mix of species within a functional group affects the way the function varies with environmental conditions, and second, how much people care about variability. This depends on peoples' risk preferences. The dominant economic approach to analyzing problems of this form is the expected utility approach. The expected utility hypothesis holds that individuals evaluate a risky prospect in terms of the mathematical expectation of the utility induced by the prospect. So the attractiveness of a gamble offering the payoffs $(x_1,...,x_n)$ with probabilities $(p_1,...,p_n)$ is evaluated not by the expected value of the payoffs, but by the expected utility associated with those payoffs, $EU = \sum_{j=1}^{n} U(x_j)p_j$, where $U(x_1,...,x_n)$ is referred to as a von Neumann-Morgenstern utility function.

This function assumes three things. The first is a complete ordering of options. For two alternatives A and B one of the following must be true: the consumer either prefers A to B, prefers B to A, or is indifferent between them. The consumer's evaluation of alternatives is also transitive. If they prefer A to B and B to C, then they prefer A to C. The second is continuity. If A is preferred to B and B to C, then there exists some probability p, $0 < p < 1$, such that the consumer will be indifferent between outcome B with certainty and a lottery (p, A, C). The third is independence. If A is preferred to B, and C is any outcome whatever, then if one lottery offers outcomes A and C with probabilities p and $1 - p$ respectively, and a second lottery offers the outcomes B and C with the same probabilities p and $1 - p$, the consumer will prefer the first lottery.

The expected utility approach is not unproblematic. The Allais and Ellsberg paradoxes reflect the tendency of individuals to overweight high-consequence low-probability events and to show aversion to ambiguity, respectively. More particularly, while people prefer a lower valued but certain outcome to a more valuable lottery that includes the possibility of total loss, they also prefer the higher valued of two uncertain outcomes (Allais). Similarly, people strongly prefer risks where the odds are known over risks where the odds are ambiguous, even if the expected payoff in the second case is much greater than the first (Ellsberg). Evidence has since been accumulating that people make many other decisions that are inconsistent with the expected utility approach (Shaw

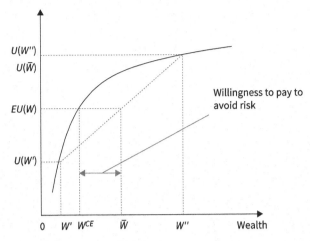

Figure 5.6 Willingness to pay to avoid risk.

Utility, measured on the vertical axis, is increasing in wealth at a diminishing rate. The indifference curve shows the utility associated with a lottery comprising wealth levels W' and W'' occurring with equal probability. The utility associated with expected level of wealth is $U(\bar{W})$ while the expected utility is denoted $EU(W)$. The certain level of wealth that delivers $EU(W)$ is W_{CE}. The difference between $\bar{W}$ and W_{CE} is a measure of the decision-maker's willingness to pay to avoid risk.

and Woodward 2008). Nonetheless, expected utility remains dominant. If we think of the payoffs to different gambles as different levels of wealth, an indifference curve from the preference function of a risk averse individual with a von Neumann-Morgenstern utility function takes the form shown in Figure 5.6. The greater is the curvature of the indifference curve, the greater is the degree of risk aversion.

To illustrate, suppose that the decision-maker has to choose the level of effort given to the promotion of just two species, s_1 and s_2, each of which offers some benefit $y_1 = y_1(s_1)$ and $y_2 = y_2(s_2)$. The expected yield of a portfolio comprising the two species is

$$E(y) = \sum_i \rho_i E(y_i), i = 1,2$$

in which ρ_i is the share of total biomass accounted for by the ith species. The variance in the yield of the portfolio would then be:

$$\sigma_p^2 = \rho_1^2 \sigma_1^2 + \rho_2^2 \sigma_2^2 + 2\rho_1^2 \rho_2^2 \sigma_1 \sigma_2 r_{12}$$

where σ_1, σ_2 are the standard deviations of the yield associated with each of the two species, and r_{12} is the correlation coefficient between yields from species 1 and 2. Now suppose that the yields of the two species vary with the state of nature in different ways. Let there be three states of nature that occur with known probabilities, p, as follows:

	p	y_1	y_2
State 1	0.2	1.2	2
State 2	0.6	1.3	1.4
State 3	0.2	1.4	0.6

Species 1 has relatively constant yields over all conditions, but does best in state 3. Species 2 has more variable yield, and does best in state 1. The expected yields from the ith species in this case is $E(y_i) = p_1 y_{1i} + p_2 y_{2i} + p_3 y_{3i}$, implying that $E(y_1) = 1.3$ and $E(y_2) = 1.36$. The correlation coefficient is $r_{12} = -0.994$, implying that the two species are substitutes in the production of y. This means that a combination of the species will generate more stable yields than specialization in just one or the other. For our numerical example the expected yield and the standard deviation in yields for each combination of species is shown in Figure 5.7.

The diversity of species in either natural or managed ecosystems, like the diversity of assets in a financial portfolio, helps people negotiate a risky world. How much diversity is needed within a portfolio of species depends on peoples' attitudes to risk, to the expected range of environmental conditions, and to the covariance in the response of distinct species to differences in environmental conditions. The greater the expected variation in conditions, the less the covariance in species responses, and the more risk averse people are, the greater will be the required diversity (Elmqvist et al. 2003). The optimal balance between the two species in Figure 5.7 then depends on the decision-maker's preferences between yield (good) and risk (bad).

While there is considerable interest in developing stated preference methods capable of accommodating the kind of uncertainty that dogs most conservation problems, there are as yet relatively few studies that incorporate uncertainty directly into survey instruments. The most common approach to estimating the effect of uncertainty has been to split the sample of respondents, presenting the same outcomes as certain in one subsample and uncertain in another (Wielgus et al. 2009, Faccioli et al. 2017). Interestingly, this work has revealed that attitudes to environmental risk are far from consistent. Risk attitudes are shown to depend on sociodemographic characteristics and the assets at risk. Health, financial, and environmental assets attract quite different responses (Weber et al. 2002, Roberts et al. 2008, Riddel 2012). One choice experiment conducted along these lines found that respondents were risk averse toward environmental losses but risk avid toward environmental

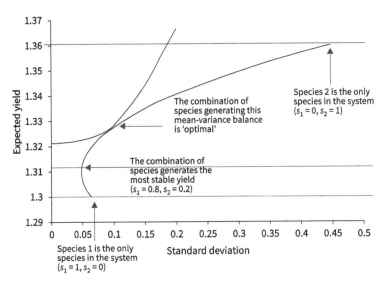

Figure 5.7 The portfolio effect and the trade-off between mean and variance in yields. This shows the effect of diversity on the trade-off between expected yield and variance in yields. If only species 2 is present the expected yield is high, but so is the variance in yield. If only species 1 is present expected yield is lower, but so is the variance in yields.

gains (Faccioli et al. 2017). There is nonetheless consensus that it is important to present risks in stated preference studies, and it is clear that the valuation of the regulating services is critically dependent on the way that risk is both calculated and presented.

5.8 Summary and conclusions

The origins of value lie in the trade-offs people are willing to make between different goods and services, whether priced or not. Economists typically identify two measures of the value of one good in terms of another: compensating and equivalent variation. For goods x and y, compensating variation, also known as willingness to pay, is the amount of y that, if given up to acquire some increase in x, leaves utility or well-being unchanged. Equivalent variation, also known as willingness to accept, is the quantity of y that yields the same increase in utility or well-being as the change in x. In this chapter we showed that the same concepts can be used to measure the value of x in terms of y even if both are unpriced. The chapter describes the various methods developed by economists to estimate either willingness to pay or willingness to accept measures for nonmarketed ecosystem services.

The value of individual ecosystem services may be either direct or indirect. An ecosystem service has direct value if it enters directly into the utility function. For example, an individual organism may have traits that appeal directly to consumers. It may be cute or charismatic, ornamental, rare, endangered, or endemic. It may have physical or chemical properties that make it valuable as food, fuel or fiber. It may have totemic, cultural, or spiritual significance. In all such cases utility is likely to be increasing in the abundance of the organism, at least up to a point. Ecosystem services have indirect value if they support production of environmental goods and services that are directly valuable, but are not themselves directly valued. For example, the habitats in which directly valued species are found derive value from those directly valued species. The value of biodiversity—the mix of species—derives from its role in the supply of directly valued ecosystem services such as pollination. It therefore depends on the links between biodiversity, ecosystem functioning and the supply of ecosystem services within a given system (Hanley and Perrings 2019).

It follows that ecosystem services that do not enter directly into the utility function have indirect value. Both the supporting and regulating ecosystem services fall into this category. The chapter addressed the case of the regulating services directly. These comprise the buffering functions of nature—such as air quality regulation, macroclimatic regulation through carbon sequestration, soil erosion control, water purification, storm damage reduction, and zoonotic disease mitigation. The value of these functions lies in their impact on the risks born by people. For example, the biodiversity underpinning a regulating service such as coastal storm damage mitigation derives value from its effect on the damage from hurricanes. Similarly, the biodiversity supporting the resilience of agroecosystem derives value from its effect on the supply of foods over a range of climatic conditions (Baumgärtner and Strunz 2014).

Because nonmarket valuation makes it possible to identify the economic impacts of environmental change, it supports application of the Hotelling approach to conservation. More particularly, it makes it possible to project the value of the environmental assets that underpin production of the provisioning and other ecosystem services. We consider environmental assets in more detail in the next chapter, but note here that asset values reflect the discounted stream of services those assets yield. Valuation of ecosystem services is therefore an important step in determining whether or not to conserve the underlying environmental assets.

References

Allen, B. P., and J. B. Loomis. 2006. Deriving values for the ecological support function of wildlife: an indirect valuation approach. Ecological Economics 56:49–57.

Barbier, E. B. 2007. Valuing ecosystem services as productive inputs. Economic Policy 49:178–229.

Barbier, E. B. 2011. Pricing nature. Annual Review of Resource Economics 3:337–353.

Barbier, E. B., S. Baumgärtner, K. Chopra, C. Costello, A. Duraiappah, R. Hassan, A. Kinzig, M. Lehman, U. Pascual, S. Polasky, and C. Perrings. 2009. The valuation of ecosystem services. Pages 248–262 in S. Naeem, D. Bunker, A. Hector, M. Loreau, and C. Perrings, editors. Biodiversity, ecosystem functioning, and human wellbeing: an ecological and economic perspective. Oxford University Press, Oxford.

Bateman, I. J., R. T. Carson, B. Day, M. Hanemann, N. Hanley, T. Hett, M. Jones-Lee, G. Loomes, S. Mourato, and D. W. Pearce. 2002. Economic valuation with stated preference techniques: a manual. Edward Elgar, Cheltenham.

Baumgärtner, S., and S. Strunz. 2014. The economic insurance value of ecosystem resilience. Ecological Economics 101:21–32.

Brunsdon, C., and K. G. Willis. 2002. Meta-analysis: a Bayesian perspective. Pages 208–234 in R. J. G. M. Florax, P. Nijkamp, and K. G. Willis, editors. Comparative environmental economic assessment. Edward Elgar, Cheltenham.

Brock, W. A., and A. Xepapadeas. 2003. Valuing Biodiversity from an Economic Perspective: A Unified Economic, Ecological, and Genetic Approach. American Economic Review 93:1597–1614.

Cardinale, B. J., J. E. Duffy, A. Gonzalez, D. U. Hooper, C. Perrings, P. Venail, A. Narwani, G. M. Mace, D. Tilman, D. A. Wardle, A. P. Kinzig, G. C. Daily, M. Loreau, J. B. Grace, A. Larigauderie, D. S. Srivastava, and S. Naeem. 2012. Biodiversity loss and its impact on humanity. Nature 486:59–67.

Carpenter, S. R., and L. H. Gunderson. 2001. Coping with collapse: ecological and social dynamics in ecosystem management. Bioscience 51:451.

Carson, R. 2012. Contingent valuation: a comprehensive bibliography and history. Edward Elgar, Cheltenham.

Carson, R. T., and W. M. Hanemann. 2005. Contingent valuation. Handbook of environmental economics 2:821–936.

Chichilnisky, G., and G. M. Heal. 1998. Economic returns from the biosphere. Nature 391:629–630.

di Falco, S., and J. P. Chavas. 2007. On the role of crop biodiversity in the management of environmental risk. Pages 581–593 in A. Kontoleon, U. Pascual, and T. Swanson, editors. Biodiversity economics: principles, methods, and applications. Cambridge University Press, Cambridge.

di Falco, S., and C. Perrings. 2005. Crop biodiversity, risk management and the implications of agricultural assistance. Ecological Economics 55:459–466.

Elmqvist, T., C. Folke, M. Nystrom, G. Peterson, J. Bengtsson, B. Walker, and J. Norberg. 2003. Response diversity, ecosystem change, and resilience. Frontiers in Ecology and the Environment 1:488–494.

Faccioli, M., L. Kuhfuss, and M. Czajkowski. 2017. Stated preferences for conservation policies under uncertainty: insights on individuals' risk attitudes in the environmental domain. Environmental and Resource Economics 73:627–659.

Freeman III, A. M., J. A. Herriges, and C. L. Kling. 2014. The measurement of environmental and resource values: theory and methods. Routledge, London.

Hanley, N., D. Bell, and B. Alvarez-Farizo. 2003. Valuing the benefits of coastal water quality improvements using contingent and real behaviour. Environmental and Resource Economics 24:273–285.

Hanley, N., S. Mourato, and R. E. Wright. 2001. Choice modelling approaches: a superior alternative for environmental valuation? Journal of Economic Surveys 15:435–462.

Hanley, N., and C. Perrings. 2019. The economic value of biodiversity. Annual Review of Resource Economics 11:355–375.

Heal, G. M., E. B. Barbier, K. J. Boyle, A. P. Covich, S. P. Gloss, C. H. Hershner, J. P. Hoehn, C. M. Pringle, S. Polasky, K. Segerson, and K. Shrader-Frechette. 2005. Valuing ecosystem services: toward better environmental decision making. The National Academies Press, Washington, DC.

Hector, A. 2011. Ecology: diversity favours productivity. Nature 472:45–46.

Hector, A., and R. Bagchi. 2007. Biodiversity and ecosystem multifunctionality. Nature 448:188–190.

Hector, A., Y. Hautier, P. Saner, L. Wacker, R. Bagchi, J. Joshi, M. Scherer-Lorenzen, E. Spehn, E. Bazeley-White, and M. Weilenmann. 2010. General stabilizing effects of plant diversity on grassland productivity through population asynchrony and overyielding. Ecology 91:2213–2220.

Hooper, D. U., F. S. Chapin, J. J. Ewel, A. Hector, P. Inchausti, S. Lavorel, J. H. Lawton, D. M. Lodge, M. Loreau, S. Naeem, B. Schmid, H. Setälä, A. J. Symstad, J. Vandermeer, and D. A. Wardle. 2005. Effects of biodiversity on ecosystem functioning: a consensus of current knowledge. Ecological Monographs 75:3–35.

Johnston, R. J., E. Y. Besedin, R. Iovanna, C. J. Miller, R. F. Wardwell, and M. H. Ranson. 2005. Systematic variation in willingness to pay for aquatic resource improvements and implications for benefit transfer: a meta-analysis. Canadian Journal of Agricultural Economics 53:221–248.

Johnston, R. J., M. H. Ranson, E. Y. Besedin, and E. C. Helm. 2006. What determines willingness to pay for fish? a meta-analysis of recreational fishing values. Marine Resource Economics 21:1–32.

Krutilla, J. V. 1967. Conservation reconsidered. American Economic Review 57:777–786.

Kumar, P., editor. 2010. The economics of ecosystems and biodiversity. Earthscan, London.

Loreau, M., S. Naeem, and P. Inchausti. 2002. Biodiversity and ecosystem functioning: synthesis and perspectives. Oxford University Press, Oxford.

Millennium Ecosystem Assessment. 2005. Ecosystems and human well-being: general synthesis. Island Press, Washington, DC.

Moeltner, K., K. J. Boyle, and R. W. Paterson. 2007. Meta-analysis and benefit transfer for resource valuation: addressing classical challenges with Bayesian modeling. Journal of Environmental Economics and Management 53:250–269.

Naeem, S., and S. Li. 1997. Biodiversity enhances ecosystem reliability. Nature 390:507–509.

Naeem, S., L. J. Thomspon, S. P. Lawler, J. H. Lawton, and R. M. Woodfin. 1995. Biodiversity and ecosystem functioning: empirical evidence from experimental microcosms. Philosophical Transactions of the Royal Society, London B, 347:249–262.

Ricketts, T. H., G. C. Daily, P. R. Ehrlich, and C. D. Michener. 2004. Economic value of tropical forest to coffee production. Proceedings of the National Academy of Sciences 101:12579–12582.

Riddel, M. 2012. Comparing risk preferences over financial and environmental lotteries. Journal of Risk and Uncertainty 45:135–157.

Roberts, D. C., T. A. Boyer, and J. L. Lusk. 2008. Preferences for environmental quality under uncertainty. Ecological Economics 66:584–593.

Rosenberger, R. S., and J. B. Loomis. 2000. Using meta-analysis for benefit transfer: in-sample convergent validity tests of an outdoor recreation database. Water Resources Res. 36:1097–1107.

Schläpfer, F., M. Tucker, and I. Seidl. 2002. Returns from hay cultivation in fertilized low diversity and non-fertilized high diversity grassland. Environmental and Resource Economics 21:89–100.

Shaw, W. D., and R. T. Woodward. 2008. Why environmental and resource economists should care about non-expected utility models. Resource and Energy Economics 30:66–89.

Shrestha, R. K., and J. B. Loomis. 2001. Testing a meta-analysis model for benefit transfer in international outdoor recreation. Ecological Economics 39:67–83.

Simon, H. A. 1957. Administrative behaviour. MacMillan, New York.

Smale, M., J. Hartell, P. W. Heisey, and B. Senauer. 1998. The contribution of genetic resources and diversity to wheat production in the Punjab of Pakistan. American Journal of Agricultural Economics 80:482–493.

Smith, V. K., and S. K. Pattanayak. 2002. Is meta-analysis a Noah's ark for non-market valuation? Environmental and Resource Economics 22:271–296.

Smith, V. K., S. K. Pattanayak, and G. L. Van Houtven. 2006. Structural benefit transfer: an example using VSL estimates. Ecological Economics 60:361–371.

Tilman, D., R. M. May, S. Polasky, and C. L. Lehman. 2005. Diversity, productivity and temporal stability in the economies of humans and nature. Journal of Environmental Economics and Management 49:405–426.

Tilman, D., P. Reich, J. Knops, D. Wedin, T. Mielke, and C. Lehman. 2001. Diversity and productivity in a long-term grassland experiment. Science 294:843–845.

Tilman, D., D. Wedin, and J. Knops. 1996. Productivity and sustainability influenced by biodiversity in grassland ecosystems. Nature 379:718–720.

Trice, A. H., and S. E. Wood. 1958. Measurement of recreation benefits. Land Economics 34:195–207.

Turner, R. K. 1999. The place of economic values in environmental valuation. Pages 17–41 in I. Batemen and K. Willis, editors. Valuing Environmental Preferences. Oxford University Press, Oxford.

Weber, E. U., A. R. Blais, and N. E. Betz. 2002. A domain-specific risk-attitude scale: measuring risk perceptions and risk behaviors. Journal of behavioral decision making 15:263–290.

Weisbrod, B. A. 1964. Collective-consumption services of individualized-consumption goods. Quarterly Journal of Economics LXXVIII:471–477.

Wielgus, J., L. R. Gerber, E. Sala, and J. Bennett. 2009. Including risk in stated-preference economic valuations: experiments on choices for marine recreation. Journal of Environmental Management 90:3401–3409.

6

The Valuation of Environmental Assets

The labour of Nature is paid, not because she does much, but because she does little. In proportion as she becomes niggardly in her gifts, she exacts a greater price for her work. Where she is munificently beneficent, she always works gratis.

—David Ricardo, *Principles of Political Economy and Taxation*, 1817

6.1 Introduction

The value of environmental assets, like the value of other assets, lies in the discounted stream of services they offer. The decision as to whether environmental assets should be conserved then depends on the expected rate of change in their value relative to the rate of return on alternative assets. The Hotelling principle indicates that the conservation of any asset will be optimal wherever the proportional growth in its expected value is greater than the rate of return on alternative assets. It follows that while the valuation of the services yielded by ecosystems, mineral reserves, water bodies, and the like is a necessary step toward their conservation, it is not sufficient. The information still needs to be used to estimate the value of the underlying stocks.

The most common method for estimating environmental assets values is the net present value approach, which relies on projections of future net returns from the use made of the asset. For many resources net returns depend on the proceeds from extraction or harvest. For others they depend on estimates of the flow of ecosystem services. Future returns are then discounted back to the present and summed to give the present value of the asset. As a first approximation, the value of an environmental asset is the discounted stream of resource rents it yields—resource rents being defined as the difference between gross operating surplus adjusting for subsidies and taxes and the user costs of produced assets.

Environmental assets are frequently poorly understood components of wealth. Many of the services they offer lie outside the market, and many nonmarketed ecosystem services are public goods of one kind or another. Nevertheless, economists have begun the work of estimating changes in the

Conservation. Charles Perrings and Ann Kinzig, Oxford University Press (2021). © Oxford University Press.
DOI: 10.1093/oso/9780190613600.003.0006

value of the environmental assets that yield ecosystem services. Most work to date has focused on low-hanging fruit such as water resources, forests, fish stocks, and minerals. While estimates of the value of forests includes climate-related services such as carbon sequestration, comparatively little attention has been paid to the ecosystem services that conservationists tend to worry about.

In this chapter we consider what has been done to measure changes in the value of environmental stocks of one kind or another, and what this implies for the value of a collection or portfolio of environmental assets. At the largest scale we consider the set of all environmental assets available to a country—its natural capital—and consider how nations are currently calculating the value of natural capital. We then consider what this tells us about conservation priorities in several areas.

The main motivation for developing natural capital accounts has been to test not the efficiency of conservation—the Hotelling problem—but the sustainability of investment. We therefore begin, in Section 6.2, by reviewing the sustainability problem and its relation to natural capital, and the way in which this problem connects to the Hotelling principle. We then consider the empirical evidence on the value of natural capital stocks, and what it tells us both about the sustainability of economic development strategies in different parts of the world, and about the efficiency of conservation strategies. There are two main approaches to the valuation of environmental assets. In Section 6.3 we consider the first of these, the United Nations' System of Environmental-Economic Accounts (SEEA). In Section 6.4 we consider the second, the World Bank's (Inclusive) Wealth Accounts. Section 6.5 then considers what evidence there is for the role of environmental assets within the system of national accounts (SNA), focusing on the role of environmental factors in the residual: total factor productivity (TFP). We note that the residual has been assigned to different things at different times, but since it is the growth left unexplained after measured factors of production have been taken into account, it necessarily includes environmental conditions. A final section offers a summary and conclusions.

6.2 Sustainability and the value of environmental assets

In 1987 the Brundtland Commission defined sustainable development to be "development that meets the needs of the present without compromising the ability of future generations to meet their own needs" (World Commission on

Environment and Development 1987). This definition ruled out development strategies that boost current consumption levels by running down the assets available to future generations. It reflected the long-held understanding that for national income to be nondeclining, the value of a nation's wealth or aggregate capital stocks should also be nondeclining. Indeed the idea is embedded in the very concept of income: the maximum amount that can be spent on consumption in one period without reducing consumption in future periods (Hicks 1939).

The Brundtland Commission was particularly interested in what maintaining national wealth implied for environmental assets. This question had attracted considerable attention in the two decades before the report appeared. The conditions under which wealth could be nondeclining, even if it included potentially exhaustible natural resources, had already been worked out by economists Robert Solow (Solow 1974, Solow 1986) and John Hartwick (Hartwick 1977, Hartwick 1978). They had shown that the value of capital stocks could be held constant only if the rents earned on the extraction of exhaustible resources were reinvested in reproducible capital. That is, a necessary condition for consumption based on the exploitation of natural resources to be sustainable was that investment should compensate for the depletion of those resources.

To see this, and the way it relates to the Hotelling principle, consider the approach taken by Hartwick (1977). He supposed that per capita output at time t, $y(t)$, depends on inputs of reproducible capital, $k(t)$, natural capital, $n(t)$, and labor, $\ell(t)$, and that it may be described by a constant returns to scale (homogeneous of degree one) Cobb-Douglas production function—that is, a function of the form:

$$y(t) = f\big(k(t), n(t), \ell(t)\big) = k(t)^{\alpha} n(t)^{\beta} 1^{\gamma} \qquad (6.1)$$

Since labor was assumed constant, $\ell(t) = 1$, and growth in output depends on growth in stocks of produced and natural capital, and on the productivity of each:

$$\dot{y} = f_k \dot{k} + f_n \dot{n}$$

$f_k = \alpha y(t)/k(t)$, and $f_n = \beta y(t)/n(t)$ in this expression describe the marginal products of produced and natural capital respectively. Hartwick took the price of output to be the numeraire of the system.

If consumption at time t is denoted $c(t)$, and if natural resource extraction costs are denoted z, the identity between income, consumption, and investment then takes the form:

$$y(t) = \dot{k} + c(t) + zn(t) \tag{6.2}$$

Income is identically equal to investment, consumption, and the cost of accessing natural resources.

Hartwick argued that consumption could be nondeclining only if the rents earned on natural resources, the difference between the price of those resources and extraction/production costs, were reinvested in reproducible capital. Since the price paid for natural resources, like the price paid for any other input in production, is just the value of the marginal physical product of those resources, this implies that:

$$\dot{k} = (f_n - z)n(t) \tag{6.3}$$

Investment, $\dot{k}$, should be equal to the rent earned on the stock of natural capital, $(f_n - z)n(t)$. This is referred to as the Hartwick rule.

Now consider the Hotelling arbitrage condition for the same natural resources. This states that the decision-maker will be indifferent between conserving the resource and converting it (extracting it) if the proportional rate of growth in the value of the resource in situ is the same as the rate of return on alternative assets. In Hartwick's one-commodity world the rate of return on alternative assets is equivalent to the value of the marginal product of reproducible capital. Since the price of output is the numeraire, the value of the marginal product of reproducible capital is just f_k. So the arbitrage condition for this economy is that the proportional rate of growth in the net price or rent on natural resources, $\frac{d}{dt}(f_n - z)\big/(f_n - z)$, should be equal to the value of the marginal product of capital, f_k, implying that:

$$f_{nn}\dot{n} + f_{nk}\dot{k} = f_k(f_n - z) \tag{6.4}$$

where $f_{nn} = \beta y(t)(\beta - 1)\big/n(t)^2$, $f_{nk} = \alpha\beta y(t)\big/n(t)k(t)$ are the second and cross partial derivatives of the production function with respect natural capital. These describe the rate of change in the marginal product of natural capital as natural and produced capital are varied. Since $f_k = \alpha y(t)\big/k(t)$, $f_n = \beta y(t)\big/n(t)$ this condition can be written in the form

$$\frac{\beta}{n(t)}\left[f_k \dot{k} + f_n \dot{n} - f_n \frac{\dot{n}}{\beta}\right] = f_k\left(f_n - z\right)$$

Substituting for $\dot{k}$ from (6.3) and rearranging yields

$$\beta\left[f_k\left(f_n - z\right)n(t) + f_n \dot{n}\right] = f_k\left(f_n - z\right)n(t) + f_n \dot{n} \tag{6.5}$$

Since $\beta > 0$ it follows that $f_k\left(f_n - z\right)n(t) + f_n \dot{n} = 0$, and since

$$f_k\left(f_n - z\right)n(t) + f_n \dot{n} = f_k \dot{k} + f_n \dot{n} = \dot{y}$$

we conclude that $\dot{y} = 0$. Application of the Hartwick rule ensures that output is constant. Moreover, since

$$c(t) = y(t) - \dot{k} - zn(t) = y(t)\left(1 - \beta\right)$$

it follows that application of the Hartwick rule will, if the Hotelling principle is applied, generate constant consumption as well.

What the Hartwick rule does is to ensure that enough resources are invested to maintain the value (the discounted stream of benefits) of the stock of all assets available to a society. It allows substitution between stocks. Denoting the value of all stocks by $V(t)$ it ensures that

$$\dot{V} = \sum_i p_i \dot{k}_i \geq 0$$

where $k_i(t)$ is the ith capital stock. If one stock is run down others will be built up to compensate. The presumption is that all stocks are valued at their true social opportunity cost, referred to variously as the shadow or accounting price of the stock.

Revealed and stated preference methods to estimate the value of nonmarketed ecosystem services were discussed in Chapter 5. These signal peoples' willingness to pay to consume such services. The present value of the services generated by any stock—the discounted stream of services—then defines the value of the stock. In recent years methods have been developed to estimate the value of natural capital stocks from the contribution they make to consumption via an asset pricing equation (Fenichel and Abbott 2014, Fenichel et al. 2016). Denoting consumption of all goods and services at time t, including nonmarketed ecosystem services, by $c(t)$ and the stock of natural capital by $n(t)$, it is argued that natural capital dynamics can be written as:

$$\dot{n} = g\big(n(t)\big) - f\big(n(t), c\big(n(t)\big)\big) \tag{6.6}$$

In which the function $g\big(n(t)\big)$ describes the natural growth of the resource and the function $f\big(n(t), c\big(n(t)\big)\big)$ describes anthropogenic effects on the growth/ decline of $n(t)$. The present value of consumption is

$$V\big(n(t)\big) = \int_{\tau=t}^{\infty} e^{-\delta(\tau-t)} W\big(n(\tau), c\big(n(\tau)\big)\big) d\tau$$

and the "price" paid for natural capital is $p\big(n(t)\big) = \dfrac{dV\big(n(t)\big)}{dn(t)}$. Since

$$V_n = \delta V\big(n(t)\big) - W\big(n(\tau), c\big(n(\tau)\big)\big) = p\big(n(t)\big)\dot{n}$$

it follows that in the steady state

$$V\big(n(t)\big) = \frac{1}{\delta} W\big(n(\tau), c\big(n(\tau)\big)\big) + p\big(n(t)\big)\dot{n} \tag{6.7}$$

Differentiation of (6.7) with respect to $n(t)$ then gives the asset pricing equation:

$$\dot{p} = \delta p - W_n\big(n(\tau), c\big(n(\tau)\big)\big) - p\big(g_n\big(n(\tau)\big) - f_n\big(n(\tau), c\big(n(\tau)\big)\big)\big) \tag{6.8}$$

This determines the way that the shadow price of natural capital may be expected to change over time. From the Hotelling principle, if it is possible to calculate the change in the shadow value of resource stocks, then it is also possible to determine both the extent to which they should be conserved (the efficiency problem) and whether aggregate stocks are increasing or declining in value (the sustainability problem).

6.3 The value of environmental assets in the national accounts

A long-standing issue with the SNA, developed in the postwar years and used to track national economic well-being ever since, is that they do a poor job of tracking changes in assets. From a conservation perspective, what is more worrying is that they do an especially poor job of tracking changes in the value of nonmarketed environmental assets. Current measures of *net* product, net domestic product (NDP) and net national product (NNP), do include estimates of the depreciation of capital. However, most estimates of NNP still exclude depreciation of environmental capital. Whereas produced assets are positively valued at a market rate and written off against the value of current output as they depreciate, environmental assets (natural capital) are zero valued and are not written off against the value of current output as they depreciate, degrade or are otherwise depleted. One consequence of this is that while the sale of environmental assets augments current income, there is no indication that it may also involves costs in terms of the future capacity of the economy. In particular, there is no indication that the sale of environmental assets will reduce the future capacity of the economy (unless environmental assets are nonscarce).

This weakness of the accounts has been recognized for decades. There are currently two main approaches to address the problem. The first is to develop a system of environmentally adjusted accounts parallel to the main income and product accounts. The second is to develop a set of wealth accounts that track changes in the value of both produced and natural stocks. We take each of these in turn.

The first approach has involved a 35-year effort by the United Nations, the European Community, the Organization for Economic Cooperation and Development (OECD), the International Monetary Fund (IMF), and the World Bank to produce a satellite SEEA. At the time of writing the SEEA is undergoing a substantial revision, but the preceding version of the SEEA, called the SEEA Central Framework (United Nations et al. 2014), envisaged the construction of four sets of accounts. The first is a set of asset accounts that record the volume and value of natural resource stocks, along with changes in those stocks. The second is a set of flow accounts for pollution, energy, and materials. These accounts record industrial use of energy and materials as inputs to production, and the generation of pollutants and solid waste. They do not, however, address the value of either emissions or damages. The third set of accounts is the environmental protection and resource management expenditure accounts. These accounts record expenditures incurred by industry, government and households to protect the environment or to manage natural resources. They reorganize data already recorded in the national income and product accounts, to bring out environmental taxes, fees, and charges. The final set of accounts use the information provided in the first three to generate indicators that can be integrated in the SNA. Examples include measures of "depletion-adjusted net national income" and "depletion-adjusted net savings" (Lange 2014).

Environmental assets are defined in the accounts as "the naturally occurring living and nonliving components of the Earth, together constituting the biophysical environment, which may provide benefits to humanity" (United Nations et al. 2014). However, the accounts only include a subset of these. Open access resources of the high seas, for example, are excluded. The set of assets included is given in Table 6.1. The assets of greatest interest to conservationist are captured in biological resources—defined as "timber and aquatic resources and a range of other animal and plant resources such as livestock, orchards, crops and wild animals" (United Nations et al. 2014). In principle this includes not only assets in private ownership (freehold) and time-limited use rights (leasehold), but also assets in common property (common pool resources and public lands) or undefined rights (open access). In practice it is limited to assets subject to well-defined claims. Indeed, the only value recognized in the accounts are benefits accruing to the economic owners of environmental assets. Although the interim (2003) SEEA flirted with the idea of

Table 6.1 SEEA Central Framework environmental assets.

1. **Mineral and energy resources**
    1.1. Oil resources
    1.2. Natural gas resources
    1.3. Coal and peat resources
    1.4. Nonmetallic mineral resources
    1.5. Metallic mineral resources
2. **Land**
3. **Soil resources**
4. **Timber resources**
    4.1. Cultivated timber resources
    4.2. Natural timber resources
5. **Aquatic resources**
    5.1. Cultivated aquatic resources
    5.2. Natural aquatic resources
6. **Other biological resources (excluding timber resources and aquatic resources)**
7. **Water resources**
    7.1. Surface water
    7.2. Ground water
    7.3. Soil water

Source: (United Nations et al. 2014)

accounting for ecosystems as assets, this was dropped from the SEEA Central Framework.

The SEEA approach to estimating asset values is based on the discounted value of future returns. Effectively this is the discounted stream of rents generated by the asset. It is calculated by adjusting the gross operating surplus recorded in the SNA to account for any taxes and subsidies on extraction, depreciation of fixed capital (depreciation) and the "normal" return to produced assets. More particularly, net subsidies and the user cost of capital are subtracted from the gross operating surplus to get a measure of resource rent. The value of the asset is then taken to be the discounted stream of expected future rents—the net present value of economic rents (United Nations et al. 2014).

The main challenge with the SEEA Central Framework is that environmental stocks that lack sufficiently well-defined property rights are still excluded. This includes the many public lands, open access resources, and sea areas within the Exclusive Economic Zone that do not currently appear in the accounts. Some of the value of such resources is captured in off-site benefits to third parties, but most is not. Off-site ecosystem services that are currently neglected in the national accounts include flows mediated by water, air, trade and travel, and access. Hydrologically mediated flows include water pollution, siltation, soil loss, flooding, and so on. Atmospherically mediated flows include emissions with local (PM10, photochemical smog), regional (sulfur dioxide), and global (carbon dioxide, nitrous oxide, methane) consequences. Human travel and transport are associated with the transmission of pests and pathogens through local, regional and global goods transport and travel networks. Access mediated flows include, for example, the external benefits or costs to people elsewhere of biodiversity conservation/loss in some particular country (Perrings 2014).

The effects of some of these flows may be reflected in asset values that are already included in the accounts (Nordhaus 2006). Some of the benefits of access to protected areas, for example, may be capitalized into the price of adjacent private properties. However, many of the benefits of public lands are not captured in private asset values. This is partly because they are public goods and so are nonexclusive and nonrival in their effects. Although capturing such flows is critical to the correct estimation of the value of the assets involved, doing so is beyond the SEEA Central Framework.

6.4 Inclusive wealth

The second approach to this problem uses SNA concepts to generate inclusive wealth accounts, while sidestepping the difficulties of working within the

SNA framework. Known variously as genuine savings (Dasgupta 2001) or adjusted net savings (World Bank 2011), the approach asks whether countries are investing sufficient amounts to maintain the value of the aggregate capital stock when changes in natural capital are taken into account—as required by the Hartwick rule (Hamilton and Clemens 1999, Hamilton and Hartwick 2005). To obtain adjusted net savings the World Bank starts with the measure of gross saving recorded in the national income and product accounts, and then makes four adjustments. First, consumption of fixed capital is deducted to obtain a measure of net national saving. Second, current public expenditure on education is added as a proxy for investment in human capital. Third, estimates of the depletion or degradation of natural resources are deducted as a proxy for the depreciation of natural capital. Fourth, deductions are made for damages from carbon dioxide and particulate emissions. Adjusted net savings are then expressed as a percentage of gross national income (World Bank 2011).

In principle, adjusted net savings provide a simple and intuitive test of sustainability. If net savings are positive the aggregate value of all capital stocks—inclusive wealth—is increasing, and current consumption is therefore sustainable. If net savings are negative current consumption is unsustainable. Two caveats to this are, first, that population growth matters, and second, that the measure of wealth should be fully inclusive. If the population is growing, the appropriate test of sustainability is the rate of change in wealth per capita. Consumption levels in several countries that reported positive adjusted net savings rates in the last quarter of the twentieth century were shown to be unsustainable when population growth was taken into account (Dasgupta 2001). The list of environmental assets recorded in the World Bank's adjusted net savings measure is also quite limited. Natural capital is defined as agricultural land, protected areas, forests, minerals, and energy, which leaves out many important environmental assets. Moreover, many assets within the listed categories are omitted. Omitted assets include several important minerals, such as diamonds, uranium, and lithium, together with hydropower, much agricultural water, wetlands, most of the regulating services, carbon storage, and habitat for biodiversity conservation (World Bank 2011).

Whether the depletion or degradation of natural capital affects adjusted net savings depends, at least in part, on the importance of natural capital in the aggregate capital stock. This differs markedly between rich and poor countries. In South Asia and sub-Saharan Africa, for example, natural capital accounted for around 25% of all capital stocks in 2010. In the United States, by contrast, natural capital accounted for only 2.5% of total wealth in that year. It follows that natural capital depletion or degradation is potentially most challenging to

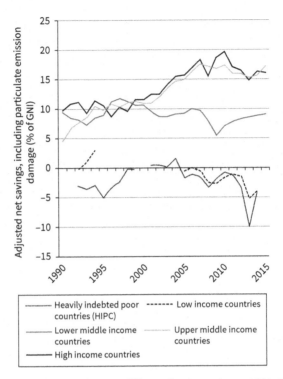

Figure 6.1 Adjusted net savings rates in different income groups, 1990–2015.

Adjusted net savings (ANS) are shown for five groups of countries: heavily indebted poor countries, low-income countries, lower-middle-income countries, upper-middle-income countries, and high-income countries.

Source: Compiled from data derived from World Bank (2017).

the sustainability of economic development in countries that depend heavily on the exploitation of natural resources.

Figure 6.1 shows adjusted net savings rates (inclusive of particulate damage) between 1990 and 2015 for five groups of countries: high-income countries, upper-middle-income countries, lower-middle-income countries, low-income countries and heavily indebted poor countries. The latter, mainly in sub-Saharan Africa, comprise a subset of low-income countries eligible to receive full or partial debt relief in addition to concessional loans from the International Development Association within the World Bank.[1] They are the poorest of the poor.

---

[1] Afghanistan, Benin, Bolivia, Burkina Faso, Burundi, Cameroon, Central African Republic, Chad, Republic of the Congo, Democratic Republic of the Congo, Comoros, Ivory Coast, Ethiopia, Gambia, Ghana, Guinea, Guinea-Bissau, Guyana, Haiti, Honduras, Liberia, Madagascar, Mali, Mauritania, Malawi, Mozambique, Nicaragua, Niger, Rwanda, São Tomé and Príncipe, Senegal, Sierra Leone, Togo, Uganda, Zambia.

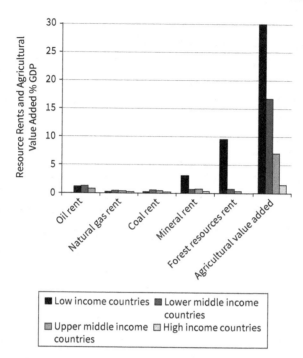

Figure 6.2 Natural resource rents and agricultural value added as a percentage of GDP by income group, 2015.

Source: Compiled from data derived from World Bank (2018).

Adjusted net savings rates below zero imply that the value of aggregate capital stocks or inclusive wealth is declining. The figure shows that for the poorest countries, net savings rates were negative and aggregate capital stocks were declining for the most of the period 1990–2015. The gap between gross and adjusted net savings was also largest for the poorest countries in this period, in part because they are among the most dependent on natural capital, and so most affected by the physical depletion or degradation of natural resource stocks. The dependence of nonoil exporting low-income countries on particular natural resources is shown in Figure 6.2, which reports agricultural value added and rents from natural resources as a percentage of GDP in 2015.

Low-income countries are most dependent on mineral and forest rents. They are also more dependent on agriculture than other countries. The measures used for forest resources and agriculture are different. But both indicate the relative importance of the assets. There are many dimensions to the dependence of poor countries on natural resources, aside from the returns their exploitation. Other commonly used indicators include contributions to employment and land area. As much as 75% of the population in the poorest countries is engaged in agriculture or the exploitation of forest products. The proportion of land area under forest is also a common indicator. It is frequently motivated by the fact that declining forest cover is a proxy for the loss of habitat for wild species. For similar reasons, data on the proportion of land in protected areas is taken as a proxy for the importance accorded to biodiversity conservation. Figure 6.3 shows the proportion of land area accounted for by forest cover (panel A) and protected areas (panel B) within the same four income groups.

Neither forest cover nor the extent of protected areas is a good proxy for the value of such resources, but both are related to value. The need for physical indicators of this kind lies in the incompleteness of value estimates. For example, of the five components of natural capital reported in the World Bank estimates—agricultural land, protected areas, forests, minerals, and energy—forests, minerals, and energy are valued on the basis of rents, but agricultural land and protected areas are both valued on the basis of the market price of farmland. For protected areas this is motivated by the fact that the opportunity cost of protection is foregone agricultural production. But as the World Bank itself observes, this leaves out many of the ecosystem services that drive the establishment of protected areas.

Protected areas provide a range of ecosystem services, many of which lie outside the market, and most of which are public goods. In some cases, such as macroclimatic regulation through carbon fixation, the value of the service is independent of the location of the protected area. But in most others, the important services are highly site-specific. The value of soil erosion control, or water quality, is always site specific, as is the value of the provision of habitat for rare or endangered species. Although there are case studies of particular protected areas, the results of these cannot easily be scaled up to a national level (World Bank 2011). It follows that the estimates of the value of protected areas used by the World Bank are lower bounds only. Other efforts to use World Bank data to estimate the value of natural capital run into essentially the same problem—that observed rents necessarily ignore any external effects of production on nonmarketed ecosystem services (Arrow et al. 2012, UNU-IHDP and UNEP 2014).

6.5 Environmental assets and total factor productivity

Given the widespread lack of confidence in current estimates of the value of environmental assets, it is not surprising that the dominant approach involves

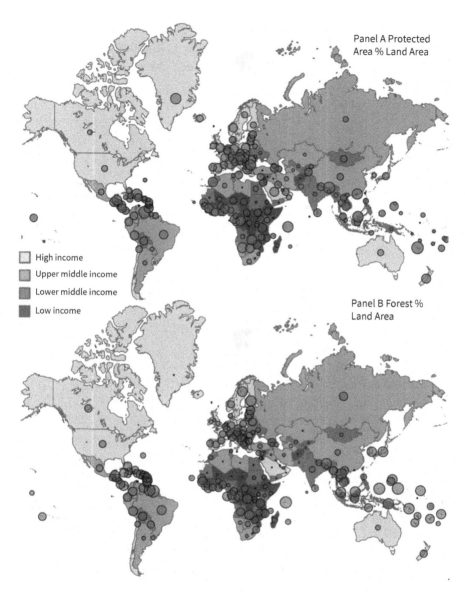

Figure 6.3 Share of land area accounted for by protected areas (panel A) and forest (panel B) across income groups.

The size of the circle indicates the share of the land surface accounted for by protected areas and forest. Since some protected areas fall in forests the two measures overlap.

Source: Compiled from data derived from World Bank (2018).

a mix of indicators—some value-based and some not. We have already noted that the System of Environmentally Adjusted Accounts has retreated from valuation in its most recent iteration. The problem this poses is that while bio-physical indicators of environmental assets may be useful in tracking volume changes over time, they do not necessarily provide good measures of the importance of environmental relative to other assets. The wealth accounts generated from the SNA by the World Bank and others persist with valuation, but then include only a small subset of environmental assets. So are the value of environmental assets captured anywhere in the accounts?

This is a question that has been posed for other assets, and the answer is generally to be found in a residual—what is left when all other known assets are taken into account. In the World Bank's wealth accounts, the residual set of assets is referred to as intangible capital. It is the difference between total wealth and the sum of produced and (measured) natural capital, and is described as a combination of institutions and human capital (World Bank 2011). As we have already seen, however, it is likely to be more than this.

For assets regulated by well-functioning markets the value of the services they yield is already recorded in the SNA through the product accounts for agriculture, industry and services. For services not supplied through the market and so not currently captured in the national income accounts, the accounts may be quite misleading. The production of food, for example, relies on a range of nonmarketed ecosystem services such as the regulation of soil and water flows, pest and disease regulation, pollination, and nutrient cycling that are not explicitly accounted for. To the extent that such services are reflected in the price of the land, they will be at least indirectly measured in the SNA. This will be the case, for example, if all such services are delivered on-site. Off-site flows of nutrients, pests and pesticides, siltation of rivers, and the like are externalities of land management and will ordinarily be missing from the accounts.

The residual left over after taking account of all marketed inputs in production is total factor productivity (TFP). TFP measures the part of output not explained by the amount of inputs used in production. Frequently measured by the Solow residual (Solow 1956), TFP has historically been associated with the efficiency of resource allocation and the technology applied—the skills and know-how of the population (World Bank 2006). If $y(t)$ is output, $k(t)$ is produced capital, and $n(t)$ natural capital, and if κ is the produced capital share, then the Solow residual is just $\dot{y} - \kappa\dot{k} - (1-\kappa)\dot{n}$.

Since TFP was seen to be the main driver of growth, economists developed models designed to explain the role of technological innovation in TFP growth. These "endogenous" growth models linked TFP growth to research and development expenditures, the availability of skilled labor, and innovation (Romer 1990). While differences in technology are important, however, there is no reason to believe that technology is the only thing behind cross-country differences in TFP. By definition, all of the things that make factors of production more efficient in one setting than in another are captured in TFP. This includes both the social and physical infrastructure of a country, its institutions, the regulatory environment and the rule of law, the quality and availability of information, social norms, the stability of the political system, and a range of environmental conditions. These are among the assets summarized as intangible capital in the World Bank's wealth accounts (World Bank 2011). What characterizes them is that they are public goods conferring nonrival and nonexclusive benefits on private factors of production. The science that underpins technology is among them, but it is only one among many.

The productivity of environmental assets not directly included in the wealth accounts is contained within TFP. This includes the effect of climatic differences; the impact of extreme events' the effect of human, animal, and plant diseases' the impact of topography and hydrology; and so on. It includes the off-site costs and benefits provided by public terrestrial and marine resources, whether mediated by water or air. It includes the transmission of pests and pathogens through local, regional, and global transport and travel networks. It follows that the environmental elements within TFP may be either positive (productivity-enhancing) or negative (productivity-reducing). Like other elements, they are typically in the public domain, and as long as they are not explicitly accounted for, they are ignored in private resource allocation decisions (Perrings 2014). In some studies, environmental conditions have been argued to modify the effects of technology on TFP growth (Vouvaki and Xepapadeas 2008, Vouvaki and Xepapadeas 2009). A more general interpretation of the role of the range of assets behind TFP is that they condition the effectiveness with which measured factors of production are used.

While increasing effort is now being given to the estimation of environmental TFP, most work focuses on the negative effects of, for example, disease (Cole and Neumayer 2006) or emissions to air (Zhang and Ye 2015). But many environmental assets have positive effects on the production of valued goods and services. The regulation of water quantity provided by the mix of plants in watersheds, or the buffering of storm damage by mangroves in coastal systems are good examples. Although less work has been done to identify the contribution of services of this kind to TFP, there are now a number of mechanisms designed to encourage their conservation. Indeed, mechanisms such as payments for ecosystem services (PES), discussed in Chapter 9, are among the most important conservation tools available.

6.6 Summary and conclusions

The valuation of environmental assets is an essential element of the Hotelling approach to the conservation of natural resources. Identification of the positive or negative effects of changes in environmental assets helps quantify the external costs or benefits of private resource allocation decisions that alter those assets. It also makes it possible to confront decision-makers with the costs of their actions, or to compensate them for benefits conferred on others. But as long as the assets are not themselves valued, it is impossible to test the efficiency of their conservation. We have shown that the Hotelling principle requires an understanding of the growth in value of environmental assets relative to produced assets if it is to guide environmental conservation decisions. We have also shown that the Hartwick rule requires an understanding of the rents earned on stocks of natural capital if it is to guide investment decisions. In both cases, information on the marginal value of the range of services/disservices provided by environmental assets is needed.

The chapter reviewed the efforts currently being made to estimate the value of environmental assets at the national level. Both the United Nations' System of Environmental-Economic Accounts and the World Bank's Wealth Accounts aim to track changes in the aggregate value of particular environmental stocks, just as the SNA (the National Income and Product Accounts in the United States) aims to identify time trends in output, employment, and other macroeconomic indicators. While the focus on national aggregates makes the information of limited value in making decisions about the conservation of particular environmental stocks, the time trends do provide information about the trade-offs currently being made between measured natural and produced capital. For example, a decline in the aggregate value of forest or mineral resources in some country is evidence of a decline in the conservation or an increase in the conversion of those resources. It may also signal a reduction in national efforts to encourage resource users to conserve the same resources.

Of course, where valuation efforts neglect the benefits generated by natural resources, the measures may be misleading. At present they are the best we have got, but the bundling of all unmeasured environmental assets into the intangible capital residual in the World Bank's Wealth Accounts is worrying. The retreat from valuation in the satellite System of Environmental-Economic

Accounts is also problematic. If a society is to be able to make sensible decisions about what environment assets to conserve and when to do so, it needs information on the consequences—in terms of the loss of benefits to both producers and consumers—of environmental change. In the absence of such information, conservation decisions will be determined in the political arena, and so depend on the sway of interest groups on different sides of the question.

References

Arrow, K. J., P. Dasgupta, L. H. Goulder, K. J. Mumford, and K. Oleson. 2012. Sustainability and the measurement of wealth. Environment and Development Economics 17:317–353.

Cole, M. A., and E. Neumayer. 2006. The impact of poor health on total factor productivity. Journal of Development Studies 42:918–938.

Dasgupta, P. 2001. Human well-being and the natural environment. Oxford University Press, Oxford.

Fenichel, E. P., and J. K. Abbott. 2014. Natural capital: From metaphor to measurement. Journal of the Association of Environmental and Resource Economists 1:1–27.

Fenichel, E. P., J. K. Abbott, J. Bayham, W. Boone, E. M. K. Haacker, and L. Pfeiffer. 2016. Measuring the value of groundwater and other forms of natural capital. Proceedings of the National Academy of Sciences 113:2382–2387.

Hamilton, K., and M. Clemens. 1999. Genuine savings rates in developing countries. World Bank Economic Review 13:333–356.

Hamilton, K., and J. M. Hartwick. 2005. Investing exhaustible resource rents and the path of consumption. Canadian Journal of Economics/Revue canadienne d'économique 38:615 621.

Hartwick, J. 1977. Intergenerational equity and the investing of rents from exhaustible resources. American Economic Review 66:972–974.

Hartwick, J. 1978. Substitution among exhaustible resources and intergenerational equity. Review of Economic Studies 45:347–354.

Hicks, J. R. 1939. Value and capital. Clarendon Press, Oxford.

Lange, G.-M. 2014. Environmental accounting. Page 319–335 in G. Atkinson, S. Dietz, and E. Neumayer, editors. Handbook of sustainable development. Edward Elgar, Cheltenham.

Nordhaus, W. D. 2006. Principles of national accounting for non-market accounts. Pages 143–160 in D. W. Jorgenson, J. S. Landefield, and W. D. Nordhaus, editors.

A new architecture for the U.S. national accounts. University of Chicago Press, Chicago.

Perrings, C. 2014. Our uncommon heritage: biodiversity, ecosystem services and human wellbeing. Cambridge University Press, Cambridge.

Romer, P. M. 1990. Endogenous technological change. Journal of Political Economy 98:S71–S102.

Solow, R. 1956. A contribution to the theory of economic growth. Quarterly Journal of Economics 70:65–94.

Solow, R. M. 1974. Intergenerational equity and exhaustible resources. Review of Economic Studies 41:29–45.

Solow, R. M. 1986. On the intergenerational allocation of exhaustible resources. Scandinavian Journal of Economics 88:141–149.

United Nations, European Union, Food and Agriculture Organization, International Monetary Fund, Organisation for Economic Co-operation and Development, and W. Bank. 2014. System of environmental-economic accounting 2012: central framework. United Nations, New York.

UNU-IHDP and UNEP. 2014. Inclusive wealth report 2014: measuring progress toward sustainability. Cambridge University Press, Cambridge.

Vouvaki, D., and A. Xepapadeas. 2008. Changes in social welfare and sustainability: theoretical issues and empirical evidence. Ecological Economics 67:473–484.

Vouvaki, D., and A. Xepapadeas. 2009. Total factor productivity growth when factors of production generate environmental externalities. FEEM Working Papers 281. Fondazione Eni Enrico Mattei, Milan.

World Bank. 2006. Where is the wealth of nations?: measuring capital for the 21st century. World Bank, Washington, DC.

World Bank. 2011. The changing wealth of nations: measuring sustainable development in the new millennium. World Bank, Washington, DC.

World Bank. 2017. Adjusted net savings, including particulate emission damage (% of GNI). World Bank, Washington, DC.

World Bank. 2018. World development indicators. World Bank, Washington, DC.

World Commission on Environment and Development. 1987. Our common future. Island Press, Washington, DC.

Zhang, Z., and J. Ye. 2015. Decomposition of environmental total factor productivity growth using hyperbolic distance functions: a panel data analysis for China. Energy Economics 47:87–97.

7
Substitutability and the Valuation of Natural Capital

> I do not deny that if our coal were gone, or nearly so, and of high price, we might find wind, water, or tidal mills, a profitable substitute for coal.
>
> —William Stanley Jevons, *The Coal Question*, 1866

7.1 Introduction

We have seen throughout that the degree of substitutability between different types of assets is at the heart of the conservation problem. It is because there is limited substitutability between different inputs in the production of goods and services, and between different goods and services, that the problems explored by Hotelling, Hicks, Solow, and Hartwick are meaningful. If there were no substitutability between produced and natural capital—if they were perfect complements—there would be no incentive to deplete stocks of natural capital. If there were perfect substitutability between produced and natural capital, there would be no incentive to conserve stocks of natural capital. The degree of substitutability is what determines how much natural capital can be lost (while gaining produced capital) without compromising human well-being. The degree of substitutability is also among the most hotly contested issues in conservation.

Consider just one of the many ways in which the debate over substitutability has played out. Following publication of the Brundtland Report in 1987, the approach developed by Solow and Hartwick to deal with substitution between produced and natural capital came to be styled "weak sustainability." The approach gives the conditions under which the value of a portfolio might be held constant by reinvesting the rents earned on exhaustible resources in reproducible capital. It assumes a degree of substitutability between produced and natural capital (Hartwick 1977). Against this, an approach developed—based on the proposition that produced and natural capital are complements—that was styled "strong sustainability" (Neumayer 2003). Strong sustainability

Conservation. Charles Perrings and Ann Kinzig, Oxford University Press (2021). © Oxford University Press.
DOI: 10.1093/oso/9780190613600.003.0007

rests on the assertion that since there are no substitutes for many environmental assets, there is also no case for their conversion. The justification for this assertion draws on arguments from conservation biology about the existence of critical components of ecosystems, and from environmental ethics about the obligations people have to other species (Doak, Bakker, Goldstein, and Hale 2015, Farley 2008).

In this chapter we consider the problem of substitutability in more detail. We revisit the substitutability between different assets used in the production of goods and services, and between different goods and services. We have two aims. The first is to understand the ways in which the limits of substitutability are captured in the functions ordinarily used to characterize the production of goods and services, and the utility functions ordinarily used to describe peoples' preferences over goods and services. The second is to use this understanding to explore the limits of substitutability between ecosystem components, and to draw out the implications of this for conservation and investment.

7.2 Substitution in production

Consider a production function of the general form $Q = f(K,N)$ in which K and N denote produced and natural capital respectively. We have seen that an isoquant of the function, $Q_0 = f(K,N)$, describes the combinations of K and N that will produce quantity Q_0, and that the slope of that function indicates the marginal rate of technical substitution between K and N. That is $-\dfrac{dK}{dN}\bigg|_{Q=Q_0}$

defines the rate at which natural capital can be substituted for produced capital, holding output constant at Q_0. The extreme cases, where the marginal rate of technical substitution is either zero (no substitution) or one (perfect substitutes) imply isoquants of the form shown in the first two panels of Figure 7.1. In the more general case (partial substitutability), isoquants take the form shown in third panel. The marginal rate of technical substitution in this case varies as the relative quantities of the two assets change. When we have very little of one asset, the other can only weakly serve as a substitute. We recall that marginal technical rate of substitution can be obtained by taking the total differential of the production function at Q_0, $dQ_0 = \dfrac{\partial f}{\partial K}dK + \dfrac{\partial f}{\partial N}dN = 0$,

implying that $-\dfrac{dK}{dN} = \dfrac{\partial f}{\partial K}\bigg/\dfrac{\partial f}{\partial N}$. This says that the marginal rate of technical substitution—the rate at which produced capital can be substituted for natural

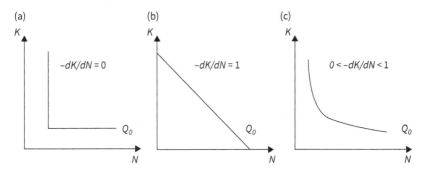

Figure 7.1 Marginal rates of technical substitution between natural and produced capital.

Isoquants correspond to different marginal rates of technical substitution. Panel A denotes zero substitutability. Panel B denotes perfect substitutability. Panel C denotes limited substitutability.

capital—is equal to the ratio between the marginal products of natural and produced capital.

In the zero substitutability case, produced and natural capital are perfect complements. They must be used in fixed proportions. The production function takes the form:

$$Q = \min(\alpha K, \beta N), \alpha\beta > 0 \tag{7.1}$$

$Q = \min(\alpha K, \beta N), \alpha\beta > 0$ implying that production will always take place along a ray at which K/N is constant. Any change in output implies a proportionate change in both inputs. In the perfect substitutability case, the production function takes the linear form:

$$Q = \alpha K + \beta N \tag{7.2}$$

Since the marginal products of produced and natural capital are α and β respectively, the marginal rate of technical substitution is constant at β/α.

In the general case, where there is some substitutability, the marginal rate of technical substitution of produced capital for natural capital will depend on the quantity of natural capital employed. Without yet thinking about particular functional forms, if (a)$Q = f(K,N)$ is monotone (meaning that output is strictly increasing in both inputs), and (b)$f(K,N)$ is at least quasi-concave (meaning that if $R = (K,N)$ and $R' = (K',N')$ are two input bundles and $R \geq R'$ then $f(aR + (1-a)R') \geq f(R')$), then the marginal rate of technical substitution of produced capital for natural capital is decreasing in natural capital. That is, the more natural capital is used in production, the smaller is the quantity of produced capital needed to compensate for a given change in the quantity of natural capital. Conversely, the less natural capital is used in production, the larger is the quantity of produced capital needed to compensate for the same change (Figure 7.2).

The elasticity of substitution in the polar cases described in panels A and B of Figure 7.1 is, respectively, zero and infinity. We now consider the elasticity of substitution in widely used production functions that lie between the polar cases. One of these that we have already encountered is the Cobb-Douglas function:

$$Q = AK^{\alpha}N^{\beta} \tag{7.3}$$

where A, α, β are positive constants. This function generates isoquants of the form shown in Panel C of Figure 7.1. Whether it exhibits increasing, decreasing, or constant returns to scale depends on the sum of α and β. $\alpha + \beta > 1$ indicates increasing returns, $\alpha + \beta < 1$ indicates decreasing returns, and $\alpha + \beta = 1$ indicates constant returns. The elasticity of substitution in the Cobb-Douglas case is everywhere

$$\sigma = \frac{d(K/N)}{d(f_N/f_K)} \frac{f_N/f_K}{K/N} = \frac{\alpha/\beta}{\alpha/\beta} = 1 \tag{7.4}$$

That is, it does not depend on the relative quantities of produced and natural capital employed in production.

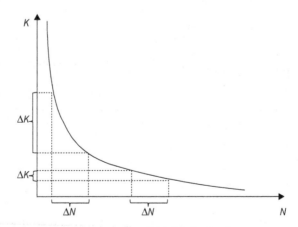

Figure 7.2 Diminishing marginal rates of technical substitution.
A given change in natural capital can be compensated by the employment of more or less produced capital, depending on whether the technology applied is natural capital intensive or not.

A second more general and equally widely used production function is the constant elasticity of substitution (CES) production function:

$$Q = A\left[\alpha K^{-\beta} + (1-\alpha)N^{-\beta}\right]^{-1/\beta} \tag{7.5}$$

in which

$$\sigma = \frac{d(K/N)}{d(f_N/f_K)}\frac{f_N/f_K}{K/N} = \frac{1}{1+\beta} \tag{7.6}$$

It follows that $\sigma = 0$, $\sigma = \infty$, $\sigma = 1$ are all possible in this case, specifically, if $\beta = \infty$, $\sigma = 0$ and there is no substitutability between produced and natural capital; if $\beta = -1$, $\sigma = \infty$ and there is perfect substitutability; if $\beta = 0$, $\sigma = 1$, and we have the Cobb-Douglas case (which can be shown using L'Hôpital's rule).

Consider what this means for the conservation of natural capital. We saw in Chapter 6 that the World Bank's wealth accounts show that the countries most dependent on natural capital are also among the poorest, where dependence is measured by the ratio of natural to produced capital. This is often argued to mean that arresting the decline of natural capital is most important in poor countries (Sachs et al. 2009). But Figure 7.2 shows that if production functions are concave and monotone, and if the technology applied depends heavily on natural capital, the produced capital needed to compensate for the loss of natural capital may be quite low. So in countries where natural capital is used most intensively, if there is some substitutability between natural and produced capital, the loss of natural capital may be offset (in the sense of the overall wealth of society) through a small increase in produced capital. This general statement is naturally qualified if the loss of natural capital is irreversible (species extinction) or involves significant externalities (e.g., pollution from mining), or if capital markets are only poorly developed. But the important point is that it may be easiest to find produced substitutes for the loss of natural capital precisely where people are most dependent on the use of natural capital—as measured by the ratio between types of capital.

Whether people elect to use natural capital more or less intensively depends both on the technological possibilities, and on the relative cost of accessing natural and produced capital. For example, slash-and-burn or swidden agriculture[1] is a production method applied in tropical and subtropical regions

---

[1] Also known as swidden agriculture, shifting cultivation, forest fallow, or fire-fallow cultivation.

that relies on an extensive land footprint. Forested land is clear-cut and vegetation burned in place. The resulting layer of ash provides nutrients for crops, while weeds are at least temporarily suppressed. Yields may be initially high but fall off as nutrients are depleted and weedy species return, leading to abandonment of the fields and the clearance of new land or to previously cultivated areas that have been allowed to revert. Where potentially cultivable land becomes scarce due to population growth or conversion to alternative economic activities, the length of the rotation shortens, and farmers substitute produced capital (in the form of commercial fertilizers or herbicides) for natural capital.

What has made slash-and-burn agriculture a feasible technology for many farmers is a structure of property rights that allows free access to forest resources. The private cost of land access—the cost to the farmer—is limited to the effort required to clear it. Only where the relative private cost of land access has risen have farmers had an incentive to adopt less land intensive methods. The point here is that moving from shifting to permanent cultivation dramatically reduces the land required per unit of output at the cost of small outlays on fertilizers and weed control. The elasticity of substitution or the ease with which produced capital can be substituted for natural capital is high.

It follows that we should expect to be able to calculate the elasticity of substitution between produced and natural capital as a function of the costs of each asset type. Suppose that a producer aims to maximize output, described by a Cobb-Douglas production function of the form given in equation (7.6), subject to a maximum cost constraint of the form $C_{max} = p_k K + p_N N$. From the Lagrangian function

$$L = AK^\alpha N^\beta + \lambda \left(C_{max} - p_K K - p_N N \right) \tag{7.7}$$

we obtain the following first order necessary conditions:

$$\begin{aligned}
L_K &= \alpha K^{\alpha-1} N^\beta - \lambda p_K = 0 \\
L_N &= \beta K^\alpha N^{\beta-1} - \lambda p_N = 0 \\
L_\lambda &= C_{max} - p_K K - p_N N = 0
\end{aligned} \tag{7.8}$$

from which it follows that

$$\lambda = \frac{\alpha K^{\alpha-1} N^\beta}{p_K} = \frac{\beta K^\alpha N^{\beta-1}}{p_N}$$

and, since $N^{\beta-1} = N^\beta/N$ and $K^{\alpha-1} = K^\alpha/K$

$$\frac{K}{N} = \frac{\alpha p_L}{\beta p_K} \tag{7.9}$$

Taking the derivative of the ratio K/N with respect to the ratio p_N/p_K gives

$$\frac{d(K/N)}{d(p_N/p_K)} = \frac{\alpha}{\beta}$$

and since (7.9) implies that

$$\frac{K/N}{p_N/p_K} = \frac{\alpha}{\beta}$$

we are able to write the elasticity of substitution between produced and natural capital in the form:

$$s = \frac{d(K/N)}{d(p_N/p_K)} \frac{p_N/p_K}{K/N} = \frac{\alpha/\beta}{\alpha/\beta} = 1 \tag{7.10}$$

That is, we have a measure of the rate at which a change in the relative cost of natural capital will induce substitution toward or away from produced capital, and we see that it is entirely determined by the characteristics of the production function.

Of course, the private cost of slash-and-burn agriculture may be quite different from its social cost. The production method involves a number of external effects including the negative effects of land clearance on soil erosion, water quality, flood risk, carbon emissions, and loss of habitat—all of which affect people other than the farmers themselves (Noble and Dirzo 1997). Therefore, the balance between produced and natural capital that is best from the perspective of the farmers may not be best from the perspective of society. Figure 7.3 takes the case where the private cost of the use made of natural capital, p_{N0}, is less than the social cost, p_{N1}, implying that the socially optimal use of natural capital, N_1, is less than the privately optimal use, N_0. If natural resource owners were confronted by the social cost of the resource, this would be expected to induce both a substitution effect, from a to b, and an output effect, from b to c.

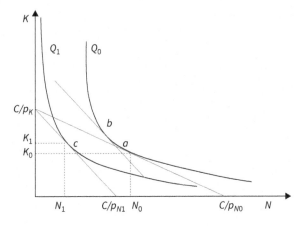

Figure 7.3 Substitution and output effects, and differences in the private and social cost of natural capital for budget-constrained output maximizers.

The output effect occurs because of the way that the problem has been posed—as a problem in output maximization subject to a budget constraint. If producers maximized profit rather than output we would not expect to see an output effect. Suppose, for example, that producers sought to maximize a profit function of the following form

$$\pi = p_Q A K^\alpha N^\beta - p_K K - p_N N \qquad (7.11)$$

by selection of the level at which produced and natural capital were used. The first order necessary conditions would then include the requirement that

$$\frac{\partial \pi}{\partial K} = p_Q A K^{\alpha-1} N^\beta - p_K = 0$$

$$\frac{\partial \pi}{\partial N} = p_Q A K^\alpha N^{\beta-1} - p_N = 0 \qquad (7.12)$$

which can be solved for K and N to give the demand functions:

$$K = \left(\frac{\alpha}{p_K}\right)^{(1-\beta)/(1-\alpha-\beta)} \left(\frac{\beta}{p_N}\right)^{\beta/(1-\alpha-\beta)} \left(p_Q A\right)^{1/(1-\alpha-\beta)}$$

$$N = \left(\frac{\alpha}{p_K}\right)^{\alpha/(1-\alpha-\beta)} \left(\frac{\beta}{p_N}\right)^{(1-\alpha)/(1-\alpha-\beta)} \left(p_Q A\right)^{1/(1-\alpha-\beta)} \qquad (7.13)$$

These show that demand for natural capital will be decreasing in the price of both natural and produced capital, and increasing in the price of output.

An increase in the price of natural capital, holding the price of produced capital constant, will lead to a reduction in the use made of natural capital and an increase in the use made of produced capital through a substitution effect. In fact, the price elasticity of demand for natural capital will be greater, the greater is the elasticity of substitution of natural for produced capital.

Two final comments on the elasticity of substitution of produced for natural capital relate to an important distinction in economics between the short run, in which capital is fixed, and the long run, in which capital is variable. The first comment is that while the fixed coefficients case (Figure 7.1, panel A) seems highly restrictive, it is frequently the case that even if producers planning a production process may be able to choose from a wide range of possible input combinations, once they have made the choice they become committed to a process that requires fixed combinations of inputs. This is sometimes styled a "putty-clay" view of capital. Before the input choice is made the different assets available to the producer are quite malleable, but once the choice has been made they are not. Putty has hardened into clay. Before land is designated as a protected area, for example, options may include a number of different landscape attributes, different scales and different locations. Once the land has been designated the set of attributes, the size, and the location are all fixed—along with the species the area can serve.

The second comment follows directly. Just as there may be a significant difference between the *ex ante* and *ex post* elasticity of substitution between produced and natural capital, so there may be a significant difference between the short and long run elasticity of substitution. In the short run, precisely because a commitment has already been made to a particular configuration of assets, it may be difficult to respond to a change in the relative costs of produced and natural capital by substituting between them. In the long run, when decisions have to be taken about which assets should be maintained and which should be replaced, substitution is much easier. If $K = K_0$ is fixed in the short run, for example, and if the relative costs of produced and natural capital are as shown in Figure 7.4, the marginal rate of technical substitution cannot be brought into line with the relative costs of the two capital types until K_0 is allowed to adjust—upward in the case of Q_1 and downward in the case of Q_2. In the long run K/L can be brought into line with the marginal rate of technical substitution by altering the quantity of produced capital employed. The short run and the long run do not imply particular time periods. They are measures of the time needed to adjust capital stocks, and will typically be different for different types of stocks. In many cases this will depend on the frequency of windows of opportunity—moments when it is possible to implement change.

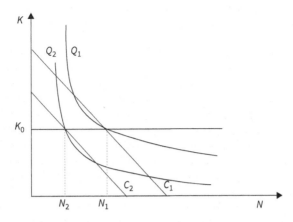

Figure 7.4 Short-run limitations on the substitutability of natural and produced capital.

7.3 Substitution in a generalized model of joint production

Our discussion of substitution in production has so far assumed that a single output, Q, is produced using two capital inputs, K and N. In reality, though, most production processes involve multiple inputs and outputs. Indeed, the rationale for the conservation of natural capital stocks frequently rests on the argument that they generate multiple ecosystem services, some consumptive (the provisioning services) and some not (the cultural and regulating services). Ecosystem services are joint products of production processes that combine sets of natural and produced assets. Many of the negative environmental effects of production, such as emissions to land, air, and water, are similarly joint products of production processes that combine natural and produced assets.

One way of describing such production processes is via an implicit production function of the form:

$$F\left(Q_1,...,Q_m, X_1,...,X_n\right)=0 \tag{7.14}$$

in which the derivatives $\partial F/\partial Q_i, i=1,...,m$ are positive, and $\partial F/\partial X_i, i=1,...,n$ are negative. The list of inputs, $X_1,...,X_n$, subsumes both produced and natural assets. The implicit production function (sometimes termed a transformation function) specifies the way in which m outputs are produced by n inputs. Profits are simply the difference between the revenue/benefits generated by the m outputs and the cost of the n inputs:

$$\pi = \sum_{i=1}^{m} p_i Q_i - \sum_{j=1}^{n} w_j X_j \qquad (7.15)$$

where p_i is the price/benefit of the ith output, and w_j is the price/cost of the jth input. Solving the problem using the Lagrangian method we form the function:

$$L = \sum_{i=1}^{m} p_i Q_i - \sum_{j=1}^{n} w_j X_j + \lambda F\left(Q_1, ..., Q_m, X_1, ..., X_n\right)$$

and set the partial derivatives of the function equal to zero to get the first order necessary conditions:

$$\frac{\partial L}{\partial Q_i} = p_i + \lambda \frac{\partial F}{\partial Q_i} = 0, \quad i = 1, ..., m$$

$$\frac{\partial L}{\partial X_j} = w_j + \lambda \frac{\partial F}{\partial X_j} = 0, \quad j = 1, ..., n \qquad (7.16)$$

$$\frac{\partial L}{\partial \lambda} = F\left(Q_1, ..., Q_m, X_1, ..., X_n\right) = 0$$

It follows that for any pair of outputs we require that

$$\frac{p_i}{p_h} = \frac{\partial F / \partial Q_i}{\partial F / \partial Q_h} = -\frac{\partial Q_i}{\partial Q_h}, \quad i, h = 1, ..., m \qquad (7.17)$$

and for any pair of inputs

$$\frac{w_j}{w_h} = \frac{\partial F / \partial X_j}{\partial F / \partial X_h} = -\frac{\partial X_j}{\partial X_h}, \quad j, h = 1, ..., n \qquad (7.18)$$

Equation (7.17) implies that the marginal rate of product transformation between every pair of outputs should be equal to the ratio of their prices. Equation (7.18) implies that the marginal rate of technical substitution between every pair of inputs should also be equal to the ratio of their prices. These conditions also imply that for any output and input, the following must be true:

$$\frac{w_j}{p_i} = \frac{\partial Q_i}{\partial X_j} \Rightarrow w_j = p_i \frac{\partial Q_i}{\partial X_j} \qquad (7.19)$$

for all i and j. That is, the value of the marginal physical product of each input with respect to each output should be equal to the input price/cost.

We can also use the first order necessary conditions to tell how a profit maximizing producer will vary both inputs and outputs as relative prices/benefits/costs change. Total differentiation of (7.16) generates a system of m + n + 1 equations in m + n + 1 variables, the changes in inputs, outputs, and the Lagrange multiplier:

$$
\begin{array}{llll}
\lambda F_{11}dQ_1 +... & +\lambda F_{1,m+n}dX_n & +F_1 d\lambda & =-dp_1 \\
\vdots & \vdots & \vdots & \vdots \\
\lambda F_{m+n,1}dQ_1 +... & +\lambda F_{m+n,m+n}dX_n & +F_{m+n}d\lambda & =-dw_m \\
F_1 dQ_1 +... & +\lambda F_{m+n}dX_n & & =0
\end{array} \tag{7.20}
$$

which may be solved (using Cramer's rule) for dQ_i, dX_j and hence for measures of the change in quantities of both outputs and inputs with respect to prices/benefits/costs. The solution implies that

$$
\begin{aligned}
\partial Q_i / \partial p_h &= -D_{hi}/D, & i,h &= 1,...,m \\
\partial Q_i / \partial w_j &= -D_{m+j,i}/D, & i &= 1,...,m, j = 1,...,n \\
\partial X_j / \partial w_k &= -D_{m+k,m+j}/D, & j,k &= 1,...,n \\
\partial X_j / \partial p_h &= -D_{h,m+j}/D, & j &= 1,...,n, h = 1,...,m
\end{aligned} \tag{7.21}
$$

where and D_{ij} is the cofactor of the element in the ith row and j^{th} column of (7.21), and D is the determinant of the coefficients in the same array. Note that the own-price effects are positive for (positively valued) outputs and negative for inputs, but otherwise the sign of these derivatives depends on the nature of the implicit production function.

One of the best-known examples of substitution of natural for produced capital is the investment by the Catskill Watershed Corporation in the New York City Catskill-Delaware Watershed, which supplies water to nine million people in New York City and its suburbs. Land purchases in the watershed, and incentives to private landowners in the area to adopt management practices that enhance water quality, was seen as a better option than investment in a downstream water treatment plant (Heal 1999, Pires 2004). But there are many other examples of decisions to conserve environmental assets for the services they deliver, all of which imply that conservation yields greater value growth than conversion.

7.4 Substitution and public goods

The example of the Catskills illustrates a common property of many conservation decisions—that they involve public goods: goods that are nonexclusive and nonrival in consumption. We consider the general problem of

environmental public goods in more detail in Chapter 7. Here we are interested only in the scope for substitution between private and public assets.
Public goods generate benefits to a sometimes very large number of people.
The social marginal utility of an extra unit of public goods is therefore the
sum of the marginal utilities of all who benefit. So, for example, a watershed enhancement scheme that delivers enhanced water quality to n people
(n = 9 million in the case of the Catskills) from N_s acres committed to the
scheme generates a social marginal utility of $\sum_{i=1}^{n} \partial U_i / \partial N_s$. We can use this to
identify the conditions that would have to hold for it to be efficient to trade
off water quality enhancement against the production of private goods from
the same land. If we denote the marginal utility of the land when committed
to the production of private goods by the ith individual by $\partial U_i / \partial N_p$, the social
marginal rate of substitution of the public good for the private good is:

$$\frac{\sum_{i=1}^{n} \partial U_i / \partial N_s}{\partial U_i / \partial N_p} \tag{7.22}$$

It is the ratio of the marginal utility gained by all who have access to the public
good to the marginal utility to the individual who gains from production of
the private good.

The condition for the allocation of land to the production of the public good
to be efficient is then that the rate of product transformation of the public
good for the private good is equal to the social marginal rate of substitution.
That is:

$$\frac{\partial F / \partial N_s}{\partial F / \partial N_p} = \frac{\sum_{i=1}^{n} \partial U_i / \partial N_s}{\partial U_i / \partial N_p} \tag{7.23}$$

Since the best that the free market can achieve is

$$\frac{\partial F / \partial N_s}{\partial F / \partial N_p} = \frac{\partial U_i / \partial N_s}{\partial U_i / \partial N_p} < \frac{\sum_{i=1}^{n} \partial U_i / \partial N_s}{\partial U_i / \partial N_p} \tag{7.24}$$

the public good will be undersupplied in the absence of collective action. To
see what optimality conditions should apply in this case we suppose that the ith
consumer's utility function is of the form

$$U_i = U_i\left(Q_{Pi}, Q_S, N_i\right) \qquad (7.25)$$

where Q_{Pi} denotes consumption of the private good by the ith consumer, Q_S denotes consumption of the public good, and N_i denotes the consumer's endowment of land. The implicit production function is:

$$0 = F\left(Q_P, Q_S, N\right) \qquad (7.26)$$

To make things simple we may suppose that the society comprises only individuals i and j, so $Q_P = Q_{Pi} + Q_{Pj}$ and $N = N_i + N_j$. To obtain the conditions that should hold if the allocation of both public and private goods is efficient, consider the problem faced by individual i and solve for some given level of utility to individual j, U_j^0. Forming the Lagrangian function

$$
\begin{aligned}
L_i = U_i\left(Q_{Pi}, Q_S, N_i\right) + \lambda\left(U_j\left(Q_{Pj}, Q_S, N_j\right) - U_j^0\right) + \\
\gamma F\left(Q_P, Q_S, N\right) + \mu\left(Q_{Pi} + Q_{Pj} - Q_P\right) + v\left(N_i + N_j - N\right)
\end{aligned}
\qquad (7.27)
$$

we can see that the first order necessary conditions include

$$
\begin{aligned}
\partial L / \partial Q_{Pi} &= \partial U_i / \partial Q_{Pi} + \mu = 0 \\
\partial L / \partial Q_{Pj} &= \lambda \partial U_j / \partial Q_{Pj} + \mu = 0 \\
\partial L / \partial Q_P &= \gamma \, \partial F / \partial Q_P - \mu = 0 \\
\partial L / \partial Q_S &= \partial U_i / \partial Q_S + \lambda \partial U_j / \partial Q_S + \gamma \, \partial F / \partial Q_S = 0 \\
\partial L / \partial N_i &= \partial U_i / \partial N_i + v = 0 \\
\partial L / \partial N_j &= \lambda \partial U_j / \partial N_j + v = 0 \\
\partial L / \partial N &= \gamma \, \partial F / \partial N + v = 0
\end{aligned}
\qquad (7.28)
$$

From which it follows that

$$
\begin{aligned}
\frac{\partial U_i / \partial Q_S}{\partial U_i / \partial Q_{Pi}} + \frac{\partial U_j / \partial Q_S}{\partial U_j / \partial Q_{Pj}} &= \frac{\partial F / \partial Q_S}{\partial F / \partial Q_P} \\
\frac{\partial U_i / \partial Q_S}{\partial U_i / \partial N_i} + \frac{\partial U_j / \partial Q_S}{\partial U_j / \partial N_j} &= -\frac{\partial F / \partial Q_S}{\partial F / \partial N}
\end{aligned}
\qquad (7.29)
$$

Formally, the first of these expressions says that the sum of the social marginal rate of substitution of the public good for the private good for both individuals should equal the marginal rate of product transformation of the public good for the private good. The second says that the sum of the marginal rates of substitution of the public good for the available resource, N, should vary inversely with the marginal productivity of N in the production of the public good.

Let us unpack these two statements. The first implies a relation between the rate at which it is technically possible to substitute public for private goods and the rate at which people prefer to do so. The rate of product transformation is the slope of the production possibility frontier. It shows the combinations of the private and public good that can be efficiently produced with a fixed set of resources (Figure 7.5). The rate of product transformation shown in the figure is increasing in the public good. At low levels of the public good an increment in provision requires only a small reduction in the provision of the private good. At high levels of the public good the same increment in provision requires a much greater reduction in the provision of the private good. The first statement says that the balance between public and private goods will be efficient where this rate is equal to the marginal rate at which society prefers to substitute public for private goods—or the ratio of the sum of the marginal utilities generated by the private good to the marginal utility generated by the public good. Societies that place a relatively high weight on private goods will opt for a balance between public and private goods that favors private goods.

The second statement says that the social marginal rate of substitution of the public good for the capital stock available to produce both public and private goods, say land, should vary inversely with the marginal productivity of land in the production of the public good. That is, the higher the marginal productivity of land in the production of the public good, the lower the rate at which society would elect to trade off the public good for land. By the same token, the greater the marginal utility of land relative to the marginal utility of the public good, the greater the marginal productivity of land in the production of the public good society would require.

7.5 Net substitutes and complements

We have seen that the substitutability of produced and natural capital inputs reflects the shape of the isoquants describing combinations of inputs that yield a given level of output. Where isoquants are L-shaped there is no scope for substitution, and all inputs are required in fixed proportions. Inputs in this case are said to be complements. In all other cases there is at least some substitutability between inputs and, except in the case where inputs are perfect substitutes, the marginal rate of technical substitution for any one input diminishes as the quantity of that input increases.

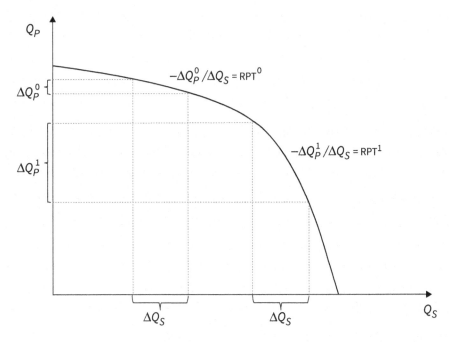

Figure 7.5 The production possibility frontier and the rate of product transformation.
The production possibility frontier shows the combinations of Q_P and Q_S that can be produced with fixed stocks of N and K. The slope of the production possibility frontier defines the rate of product transformation—the reduction in the private good needed to acquire an extra unit of the social good, holding technology, and factors of production constant.

We have also seen that substitutability in the production of goods and services reflects the shape of the production possibility frontier, and that the rate of product transformation for any one output increases as the quantity produced of that output increases. There is in fact an output analog to the fixed proportions of inputs, in that some combinations of outputs are produced in fixed proportions. These are generally byproducts of processes aimed at producing some target output, and while they may include positively valued commodities, they mostly consist of waste streams. The production of steel, for example, is accompanied by the production of a range of solid wastes— slags, dusts, and sludges—depending on the production method used. Slags are the main byproduct of blast furnaces, dusts are the main byproduct of arc furnaces. Steel making is also associated with a range of emissions to air, especially CO, SOx, NOx, and particulates. As in the fixed proportions case as well, byproducts of this kind tend to be set once a technology has been chosen. Producers select from a range of input combinations at the production planning stage, but may lose all flexibility once a plan is implemented. Similarly, they select from a range of waste-products at the planning stage, but may be committed to a particular bundle once a plan is implemented. There is a putty-clay analog in waste generation.

We will consider the broader conservation implications of waste products and emissions to land, air, and water in Chapters 7 and 8. At this point, we wish to connect the substitutability of inputs and outputs to the value of resources. Note that two goods, Q_i and Q_j, are said to be gross substitutes if an increase in the price of one leads to an increase in consumption of the other that is if $\partial Q_i / \partial p_j > 0$, and gross complements if an increase in the price of one leads to a decrease in consumption of the other, that is if $\partial Q_i / \partial p_j < 0$. The relation is "gross" in the sense that it includes both substitution and income effects. Since income effects can potentially dominate substitution effects it is common to isolate the substitution effect. Q_i and Q_j are said to be net substitutes if an increase in the price of one leads to an increase in consumption of the other, holding utility constant:

$$\left. \frac{\partial Q_i}{\partial p_j} > 0 \right|_{U \text{ constant}} \tag{7.30}$$

and net complements if an increase in the price of one leads to a decrease in consumption of the other, holding utility constant:

$$\left. \frac{\partial Q_i}{\partial p_j} < 0 \right|_{U \text{ constant}} \tag{7.31}$$

Since cross substitution effects are symmetric, the relation holds whether we are interested in the impact of p_j on Q_i, or of p_i on Q_j. Symmetrically, X_i and X_j are said to be net substitutes if an increase in the price of one leads to an increase in demand the other, holding output constant:

$$\left. \frac{\partial X_i}{\partial w_j} > 0 \right|_{Q \text{ constant}} \tag{7.32}$$

and net complements if an increase in the price of one leads to a decrease in demand the other, holding output constant:

$$\left. \frac{\partial X_i}{\partial w_j} < 0 \right|_{Q \text{ constant}} \tag{7.33}$$

Note that the relation between net substitutes and complements described here refers to positively valued inputs and outputs only. The idea can, however, be readily extended to the case where complementary inputs or outputs are negatively valued—where they are "bads" rather than "goods." Many waste products, for example, effectively carry a negative price. Their destruction is more valuable than their production. This may be because of some inherent property of the waste—perhaps it is toxic—or it may be because there is no positive use it can be put to. In some electricity markets, for example, excess electricity production is negatively priced. This occurs where electricity is a byproduct of combined cycle facilities installed to generate heat, or where the cost of shutting down large inflexible generators exceeds the benefits of reducing output. In such cases an increase in the damage cost associated with the byproduct of a process producing a positively valued good will cause a reduction in the supply of the positively valued good. Q_i and Q_j would then be said to be net substitutes if

$$\frac{\partial Q_i}{\partial |p_j|} > 0 \bigg|_{U \text{ constant}} \tag{7.34}$$

where $|p_j|$ is the absolute value of the (negative) price of Q_j, and net complements if:

$$\frac{\partial Q_i}{\partial |p_j|} < 0 \bigg|_{U \text{ constant}} \tag{7.35}$$

An increase in the damage cost imposed by production of the complementary output Q_j leads to a decrease in consumption of Q_i, holding utility constant.

The way in which harmful byproducts are normally analyzed is not to treat them as a separate elements, but to bundle them together with the positively valued inputs or outputs, and then to price the bundle net of the costs associated with management or disposal of those byproducts.

7.6 Conditional substitutes and complements

Finally, we have observed that the relative value of the inputs to and outputs from production processes is frequently conditional. It depends on the environmental conditions under which production takes place. This is equally true of the harmful byproducts of production. Emissions to air or water that are highly damaging in one set of conditions may be harmless in other conditions. Wind patterns and water currents often determine whether pollutants remain in an airshed or water body, or are moved out of the system. The structure of landscapes and the composition of ecological communities often determine whether land-use change threatens species richness and abundance. Stress on particular subcommunities in a meta-community, for example, may be more or less damaging depending on the rate at which species move between subcommunities.

The substitutability between species also turns out to depend on environmental conditions, and may change both with changes in environmental conditions and with levels of anthropogenic stress. Consider the example of grass and sedge species in rangelands. A study of lightly and heavily grazed rangelands in Australia considered the functional similarities between more and less abundant species, and the relation between abundance, environmental conditions, and grazing pressure (Walker, Kinzig, and Langridge 1999). It showed that there were functional similarities between the dominant species and many of the minor species in the system, and that the relative abundance of species depended on environmental conditions. Minor species typically had different responses to fluctuations in environmental conditions than dominant species. They also found that community composition was sensitive to grazing pressure. Dominant species were functionally more dissimilar to each other in lightly grazed communities than in heavily grazed communities. The abundance of functionally similar species was also more dissimilar in lightly grazed communities than in heavily grazed communities.

Figure 7.6 shows rank abundance and functional similarity between groups of species identified in lightly grazed communities. Groups identified by letter share functional traits with other species in the community. Remaining groups did not share any functional traits. In heavily grazed communities they found that the abundance of particular dominants decreased more than others—a function of the palatability of the species. But they also found that the abundance of a number of functionally similar groups of species increased, and that this number was greater than would have been expected from the ecological distance between species alone.

The authors concluded that dominant species were responsible for community function, being functionally dissimilar, while minor species provided resilience in that they were functionally similar to dominant groups and could increase in abundance if the dominant groups were to disappear through either environmental or grazing conditions. The results led the authors to argue that differences of this kind enhance the resilience of the system to environmental stresses and to grazing pressure.

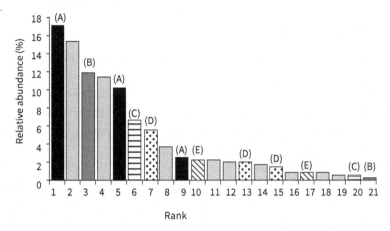

Figure 7.6 Functional similarities between dominant and minor species.
Source: Walker et al. (1999).

In the language of economics, the members of functionally similar groups of grass species in this study are substitutes, while the elasticity of substitution is a function of environmental conditions and grazing pressure. It is still possible to identify the trade-off between species in average (expected) conditions, but it is also possible to see how the trade-offs might vary if environmental conditions were nonstationary—that is, trending in some direction, such as to warmer, drier climates. The slope and location of isoquants might vary with environmental conditions. In Figure 7.7, if N_1 were less productive in dry conditions (indicated by E'), and N_2 in wet conditions (indicated by E''), achieving a given level of output in the two sets of conditions might imply quite different combinations of inputs.

The connection between this and the portfolio effect described in Chapter 5 is obvious. If two palatable grass species respond to changes in environmental conditions in dissimilar ways, then landholders have an interest in ensuring that both remain in the system. More than this, they have an interest in increasing access to currently productive species, and reducing access to currently unproductive species. Put another way, producers have an interest in maintaining the flexibility to implement a range of production processes depending on environmental conditions. Most rainfed agriculture has elements of this approach, as do many wild capture fisheries.

7.7 Summary and conclusions

The Hotelling approach to conservation presupposes a degree of substitutability between produced and natural assets. Assets may be substitutes in

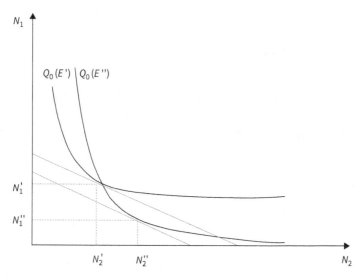

Figure 7.7 The impact of environmental conditions on production.

some respects only, and their substitutability may be limited by technology or environmental conditions. But there is an implicit assumption that not all assets are complements. The substitutability of assets also depends on the perspective of the user. From an ecological perspective, what is interesting is the degree to which species are substitutes in the provision of ecological functions and processes. From a systematics perspective, what matters is the phylogenetic distance between species rather than their substitutability in the provision of ecological functions or processes—there is only a weak link between phylogeny and ecological functioning. Which aspect of substitutability matters depends on the problem being posed. The distinction between weak and strong sustainability mentioned at the start of this chapter is largely about the degree of substitutability between natural and produced capital in the provision of ecosystem services. The distinction between functional groups discussed by Walker et al. (1999) is about the complementarity between functionally similar species that thrive in different environmental conditions. The phylogenetic approach to protected area design adopted by many conservation biologists (e.g., Pellens and Grandcolas 2016) is effectively about the substitutability of species with similar evolutionary histories.

While context is important, all substitutability problems can be analyzed using very similar concepts. An understanding of the elasticity of substitution and its relation to time, for example, is helpful in analyzing substitutability between all kinds of assets. The elasticity of substitution between natural and produced capital stocks depends not only on the productive potential of each, but also on the time it takes for investment decisions to be made and implemented.

The difference between the short and long period in economics is just the difference between the period in which no new investment is possible (the elasticity of substitution is low), and the period in which new investments can be completed (the elasticity of substitution is high). Similarly, the elasticity of substitution between species within a functional group depends on the regeneration time of those species. Species with fast regeneration times—such as insects and microbes—respond to environmental changes more rapidly than species with slow regeneration times. The elasticity of substitution between species will be increasing both in the time allowed for a response, and in the regeneration rate.

Where assets are perfect substitutes it follows that there is no incentive to conserve one rather than the other. If assets are perfect complements it follows that the incentive is conserve both or neither. For assets that lie somewhere in between these polar cases, the incentive to conserve one or both will depend on the elasticity of substitution between them. The degree of substitutability between assets constrains their potential value to users. As we saw when we introduced the Hotelling price path, the existence of substitutes can limit the potential value of natural assets, and hence the likelihood that it will be optimal to conserve those assets.

Before we consider conservation policy and conservation instruments, it is important to enter two caveats that follow from our discussion of the conditionality of substitution. First, assets that are substitutes in the provision of one thing may not be substitutes in the provision of something else. For example, species that belong to some functional group may be close substitutes in the performance of a particular ecological function, but may be very poor substitutes in terms of another ecological function. The second is that assets that are close substitutes in the provision of some good or service may have very different effects on the provision of other goods and services. For example, watershed protection and watershed treatment plants may both deliver clean water supplies, but have very different implications for habitat, flood risk, siltation, and so on. The decision about which assets to conserve should include information not only on the degree to which they are substitutes, but also on their wider social effect—as we shall see in the following chapters.

References

Doak, D. F., Bakker, V. J., Goldstein, B. E., and Hale, B. 2015. What is the future of conservation? Trends in Ecology & Evolution 29:77–81.

Farley, J. 2008. The role of prices in conserving critical natural capital. Conservation Biology 22:1399–1408.

Hartwick, J. 1977. Intergenerational equity and the investing of rents from exhaustible resources. American Economic Review 66:972–974.

Heal, G. 1999. Markets and sustainability. Science of the Total Environment 240:75–89.

Neumayer, E. 2003. Weak versus strong sustainability: exploring the limits of two opposing paradigms: Edward Elgar, Cheltenham.

Noble, I. R., and Dirzo, R. 1997. Forests as human-dominated ecosystems. Science 277:522–525.

Pellens, R., and Grandcolas, P., eds. 2016. Biodiversity conservation and phylogenetic systematics: preserving our evolutionary heritage in an extinction crisis. Springer, New York.

Pires, M. 2004. Watershed protection for a world city: the case of New York. Land Use Policy 21:161–175.

Sachs, J. D., J. E. M. Baillie, W. J. Sutherland, P. R. Armsworth, N. Ash, J. Beddington, T. M. Blackburn, B. Collen, B. Gardiner, K. J. Gaston, H. C. J. Godfray, R. E. Green, P. H. Harvey, B. House, S. Knapp, N. F. Kumpel, D. W. Macdonald, G. M. Mace, J. Mallet, A. Matthews, R. M. May, O. Petchey, A. Purvis, D. Roe, K. Safi, K. Turner, M. Walpole, R. Watson, and K. E. Jones. 2009. Biodiversity Conservation and the Millennium Development Goals. Science 325:1502–1503.

Walker, B. H., Kinzig, A. P., and Langridge, J. 1999. Plant attribute diversity, resilience, and ecosystem function: the nature and significance of dominant and minor species. Ecosystems 2:95–113.

PART III

ALIGNING THE PRIVATE AND SOCIAL VALUE OF NATURAL RESOURCES

8

Environmental Public Goods

Defenders of the short-sighted men who in their greed and selfishness will, if permitted, rob our country of half its charm by their reckless extermination of all useful and beautiful wild things sometimes seek to champion them by saying the "the game belongs to the people." So it does; and not merely to the people now alive, but to the unborn people. The "greatest good for the greatest number" applies to the number within the womb of time, compared to which those now alive form but an insignificant fraction. Our duty to the whole, including the unborn generations, bids us restrain an unprincipled present-day minority from wasting the heritage of these unborn generations. The movement for the conservation of wild life and the larger movement for the conservation of all our natural resources are essentially democratic in spirit, purpose, and method.
—Theodore Roosevelt, *A Book-Lover's Holidays in the Open*, 1916

8.1 Introduction

The Hotelling principle holds that it will be optimal for society to conserve any natural resource if the social value of that resource, when kept, is expected to grow faster than the rate of return on the best alternative investment. We have seen that efforts to value nonmarketed ecosystem services have made it possible to value the underlying environmental assets. Ecosystem service values have been used to generate estimates of the resource rents on the underlying assets, which have then been converted to asset values via the net present value approach. Nevertheless, estimates of asset values continue to be compromised by two things. One, addressed in this chapter, is the public good nature of many of ecosystem services and the underlying assets. A second, addressed in the next chapter, is the existence of incidental, often unrecognized consequences of resource use.

In what follows we consider the problem of environmental public goods. We consider how people value public goods, and what this means for their

Conservation. Charles Perrings and Ann Kinzig, Oxford University Press (2021). © Oxford University Press.
DOI: 10.1093/oso/9780190613600.003.0008

conservation. The core characteristics of public goods are that they are non-exclusive, at least to some degree, and nonrival, also at least to some degree. The nonexclusiveness of public goods means that none of the population of beneficiaries can be excluded from the benefits it offers. In some cases, such as the climate regulatory functions of the atmosphere, the population of beneficiaries comprises everyone on the planet. In other cases, public goods associated with a particular jurisdiction, say, it might include only members of certain national, cultural, religious, or social groups. In yet other cases it might include only the members of a particular club. National security, for example, once provided, protects all in the nation without exclusion, but not those living outside the nation's borders.

The nonrival nature of public goods means that consumption by one person does not increase the cost to others. In extreme cases, it implies that access by one individual has no consequences for the cost of access by other individuals. Information in the public domain would be one example. The weather effects of solar flares would be another. Many public goods are, however, only partially nonrival. Congestible public goods such as parks, roads, public buildings and the like may be nonrival at low levels of use, but increasingly involve access costs at higher levels of use. While we will assume both nonexclusiveness and nonrivalry in discussing the theory of public goods, we will relax both assumptions when dealing with particular cases.

We are particularly concerned with public goods secured through conservation decisions. Many examples of these have already been identified. As we saw in Chapter 5, a number of the provisioning, cultural, and regulating services identified by the Millennium Ecosystem Assessment are public goods secured through decisions to protect particular landscapes or species. Examples include the regulation of water supplies and water quality through the conservation of watersheds or catchments, the control of soil erosion through the conservation of upland forests, the genetic information secured through the in situ conservation of particular species, the reduction of fire risk through the exclusion of introduced fire-prone species from certain ecosystems, or the mitigation of disease risk through the isolation of wild disease reservoirs. None within the set of potential beneficiaries can be excluded from the benefits such public goods offer, and adding a beneficiary has no implications for the cost to all others.

The nonexclusive and nonrival nature of such public goods has important implications for their conservation. When none can be excluded from the benefits of a public good, all have an incentive to free-ride on the efforts of others. If those who do not pay to obtain a public good enjoy exactly the same benefits as those who do pay, nobody has an incentive to pay. The result is that such public goods are systematically undervalued and the underlying environmental assets—watersheds, habitats, ecological communities, and the like—are underconserved. Fortunately, not all public goods are equally plagued by the free-rider problem. Indeed, some public goods are provided in a relatively efficient manner. Knowing what institutional arrangements work best can help reduce the impact of free-riding on conservation.

We first rehearse the theory of public goods to tie down the source of the problem, and to identify which types of public good are most susceptible to free-riding. To do this we consider the relation between types of public good, the strategic behavior of potential providers, and public goods provision. The art of free-riding turns out to depend on the nature of the game at hand—the strategies available to different parties and the payoffs to different strategies. We consider the importance of differences between games that offer more or less incentive to cooperate in the provision of public goods, and give examples using evidence from the conservation of environmental assets at multiple scales—extending from informal rules for the protection of quite local environmental public goods to multilateral agreements for the collective provision of global environmental public goods.

8.2 The optimal provision of public goods

To get a clear idea of the origin of the free-rider problem, and to see when it leads to underconservation, we need to distinguish between different types of public good. In the most general case we may suppose that the ith individual obtains benefits from consumption of a bundle of private goods, denoted by the vector x_i, and a public good available to all n members of the community, Y, to which their contribution is y_i. If the ith individual maximizes their well-being by choosing the components of x_i and their contribution to the public good, y_i, the problem is of the form:

$$\max_{x, y_i} U_i\left(x, y_i \middle| y_j\right), j \in \{1, 2, ..., n\}, j \neq i \tag{8.1}$$

That is, the ith individual takes the contributions of all others to the public good as given, and decides their own contribution accordingly. Without losing anything of importance we can suppose that there is just a single private good, x, the price of which is taken to be the numeraire (all other prices are denominated in terms of that price). The ith individual has a budget, B_i, and the price of the public good in terms of the private good is $p_y/p_x = p$. The ith individual maximizes (8.1) subject to a budget constraint:

$$x + py_i = B_i \qquad (8.2)$$

Setting the derivatives of the Lagrangian function

$$L = U_i\left(\mathbf{x}, y_i \middle| y_j\right) + \lambda\left(B_i - x - py_i\right) \qquad (8.3)$$

to zero

$$
\begin{aligned}
L_x &= \frac{\partial U_i}{\partial x} - \lambda = 0 \\
L_{y_i} &= \frac{\partial U_i}{\partial y_i} - \lambda p = 0
\end{aligned}
\qquad (8.4)
$$

allows us to see that the individual will contribute to the public good up to the point where the marginal rate of substitution between the public and private good is equal to the price of the public good in terms of the private good, that is:

$$\frac{\partial U_i}{\partial p_i} \middle/ \frac{\partial U_i}{\partial x} = p \qquad (8.5)$$

In other words, the ith individual will trade off the public for the private good at the ratio between the prices of public and private goods. Now we know that if the ith individual contributes y_i toward the public good all other individuals in society will gain. That is, $\partial U_j/\partial y_i > 0, j = 1,...,n, j \neq i$. But since the ith individual has no incentive to take these benefits into account, they will contribute too little. Symmetrically, since the ith individual benefits from the contributions made by all others in society, $\partial U_i/\partial y_j > 0, j = 1,...,n, j \neq i$, whether or not they themselves contribute, they will have an incentive to free-ride on the efforts of others. Once again, they will contribute too little.

To see the trade-off between contributions made by the ith individual and all others in society, we can define the share of the public good provided by the rest of society as $\hat{Y} = Y - y_i$. We can then rewrite the utility function described in 8.1:

$$U_i\left(\mathbf{x}, y_i \middle| y_j\right) = U_i\left(B_i - py_i, y_i, \hat{Y}\right) = V_i\left(y_i, \hat{Y} \middle| B_i, p\right) \qquad (8.6)$$

where $V_i\left(y_i, \hat{Y} \middle| B_i, p\right)$, the ith individual's indirect utility function, gives the maximum utility possible given the relative prices of the public and private good, and the available income, B_i.

The indifference curves corresponding to this utility function would ordinarily be of the form shown in Figure 8.1. As the ith individual increases their contribution to the public good from zero they require less of the public good provided by others to yield the same utility, but beyond some point additional expenditure on the public good by the ith individual can only be balanced by additional expenditure by others. The locus of minimum points of this set of indifference curves defines what is called a Nash-Cournot reaction curve. This locus gives the individual's best response to the level of the public good provided by others. It is intuitive that the privately optimal provision of y_i is going to be less than the socially optimal provision of y_i since, from the perspective of society, the decisions of each person to contribute to the public good should take account of the costs and benefits to all people.

To see how much should be contributed to the public good if resources were being allocated efficiently from the perspective of society, denote the ith individual's share of the public good by $Y_i = y_i/Y$ and substitute this into the objective function to obtain

$$\max\nolimits_{x, y_i} U_i\left(x, y_i/Y_i\right) \tag{8.7}$$

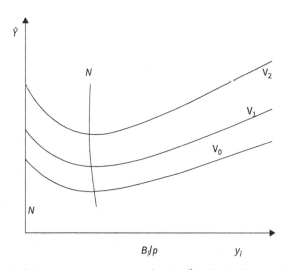

Figure 8.1 The Nash-Cournot reaction curve for the ith individual's contribution to the public good.

Since Y_i is a share, it follows that $\sum_{i=1}^{n} Y_i = 1$. Maximization of (8.7) subject to equation (8.2) now yields the following first order necessary conditions:

$$L_x = \frac{\partial U_i}{\partial x} - \lambda = 0$$

$$L_{y_i} = \frac{\partial U_i}{\partial y_i}\frac{1}{Y_i} - \lambda p = 0 \qquad (8.8)$$

$$\Rightarrow \frac{\partial U_i}{\partial y_i} \Big/ \frac{\partial U_i}{\partial x} = Y_i p$$

If we then sum over all individuals in society we get

$$\sum_{i=1}^{n} \frac{\partial U_i}{\partial y_i} \Big/ \frac{\partial U_i}{\partial x} = \sum_{i=1}^{n} Y_i p = p \qquad (8.9)$$

That is, individuals should increase their contribution to the public good up to the point where the sum of the n marginal rates of substitution of the public for the private good should be equal to the ratio of the price of the public good to the price of the private good. This condition, known as the Samuelson condition, equates the relative marginal benefit and marginal cost of public good provision.

Suppose, for example, that Y is a planned national park that, once established, would benefit 1,000,000 people, and that x is a composite consumption bundle that meets average needs of one person for one week. Suppose also that each individual would be willing to give up one week's consumption, a unit of the composite consumption bundle, to secure the national park. It is easy to see that if development of the national park were left to the market it would never be established. The social marginal rate of substitution of the national park for the composite consumption bundle in this case would be 1,000,000 to 1. That is, taken together, the population would be willing to give up 1,000,000 units of the consumption bundle to secure the park. If the cost of establishing the national park were 500,000 units of the consumption bundle, however, it is obvious that no one individual would be willing to fund the park. They would rather choose the composite consumption bundle. Since the rate of product transformation—the rate at which the national park could be transformed into the consumption bundle—is 500,000 to 1, while the social marginal rate of substitution is 1,000,000 to 1, it would make a lot of sense for the society to invest in the national park, but no sense for an individual within that society to do so.

The free-rider problem also characterizes public good provision by groups of people, whether local communities or nation-states. Suppose that there are two communities adjacent to a wilderness area that each community has some interest in conserving. Suppose demand for conservation by community 1 is given by $Y = 2000 - p$ where p is the cost of an acre of conserved land, and 2000, the intercept, is the maximum dollar amount the community is willing to pay for an acre of protected wilderness. Suppose also that demand for conservation by community 2 is $Y = 4000 - p$. It follows that community 2 is either more affluent, more committed to conservation, or both. Now suppose that, once protected, both communities have equal rights of access to the wilderness area (i.e., it is nonexclusive).

The two demand functions can be expressed in inverse form as $p = 2000 - Y, p = 4000 - Y$ implying that for $p > 2000$ the joint or aggregate demand for conservation would be $p = 6000 - Y$, while for $p \leq 2000$ it would be $p = 4000 - Y$ (see Figure 8.2). That is for any cost of conservation greater than the maximum amount that community 1 was willing to pay, demand would

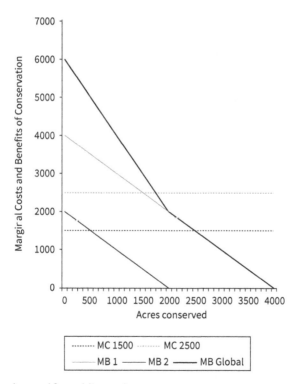

Figure 8.2 The demand for public goods.
The demand curve for a public good accessed by two communities is the vertical sum of the demand curves for each community.

be determined by community 2 alone. For any cost of conservation less than the maximum amount that community 1 was willing to pay, demand would be determined by both communities. Specifically, aggregate demand would be the vertical sum of demand by each community. In Figure 8.2 we ask what would be the optimal area conserved if it could be acquired at $1,500 and $2,500 per acre. At $1,500 per acre only community 1 would contribute 2,500 acres. At $2,500 per acre the socially efficient level of conservation would be 1,750 acres, which includes contributions from both communities.

The socially efficient level of conservation is given by the intersection of the aggregate demand curve and the supply curve, and equates marginal cost and marginal global benefit—that is, the sum of the marginal benefits to each community. The aggregate demand curve is the vertical sum of the demand curves of the two communities reflecting the fact that each derives benefit from accessing the same area of land. Each acre of conserved land delivers benefits to both communities.

Both cases provide at least a partial free-ride to one of the communities. Whether or not that involves a social cost depends on the case. If the cost of conservation was $2,500 per acre and production of the public good was left to the market (i.e., the two communities made decisions independently), community 1 would conserve 1,500 acres and community 2 would conserve nothing while free-riding on the efforts of community 1. Since the socially efficient level of conservation is 1,750 acres this would involve a social cost. For conservation to be socially efficient, community 2 should provide 250 acres at $250. If the cost of conservation were $1,500 per acre, community 1 would provide 2,500 acres and community 2 nothing. Community 2 would free-ride on the efforts of community 1, but without any loss of social efficiency.

8.3 Types of public goods

Whether or not free-riding matters depends, in part, on what has been called the technology of public good supply (Sandler 2004). The technology of public good supply determines the relative importance of different actors in the provision of public goods. As our numerical example shows, this depends on more than technical conditions. Whether the socially efficient level of conservation involves one or both communities depends on the cost of conservation and the strength of demand from each community. If the marginal cost of conservation is low, community 1 is the sole provider, but free-riding by community 2 is costless. If the marginal cost of conservation is high, both communities should contribute, and free-riding by community 2 is socially costly.

We can capture the differences between the two cases in a stylized way by defining a number of particular types of technology of supply.

Simple sum public goods: In the first technology of supply, the level of the public good is the sum of the contributions made by all people (or communities) in the system. The problem to be solved by the ith individual or community in this case takes the form

$$\max_{\mathbf{x},y_i} U_i\left(\mathbf{x},y_i\middle|y_j\right)=U_i\left(\mathbf{x},y_1+\dots+y_i+\dots+y_n\right) \tag{8.10}$$

Utility is increasing in the sum of the contributions of all decision-makers. Every contribution counts. A frequently cited example of a public good of this type is macroclimatic regulation through carbon sequestration. Every ton of carbon sequestered makes the same contribution to macroclimatic regulation, no matter where it takes place.

In the same way, cross-border game reserves are the sum of the areas contributed by each nation-state. The Great Limpopo Transfrontier Park in Southern Africa, for example, links the Limpopo National Park in Mozambique, Kruger National Park in South Africa, Gonarezhou National Park, Manjinji Pan Sanctuary and Malipati Safari Area in Zimbabwe, plus the Sengwe communal land in Zimbabwe and the Makuleke region in South Africa, into one 35 000 km² conservation area (Figure 8.3). A decision not to contribute in such cases reduces the benefits to all. Free-riding imposes a social cost.

Best-shot public goods: In the second technology of supply, utility to the ith individual or community depends only the contribution made by the most effective provider. In this case the problem to be solved by the ith individual or community takes the form

$$\max_{\mathbf{x},y_i} U_i\left(\mathbf{x},y_i\middle|y_i\right)=U_i\left(\mathbf{x},\arg\max\left(y_1,\dots,y_i,\dots,y_n\right)\right) \tag{8.11}$$

Utility is increasing only in the contribution of the most effective provider. No other contribution counts. So if the ith individual or community is not the most effective provider, they have no incentive to contribute. If a decision not to contribute has no implications for the benefits to others, however, there is no social cost involved. Free-riding, in this case, is costless. There are a number of examples of public goods of this type. Defense shields are one of the most frequently cited, but there are close analogs in conservation. In human and animal health, for example, monitoring services by the Centers for Disease Control (CDC) in the United States provide benefits worldwide (Sandler 2004). While CDC services are not a pure best-shot public good—a

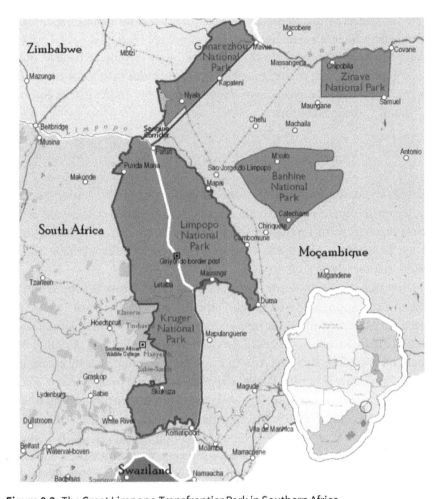

Figure 8.3 The Great Limpopo Transfrontier Park in Southern Africa.

This is an example of an additive conservation public good. If the abundance of conserved species is increasing in range size, and if the nonexclusive and nonrival benefits are increasing in abundance, each additional unit of land committed to conservation offers benefits to all contributing countries.

Source: South African National Parks (2018).

number of other international agencies provide important infectious disease monitoring services, including the World Health Organization (WHO) and the World Animal Health Organization (OIE)—the example illustrates the central feature of this technology of supply. The efforts of a country with little capacity to monitor disease outbreaks have few implications for the well-being of others.

Weakest-link public goods: In the third technology of supply, utility to the ith individual or community depends only the contribution made by the least effective provider. In this case the problem to be solved by the ith individual or community takes the form

$$\max_{x,y_i} U_i\left(x, y_i \middle| y_j\right) = U_i\left(x, \arg\min\left(y_1, ..., y_i, ..., y_n\right)\right) \qquad (8.12)$$

Utility is increasing only in the contribution of the least effective provider. No other contribution counts. The incentive effects in this case are mixed. While it can lead many to reduce their own contribution to match the efforts of the least effective provider, it can also lead to a concerted effort to strengthen the least effective provider.

The most frequently cited example of a weakest link public good is a dike, sea wall, or levee maintained by the communities who benefit from the flood protection it offers. If the integrity of the whole structure depends on the maintenance efforts of all communities, maintenance is only as good as that provided by the least effective community—the weakest link in the chain. This is because the structure has to fail in one place only to put all at risk. There are many similar examples of barriers in nature. Coastal mangrove systems, for instance, provide (among other things) protection against storm damage inland. The 2004 Indian Ocean earthquake and tsunami resulted in extensive coastal damage in Indonesia, Thailand, India, Sri Lanka, and Somalia, with the loss of around 250,000 lives. The degree of the damage and the loss of life was, however, lower in areas protected by intact mangrove systems than in areas where mangroves had been cleared for shrimp ponds or coastal development (Dahdouh-Guebas et al. 2005). Since decisions to conserve or convert mangroves are frequently made at the community level, mangrove conservation has many of the attributes of a weakest link public good.

Other examples of weakest or weaker link public goods include the control of invasive species and infectious disease. In both cases the protection all enjoy is only as good as that offered by the weakest link in the chain. Many emerging zoonotic diseases have their origins in contact between people or domestic animals and wild species at the edges of natural forests (Jones et al. 2008). The conversion of forests for the production of crops or the raising of livestock brings susceptible individuals into contact with infected wildlife, so risking cross species infection and the emergence of new diseases. Biosecurity measures in such cases are generally poorly developed, but once again the risk to all is determined by the weakest link in the chain. Similarly, the international spread of infectious disease outbreaks depends on measures taken by public health authorities to isolate and treat the infected population—including quarantines, school closures, and travel and border health controls. The capacity to bring a pandemic, such as the 2020 coronavirus, under control is limited by the weakest public health authorities.

Impure public goods: The fourth technology of supply occurs when contributions to a public good generate exclusive benefits to the contributor in addition to nonexclusive benefits to all those accessing the public good. That is, utility to the ith individual or community depends both on the level of the public good, and on their own contribution to the public good. In this case the problem to be solved by the ith individual or community takes the form

$$\max_{\mathbf{x}, y_i} U_i\left(\mathbf{x}, y_i \middle| y_j\right) = U_i\left(\mathbf{x}, y_i, Y\right) \tag{8.13}$$

Utility is increasing in the ith individual or community's own contribution to the public good, as well the contributions of all others. They get a double benefit from their contribution. We see this at many different scales. The engagement of the private sector in the provision of public goods at many scales is often promoted on efficiency grounds, but the main motivation is as often to generate private benefits in the form of the value added in the production of public goods. That is, the return to labor and capital in the production of some public good may be as important a motive for contributing as the benefits offered by the public good itself.

At the smallest scale, a good example of the double benefit individual's get from contribution to a public good is vaccination against an infectious disease. The decision that individuals make to vaccinate against influenza, for example, includes both a private benefit (they are less likely will to ill if they encounter an infected person), and a public benefit (fewer people in total will fall ill). By strengthening their own immune response to the virus, people who get vaccinated gain themselves. By reducing the likelihood that they will infect others, their action allows society to gain. From a social perspective the individual should take account of the benefits to all individuals in their decision to get vaccinated. But even if they are not swayed by the wider benefits of the immunization program, they might still choose to get vaccinated if it increased their own protection.

Many conservation efforts similarly involve both private and public benefits. For example, conservation of endangered species on private lands may offer a range of private benefits in addition to the public benefit offered by protection of the global gene pool. The survival of the Pere David's deer, for example, is solely due to the existence of private collections in the Nanyuan Royal Hunting Garden in Nan Haizi, China, and later in Woburn Abbey, Britain (Gibson and Yong 2017). In both cases protection of the species offered a direct benefit to the curator in addition to wider benefits to all humankind.

Local public goods

Finally, the fifth technology of supply occurs when the benefits offered by a public good depend on the size of the population having rights of access. That is, utility to the ith individual or community depends both on their own contribution to the public good, and on the number of others also contributing. In this case the problem to be solved by the ith individual or community takes the form

$$\max_{\mathbf{x}, y_i} U_i\left(\mathbf{x}, y_i \middle| y_j\right) = U_i\left(\mathbf{x}, y_i, n\right) \tag{8.14}$$

where n denotes the number of those contributing to and having access to the public good. This type of public good occurs where consumption of the public good is rival, but nonexclusive. Such public goods are frequently referred to as congestible. The public good has a limited capacity such that beyond some point, adding one more user imposes costs on all. Public roads, bridges, railways, airports, parks, recreation areas, and so on all have this feature. As they become more and more congested, the value of the facility to users declines. The solution, in all cases, involves measures either to increase the carrying capacity of the public good, or more commonly, to limit access.

Small-scale examples of local public goods include clubs of one kind or another. The facilities of the club are freely available to members, but since they are congestible, membership is restricted. There is, however, a very wide range of public goods of this type that extends well beyond sporting, recreational, or social clubs. Many are designed to regulate access to common pool resources of one kind or another. Examples include artisanal fisheries, forests exploited for timber and nontimber forest products, hunting grounds, sacred groves, medicinal resources, water bodies, and so on. There is also a very extensive body of literature on the characteristics of the more or less informal institutional arrangements established to regulate access to such resources (Ostrom 2015).

8.4 Strategic behavior and the provision of public goods

In all the cases discussed in Section 8.3 the problem has been posed as one where the ith individual or community makes a decision about their contribution to a public good, *given* the decisions made by other individuals or other communities. The Nash-Cournot reaction function describes the best response *given* the amount of the public good provided by others. The implication of this is that people are assumed to behave strategically. If a protected area is nonrival and nonexclusive in consumption (at least over some range) then every acre provides benefits to all, but each is better off if others carry the cost of conservation. The payoff from conservation effort to one community is conditioned by the conservation effort of others. If we think of the establishment of a protected area as resulting from a single irreversible act, we can cast the two-community problem as a binary nonrepeated game. The conditional payoffs to alternative actions, protect or not protect, then determine what each community will do.

Consider the numerical example illustrated in Figure 8.4. The numbers in each cell represent the payoffs (net benefits) to each community of an action they might undertake, given the actions of the other community.

So, for example, if community 2 were to protect a common area, the payoff to community 1 would be 2 if it also invested in protection, but 3 if it did not. Community 1 would therefore choose not to protect. If community 2 chose not to protect on the other hand, the payoff to community 1 would be 0 if it also chose to protect, and 2 if it did not. Once again, community 2 would choose not to protect. Symmetrically, if community 1 chose to protect the payoffs to community 2 would be 3 if it also chose to protect, and 1 if it did not. So community 2 would choose to protect. If community 1 chose not to protect, the payoffs to community 2 would be 1 if it chose to protect and 0 if it did not. So we see that in this problem it would always be optimal for community 1 not to protect, and for community 2 to protect. Since the payoff to society in this case—both communities taken together—would be 4 if only community 2 contributed, and 5 if both contributed, there is a social cost to

	Payoffs to community 2	
Action	Protect	Not protect
Protect	2,3	0,1
Not protect	3,1	2,0

Payoffs to community 1 (label to the left of the "Not protect" row / Action column)

Figure 8.4 Payoffs to conservation in a binary nonrepeated game.

the strategic choice of community 1 not to contribute. This loosely corresponds to the MC = $2,500 case in Figure 8.2. Although the payoff to society would be at a maximum when both communities invest in protection, this will not happen if the decision is left to the market.

For most public goods the payoff to alternative actions depends both on the institutional conditions that determine access, and the characteristics of the public good that determine the degree to which it is rival in consumption. Access depends on property rights and access rules—minimal in the case of open access resources beyond any national jurisdiction, substantial in the case of regulated access common pool resources within a single jurisdiction. To get a sense of the range of possible outcomes we take the most common of the results generated in a two-by-two nonrepeated game of the form given in Figure 8.4. The choices available to each party are generally characterized as cooperation and defection, the payoff structure being denoted CC (R) if both cooperate, DD (P) if both defect, DC (S) if only the first country defects, and CD (T) if only the second country defects. They involve three main types of collective action problem: (a) coordination, captured in "pure coordination" and "assurance" games, (b) disagreement, captured in "chicken" and "battle of the sexes" games, and (c) defection, captured in the classical "prisoners' dilemma" (Holzinger 2001, Holzinger 2008). To see how different payoff structures relate to these collective action problems and associated games, we adapt a figure due to (Hauert 2001) in Figure 8.5.

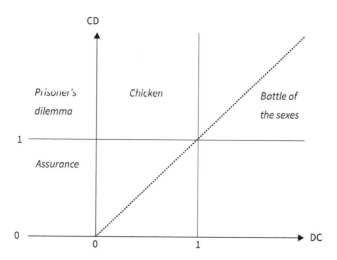

Figure 8.5 Types of two-by-two nonrepeated games.
Games are shown in the DC, CD plane, CC normalized to 1, and DD normalized to 0.
Source: Adapted from Hauert (2001).

Payoff structures associated with each type of game are illustrated in Figure 8.6. In the classic prisoner's dilemma while both parties would be better off if they cooperated in providing the public good, the payoff structure leads each to defect. In the assurance game, the collectively best outcome is similarly attained only if both cooperate. Defection by either party is sufficient for the effort to fail. The worst outcome is if one cooperates and the other does not. In the chicken game, the worst outcome is where neither contributes to the public good. As a result, each has an incentive to contribute if they believe that the other will not. Finally, in the battle of the sexes game, the two parties have different preferences about the provision of the public good, but each would rather cooperate with the other than proceed on their own.

The choices parties make are a Nash equilibrium if, once the choice is made, neither party would wish to change that choice. At the Nash equilibrium, no party can improve their position by unilaterally switching strategies once others have made their choice. The prisoners' dilemma, for example, has a single Nash equilibrium at which each party chooses not to cooperate regardless of what the other party chooses to do, even though both would be better off cooperating.

The other games are characterized by multiple equilibria. As in the prisoner's dilemma, the highest payoff to each party in a chicken game occurs when they defect while the other party cooperates. However, unlike the prisoner's dilemma, the unilateral provision of the public good is preferred to a situation where both defect. The result is that while mutual cooperation is the best outcome, the equilibrium outcome is that only one of the two parties

(a) Prisoner's dilemma

	Community 2	
Action	Cooperate	Defect
Cooperate	3,3	1,4
Defect	4,1	2,2

Community 1 labels the rows (Cooperate, Defect).

(b) Chicken

	Community 2	
Action	Cooperate	Defect
Cooperate	3,3	2,4
Defect	4,2	1,1

(c) Assurance

	Community 2	
Action	Cooperate	Defect
Cooperate	3,3	0,1
Defect	1,0	1,1

Community 1 labels the rows (Cooperate, Defect).

(d) Battle of the sexes

	Community 2	
Action	Cooperate	Defect
Cooperate	3,2	0,0
Defect	0,0	2,3

Figure 8.6 Payoff structures in two-by-two nonrepeated games.
Examples of payoff structures associated with (a) prisoner's dilemma, (b) chicken, (c) assurance and (d) battle of the sexes games.

will choose to cooperate, allowing the other to defect. CD and DC are both Nash equilibria.

Assurance and battle-of-the-sexes games are similarly characterized by multiple equilibria. Unlike prisoners' dilemma or chicken games, both involve coordinated outcomes that are preferred to uncoordinated outcomes. At the coordination equilibria no party can improve their position by changing their response. In assurance games, while each party prefers the social benefit secured through cooperation, mutual defection is also an equilibrium in which the public good is not provided and any unilateral efforts are wasted. In the battle of the sexes games, there is no agreement as to which of two coordinated outcomes is better—one outcome is preferred by the first party, the other is preferred by the second. The game therefore has two pure strategy Nash equilibria, one where both cooperate and another where both defect.

What we see is that the nature of the game, and therefore the outcomes that might be expected, are both sensitive to the structure of payoffs. Small changes in the structure of payoffs can transform the game from one form to another, and hence can change the outcome. The characteristics of the public good itself may be part of the explanation for the structure of payoffs, but it also reflects demand, institutional and regulatory conditions (the rules of the game), whether the game is repeated or not, the scope for negotiation between parties, and the scope for punishing defectors. There is now a large body of experimental research exploring the conditions under which people will or will not contribute to public goods in a laboratory setting. It has been shown, for example, that participants in laboratory public goods experiments are frequently conditional cooperators. That is, their own contributions to the public good are positively correlated with their beliefs about the average contribution of others in the group. In many cases those beliefs are reinforced by their willingness to punish free-riders in ways that change the payoff to defection (Fehr and Gachter 2000), although willingness to commit resources to the provision of public goods also declines over time (Fischbacher and Gachter 2010).

Whether decision-makers invest resources in changing the structure of payoffs in the real world depends on the costs of free-riding. If public goods are lumpy or step public goods—in the sense that there is both a minimum size required for any benefit to be delivered, and expansion beyond that size delivers no additional benefit—free-riding may be costly before the step is achieved, but costless once it has been achieved. The eradication of a harmful infectious disease would be an example. The eradication of smallpox and rinderpest, for instance, was not complete until both diseases had been eliminated in every country in the world.

In most other cases free-riding is at least potentially costly. Many public goods are neither step goods nor additive goods, but are threshold goods. That is, there is some minimum level of provision before they start to yield any benefit, but benefits continue to increase with enhancements in provision beyond the threshold. One example is the control of infectious diseases. The control necessary to bring the basic reproduction ratio (R0), the number of individuals infected by each infected individual, below 1 is the threshold. Beyond the threshold, however, further reductions in R0 will still offer benefits in the speed with which an epidemic is brought under control, and/or benefits in terms of the number of people infected. Similarly, the adoption of minimum standards for water quality provides a threshold at which basic health standards are met, but further improvements in water quality can offer additional benefits in terms of further improved health, recreation, aesthetic appeal and so on. Conservation thresholds include critical minimum population sizes, or critical habitat sizes of endangered species, but increasing provision beyond these thresholds builds in a safety margin that enhances the value of the public good.

8.5 Resolving the public goods problem

While the provision of public goods is the business of government, governments are not the only sources of public goods. Many government-funded public goods are provided by private entities, and in places where private philanthropy is underpinned by a supportive tax system, such as the United States, many public goods are funded not from tax revenue but from private donations. Moreover, a number of public goods are both funded and produced by nongovernmental organizations or private foundations. The public good problem is to ensure that provision is at a level that satisfies the Samuelson conditions—that equates social marginal costs and benefits. This requires two mechanisms: one to encourage the beneficiaries of public goods to reveal the strength of their demand, the other to encourage the providers of public goods to meet social demand. Methods for getting individuals to reveal their demand for public goods were discussed in Chapter 5. Here we consider methods for encouraging the providers of public goods to meet social demand.

To fix ideas, suppose that the preservation of some endangered endemic species is in the hands of a local community, whose members derive some benefit from the conservation of that species. Suppose also that there exists a wider community whose members also derive benefit from the conservation of the same species. Suppose further that we are able to specify demand for conservation efforts by both the local and wider communities. In the absence of any mechanism to express the strength of global demand for conservation, the local community will conserve up to the point where the marginal local cost of conservation is equal to the local marginal benefit of conservation. Figure 8.7 illustrates the problem. It shows that local conservation effort would be equal to C_L. At that level, conservation effort would be undersupplied. If there were a mechanism to express the strength of global demand for conservation, however, the local community would conserve up to the point at which the marginal local cost of conservation was equal to the marginal global benefit of conservation, that is, at C_G. It is clear that any such mechanism would have to cover the increment in the cost of provision involved in moving from C_L to C_G (the stippled area in Figure 8.7).

As we will see in the next chapter, this is a mechanism for internalizing the global external benefits of local conservation effort. The imposition of penalties for those responsible for imposing global external costs is symmetric. In both cases the public nature of the external benefits/costs implies that none can be excluded from the benefits/can evade the costs. Absent collective treaties or other institutions (e.g., the Global Environment Facility, the Law of the Seas), public goods will be undersupplied and public bads oversupplied. The management challenge is to adjust activity levels to bring the private and social costs and benefits into line.

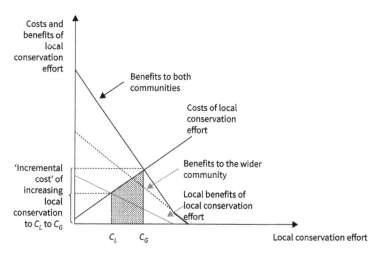

Figure 8.7 The incremental cost of increasing supply of local conservation effort.

8.6 Summary and conclusions

The Hotelling principle holds that it will be optimal for society to conserve any natural resource if it's value to society, when conserved, is expected to grow faster than it's value when converted. This chapter addressed one reason why the value of many natural resources to individuals and communities is systematically underestimated. It is the public good nature of those resources and the services they generate. Whenever ecosystem services are nonexclusive and/or nonrival in consumption (public goods), those who benefit from the services have an incentive to free-ride on the efforts of others. In very many cases, such services will be underprovided, and the environmental assets that generate them will be underconserved. The public good nature of such services also ensures that those who do provide them will take no account of the impact of their own behavior on the welfare of others. Absent corrective measures, the underlying assets will therefore be underconserved.

The chapter reviewed the characteristics of public goods, and the conditions under which free-riding behavior is problematic. It showed why the Samuelson condition for the socially optimal provision of public goods is efficient, and when decision-makers are likely to deviate from that condition. Specifically, it showed that what any one decision-maker does depends on the decisions made by others. The Nash-Cournot reaction curve describes the individual's best response to the level of the public good provided by others. It results in a level of provision that is generally below the socially optimal level of provision.

We showed that the extent of the free-riding problem depends both on what has been termed the technology of public good supply, and the way in which pay-offs to strategic behavior vary. The technology of public good supply distinguishes between different types of public goods. The range considered in the chapter includes additive, best and better shot, weakest and weaker link, impure, local or club, step and threshold public goods. We saw how the incentive to free-ride varies with each of these, and is more problematic in some cases (e.g., additive public goods like the macro-climatic regulation from carbon sequestration) than others (e.g., best-shot public goods like the provision of information on infectious disease outbreaks). Step public goods (e.g., pest eradication) have a minimum size for any benefit to be delivered, but expansion beyond that size delivers no additional benefit. It follows that while free-riding is costly before the step is achieved, it is costless beyond that point. Threshold public goods (e.g., securing the critical minimum population for an endangered species) similarly require a minimum size before any benefit is delivered, but the benefits continue to grow with expansion beyond the threshold. It follows that free-riding is costly both before and after the threshold is achieved.

We also saw how pay-offs to strategic behavior depend on the nature of the game. Many environmental public goods involve prisoners' dillemmas, where the Nash equilibria can be socially undesirable. The collective action problem in this case lies in the fact that people have an incentive to defect from the socially optimal outcome. The collective action problem in other games may involve either coordination (as in assurance games), or disagreement (as in chicken or battle of the sexes games). Where decision-makers fail to cooperate, the outcome is almost always suboptimal.

In general, the social cost of free-riding on the provision of environmental public goods rises with the number of people involved. This is not necessarily true for best-shot public goods, but is for all others. In the case of global environmental public goods that depend on local actions, where billions of beneficiaries of local action make no contribution to local effort, the undervaluation and underprovision of environmental public goods/overprovision of environmental public bads can be extreme.

As we shall see in later chapters, this makes the issue of governance central to the solution of environmental public goods problems. For environmental public goods that are supplied by private individuals, households, or firms, optimal provision relies on interventions that bring the private and social value of the underlying assets into alignment. For environmental public goods supplied by collective action, it requires the resolution of the collective action problems involved. While the subsidiarity principle applied in many states favors devolution of responsibility for public good provision to the lowest level possible, it also favors higher-level collective approaches to public good provision where necessary. We return to the implications of the principle in the final chapter.

References

Dahdouh-Guebas, F., L. P. Jayatissa, D. Di Nitto, J. O. Bosire, D. L. Seen, and N. Koedam. 2005. How effective were mangroves as a defence against the recent tsunami? Current Biology 15:R443–R447.

Fehr, E., and S. Gachter. 2000. Cooperation and punishment in public goods experiments. American Economic Review 90:980–994.

Fischbacher, U., and S. Gachter. 2010. Social preferences, beliefs, and the dynamics of free riding in public goods experiments. American Economic Review 100:541–556.

Gibson, L., and D. L. Yong. 2017. Saving two birds with one stone: solving the quandary of introduced, threatened species. Frontiers in Ecology and the Environment 15:35–41.

Hauert, C. 2001. Fundamental clusters in spatial 2 × 2 games. Proceedings of the Royal Society of London B: Biological Sciences 268:761–769.

Holzinger, K. 2001. Aggregation technology of common goods and its strategic consequences: global warming, biodiversity, and sitting conflicts. European Journal of Political Research 40:117–138.

Holzinger, K. 2008. Treaty formation and strategic constellations: a comment on treaties: strategic considerations. University of Illinois Law Review 1:187–200.

Jones, K. E., N. G. Patel, M. A. Levy, A. Storeygard, D. Balk, J. L. Gittleman, and P. Daszak. 2008. Global trends in emerging infectious diseases. Nature 451:990–993.

Ostrom, E. 2015. Governing the commons. Cambridge University Press, Cambridge.

Sandler, T. 2004. Global collective action. Cambridge University Press, Cambridge.

South African National Parks. 2018. Great Limpopo Transfrontier Park. South African National Parks, Pretoria.

9

Environmental Externalities

> The problem which we face in dealing with actions which have
> harmful effects is not simply one of restraining those responsible for
> them. What has to be decided is whether the gain from preventing the
> harm is greater that the loss which would be suffered elsewhere as a
> result of stopping the action which produces the harm.
>
> —Ronald Coase, *The Problem of Social Cost*, 1960

9.1 Introduction

An externality or external effect occurs when actions undertaken by one
person or one community affect others, and the effect is neglected in the
decisions leading to those actions. If the actions impose costs or confer
benefits on others, and no compensation is given or received, the costs or
benefits are said to be externalities of the action. Many of the environmental
changes that threaten individual species, ecological communities, landscapes,
and ecosystems are negative externalities of agriculture, forestry, industrial
production, infrastructural development, and urban growth. Climate change
from the emission of greenhouse gases; habitat loss from land-use change;
habitat fragmentation from the construction of roads, railways, power lines,
and canals; and the spread of pests and pathogens from trade and travel are all
examples of externalities of economic development that pose challenges for
conservation.

In Chapter 8 we saw that the public good nature of many ecosystem services
means that providers take little account of the wider benefits of their actions.
This leads to the undervaluation and hence undersupply of those services, and
to the underconservation of the environmental assets from which the services
derive. By the Hotelling principle, decision-makers will conserve assets up to
the point where the discounted value of the stream of services they deliver
is expected to grow at least as fast as the rate of return on the best alternative
investment. So private land that is the source of public goods is likely to be
undervalued by the landowner, and hence underconserved. In this chapter

Conservation. Charles Perrings and Ann Kinzig, Oxford University Press (2021). © Oxford University Press.
DOI: 10.1093/oso/9780190613600.003.0009

we consider the general problem of environmental externalities, their measurement, and the design of instruments to bring the private and social value of ecosystem services and underlying environmental assets into alignment. More particularly, we consider instruments aimed at internalizing environmental externalities by confronting private decision-makers with the wider costs or benefits of their actions.

Internalization of the environmental externalities involves both carrots and sticks. The carrots comprise compensation for actions that enhances the survival prospects of threatened species, or that restores ecosystem functionality. This includes the payments for ecosystem services, along with a range of other instruments. The sticks comprise charges or penalties that confront people with the costs of actions that displace populations and species, that disrupt and degrade habitat, or that compromise the health and functions of ecosystems. The chapter first considers the nature of environmental externalities in general, why they are important sources of inefficiency and inequity, and how they may be internalized. It then focuses on conservation-relevant externalities, and discusses the merits of different options for dealing with them.

Chapter 1 described the main drivers of environmental change over the last few hundred years. Many of these drivers have involved externalities. For example, the costs of introduced pests and pathogens during the Columbian Exchange would now be described as externalities of the decisions Europeans made to engage with Native Americans. Today, 500 years later, the introduction of invasive pests and pathogens remains among the greatest external costs of trade and travel. The threat posed by invasive species has been found to increase with the opening of new trade routes and with the growth of trade along existing routes, although the effect does saturate (Dalmazzone 2000, Costello et al. 2007). As the global economy has grown, and as world markets have become more closely integrated, the rate at which new pests and pathogens have been introduced and reintroduced have both increased (Perrings et al. 2010). Effects extend from localized harms to global disruption—as evidenced by COVID-19 at the time of writing. From an ecological perspective, the establishment and spread of introduced species have had numerous effects, including stress on the richness and abundance of native species. While biological invasions have been claimed to be a leading factor in extinctions, and while they are certainly implicated in the decline of many island species, it is not clear how many extinctions have been directly caused by invasive species (Gurevitch and Padilla 2004). We will nevertheless see that it is critical to account for external effects such as these in balancing the relative advantages of conservation or conversion.

Like the impact of invasive species, other anthropogenic drivers of environmental change—land-use change, freshwater withdrawal and diversion, and emissions to land, air, and water—are also external effects of the decisions people have made to use resources in particular ways. Take the diversion of surface water, for example. Globally, the four main sources of anthropogenic demand for water are agriculture, energy, industrial production, and household consumption. Of these, agriculture accounts for around 70% of global freshwater withdrawals (and more than 90% in the least developed countries), while energy accounts for around 15% (United Nations World Water Assessment Programme 2015). The diversion of both surface and groundwater for human use has had direct negative effects on wetlands, rivers, streams, and riparian systems. In many cases it has also increased soil erosion, and reduced soil water-holding capacity and the recharge of groundwater and surface-water storage capacity (United Nations World Water Assessment Programme 2012).

Changes in nitrogen and phosphorus fluxes are among the main forms of pollution of terrestrial, freshwater, and marine ecosystems. The intensification of agriculture has been associated not only with increased use of water, but also with increased applications of synthetic nitrogen and inorganic phosphorus fertilizers. It is estimated that nitrogen and phosphorus applications per unit of cropland use rates on per unit cropland area increased by factors of eight and three in the last 50 years alone (Lu and Tian 2017). Environmental effects include the eutrophication of coastal marine ecosystems and freshwater lakes, the production of ground-level ozone and the destruction of stratospheric ozone with well understood consequences for UV-B radiation, and the loss of biodiversity in aquatic and terrestrial ecosystems (Galloway et al. 2004, Bobbink et al. 2010, Vitousek et al. 2010).

Few such effects are taken into account in the decisions of those who cause them. Most are externalities of market transactions that balance the private costs and benefits of agricultural or industrial production. In many cases, the effects are the cumulative result of millions of independent decisions. The dead zone in the Gulf of Mexico, for example, is the product of nitrogen and phosphorus applications by farmers over much of the American Midwest. Each individual farmer can legitimately claim that runoff from their land has a vanishingly small impact on the Gulf, but the cumulative effect of agricultural runoff everywhere is among the most severe threat to coastal ecosystems globally (Diaz and Rosenberg 2008).

The next four sections of this chapter consider the nature of environmental externalities—whether they are public or private, whether unidirectional or reciprocal, and the degree to which they are determined by wider environmental and socioeconomic conditions. In Section 9.6 we consider the instruments available to internalize externalities at different scales, either by confronting those whose actions harm others with the full cost of the actions, or by compensating those whose actions confer benefits on others. A final section offers a summary and conclusions. If it is possible to ensure that the users of natural resources base conservation decisions on the value of those resources to society as a whole, then by the Hotelling principle, the resources should be optimally conserved.

9.2　The nature of environmental externalities

The external effects of the resource allocation decisions people make may or may not be intended. Those who cause an external effect may have little idea that their actions potentially affect others. They may also be fully aware of what effect they are having, but care little about the consequences for others (either through indifference or because they cannot afford to). In what follows we will suppose that there is enough information to calculate the welfare effects of environmental externalities. However, we add the rider that many of the most important historical externalities were, at least initially, the product of ignorance rather than informed malicious or benign behavior. It has frequently taken science to uncover the causal pathways by which particular actions drive particular effects. John Snow's establishment of contaminated water as the source of the 1848 cholera outbreak in London is a well-known early example, but many of the environmental external effects of economic development that concern us today—greenhouse gas emissions and climate change; halocarbons and depletion of the ozone layer; the health effects of radiation, PCBs, and other substances on human health; the environmental consequences of Tributyltin—were unknown until discovered by science. Interestingly, in almost every case the immediate response of those responsible has been to deny the science, an issue we consider later in this book.

From an economic perspective externality matters because it affects both efficiency (it is said to be "Pareto relevant") and equity (some people are harmed or benefit more than others). By the Pareto criterion, one allocation of resources, A, is socially preferred to another allocation, B, if at least one individual is better off with A and no one is worse off with A relative to B. That is, an allocation is Pareto optimal if it is not possible to improve the well-being of one individual by changing that allocation without harming other individuals. Wherever an externality has consequences for well-being that are not taken into account in the allocation of resources, that allocation cannot be Pareto optimal. Society as a whole carries a cost. Whenever external costs or benefits weigh more heavily on some people than others, the cost is skewed in ways that may be inequitable.

Environmental externalities are those in which the effect of an action on others is mediated by the environment. For example, the effect of carbon emissions in one location and climatic conditions elsewhere is mediated by the general circulation system. The effect of fertilizer applications in the American Midwest on dissolved oxygen levels in the Gulf of Mexico is mediated by water flows through the Mississippi basin. The effect of land-use change on the abundance and richness of wild species is mediated by alterations in the extent, structure, and connectedness of habitat.

It is possible to identify a number of different types of environmental externalities depending on the properties of the systems linking source and sink. Externalities may be characterized as unidirectional or reciprocal depending on the direction of flow between those who are the source of the externality and those who experience the effects. Depending on the spatial and temporal spread of effects, externalities may be local and short term, at one extreme, or global and long-term at the other. They may affect only a few people or many. They may have their origin in either the production or consumption of goods and services, and on the number of people affected.

9.3 Unidirectional externalities

Consider the case where the system comprises just two industries linked through a common environment. Suppose that the net benefits of production in two industries can be described by the equations:

$$\pi_x = p_x x(K_x) - rK_x$$
$$\pi_y = p_y y(K_y, e(K_x)) - rK_y \tag{9.1}$$

where π_x, π_y denote net benefits in each industry, x, y denote outputs of each industry, K_x, K_y denote capital employed in each industry, p_x, p_y, r denote the prices of x, y, K_x, K_y, and $e(K_x)$ denotes the environmental impacts of the use of K_x. From the production functions for the two outputs, $x(K_x), y(K_y, e(K_x))$, we see that while the production of x depends only on K_x, production of y depends both on K_y and K_x. If the impact of output of K_x on output of y lies outside the market, it is said to be an externality of the production of the employment of K_x. If $\dfrac{\partial y}{\partial e}\dfrac{\partial e}{\partial K_x} > 0$ the externality is positive. An increase

in K_x increases y. If $\dfrac{\partial y}{\partial e}\dfrac{\partial e}{\partial K_x} < 0$ the externality is negative. An increase in K_x

decreases y. If we assume that $\partial y/\partial e > 0$—that output of y is increasing in our measure of environmental quality—then the direction of the effect depends on $\partial e/\partial K_x$. This will be positive if employment of K_x is environmentally beneficial and negative if environmentally damaging.

A good example of conservation-relevant externalities of this sort, already referred to, is the effect of fertilizer runoff from farms in Mississippi basin on fisheries in the Gulf of Mexico. We can use the simple fisheries model described in Chapter 4 to explore two potential pathways for the externality. Suppose, first, that the carrying capacity of the marine environment, denoted k, was directly affected by land-based activities that generate flows of nitrogen or phosphates. If output of the land-based activity at time t is denoted $x(t)$ this implies that $k = k(x)$, and the equation describing the growth of fish stocks

might take the form $\dot{y} = ry(t)\left(1 - \dfrac{y(t)}{k(x(t))}\right)$. The carrying capacity of the ma-

rine resource in this case depends on land-based activity. The effect of land-based output of $x(t)$ on fishery profits, $d\pi_Y(t)/dx(t)$, is a measure of the value of the fishery externality. If the externality is negative an increase in land-based output reduces the equilibrium size of the fish stock, and hence fish harvest (see Figure 9.1). Since carrying capacity in dead zones is close to zero, the value of the fishery externality in such dead zones would be the forgone profit of fishing activity. Of course, the existence of dead zones in many of the worlds coastal systems has impacts far beyond the loss of value added in the fishing industry, but this illustrates the problem.

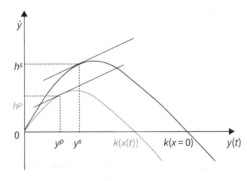

Figure 9.1 Externalities of land-based output on capture fisheries via the carrying capacity of marine ecosystems.

A second potential pathway is more direct. Suppose that land-based emissions directly increased fish mortality, so $\dot{y} = ry(t)\left(1 - \dfrac{y(t)}{k(x(t))}\right) - m\big(y(t), x(t)\big)$.

This would capture the effect of oil or chemical spills, for example, or the introduction of an infectious disease. Mortality would then depend both on the level of emissions and the density of the harvested stock, the specific form of the functions depending on the way that land based activities impact the species affected.

The effect of this on fish stocks is illustrated in Figure 9.2, the negative impact of increased mortality being shown in grey. As in the first case considered, the effect is to reduce the sustainable yield on fish stocks. The size of both harvest and stock would be affected in ways similar to those illustrated in Figure 9.1. Using the methods described in Chapter 4 to find the optimal level of harvest and stock size, we can identify the marginal cost to the fishery of the land-based activity in both of these cases. If land-based pollution affects carrying capacity this is:

$$\frac{d\pi_y}{dx(t)} = \frac{\lambda(t)ry(t)^2\, dk/dx(t)}{k^2}$$

If land-based pollution directly affects fish mortality it is:

$$\frac{d\pi_y}{dx(t)} = \lambda(t)\frac{dm}{dx(t)}$$

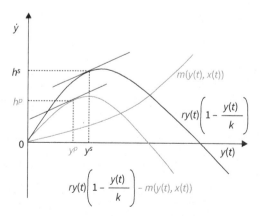

Figure 9.2 Pollution externalities affecting fish mortality alter marine stock dynamics.

where $\lambda(t)$ is the shadow value of the fish stock at time t. That is, the effect of the externality will be to reduce both harvest and stock size in the Y industry, and this will in turn affect profits in that industry.

If the external effects of K_x are not taken into account by the industry producing x, the decision problem in that industry is of the form:

$$\max_{K_x} \pi_x = p_x x(K_x) - rK_x \qquad (9.2)$$

and the first order necessary conditions for an optimum of the problem require only that $p_x \dfrac{dx}{dK_x} - r = 0$, that is, that the producer of x increase employ-

ment of K_x up to the point where its marginal cost is exactly equal to the value of its marginal physical product. This is indicated by K_x^p in Figure 9.3.

To see the effect of the externality we need to consider both producers together. Suppose that society's interests are best served by maximizing the sum of profits in each of the two industries. The social decision problem then takes the form:

$$\max_{K_x, K_y} \pi_s = p_x x(K_x) + p_y y(K_y, e(K_x)) - r(K_x + K_y) \qquad (9.3)$$

which requires that the following two conditions be satisfied:

$$p_y \frac{dy}{dK_y} - r = 0$$

$$p_x \frac{dx}{dK_x} + p_y \frac{dY}{de} \frac{de}{dK_x} - r = 0$$

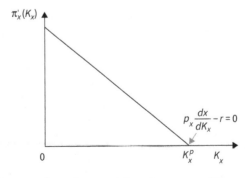

Figure 9.3 Privately optimal employment of K_x when externalities are ignored.

The term in grey is the marginal external benefit or cost of employing K_x: that is, the value of the marginal impact of employment of K_x on output of y. K_x will be employed below (above) the socially optimal level if $\dfrac{dy}{de}\dfrac{de}{dK_x} > 0(<0)$. Figure 9.4 describes the socially optimal level of employment of K_x in both cases.

If the externality is negative, that is, $de/dK_x < 0$, the difference between the privately and socially optimal level of employment of K_x is $K_x^p - K_x^s$. The socially optimal level of employment of K_x is less than the privately optimal level. Output of X will be reduced so as to equate the marginal net private benefit and marginal external cost of K_x. If the externality is positive, that is, $de/dK_x > 0$, the socially optimal level of employment of K_x is greater than the privately optimal level, and employment of K_x should be increased.

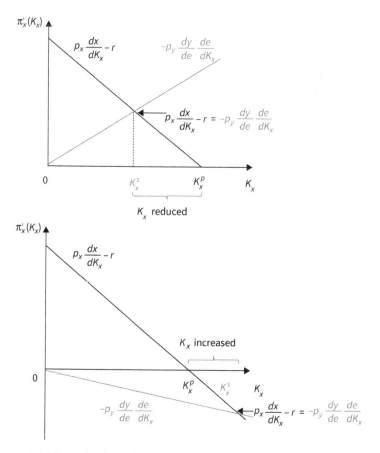

Figure 9.4 Socially optimal employment of K_x when externalities are internalized. The difference between privately and socially optimal employment of K_x where externalities are negative (upper panel) and positive (lower panel).

This example covers the simplest case—unidirectional externalities between two industries. Not surprisingly, externalities of this sort are also the easiest to resolve, particularly if the causal pathways and the consequences of actions involving external effects are known. We will consider how this may be achieved later in this chapter. Other types of environmental externality are more problematic. One example is positional externalities, in which actions by one agent or one community induces a response by others to maintain their relative position leaving everyone worse off. Another example is public externalities—externalities that are nonrival in consumption.

9.4 Positional externalities

All positional externalities involve a form of arms race (Sabin 2006). Common, albeit rather trivial examples include the progressive increase in noise at social gatherings, or the compulsion to stand at sporting events. If one person raises their voice to make themselves heard at a social gathering, all others have to follow suit. If one person stands up from their seat in a sports stadium to get a better view of the action on the field of play, those behind have to follow suit. While positional goods have been of interest to economists since the nineteenth century (Veblen 1899), the idea that their consumption involves external costs serious enough to warrant a policy response is much more recent (Hirsch 1976, Frank 1991, Frank 2005, Frank 2008). The core of the argument is that the race to the top (or to the bottom) induced by positional goods involves uncompensated and unrecoverable costs. Those whose pattern of consumption is driven by the need to avoid losing relative position end up consuming at levels that are not warranted by the marginal social cost of consumption. Environmental economists have claimed that the resulting "overconsumption" is one of the factors driving environmental degradation (Howarth 1996, Arrow et al. 2004).

Suppose that the ith community obtains utility from the absolute level of consumption of goods X_i and Y_i, and from the level of consumption of X_i relative to others. In other words, suppose that X_i is a positional good. The utility function of the ith community therefore has the form:

$$U_i = U_i\left(x_i, y_i, x_j\right) = U_i\left(x_i, y_i, f_{ij}\left(x_i, x_j\right)\right), j \neq i, j \in \{1,...,n\} \quad (9.4)$$

where $f_{ij}\left(x_i, x_j\right)$ depends on the difference in consumption of $x_j, j \neq i, j \in \{1,...,n\}$ and x_i. Since x_i is positional, growth in x_i relative to x_j would be expected to increase utility, while a decline in x_i relative to x_j would be expected to reduce utility. Suppose, further, that the ith community maximizes 9.4 through choice of x_i and y_i subject to a budget constraint of the form, $I_i = p_x x_i + p_y y_i$. Solving the problem requires that

$$\frac{\dfrac{dU_i}{dx_i} + \sum_j \dfrac{dU_i}{df_{ij}} \dfrac{df_{ij}}{dx_i}}{\dfrac{dU_i}{dy_i}} = \frac{p_y}{p_x} \tag{9.5}$$

That is, the ith community equates the marginal rate of substitution between x_i and y_i with the price ratio, taking account of both absolute and relative consumption of x_i. The positional externality in this case derives from fact that if i^{th} community changes x_i this does not only affect $f_{ij}(x_i, x_j)$, it also affects $f_{ji}(x_j, x_i)$. That is, by changing relative consumption of x_i in ways that enhance welfare in the ith community, it worsens relative consumption in all other communities. If the impact on other communities were taken into account by the ith community, the conditions for X_i to be chosen optimally would now include:

$$\frac{\dfrac{dU_i}{dX_i} + \sum_j \dfrac{dU_i}{df_{ij}} \dfrac{df_{ij}}{dx_i} + \sum_i \dfrac{\partial U_i}{\partial f_{ji}} \dfrac{\partial f_{ji}}{\partial x_i}}{\dfrac{\partial U_i}{\partial y_i}} = \frac{p_y}{p_x} \tag{9.6}$$

Since $\dfrac{df_{ji}}{dx_i} > 0, j \neq i, j \in \{1,...,n\}$, this implies that absolute levels of consumption of X_i would be lower.

The field effects involved in positional consumption are widely recognized to drive a range of "herd" behaviors—extending from fads and fashions in the choice of consumer goods to social behavioral norms. A number of these turn out to be of relevant to the conservation of environmental assets. There are surprisingly few empirical studies of positional goods, but those that do exist find that income tends to be more positional than leisure; that goods tend to be more positional than bads; that private goods tend to be more positional than public goods. The evidence is, however, far from conclusive. A rather informal US study reported in the *American Economic Review* tested responses to a range of goods across the public–private, good–bad spectrum, and found that most private goods and all private bads were not positional, and that many public goods and all public bads were not positional. The most frequently encountered positional goods were public: national defense spending, national space exploration spending, and national spending on public parks (Solnick and Hemenway 2005). The number of goods that are positional at all times and in all places is vanishingly small. Fads and fashions come and go, along with the goods and services they involve. Whether or not goods are positional depends on preferences, technology, income levels, age, and culture. Goods that are positional for people in their teens may not be positional for people in their seventies. Goods that are positional for the poor may not be positional for the rich.

So where would we expect to find positional externalities affecting conservation? First, demand for positional natural resource-based products has driven a number of species close to extinction. The demand for furs, for example, led to the extirpation of Guadalupe Fur seals from their range off the coast of California by 1825. As of now the only breeding colonies known to exist are on Guadalupe Island and the San Benito archipelago off the coast of Mexico (García-Capitanachi et al. 2017). The demand for spermaceti and ambergris similarly saw the global sperm whale population reduced by around two-thirds during the nineteenth century (Whitehead et al. 1997). In some cases, such as the Carolina parakeet, demand for its decorative feathers in the nineteenth century led to the complete extinction of the species (Ceballos et al. 2015).

What these examples all have in common is that they involved goods that conferred status on the consumer (that they were aspirational) and that they were obtained from a finite natural resource (a single species). Indeed, when Hirsch introduced the concept of positional goods he claimed that a central characteristic is that they were subject to congestion and crowding (Hirsch 1976). This has subsequently led others to claim that competition for positional goods is a zero sum game (Pagano 1999). The more that is consumed by any one person, the less is available to others. The externality in this case is the loss each person's consumption imposes on all others. Current examples include the demand for shark-fin soup on threats to sharks and shark-like rays (Dulvy et al. 2014), and the demand for status "medicines" deriving from rhino horn, tiger bone, and pangolin scales on threats to all three (Graham-Rowe 2011, Challender and MacMillan 2014).

The notion that positional goods induce competition for relative social standing suggests that status goods of natural origin may be no more than the tip of the iceberg. All actions that confer relative standing on some while causing others to lose standing are positional. Since there is a close connection between subjective well-being and relative wealth and income (McBride

2001), actions that change relative wealth and income confer a direct benefit on those whose relative standing improves and impose a direct cost on those whose relative standing deteriorates. Consider, for example, measures taken to regulate the environmental impacts of economic activities. To the extent that environmental regulations affect production costs or market access, regulators may engage in a regulatory arms race that can lead in either direction. If a jurisdiction seeks to make itself more competitive by relaxing environmental protections, for example, it can induce others to match or exceed its efforts—generating a regulatory race to the bottom (Woods 2006). Conversely, if a jurisdiction seeks to secure a market advantage by insisting on high levels of protection it can induce matching behavior through the harmonization of standards at higher levels—generating a regulatory race to the top (Prakash and Potoski 2006).

The evidence points in both directions. Where the cost of compliance with environmental regulations is high, investment tends to flow to jurisdictions with weaker environmental regulatory requirements (Konisky 2007). This in turn stimulates a regulatory race downward. However, where the cost of compliance is low, where public demand for environmental quality is high, or where regulated firms see an opportunity for limiting competition, the tendency is for jurisdictions to harmonize environmental standards at higher levels. Since some producers and many consumers benefit from higher environmental standards, there is a convergence of interest in harmonizing standards at higher levels. While there is some evidence that the level at which standards are harmonized is sensitive to economic conditions—being raised in times of prosperity and relaxed in times of hardship—standards have overall been increasing. Harmonization of environmental standards at levels consistent with those in developed countries benefits firms from those countries by limiting competition. But it also benefits consumers who experience higher levels of environmental quality (Holzinger and Sommerer 2011).

9.5 Public externalities

Public externalities, sometimes referred to as nondepletable externalities, are incidental effects of activities impacting the supply of public goods or bads. Since the underlying public goods or bads are nonexclusive and nonrival in consumption, so are the associated externalities. Emissions of greenhouse gases that are not taken into account in the decisions made by emitters, for example, involve nondepletable external costs to all those likely to be harmed by climate change. None can be excluded from the effects, and the

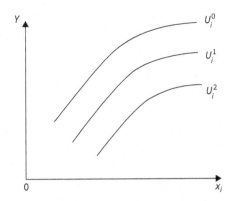

Figure 9.5 Indifference curves for a public bad, Y.

harm experienced by one person does not reduce the harm experienced by others. The description of public goods offered in Chapter 8 accordingly also applies here.

Suppose that the ith individual gains positive utility from the consumption of a bundle of goods denoted by x_i and negative utility from pollution due to the consumption of x_i, Y. That is, $U_i = U_i\left(x_i, Y(X)\right), X = \sum_j x_j$. Their indifference curves accordingly take the form given in Figure 9.5. Since the curves are upward sloping, the consumer is indifferent between combinations that involve more or less of both x_i and Y. Increased consumption of the bad can only be compensated by increased consumption of the good. The steeper the indifference curve, the less is the quantity of the good required to compensate for a unit increase in the bad, the flatter the indifference curve the more is the quantity of the good required to compensate for a unit increase in the bad. If the indifference curves flatten as consumption of x_i grows, as in Figure 9.5, marginal disutility of the bad is increasing in x_i.

If the ith individual faces the budget constraint $I_i = p_x x_i$ we can identify the indirect utility function:

$$V_i = V_i\left(p, I_i, Y(X)\right) = Max_{x_i} U_i\left(x_i, Y(X) | px_i = I, Y(X) = Y\right)$$

This is continuous, convex, decreasing in prices and increasing in income. It defines the maximum utility obtainable given $p, I_i, Y(X)$. We can use this to obtain measures of the value of a change in the quantity of the public bad. As we saw in Chapter 5, there are two potential measures of the value of a change in a nonmarketed environmental good or bad: compensating and equivalent surplus. Suppose that there is a change in the public bad associated with consumption from Y^0 to Y^1. This might, for example, be an increase in the pollution due to the consumption of a unit of x. The compensating surplus of the change would be the increase in income that would leave the individual with their original level of utility given the new, higher level of the public bad.

$$V^0\left(p, I^0, Y^0\right) = V^0\left(p, I^0 + CS, Y^1\right)$$

The equivalent surplus of the change would be the decrease in income that generates the same loss of utility as the change in the public bad:

$$V^1\left(p, I^0 - EV, Y^0\right) = V^1\left(p, I^0, Y^1\right)$$

The two measures are illustrated in Figure 9.6.

They give the change in income corresponding to a change in the public good, albeit at different levels of utility. The ratio of each measure to the change in the public good is therefore a discrete approximation to the slope of the indifference curves associated with each level of utility, that is:

$$CS\left(I^0, \Delta Y, V^0\right)\big/\Delta Y = \frac{\Delta I}{\Delta Y} \approx p\frac{dx}{dy}\bigg|_{V=V^0}, ES\left(I^0, \Delta Y, V^1\right)\big/\Delta Y = \frac{\Delta I}{\Delta Y} \approx p\frac{dx}{dy}\bigg|_{V=V^1}$$

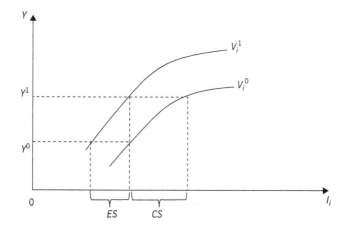

Figure 9.6 Compensating and equivalent surplus for public bads.
ES, CS shows the equivalent and compensating surplus associated with an increase in Y from Y^0 to Y^1.

Left to themselves the ith individual will equate the marginal benefits and costs of the consumption of x. That is, if the problem faced by the ith individual is

$$Max_{x_i} U_i(x_i, Y(X))$$
$$s.t$$
$$I_i = px_i + cy_i(x_i)$$

where c denotes the "price" of the public bad. From the Lagrangian function

$$L = U_i(x_i, Y(X)) + \lambda(I_i - px_i - cY)$$

the first order necessary conditions imply that

$$\frac{p}{c} = \frac{dU_i/dx_i + (dY/dy_i)(dy_i/dx_i)}{(dU_i/dY)(dY/dy_j)}$$

The ith individual should increase consumption of x_i up to the point where the ratio of the price of the marketed consumer good to the consumer surplus is equal to the marginal rate of substitution of x_i net of the negative effects of y_i. They will not, however, take account of the effects of their actions on others. If the problem is to maximize the utility of all individuals in society

$$Max_X \sum_i U_i(x_i, Y(X))$$

then the first order necessary conditions for the ith of n individuals require that

$$\frac{p}{c} = \frac{(dU_i/dx_i) + (dY/dy_i)(dy_i/dx_i) + \sum_j (dU_i/dY)(dY/dy_i)(dy_i/dx_i)}{(dU_i/dY)(dY/dy_j)} \tag{9.7}$$

That is, individuals should increase their consumption of x up to the point where the ratio of the price of the marketed consumer good to the consumer surplus of the public bad is equal to the marginal rate of substitution of x, net of the negative effects of the associated public bad on themselves and all other consumers. The public externality, given in grey in (9.7), is the harm to people everywhere caused by consumption by the ith individual.

There is a wide range of public externalities relevant to the conservation of environmental resources. In fact, any public externality that changes the value of environmental stocks falls into this category. The climatic impact of carbon, methane, and nitrous oxide emissions is an example. Changes in sea levels, in air, water, or soil temperature, or in precipitation all affect provision of ecosystem services, and hence the value of the underlying environmental assets. Actions that alter species abundance and richness similarly affect the provision of ecosystem services. In some cases, the impact is quite localized and short term. Actions that lead to the increasing abundance of disease vectors, for example, can give rise to localized disease outbreaks. In other cases, the impact is much more widespread, and plays out over a much longer period. Actions that reduce the genetic diversity of valued species—crops and their wild relatives or livestock strains, for example—limit the capacity to develop species adapted to future changes in environmental conditions. By altering the evolutionary potential of agroecosystems, such actions change the future flow of services from those systems.

We have already identified the actions that are most often implicated in changes in species richness and abundance. They include the conversion of wild lands to agricultural production, and the fragmentation of wild habitat due to infrastructural development—the construction of roads, railways, power lines, and pipelines. They include the diversion of water resources to human use, and emissions to soil, air, and water. They include the hunting or gathering of target species, as well as collateral damage to nontarget species. In all cases, actions of this kind have incidental effects on species richness and abundance that alter the flow of benefits to humans. If those effects are neither rival, nor exclusive the externality is public.

9.6 Aligning private and social value

There are a number of instruments available to internalize both private and public externalities. These include the assignment of rights (the Coase theorem); the imposition of environmental taxes, user charges, access fees, taxes and royalties; subsidies for beneficial land use and payments for ecosystem services; regulatory controls or zoning restrictions supported by penalties for noncompliance; tradable development rights, voluntary agreements, easements, and covenants. These instruments all suppose that there is a sovereign authority with the power to allocate property rights, to impose taxes or to grant subsidies, to determine what activities are allowable in particular places through zoning or land-use restrictions, to regulate the activities allowed, and to penalize those who do not comply with regulations. In other words, all of these instruments suppose the existence of a sovereign nation-state. The options available when there is no sovereign authority are discussed later.

We begin with the simplest case: unidirectional private externalities. We suppose that there are two communities affected by a forested watershed, each community being associated with an activity that generates a different output. The upstream community, associated with the production of good x, a forest product, secures that product by clear-cutting the forest. The downstream community, associated with the production of good y, an agricultural product say, suffers a loss in output due to the resulting increase in, for example, flooding or the siltation of check dams.

The first instrument for solving such problems was proposed in a rightly famous paper published in 1960 by Ronald Coase. Coase observed that the then-standard approach to the management of environmental externalities asked: If one person inflicts harm on another, how can that person be restrained? He argued that this is the wrong question, since all externalities are essentially reciprocal. In our example, while the downstream community may be harmed by the activities of the upstream community, the upstream community would also be harmed by any restriction on its activities. The question should really be whether the upstream community should be allowed to inflict harm on the downstream community, or the downstream community should be allowed to inflict harm on the upstream community. He argued that the aim should be to avoid the more serious harm (Coase 1960).

The Coase theorem states that if there are well-defined property rights in some environmental effect, if there are no transaction costs, and if wealth effects are negligible, then the outcome of bargaining between the interested parties will be Pareto optimal regardless of the distribution of those rights. Translated, it means that in certain circumstances it is possible to internalize external effects by assigning rights to the effect, and that the outcome will be efficient regardless of who receives the rights (Figure 9.7).

The various conditions attached to the proposition imply that if transaction costs are too high to motivate the establishment of a market, it may be optimal not to internalize the external effect. Similarly, if the assignment of property rights makes some people much wealthier or poorer than they were before, it may also be better to not to assign rights. Since the allocation of rights always increases the wealth of the rights-holder (just as the assignment of liability always reduces the wealth of those held to be liable), the decision to allocate rights one way or the other is generally made on political grounds. Perceptions of fairness tend to favor both the first-in-time principle and the polluter-pays

Case 1: The downstream community has a right to clean water flows

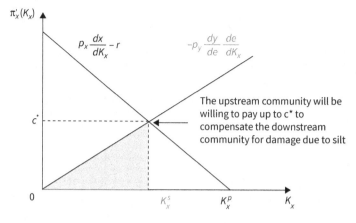

$\pi'_x(K_x)$

$p_x \dfrac{dx}{dK_x} - r$

$-p_y \dfrac{dy}{de}\dfrac{de}{dK_x}$

The upstream community will be willing to pay up to c* to compensate the downstream community for damage due to silt

c^*

0

K_x^s K_x^p K_x

Case 2: The upstream community has the right to cause downstream siltation

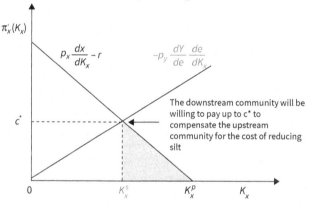

$\pi'_x(K_x)$

$p_x \dfrac{dx}{dK_x} - r$

$-p_y \dfrac{dY}{de}\dfrac{de}{dK_x}$

The downstream community will be willing to pay up to c* to compensate the upstream community for the cost of reducing silt

c^*

0

K_x^s K_x^p K_x

Figure 9.7 The efficiency of property-rights based solutions to externalities. Showing that the efficiency of the solution does not depend on who receives the rights.

principle. Rights go to those who were there first (grandfathering) and against those whose actions are the source of the externality.

A second set of instruments, economic incentives, comprises Pigovian taxes, user charges or fees, and subsidies and payments for ecosystem services. Taxes, charges, and fees are intended to confront those who are the source of negative externalities with the costs they impose on others. They have their origin in work by the economist Arthur Pigou, who proposed taxing/subsidizing private activities that were excessive/insufficient from a social perspective (Pigou 1912, Pigou 1920). In Figure 9.8, taxes equal to the marginal external cost caused by the harmful input K_x reduce employment of that input from the privately optimal level K_x^p to the socially optimal level K_x^s. Moreover,

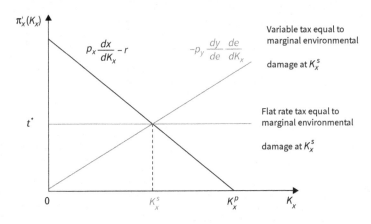

Figure 9.8 Taxation of environmentally damaging externalities.
Taxation of harmful activities at the marginal environmental damage cost can induce the socially optimal employment of K_x.

this is independent of the form of the tax—whether it is a flat or variable rate. Examples include taxes on fossil fuels that are a source of carbon emissions, or property taxes that vary with the external costs of land use.

Subsidies and payments for ecosystem services are intended to compensate those who are the source of positive externalities for the benefits they confer on others. While subsidies on inputs are still quite widespread, payments for ecosystem services have been the preferred option in recent years. One of the oldest examples of such payments are the agri-environment schemes introduced in both Europe and the United States in the 1980s. In the United States, the Conservation Reserve Program (CRP) makes payments to farmers enrolled in the program for activities that deliver one or more environmental benefits, including the control of soil erosion, enhancement of water quality, and the provision of habitat. Annual payments in the order of $2 billion encourage farmers to adopt land uses that provide off-site benefits to others. The CRP pollinator program, for example, requires farmers to develop a conservation plan that sets aside and seeds land suitable as pollinator habitat, in exchange for 10 years of annual rental payments, a payment covering 50% of the eligible costs of establishing the pollinator practice, a sign-up incentive payment of $150, and a 50% cost-share payment for mid-contract management.

Figure 9.9 shows how payments equal to the marginal external benefits associated with the employment of K_x (in grey) increase employment of that input from the privately optimal level K_x^p to the socially optimal level K_x^s.

A third set of instruments, sometimes referred to as "command and control," depend on the establishment of legal restrictions or regulations. As with

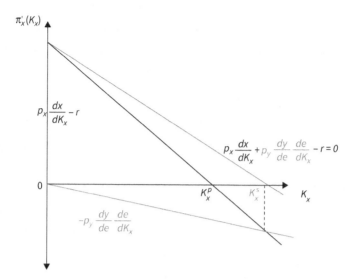

Figure 9.9 Inducing the socially optimal employment of resources with positive external effects.

Payments at the marginal external benefits associated with the employment of K_x increase employment of that input to the socially optimal level.

economic incentives, such instruments also use prices to change behavior. The only difference is that the price takes the form of a penalty for noncompliance with the regulation. One implication of this is that the price is discontinuous around a set of limits imposed by law. Resource users pay nothing up to the legal limit, but pay the penalty beyond the limit. If we take our example of a unidirectional externality, regulations may prohibit activity beyond the socially optimal level on penalty of a fine equal to the marginal external damage cost plus a factor to allow for the probability of detection and successful prosecution. Figure 9.10 illustrates the role of penalties for non compliance with a regulation in limiting employment of K_x to the socially optimal level, K_x^s.

Finally, it is worth underlining the fact that significant effort has been made around the world to apply such policies to some of the more pressing environmental problems. Examples are given in Chapter 13. As an illustration of the rate at which they are being applied consider just one: the use of payments for ecosystem services to address the externalities of land use in watersheds. The poster child for watershed payment for ecosystem services schemes, the Catskills-Delaware watershed scheme in New York, is discussed elsewhere in the book. A 2011 report by the President's Council of Advisors on Science and Technology commended the use of such instruments as an important element in the delivery of environmental public goods (Presidents Council of Advisors on Science and Technology 2011). A recent global study of the

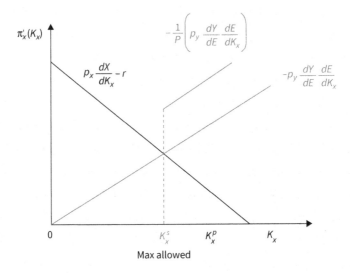

Figure 9.10 Penalties for noncompliance with a regulatory restriction.

Penalties can reduce employment of K_x to the socially optimal level. The penalty for noncompliance should exceed damage cost by 1/P, where P is the probability of detection and successful prosecution.

development payments for ecosystem services schemes in watersheds in the years since noted a rapid expansion in both the number of programs and the size of the market involved (Table 9.1).

Table 9.1 Watershed payments for ecosystem services programs, 2005–2015.

PES mechanism (category)	Definition	Example	Market size 2009–2015	Program 2005–2015	Number of countries
Subsidy watershed PES (government-financed)	Public finance rewards land managers for enhancing or protecting ecosystem services. The funders do not directly benefit from the management activities.	Chinese government's Sloping Lands Conversion Program pays farmers to stop cultivating on steep slopes. Roughly 53 million farmers receive compensation to improve water quality and flood control.	$6.3 billion– $23.7 billion (US$12.98 billion in China)	17–139, with 69 in China	39

Table 9.1 *Continued*

PES mechanism (category)	Definition	Example	Market size 2009–2015	Program 2005–2015	Number of countries
Collective action watershed PES (user- and government-financed)	An institution pools resources from multiple water users (private parties, NGOs, government bodies) to pay upstream landowners for management actions that provide water quality and other benefits.	Quito's Water Conservation Fund relies on a 1% surcharge on monthly water bills and monies from local electrical utility and beer company directed to finance projects protecting forests and grasslands in the watershed.	US$402 million– US$564 million	16–86	22
Bilateral watershed PES (user- and government-financed)	A single water user compensates one or more parties for activities that deliver hydrological benefits to the payer or serves to mitigate impacts from their activities.	In the 1990s, New York City raised a bond to pay for land-use changes in the Catskills and Delaware watersheds to ensure the quality of their drinking water at much lower cost than installing a treatment plant.	US$13 million– US$93 million	19–111	27
Instream buybacks (user- and government-financed)	Water rights are purchased or leased from historic rights-holders and retired, which leaves the water in-stream to deliver water-quality benefits and ensure healthy ecological flows.	In Australia, the Restoring the Balance programme committed over $3 billion over a ten-year period to purchase water entitlements from farmers to ensure instream flows in the Murray–Darling Basin.	US$25 million– US$60.7 million	15–20, with 18 in the United States	3

Continued

Table 9.1 *Continued*

PES mechanism (category)	Definition	Example	Market size 2009–2015	Program 2005–2015	Number of countries
Quality trading and offsets (compliance)	Water service providers comply with regulations by paying landowners for activities that improve a measure of water quality (such as nutrients, salinity or temperature) in exchange for credits.	In the Hunter River Salinity Trading Scheme, salt credits are traded among mines and power stations based on river conditions to control the salinity.	US$8.3 million– US$22.2 million	10–31, with 29 in the United States	3

Source: (Salzman et al. 2018).

9.7 Summary and conclusions

This chapter explored the second of the two main reasons why the asset values needed to inform a Hotelling conservation strategy might be compromised. Chapter 8 considered the public good nature of many such assets. In this chapter we considered the effect of externality. Externalities are a major reason why the private and social value of environmental assets might differ, and therefore why privately and socially optimal levels of asset conservation might diverge. If environmental assets are privately owned or managed, and if the private value of those assets is expected to grow at less than the social value, then too little of the asset will be conserved. In this chapter we considered the nature of environmental externalities and how they affect conservation decisions. We distinguished between types of externality in terms of the direction of effects (whether they are unidirectional or reciprocal), the degree to which effects are public or private (whether they are nonexclusive and/or nonrival in consumption), and the existence of positive feedbacks (whether they are positional).

In each case, we showed how the under- or overvaluation of goods and services whose production or consumption involves positive or negative external effects leads to their over- or underuse. Where those goods and services depend on a set of underlying environmental assets it will also lead to under- or overconservation of those assets. Land that incidentally provides habitat for beneficial species will be underconserved if no account is taken of the benefits offered by those species. Conversely, land that incidentally provides habitat for pest species will be overconserved if no account is taken of the costs imposed by those species.

We then considered the options for aligning the private and social value of goods and services affected by externalities, thereby internalizing those externalities. Options include an array of economic instruments—taxes, subsidies, payments for ecosystem services, and so on. We saw how such instruments could be used to confront decision-makers whose actions harm others with the cost of their actions, and to compensate decision-makers whose actions benefits others.

The final part of this book discusses conservation policies at different spatial and temporal scales—inside and outside of protected areas, within and beyond national jurisdictions, short- and long-term. Many of these policies, and the instruments they employ, address the kind of market failures associated with public goods and externalities described here. Although conservationists remain skeptical about market-like instruments, the principles discussed in this chapter are increasingly being applied to policies designed to change behaviors that threaten the natural environment. Moreover, this is occurring in developing as well as developed countries.

The effectiveness of instruments varies with the socioeconomic conditions in which they are applied. The degree to which people have secure land tenure, for example, affects the scope for using incentives to invest in land improvements. Whether landholders are in poverty limits the scope for using taxes or charges to internalize the external costs of land use. Willingness to pay is always constrained by ability to pay. Before we turn to conservation policies in Part IV, therefore, Chapter 10 considers the problem of poverty, and the way in which poverty affects the value of environmental assets.

References

Arrow, K., P. Dasgupta, L. Goulder, G. Daily, P. Ehrlich, G. Heal, S. Levin, K.-G. Mäler, S. Schneider, D. Starrett, and B. Walker. 2004. Are we consuming too much? Journal of Economic Perspectives 18:147–172.

Bobbink, R., K. Hicks, J. Galloway, T. Spranger, R. Alkemade, M. Ashmore, M. Bustamante, S. Cinderby, E. Davidson, F. Dentener, B. Emmett, J. W. Erisman, M. Fenn, F. Gilliam, A. Nordin, L. Pardo, and W. De Vries. 2010. Global assessment of nitrogen deposition effects on terrestrial plant diversity: a synthesis. Ecological Applications 20:30–59.

Ceballos, G., A. H. Ehrlich, and P. R. Ehrlich. 2015. The annihilation of nature: human extinction of birds and mammals. Johns Hopkins University Press, Baltimore.

Challender, D. W., and D. C. MacMillan. 2014. Poaching is more than an enforcement problem. Conservation Letters 7:484–494.

Coase, R. 1960. The problem of social cost. Journal of Law and Economics 3:1–44.

Costello, C., M. Springborn, C. McAusland, and A. Solow. 2007. Unintended biological invasions: does risk vary by trading partner? Journal of Environmental Economics and Management 54:262–276.

Dalmazzone, S. 2000. Economic factors affecting vulnerability to biological invasions. Pages 17–30 in C. Perrings, M. Williamson, and S. Dalmazzone, editors. The economics of biological invasions. Edward Elgar, Cheltenham.

Diaz, R. J., and R. Rosenberg. 2008. Spreading dead zones and consequences for marine ecosystems. Science 321:926–929.

Dulvy, N. K., S. L. Fowler, J. A. Musick, R. D. Cavanagh, P. M. Kyne, L. R. Harrison, J. K. Carlson, L. N. K. Davidson, S. V. Fordham, M. P. Francis, C. M. Pollock, C. A. Simpfendorfer, G. H. Burgess, K. E. Carpenter, L. J. V. Compagno, D. A. Ebert, C. Gibson, M. R. Heupel, S. R. Livingstone, J. C. Sanciangco, J. D. Stevens, S. Valenti, and W. T. White. 2014. Extinction risk and conservation of the world's sharks and rays. eLife 3:e00590.

Frank, R. H. 1991. Positional externalities: strategy and choice. The MIT Press, Cambridge, MA.

Frank, R. H. 2005. Positional externalities cause large and preventable welfare losses. American Economic Review 95:137–141.

Frank, R. H. 2008. Should public policy respond to positional externalities? Journal of Public Economics 92:1777–1786.

Galloway, J. N., F. J. Dentener, D. G. Capone, E. W. Boyer, R. W. Howarth, S. P. Seitzinger, G. P. Asner, C. Cleveland, P. A. Green, E. Holland, D. M. Karl, A. Michaels, J. H. Porter, A. Townsend, and C. Vorosmarty. 2004. Nitrogen cycles: past, present, and future. Biogeochemistry 70:153–226.

García-Capitanachi, B., Y. Schramm, and G. Heckel. 2017. Population fluctuations of guadalupe fur seals (arctocephalus philippii townsendi) between the San Benito Islands and Guadalupe Island, Mexico, during 2009 and 2010. Aquatic Mammals 43:492–500.

Graham-Rowe, D. 2011. Endangered and in demand. Nature 480:S101.

Gurevitch, J., and D. K. Padilla. 2004. Are invasive species a major cause of extinctions? Trends in Ecology and Evolution 19:470–474.

Hirsch, F. 1976. Social limits to growth. Harvard University Press, Cambridge, MA.

Holzinger, K., and T. Sommerer. 2011. "Race to the bottom" or "race to Brussels"? environmental competition in Europe. JCMS: Journal of Common Market Studies 49:315–339.

Howarth, R. B. 1996. Status effects and environmental externalities. Ecological Economics 16:25–34.

Konisky, D. M. 2007. Regulatory competition and environmental enforcement: is there a race to the bottom? American Journal of Political Science 51:853–872.

Lu, C. C., and H. Tian. 2017. Global nitrogen and phosphorus fertilizer use for agriculture production in the past half century: shifted hot spots and nutrient imbalance. Earth System Science Data 9:181.

Mcbride, M. 2001. Relative-income effects on subjective well-being in the cross-section. Journal of Economic Behavior and Organization 45:251–278.

Pagano, U. 1999. Is power an economic good? notes on social scarcity and the economics of positional goods. Pages 116–145 in S. Bowles, M. Franzini, and U. Pagano, editors. The politics and the economics of power. Routledge, London.

Perrings, C., H. A. Mooney, and M. Williamson. 2010. The problem of biological invasions. Pages 1–18 in C. Perrings, H. A. Mooney, and M. Williamson, editors. Globalization and bioinvasions: ecology, economics, management and policy. Oxford University Press, Oxford.

Pigou, A. C. 1912. Wealth and welfare. Macmillan, London.

Pigou, A. C. 1920. The Economics of welfare. Macmillan, London.

Prakash, A., and M. Potoski. 2006. Racing to the bottom? trade, environmental governance, and ISO 14001. American Journal of Political Science 50:350–364.

Presidents Council of Advisors on Science and Technology. 2011. Sustaining environmental capital: protecting society and the economy. Executive Office of the President, Washington, DC.

Sabin, M. 2006. Antitrust and positional arms race. Harvard Journal of Law and Public Policy 30:1023.

Salzman, J., G. Bennett, N. Carroll, A. Goldstein, and M. Jenkins. 2018. The global status and trends of payments for ecosystem services. Nature Sustainability 1:136.

Solnick, S. J., and D. Hemenway. 2005. Are positional concerns stronger in some domains than in others? American Economic Review 95:147–151.

United Nations World Water Assessment Programme. 2012. The United Nations world water development report 4: managing water under uncertainty and risk. UNESCO, Paris.

United Nations World Water Assessment Programme. 2015. The United Nations world water development report 2015: water for a sustainable world. UNESCO, Paris.

Veblen, T. 1899. The theory of the leisure class: an economic study in the evolution of institutions. Macmillan, London.

Vitousek, P. M., S. Porder, B. Z. Houlton, and O. A. Chadwick. 2010. Terrestrial phosphorus limitation: mechanisms, implications, and nitrogen–phosphorus interactions. Ecological Applications 20:5–15.

Whitehead, H., J. Christal, and S. Dufault. 1997. Past and distant whaling and the rapid decline of sperm whales off the Galápagos Islands. Conservation Biology 11:1387–1396.

Woods, N. D. 2006. Interstate competition and environmental regulation: a test of the race-to-the-bottom thesis. Social Science Quarterly 87:174–189.

10
Poverty, Value, and Conservation

> We do not wish to impoverish the environment any further and yet we cannot for a moment forget the grim poverty of large numbers of people. Are not poverty and need the greatest polluters? For instance, unless we are in a position to provide employment and purchasing power for the daily necessities of the tribal people and those who live in or around our jungles, we cannot prevent them from combing the forest for food and livelihood; from poaching and from despoiling the vegetation. When they themselves feel deprived, how can we urge the preservation of animals? How can we speak to those who live in villages and in slums about keeping the oceans, the rivers and the air clean when their own lives are contaminated at the source? The environment cannot be improved in conditions of poverty.
>
> —Indira Gandhi, Speech to the Stockholm Conference, 1972

10.1 Introduction

We have seen that peoples' willingness to pay for goods and services is always constrained by the resources available to them. Their expenditures are always limited by their budget. We have also seen that the income and wealth effects of changes in prices, taxes, and subsidies have a potentially significant impact on the use made of natural resources. In fact, income and wealth effects frequently dominate the land-use choices that people—especially poor people—make in response to changes in market conditions. The conservation decisions that poor people might make, applying the Hotelling principle to specific resources, can look very different from the conservation decisions that rich people might make about the same set of resources.

This chapter considers the relation between conservation, income, and wealth in more detail. To fix ideas, we take a particular conservation problem—the conservation of biodiversity. We identify the points at issue in the large literature on the relation between biodiversity loss and poverty. We

Conservation. Charles Perrings and Ann Kinzig, Oxford University Press (2021). © Oxford University Press.
DOI: 10.1093/oso/9780190613600.003.0010

consider when poverty alleviation and biodiversity conservation may be mutually consistent goals, and when not.

The stylized facts that lie behind many of the arguments for linking biodiversity conservation and poverty alleviation are the following. First, the highest rates of habitat loss recorded over the last five decades have been in the tropics (Millennium Ecosystem Assessment 2005). Second, there is a latitudinal gradient in species richness. Species richness is highest in the tropics, and declines along a gradient toward the poles, as does net primary productivity (Davies and Buckley 2011, Gillman et al. 2015). Third, the geographical distribution of income follows a broadly similar pattern. Most low-income and lower-middle-income countries are in the tropics, and most upper-middle and high-income countries are in the temperate regions. In other words, the regions where habitat is being lost at the greatest rate are also the regions of greatest species richness, and the regions where poverty is most widespread (Sachs et al. 2009) (Figure 10.1).

The Millennium Ecosystem Assessment concluded that the main driver of the process is the extensive growth of agriculture in the tropics, caused by population-driven demand for foods, fuels and fibers in poor countries (Millennium Ecosystem Assessment 2005). Currently, around 67% of the population in low-income countries is found in rural areas, compared to 47% in middle-income countries, and 19% in high-income countries. Rural

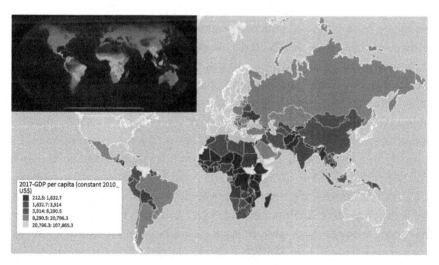

Figure 10.1 The geographical distribution of species richness (inset) and per capita GDP. Lighter areas show higher biodiversity in the inset. Darker areas show higher incidence of poverty in the main map. Most low-income and lower-middle-income countries are in areas of high biodiversity. Sources: Mannion et al. (2014), World Bank (2018).

population growth rates are falling in most low-income countries but are still increasing in some of the poorest countries (for example, Guinea-Bissau and Uganda) (World Bank 2020). Since there are few alternatives to agriculture in the poorest countries, and few options for investing in productivity-enhancing agricultural technologies, it has been argued that increasing farm income necessitates clearing and planting more land (Barrett 2013).

This is not to say that urbanization has no consequences for biodiversity. A study of the impact of urbanization on threatened species found that cities now cover more than a third of the land area in 29 ecoregions supporting 213 endemic terrestrial vertebrate species, and that 8% of terrestrial vertebrate species on the IUCN Red List are at risk because of urbanization—mostly in low-income countries (McDonald et al. 2008). Nonetheless, most projections of future habitat loss in low-income countries have been largely driven by projections of the growth of agricultural lands. At the turn of the millennium, one study projected an overall increase in agricultural land of around 18% in the first half of this century, equivalent to around one third of remaining tropical and temperate forests, savannahs, and grasslands (Tilman et al. 2001). It is argued that the extensive growth of agriculture—the expansion of agricultural lands—will directly lead to the loss of biodiversity, because less land can house fewer species according to the ecological theory known as the species area curve (Sachs et al. 2009).

The evidence provides some support for this in the case of mammals and, to a lesser extent, birds—but not in the case of plants. A study of the relation between per capita gross domestic product (GDP), land conversion, and the number of threatened IUCN Red List species in three taxonomic groups—mammals, plants, and birds—found that the relation not only differed across species groups but was sensitive to the time scale over which land conversion occurs. An increase in land area committed to agriculture was associated with an increase in the number of threatened species only on relatively short time scales. Moreover, the short-run trade-off between land conversion and biodiversity loss was found to be much stronger for mammals and birds than for plants (Perrings and Halkos 2015).

Of course land-use change may have legacy effects—what is referred to as the "extinction debt" (Tilman et al. 1994). Land-use change can drive losses that occur many decades later. It has, for example, been found that biodiversity loss in European grasslands is better explained by past than present habitat change (Krauss et al. 2010). Moreover, this is frequently sensitive to the technology applied. Agricultural intensification—the growth that derives from productivity improvements on existing agricultural lands, rather than new clearing—has the potential to reduce the amount of habitat converted

(Foley et al. 2011). In developed countries, all productivity increase in the last 50 years has come from intensification. In fact, land in agriculture declined by 6% between 1961 and 2005. In developing countries, by contrast, the growth in agricultural output in that period was due as much to growth in agricultural land (new clearing) as to productivity growth (Fuglie 2008). Both extensification and intensification have legacy effects, the first driven by habitat loss, the second by the cumulative effects of pesticides and herbicides (Dudley et al. 2017). Just as DDT applications from the 1940s to the 1960s had long-lasting negative impacts on insects, so current applications of systemic fipronil and neonicotinoid insecticides, both persistent and potent neurotoxins, are having widespread impacts on a range of species and environments (Van der Sluijs et al. 2015).

The relation between biodiversity loss and land-use change in the poorest countries accordingly centers on the external effects of farmer's decisions—and especially on decisions leading to the expansion of agricultural lands. The current consensus is that addressing the root causes of biodiversity loss and poverty can generate complementary gains in both areas. By reducing population pressure in poor regions, for example, it is argued that the threat to wild species will also be reduced (Sachs et al. 2009). But those "win-wins" may not be universal.

To get a sense of the complex relation between poverty, the value of natural resources, and conservation this chapter addresses three dimensions of the problem. The first is the role of income in the demand for natural resources. The second is the empirical relation between income and biodiversity conservation. The third brings us back to the Hotelling principle. It is the link between wealth, property rights, and the incentive to conserve. A final section offer a summary and conclusions.

10.2 Income effects and poverty

As we have already seen, any change in the price of a good or service has two effects on the purchases made by consumers: a substitution effect and an income effect. The substitution effect measures the change in demand for the good due to a change in its price relative to the price of other goods or services. The income effect measures the change in demand for the good due to the effect of the price change on the real income of the consumer. Income effects may change demand either in the same direction as substitution effects, or in the opposite direction. In some cases (e.g., the case of Giffen goods) perverse income effects can dominate substitution effects.

In general, the income effects of a price change are larger the greater the proportion of the consumer's income is spent on the affected good or service. It turns out that the proportion of income spent on individual goods and services is itself highly sensitive to the level of income. In the nineteenth century, the statistician Ernst Engel observed that the proportion of their income that people spent on food declined as incomes rose. The same relation has since been observed in every society for which we have data, and has come to be known as Engel's law. Since the poor also consume a less diverse basket of goods and services than the rich (Jackson 1984), it follows that a change in the price of any of the goods and services in that basket has a bigger effect on the real incomes of the poor than of the rich, and so has a stronger effect on demand.

The quantity of any one good or service consumed as income increases is described by an Engel curve. Figure 10.2 depicts Engel curves for three different types of commodity, y. For normal goods and services consumption of the commodity increases as income increases, but at a decreasing rate. The income elasticity of demand for such commodities is positive, but less than one. For luxury goods and services, consumption of the commodity increases at an increasing rate as income rises, implying that the income elasticity of demand for such commodities is positive and greater than one. For inferior goods, on the other hand, consumption of the commodity decreases as income increases, implying that the income elasticity of demand for such commodities is negative. An increase in the price of an inferior good, by reducing the real income of the consumer, is associated with an increase (not a decrease) in the consumption of the good. A simple example might be the allocation of a fixed income between alternative protein sources—low-priced lentils and high-priced chicken, say. Suppose lentils were regarded as inferior to chicken. A rise in the price of lentils, by increasing the cost of protein, could

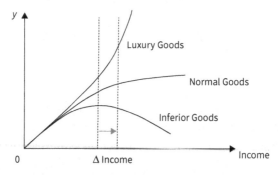

Figure 10.2 Engel curves for normal, luxury, and inferior goods and services.

induce the household to spend less of the budget on chicken, and more of the budget on lentils.

There is long-standing evidence that the price responsiveness of the poor is, for all these reasons, much greater than the price responsiveness of the rich. For example, a 1980s study of the responsiveness of poor households to an increase in the price of basic foods found the price elasticity of demand for rice of the poorest 10% of the population to be 80% higher than the average price elasticity of demand (Alderman 1986). The real income of the poor is more sensitive to fluctuations in the price of basic goods and services, and the response of the poor to price fluctuations is correspondingly stronger.

Consider, though, the relation between poverty and the demand for inferior as opposed to normal or luxury goods and services illustrated in Figure 10.3. In the case of normal or luxury goods and services, a price, tax, user fee, or access charge set at some level would be expected to induce a larger reduction in demand in low-income than in middle- or high-income countries.

One immediate implication of this is that economic instruments may be a particularly effective way of inducing a change in behavior in low-income countries. Notice, though, that if the goods and services concerned are inferior, the net impact of such economic instruments on demand may be perverse. If people access natural forest resources because they are the least costly source of food, fuels, or fibers, for example, an increase in the cost of access can potentially lead to more, not less, pressure on the resource. Suppose that a low-income consumer combines two goods (or two bundles

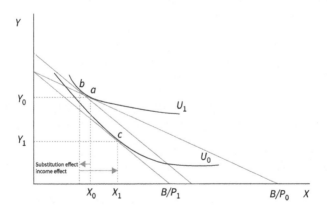

Figure 10.3 Inferior goods.

The income effects associated with an increase in the price of inferior goods can lead to an increase in demand, despite negative substitution effects. An increase in price from P_0 to P_1 is associated with an increase in the quantity consumed from X_0 to X_1.

of goods and services), one normal and one inferior. Suppose, further, that the price of the inferior good (or bundle of goods and services) increases relative to the price of the normal good. Ordinarily this would induce an increase in consumption of the normal good, and a reduction in consumption of the inferior good. But if the household is severely budget constrained, the consumption of the inferior good could rise. Figure 10.3 shows how an increase in the price of good X from P_0 to P_1 can lead to an increase in the quantity consumed from X_0 to X_1

The most frequently cited example of an inferior good is potato peels, but any good that is the least costly of a set of substitutes might induce a similar response. It is highly unlikely, for example, that biodiversity conservation would fall into this category. Studies of the income elasticity of demand for biodiversity conservation expressed in terms of existence values show it to be a normal good. Specifically, a meta-analysis of 145 willingness to pay estimates for biodiversity conservation, obtained from 46 contingent valuation studies, found that the demand for conservation was increasing in income, but also that the income elasticity of willingness to pay was less than one (Jacobsen and Hanley 2009).

A natural resource accessed by the poor, such as a forest product that is the least costly among a number of substitutes might, on the other hand, have the characteristics of inferior goods. An example would be firewood collection relative to kerosene purchase. An increase in the cost of firewood collection could, by reducing the real income of a consumer, increase consumption of firewood and reduce consumption of kerosene. There are very few studies of inferior goods, especially nonmarketed environmental goods, but all are associated with consumers at the bottom end of the income scale choosing among options that are differentiated by quality.

10.3 Poverty-population-environment

Now consider the demand for nonmarketed environmental goods and services, and the underlying environmental assets, by the rural poor. There is a widespread and long-standing perception that one of the main drivers of environmental change is population-induced growth in demand for land and other environmental resources (Ehrlich and Holdren 1971). There is an equally widespread and long-standing perception that population growth and poverty are closely linked (De Janvry and Garcia 1988). We have, for example, already seen that while rural population growth rates are generally declining, they are still increasing in some of the poorest countries.

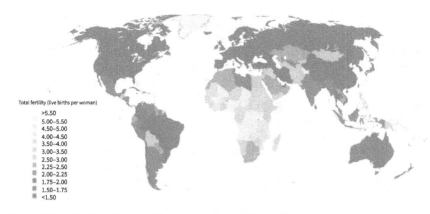

Total fertility (live births per woman)
>5.50
5.00–5.50
4.50–5.00
4.00–4.50
3.50–4.00
3.00–3.50
2.50–3.00
2.25–2.50
2.00–2.25
1.75–2.00
1.50–1.75
<1.50

Figure 10.4 Total fertility, medium projection, 2020–2025.
Source: United Nations Department of Economic and Social Affairs (2018a).

Globally, fertility rates are highest in the poorest countries. In 2015, fertility rates in the 47 least developed countries were 4.3 births per woman, more than twice the replacement rate. By 2030 the population in those countries is expected to increase by around a third. By 2050 it is expected to double (Figure 10.4) (United Nations Department of Economic and Social Affairs 2018a). That is, the same kind of latitudinal gradient that we see in species richness and per capita GDP shows up in human population growth rates.

One explanation is offered by the demographic transition hypothesis (Caldwell 1976), which built on observations by the demographer Warren Thompson that decreases in birth rates typically followed decreases in death rates, but only with a lag (Thompson 1929). In the first phase of the demographic transition, birth and death rates are argued to be high and variable, but in balance, implying stable population levels. In the second phase, death rates fall but birth rates remain high. In the third phase, birth rates fall and stabilize at replacement rates, leading to a fourth phase in which total population is once again stable (Figure 10.5).

It is argued that different countries are generally at different stages in the demographic transition. The critical factor in the second phase of the transition is the development of public health programs that have targeted the water-borne, food-borne and vector-borne diseases most implicated in child mortality. While national public health expenditures have varied a lot in poor countries, international public investment in child and maternal health has helped bring down mortality rates in those countries. The third phase of the transition depends less on public expenditures and more on decisions made by individual households. While public education programs, and especially the education of women, have been instrumental in reducing birth rates (Lutz

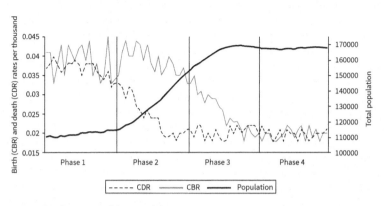

Figure 10.5 The demographic transition.

In the first phase birth (CBR) and death (CDR) rates are highly variable but balanced. In the second phase death rates fall, while birth rates remain high. In the third phase death rates fall, and in the fourth phase both are again in equilibrium balance. Total population increases at an increasing rate in the second phase and at a decreasing rate in the third phase. In the fourth phase total population is again stable.

Source: Perrings (2014).

and Samir 2010), the persistence of high fertility rates in many countries reflects the long-term security of household income. High fertility rates have been argued to be a response to future income insecurity. The less confidence people have in their ability to meet their income needs in old age, the more children they are likely to have (Dasgupta 2001). The factors that underpin income insecurity also prolong the demographic transition.

The link between population growth and environmental change is similarly dependent on institutional conditions. While a growing human population translates directly into growing demand for foods, fuels, and fibers, it does not follow that this will always lead to environmental degradation. It depends on factors such as the structure of property rights and the rule of law. As we have already seen, if a common pool resource is open to all, increasing population can lead directly to increasing pressure on the resource. Population growth in the neighborhood of open access natural forests, for example, has frequently led to an increase in the rate at which forest is converted to farmland or rangeland or forest species are hunted (Panayotou 1996). Moreover, since those who exploit open access natural forests have no security of tenure, they also have no incentive to conserve the resource.

Population growth in conditions where people do not have open access to natural resources generates a different set of outcomes. If people are unable to survive on the resources to which they do have access, the most common response is migration and, when migration is not an option, other Malthusian demographic controls kick in, such as war, disease, or famine. In the long term, Esther Boserup has argued that population pressure may also lead to technological innovation (Boserup 1981), but in the short term that is not an option. The growth of cities around the world has been fueled by migration of people no longer able to survive in increasingly congested or constrained rural areas. The open access resources being exploited in such cases are frequently the squatter communities that spring up on the edges of large cities. While these communities pose their own environmental challenges, they have fewer implications for habitat loss and predation on forest species.

10.4 Per capita income growth and conservation

The connection between income, population growth, and environmental change is a complicated one. It is strongly dependent on institutional conditions. It can be either positive or negative, and it need not be monotonic. Empirical studies have shown that for a number of environmental stresses, the relation between per capita GDP and the appropriate measure of environmental quality has an inverted U shape. In other words, at lower incomes, as income increases, so does environmental damage. Past some point further increases in income can lead to reduced environmental damage. This is attributed to increased demand for environmental amenities as necessities are met and disposable income increases. Since the economist Simon Kuznets had shown a similarly shaped relation between average income and income inequality in the 1950s, known as the Kuznets curve, the relation between average income and environmental quality has come to be known as the environmental Kuznets curve. An inverted U-shaped curve has been found, for example, for the relation between average income and several air pollutants including sulphur dioxide, but not for others, such as carbon dioxide. Nor has it been found for many water pollutants pollutants (Stern 2004).

The relation between average income and biodiversity has been approached in quite different ways in this literature. One approach uses a measure of deforestation as a proxy for biodiversity loss (justified by the species area relationship (MacArthur and Wilson 1967). However, no studies using this proxy have found a statistically significant relation between income and biodiversity loss (Dietz and Adger 2003, Mills and Waite 2009). Other proxies for biodiversity loss include the National Biodiversity Risk Assessment Index (NABRAI) (Reyers et al. 1998, Mozumder et al. 2006), and measures of threat contained in the IUCN's red list. While earlier studies using the last measure did find a statistically significant relation between average income and threats to biodiversity, it was very different for plants (linear), amphibians, reptiles,

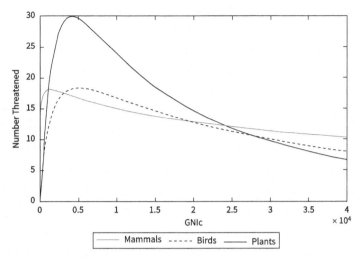

Figure 10.6 Relation between the number of threatened species and per capita income (OLS estimates).
Source: Perrings and Halkos (2012).

fishes and invertebrates (U-shaped), and birds (inverted U-shaped) (Naidoo and Adamowicz 2001).

More recently, a study of the relation between per capita gross national income and the number of threatened species found that while the number of threatened species was negatively related to income growth in high- and middle-income countries, it was positively related to income growth in the poorest countries (Perrings and Halkos 2012) (Figure 10.6).

The inverted U-shaped relation was more marked in the case of plants than in the case of either mammals or birds, but held for all three. The turning points differ, being lowest for mammals and highest for birds, as does the rate at which the number of threatened species declines with income increases after the turning point. Given the evidence of skewness and kurtosis in these curves, the authors also estimated conditional quantile regression models, and found that both the sign and magnitude of effects changed at either very low or very high levels of threat (Figure 10.7).

The conclusion they drew from this is that over some income ranges and some levels of biodiversity loss through habitat conversion may be socially efficient. At low levels of average income, the conversion of wild habitat to agriculture may be the best use of limited resources. Although there is evidence that people's willingness to pay for habitat protection is increasing in income, in poorer countries that effect is dominated by the private benefits of habitat conversion to farmland or rangeland. The implication of Section 10.3 is that

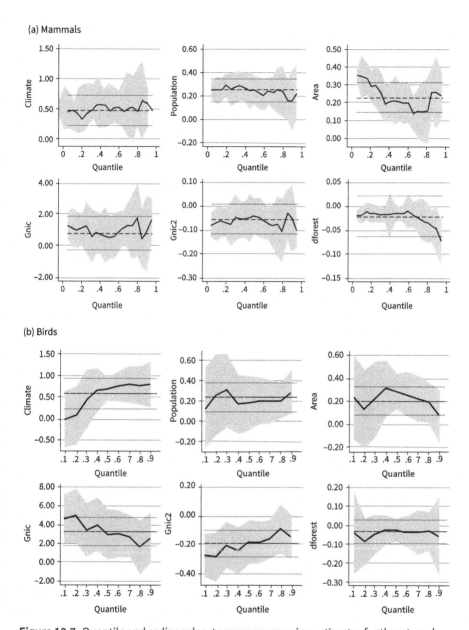

Figure 10.7 Quantile and ordinary least squares regression estimates for threatened species (including mean coefficient values and 95% confidence intervals).

The dotted lines indicates the OLS estimate and 95% confidence intervals. The solid line and grey area indicates the quantile regression estimates and 95% confidence intervals.

Source: Perrings and Halkos (2012).

(c) Plants

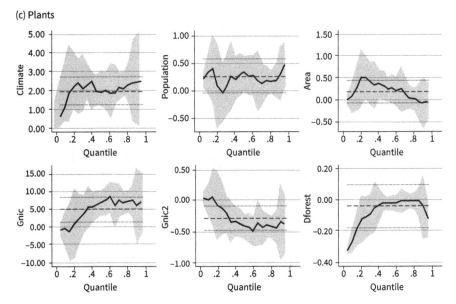

Figure 10.7 Continued

this is most likely to be the case (a) where farmers have open access to natural forest, woodland, or grassland, and (b) where property rights to natural resources are least well-defined.

10.5 Wealth, property rights, and conservation

The scope for linking poverty alleviation and biodiversity conservation remains a contested area. One line of argument is that simultaneously addressing the root causes of biodiversity loss and poverty can lead to complementary positive results—a win-win outcome in which the stress on biodiversity is reduced and incomes are boosted. For example, it is claimed that the development of policies to reduce population pressure by promoting voluntary reductions in fertility in poor countries can support both conservation of biodiversity and poverty alleviation (Sachs et al. 2009). As we have already seen, however, speeding up the demographic transition may depend more on a change in peoples' perceptions of their long-term income security than on awareness of family planning options. As long as people perceive access to land and the support of children as important to their income security, fertility levels will remain high. Moreover, as long as natural resources are subject to open or poorly regulated access, population growth will put those same resources under increasing pressure.

Historically, the most effective means of reducing population-induced pressure on natural resources has been a multifaceted attack on the problem of income insecurity, access to credit, the problem of open access, and the education and training of resource users. Only when the rural poor have been able to build other skills, and other assets, has the pressure come off remaining wild habitat. Historically, this has occurred alongside a major demographic shift away from rural and toward urban areas. This has occurred both within and between countries. The result has been a general decline in the proportion of the population living in rural areas, but occurring at very different rates in different parts of the world. Figure 10.8 shows realized and projected average annual rates of change in the size of the rural population by income group between 1970 and 2030. While the rural population has been declining in both high-income and upper-middle-income countries since the 1990s, it is projected to continue increasing in lower-middle-income countries until 2030, and in low-income countries until at least 2050.

The reasons for the persistence of high rates of growth of the rural population in low-income countries extend beyond the connection between income security and fertility. High rates of rural population growth are also associated with low rates of rural-urban migration. Once again, there are many and varied reasons for the decision to move from rural to urban areas. Current income differentials between rural and urban areas have been recognized to be an important factor since the 1960s (Todaro 1969), but other factors are also important. Migration decisions are frequently taken

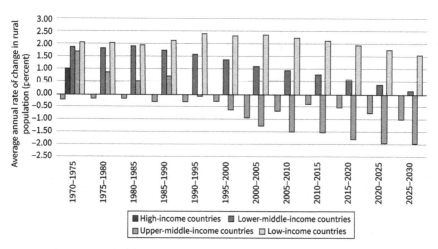

Figure 10.8 Realized and projected average annual rates of change in the size of the rural population by income group, 1970–2030.
Source: United Nations Department of Economic and Social Affairs (2018b).

by households rather than individuals, and represent one of many ways to manage risks across generations. Migrants frequently remit a part of their income to the rural areas, and this serves both to provide for children and older members of the household, but also to secure rights of access to rural resources. A study of rural-urban migration patterns in sub-Saharan Africa in the 1990s, for example, found that while the annual regional population-weighted rural-urban migration rate was positive at 1.07%, several countries had either very low or even negative rural–urban migration rates (De Brauw et al. 2014). Countries with negative rural-urban migration rates include Cote-d'Ivoire, Benin, Central African Republic, Democratic Republic of the Congo, Guinea, and a group of Southern African countries—Botswana, Swaziland, Lesotho, and Zambia. Noting that a negative rate means that people are returning from urban to rural areas, the implication is that access to land and family support systems were of increasing rather than decreasing value in these countries.

Potential reasons for this include the structure of land rights in rural areas, the rural opportunity cost of urban migration, and health and personal security risks in urban areas. Where household control over resources depends on keeping those resources in use, for example, migrants risk losing the only assets they have. A study of rural-urban migration in Ethiopia, for example, found migration to be positively associated with the security of land rights (De Brauw and Mueller 2012). The rural opportunity cost of migration can also be high if there are too few economically active adults in the rural household to maintain household production, or if other rural income earning opportunities exist. Wildlife-based ecotourism in Southern Africa, for example, has generated new sources of rural employment and income other than agriculture, so discouraging out-migration. Payments for ecosystem services schemes may have the same effect.

In recent years, the implementation of payments for ecosystem services schemes has been motivated by the fact that they have the potential both to reduce rural poverty in low-income countries, and to benefit the natural environment. Payments made to rural households are argued to alleviate their poverty, while at the same time delivering enhanced habitat protection either as the primary goal of the scheme or, more commonly, as a side effect of schemes designed to deliver other environmental benefits such as carbon sequestration, watershed protection, or erosion control (Wunder 2008).

In East Asia, Southeast Asia, and parts of Latin America, high rates of rural-urban migration have supported urbanization and the development of industrialized economies, and have reduced at least one source of pressure on natural resources. In South Asia and sub-Saharan Africa the persistence of a still-growing, largely poor rural population maintains that source of pressure. Where access to forest and other resources is largely open, this frequently means the continued loss of habitat. Attempts to reduce the environmental impacts of rural population growth by systems of payments to rural landholders has some potential to contain the threat to wild species, but only if those payments are conditional on the adoption of conservation practices (Pattanayak et al. 2010). The danger of attempts to achieve multiple goals with a single instrument, such as payments for ecosystem services, is that the instrument will fail to meet any of the goals. For example, where agri-environmental or payments for ecosystem services schemes include farmer support/poverty alleviation as an explicit goal, payments are seldom sensitive to the condition of habitats (Kinzig et al. 2011).

The challenge is that the conservation of biodiversity and poverty alleviation are tightly connected only under very particular sets of conditions. These conditions are frequently institutional—legal, social, cultural, and economic—rather than biophysical. It may be possible to find that a single instrument will deliver multiple benefits in some very special cases, but not as a general rule. In most cases, achieving both poverty alleviation and biodiversity conservation requires a range of interventions directed as much to the institutional conditions under which people access land as to income levels.

One conservation initiative that targets the factors that underpin the over-exploitation of environmental resources is a Ford Foundation initiative to improve conservation outcomes by strengthening rural communities. The goal is to give local inhabitants of forested regions clear rights over their natural resources, and follows research in Brazil and Mesoamerica which shows that the allocation of secure rights to forest resources is at least as effective a way of conserving forests as establishing protected areas. The allocation of secure rights to rural communities addresses two dimensions of the poverty-environment connection. First, it eliminates the incentives to members of those communities to overexploit open access resources. Second, it protects the most important assets in rural areas, so enhancing community wealth, and reducing community vulnerability. Secure rights encourage longer-term investments aimed at generating a sustainable flow of benefits. While these might include decisions to clear land for cattle ranching or oil palm plantations, they would at least balance the benefits of such activities against the wider benefits to the rural community of maintaining intact forest systems. Of course, any remaining external effects of land clearance would need to be addressed separately.

10.6 Summary and conclusions

Hotelling assumed that decision-makers have secure property rights in natural resources. He showed that if the expected growth in the value of some resource, if conserved, exceeded the rate of return on the best alternative asset, it would be optimal to conserve that resource. Many of the natural resources currently used by the rural poor in low-income countries are not, however, subject to well-defined property rights. Some, for example, are accessed through traditional use rights. Others are open access.

In this chapter we considered the relation between property rights, wealth, income, and resource use in low-income countries. Starting with the relation between income and the demand for natural resources, we showed how income constrains the choices people make. We also showed how the characteristics of goods and services influence responses to a change in prices and incomes. In particular, the income elasticity of demand is positive and greater than one for luxury goods, positive and less than one for normal goods, and negative for inferior goods. We saw that many open access resources are inferior in this sense—that they are the least costly and often the least desirable among a number of substitutes. If incomes fall, the demand for such goods can rise as people substitute out of more preferred, more expensive goods. While an increase in the price of inferior goods will ordinarily induce a reduction in demand for those good, in extreme cases (the case of Giffen goods) perverse income effects can dominate substitution effects. An increase in the price of such goods can, by reducing real incomes, induce consumers to increase, not decrease their consumption. Many of the products accessed by hunter-gatherer societies fall into the category of inferior goods and, at least potentially, of Giffen goods. It follows that changes in the price of such goods may have unexpected consequences for demand.

So what does this imply for the Hotelling principle and the conservation of habitat? A first point is that the principle applies whether or not decision-makers have secure property rights in natural resources. If they do not have secure property rights, however, it follows immediately that the expected gain from holding on to a resource is zero. It will always be better to convert that resource into an asset to which they have secure rights. A second point is that for rural landholders to have an incentive to conserve their land, they also need to have secure property rights. A necessary condition for land conservation to be optimal by the Hotelling principle is that the rights-holder can realize the gains to be had from conserving the resource.

If land is held in public trust, and if those who use the land have only limited use rights, the same principle applies. In this case, however, users need to be confronted by incentives that reflect the expected growth in the value of land, if conserved. In the final part of the book, we consider the two main conservation strategies adopted over the last half century: protected areas and conservation incentives. While each has frequently been adopted in isolation, we shall see that the most effective conservation efforts involve elements of both.

References

Alderman, H. 1986. The effect of food price and income changes on the acquisition of food by low-income households. International Food Policy Research Institute, Washington, DC.

Barrett, C. B. 2013. Assisting the escape from persistent ultra-poverty in rural Africa. *in* W. P. Falcon and R. L. Naylor, editors. Frontiers in Food Policy for Sub-Saharan Africa and South Asia. Stanford Center on Food Security and the Environment, Stanford.

Boserup, E. 1981. Population and Technological Change: A Study of Long Term Trends. University of Chicago Press, Chicago.

Caldwell, J. C. 1976. Toward a restatement of demographic transition theory. Population and Development Review 2: 321–366.

Dasgupta, P. 2001. Human well-being and the natural environment. Oxford University Press, Oxford ; New York.

Davies, T. J., and L. B. Buckley. 2011. Phylogenetic diversity as a window into the evolutionary and biogeographic histories of present-day richness gradients for mammals. Philosophical Transactions of the Royal Society of London B: Biological Sciences 366:2414–2425.

De Brauw, A., and V. Mueller. 2012. Do limitations in land rights transferability influence mobility rates in Ethiopia? Journal of African Economies 21:548–579.

De Brauw, A., V. Mueller, and H. L. Lee. 2014. The role of rural–urban migration in the structural transformation of Sub-Saharan Africa. World Development 63:33–42.

De Janvry, A., and R. Garcia. 1988. Rural Poverty and Environmental Degradation in Latin America: Causes, Effects and Alternative Solutions. IFAD, Rome.

Dietz, S., and N. Adger. 2003. Economic growth, biodiversity loss and conservation effort. Journal of Environmental Management 68:23–35.

Dudley, N., S. J. Attwood, D. Goulson, D. Jarvis, Z. P. Bharucha, and J. Pretty. 2017. How should conservationists respond to pesticides as a driver of biodiversity loss in agroecosystems? Biological Conservation 209:449–453.

Ehrlich, P. R., and J. P. Holdren. 1971. Impact of Population Growth. Science 171:1212–1217.

Foley, J. A., N. Ramankutty, K. A. Brauman, E. S. Cassidy, J. S. Gerber, M. Johnston, N. D. Mueller, C. O/'Connell, D. K. Ray, P. C. West, C. Balzer, E. M. Bennett, S. R. Carpenter, J. Hill, C. Monfreda, S. Polasky, J. Rockstrom, J. Sheehan, S. Siebert, D. Tilman, and D. P. M. Zaks. 2011. Solutions for a cultivated planet. Nature 478:337–342.

Fuglie, K. O. 2008. Is a slowdown in agricultural productivity growth contributing to the rise in commodity prices? Agricultural Economics 39:431–441.

Gillman, L. N., S. D. Wright, J. Cusens, P. D. Mcbride, Y. Malhi, and R. J. Whittaker. 2015. Latitude, productivity and species richness. Global Ecology and Biogeography 24:107–117.

Jackson, L. F. 1984. Hierarchic demand and the Engel curve for variety. Review of Economics and Statistics 66:8–15.

Jacobsen, J. B., and N. Hanley. 2009. Are there income effects on global willingness to pay for biodiversity conservation. Environmental and Resource Economics 43:137–160.

Kinzig, A. P., C. Perrings, F. S. Chapin, S. Polasky, V. K. Smith, D. Tilman, and B. L. Turner. 2011. Paying for Ecosystem Services: Promise and Peril. Science 334:603–604.

Krauss, J., R. Bommarco, M. Guardiola, R. K. Heikkinen, A. Helm, M. Kuussaari, R. Lindborg, E. Öckinger, M. Pärtel, J. Pino, J. Pöyry, K. M. Raatikainen, A. Sang, C. Stefanescu, T. Teder, M. Zobel, and I. Steffan-Dewenter. 2010. Habitat fragmentation causes immediate and time-delayed biodiversity loss at different trophic levels. Ecology Letters 13:597–605.

Lutz, W., and K. C. Samir. 2010. Dimensions of global population projections: what do we know about future population trends and structures? Philosophical Transactions of the Royal Society of London B, Biological Sciences 365:2779–2791.

MacArthur, R. H., and E. O. Wilson. 1967. The theory of island biogeography. Princeton University Press, Princeton, NJ.

Mannion, P. D., P. Upchurch, R. B. Benson, and A. Goswami. 2014. The latitudinal biodiversity gradient through deep time. Trends in Ecology & Evolution 29:42–50.

McDonald, R. I., P. Kareiva, and R. T. Forman. 2008. The implications of current and future urbanization for global protected areas and biodiversity conservation. Biological Conservation 141:1695–1703.

Millennium Ecosystem Assessment. 2005. Ecosystems and Human Well-being: General Synthesis. Island Press, Washington, DC.

Mills, J. H., and T. A. Waite. 2009. Economic prosperity, biodiversity conservation, and the environmental Kuznets curve. Ecological Economics 68:2087–2095.

Mozumder, P., R. P. Berrens, and A. K. Bohara. 2006. Is there an Environmental Kuznets Curve for the risk of biodiversity loss? The Journal of Developing Areas 39:175–190.

Naidoo, R., and W. L. Adamowicz. 2001. Effects of Economic Prosperity on Numbers of Threatened Species. Conservation Biology 15:1021–1029.

Panayotou, T. 1996. An inquiry into population, resources and the environment. Pages 259–298 *in* D. A. Ahlburg, A. C. Kelley, and K. O. Mason, editors. The impact of population growth on well-being in developing countries. Springer Science & Business Media, New York.

Pattanayak, S. K., S. Wunder, and P. J. Ferraro. 2010. Show Me the Money: Do Payments Supply Environmental Services in Developing Countries? Review of Environmental Economics and Policy 4:254–274.

Perrings, C. 2014. Our Uncommon Heritage: Biodiversity, Ecosystem Services and Human Wellbeing. Cambridge University Press, Cambridge.

Perrings, C., and G. Halkos. 2012. Who Cares about Biodiversity? Optimal Conservation and Transboundary Biodiversity Externalities. Environmental and Resource Economics 52:585–608.

Perrings, C., and G. Halkos. 2015. Agriculture and the threat to biodiversity in sub-Saharan Africa. Environmental Research Letters 10:095015.

Reyers, B., A. S. Van Jaarsveld, M. A. McGeoch, and A. N. James. 1998. National Biodiversity Risk Assessment: A Composite Multivariate and Index Approach. Biodiversity and Conservation 7:945–965.

Sachs, J. D., J. E. M. Baillie, W. J. Sutherland, P. R. Armsworth, N. Ash, J. Beddington, T. M. Blackburn, B. Collen, B. Gardiner, K. J. Gaston, H. C. J. Godfray, R. E. Green, P. H. Harvey, B. House, S. Knapp, N. F. Kumpel, D. W. Macdonald, G. M. Mace, J. Mallet, A. Matthews, R. M. May, O. Petchey, A. Purvis, D. Roe, K. Safi, K. Turner, M. Walpole, R. Watson, and K. E. Jones. 2009. Biodiversity Conservation and the Millennium Development Goals. Science 325:1502–1503.

Stern, D. I. 2004. The rise and fall of the Environmental Kuznets Curve. World Development 32:1419–1439.

Thompson, W. S. 1929. Population. American Journal of Sociology 34:959–975.

Tilman, D., J. Fargione, B. Wolff, C. D'Antonio, A. Dobson, R. Howarth, D. Schindler, W. H. Schlesinger, D. Simberloff, and D. Swackhamer. 2001. Forecasting Agriculturally Driven Global Environmental Change. Science 292:281–284.

Tilman, D., R. M. May, C. L. Lehman, and M. A. Nowak. 1994. Habitat Destruction and the Extinction Debt. Nature 371:65–66.

Todaro, M. P. 1969. A Model of Labor Migration and Urban Unemployment in Less Developed Countries. American Economic Review 59:138–148.

United Nations Department of Economic and Social Affairs. 2018a. World Population Prospects: The 2017 Revision. UN DESA, New York.

United Nations Department of Economic and Social Affairs. 2018b. World Urbanization Prospects 2018. UN DESA, New York.

Van der Sluijs, J. P., V. Amaral-Rogers, L. Belzunces, M. B. Van Lexmond, J.-M. Bonmatin, M. Chagnon, C. Downs, L. Furlan, D. Gibbons, and C. Giorio. 2015. Conclusions of the Worldwide Integrated Assessment on the risks of neonicotinoids and fipronil to biodiversity and ecosystem functioning. Springer.

World Bank. 2018. Data Bank, World Development Indicators. World Bank, Washington, DC.

World Bank. 2020. Rural Population. World Bank, Washington, DC.

Wunder, S. 2008. Payments for environmental services and the poor: concepts and preliminary evidence. Environment and Development Economics 13:279–297.

11
Conservation in Protected Areas

There are no words that can tell the hidden spirit of the wilderness, that can reveal its mystery, its melancholy and its charm. The nation behaves well if it treats the natural resources as assets which it must turn over to the next generation increased and not impaired in value.

—Theodore Roosevelt, Osawatomie, Kansas, 1910

11.1 Introduction

The dominant approach to the conservation of wild species since the late nineteenth century has been the establishment of protected areas. While there were lands reserved for special use in earlier times that protected particular species or landscapes—such as royal hunting preserves and community sacred sites—there were relatively few legally defined protected areas before the establishment of Yellowstone National Park in 1872. The approach spread rapidly, both through the United States and elsewhere. The Royal National Park was established in Australia in 1879, followed by El Chico in Mexico in 1882, Banff in Canada in 1885, Sabi Game Reserve (the precursor to Kruger National Park) in South Africa in 1892, and Tongariro in New Zealand in 1894. By the first world conference on national parks held in Seattle in 1962, there were nearly 10,000 parks worldwide. By the early twenty-first century there were more than 100,000 (Chape et al. 2008). Currently, around 15% of the world's land surface and 7% of the oceans are subject to some form of protection. Over 160,000 designated areas are protected at national, state, provincial, or local level (Figure 11.1)(UNEP-WCMC and IUCN 2016).

Protected areas are generally described as "a clearly defined geographical space, recognized, dedicated and managed, through legal or other effective means, to achieve the long-term conservation of nature with associated ecosystem services and cultural values" (IUCN 2008). However, not all protected areas share the same goals, and not all offer the same level of protection. The

Conservation. Charles Perrings and Ann Kinzig, Oxford University Press (2021). © Oxford University Press.
DOI: 10.1093/oso/9780190613600.003.0011

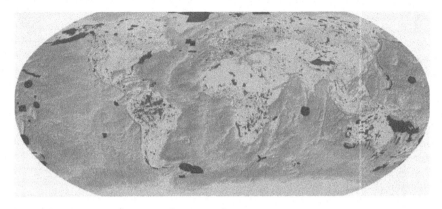

Figure 11.1 Marine and terrestrial protected areas, 2016.
Source: UNEP-WCMC and IUCN (2016).

IUCN identifies seven different categories of protected area, allowing for progressively greater levels of disturbance.

- **Category I(a):** Strict Nature Reserves are strictly protected areas set aside to protect biodiversity and sometime geological or geomorphological features. In all cases human access, use, and impacts are controlled to avoid damage to the system.
- **Category I(b):** Wilderness Areas are usually large unmodified or slightly modified tracts without permanent or significant human habitation that are protected and managed so as to preserve their natural characteristics.
- **Category II:** National Parks are large natural or near natural areas set aside to protect the species and ecosystems characteristic of the area, which also allow "environmentally and culturally compatible, spiritual, scientific, educational, recreational, and visitor opportunities."
- **Category III:** Natural Monuments are typically small terrestrial or marine protected areas set aside to protect a specific landform or geological feature, such as sea mounts, submarine caverns, caves, or living features such as sacred groves. Human access may be limited.
- **Category IV:** Habitat/Species Management Areas aim to protect particular species or habitats by appropriately limiting access and use.
- **Category V:** Protected Landscapes/Seascapes refer to tracts where the interaction of people and nature over time has produced an area of distinct ecological, biological, cultural or scenic character.
- **Category VI:** Protected areas allowing sustainable use of natural resources are generally large tracts in which much of the area is in natural

condition, but a proportion is allows low-level, nonindustrial use of natural resources.

The IUCN categories show that there are many degrees of protection, just as there are many targets of protection. Individual species, ecological communities, geological and geomorphological features, and natural and managed landscapes are all targets of protection, and the level of protection extends from the near-complete exclusion of humans to the lightest of restrictions on use and access. As we will see in the next chapter, the continuum extends well beyond formally designated protected areas to include a wide range of zoning restrictions—limitations on use—applied to land and sea areas that are not formally protected.

This chapter focuses on land and sea areas that are formally subject to some level of protection, and asks how the principles described in earlier chapters help determine the size, shape, and timing of protected areas, as well as the restrictions on use. Although management of IUCN Category I(a) protected areas is notionally driven only by conservation values, it is subject to the same conditions that apply to any resource allocation decision. The conservation of the various elements of natural capital targeted by different protected areas involves trade-offs between, for example, the area to be protected and the level of protection that can be given. The phenomenon of "paper parks"—legally designated protected areas in which use restrictions are not enforced—is frequently a consequence of the designation of areas too large to be protected. This has been a particular problem in marine systems where estimates of the proportion of marine protected areas that are not enforced are as high as 90%. We will see that the efficiency (or cost-effectiveness) of conservation through protected areas requires that trade-offs be identified and resolved in ways that balance costs and benefits (or effects per unit cost).

11.2 Protected area design: ecological principles

The IUCN protected area categories suggest that there are many reasons for establishing protected areas, only some of which relate to the conservation of endangered wild living species. While some of the earliest national parks, such as the Sabi Game Reserve (Kruger National Park), were established with the explicit goal of protecting certain animals, others such as Yellowstone, Banff, or Tongariro focused on charismatic geological and geomorphological features—as do many national monuments established later. Among game reserves there are also some that were established to protect humans as much as other species. Botswana's Central Kalahari Game Reserve, for example, was established in 1961 to protect the way of life of the San Bushmen. While that goal has subsequently changed (at considerable cost to the San), it held for around three decades. Other protected areas have been established to protect entirely human-dominated and managed landscapes. Britain's North York Moors National Park, for example, was established in 1952 to protect a landscape that was created by forest clearance starting in Neolithic times; the North York Moors are currently home to more than 20,000 people.

In all cases, the design of protected areas depends on the objectives behind their establishment. We focus on the conservation of endangered wild living species. IUCN Category I protected areas aim to preserve ecosystems and species in a state as undisturbed by human activity as possible. While this elevates wild species, Category I(a) areas also seek to protect cultural and spiritual values associated with nature, while Category I(b) areas seek to protect the rights of indigenous communities to maintain traditional lifestyles.

The core aim of the conservation of endangered wild living species involves other more specific aims: to preserve species and ecosystem diversity that will not survive outside of protected areas, and to provide reference points and study systems for long-term measurement and monitoring. The more specific aims of conservation are what lie behind the push of the last five decades to use protected areas to preserve as much biodiversity in as natural a state as possible.

From an ecological perspective, the selection of protected areas depends on the distribution and state of species. Selection normally reflects three main criteria:

- **Threat.** This criterion favors areas containing one or more threatened species or ecosystems, and favors areas containing more threatened species over areas containing less threatened species (assuming those species can still be saved).
- **Distinctness.** This criterion favors areas rich in endemic species of restricted range.
- **Representativeness.** This criterion favors areas that increase the degree to which the set of protected areas is representative of the biomes in the system.

Selection is generally implemented through a gap analysis, which typically focuses on three different types of gaps. Representation gaps occur where there are either no representations of a particular species or ecosystem in any protected area, or not enough instances to ensure long-term protection.

Ecological gaps occur if protected areas aimed at supporting particular species or ecosystems are inadequate to do so. Management gaps occur when management regimes are ineffective (Dudley et al. 2010).

Specific choices about the size and shape of individual protected areas or the structure of a protected area network depend partly on a set of ecological principles and partly, as we will see, on other factors such as surrounding land use and land ownership. As a first approximation, the minimum size of protected areas designed around a set of target species is determined by the home ranges of those species. In marine systems, for example, it has been found that fish densities are significantly higher in fully protected areas that are larger than the home range of the targeted species, but are unaffected when home ranges are larger than fully protected areas (Di Franco et al. 2018). If the intent is to protect other nontargeted species in the process, however, the home range of the targeted species will almost certainly result in an area that is too small. In these circumstances, the theory of island biogeography has been used to argue that bigger is better.

If protected areas are conceptualized as islands, the theory of island biogeography suggests that smaller protected areas will lose species at a higher rate than larger protected areas. A study of differences in rates of extinction of mammals in parks of different size in the Western United States found, for example, that extinction rates were highest in the smallest parks (Newmark 1995). The same study also showed that the permeability of protected area boundaries matters. If the species within a protected area are able to exploit resources beyond the protected area, they are less at risk.

What is less clear is whether a single large reserve of given area would hold more distinct species than a series of smaller reserves that had the same combined area. If the species contained in each smaller reserve are the same, a single large reserve could be more effective. If the species contained in each smaller reserve are different, the answer should favor multiple smaller reserves (Simberloff and Abele 1976).

Since the representativeness principle favors the distribution of protected areas across biomes, the consensus approach to the establishment of new protected areas has accordingly been to try to secure as large an area as possible, and to include as many biomes as possible. This consensus is now reflected in an agreement by parties to the Convention on Biological Diversity to establish comprehensive, effectively managed, and ecologically representative national and regional systems of protected areas.

The bigger is better principle is reflected in a progressive expansion in national conservation ambitions. At the 1992 World Parks Congress in Caracas, Venezuela, there was agreement to set a target of 10% of all biomes to be protected by the year 2000. The current goal, set out in the Aichi biodiversity targets, is for 17% of terrestrial and inland waters and 10% of coastal and marine areas to be protected by 2020. Consistent with the recommendation of the 2014 World Parks Congress in Sydney, Australia, the government of the United Kingdom has recently called for 30% of the world's oceans to be protected by 2030.

Initially, the wider landscapes within which protected areas were established were largely left out of account. Protected areas were conceived very much like islands—fragments of natural habitat in a landscape undergoing progressive conversion to states threatening to wild species. Increasingly, however, protected area design has come to take account of the relation between the protected area and the surrounding land or sea area. Interactions between species across the boundaries of protected areas have been shown to have important implications both for the species targeted for protection, and for other species. Trophic cascades due to changes in the abundance of top predators in either protected or unprotected areas have induced fundamental changes in the composition of ecological communities in both areas. One well-known example is the indirect effect of changes in grey wolf populations in Yellowstone on aspen forests, via a direct effect on elk (Ripple and Beschta 2012). Another is the indirect effect of changes in the abundance of snapper or spiny lobsters in New Zealand's Leigh Marine Reserve on kelp, via a direct effect on sea urchins (Shears and Babcock 2003).

The edge effects between protected and unprotected areas include impacts beyond the protected area that are both positive and negative. Some marine reserves have been shown to have positive effects on the abundance of species targeted by fishers outside of the protected areas. A network of five small reserves in St. Lucia, for example, were shown to have increased adjacent catches of artisanal fishers by up to 90% within five years (Roberts et al. 2001). In terrestrial systems, protected areas have led to changes in the relative abundance of mammals in areas adjacent to the protected areas—both through trophic cascades and other ecological processes—with a range of effects on resource users in those areas. The net result is that protected area design is now more likely to consider impacts that span both the protected are and the landscapes or seascapes in which it is embedded. The formal wording of the eleventh of the Aichi biodiversity targets reflects this:

By 2020, at least 17 per cent of terrestrial and inland water, and 10 per cent of coastal and marine areas, especially areas of particular importance for biodiversity and ecosystem services, are conserved through effectively and equitably managed, ecologically representative and well-connected systems of protected areas and other effective area-based conservation measures, and integrated into the wider landscapes and seascapes.

This is argued to strengthen conservation by allowing for improved connectivity between protected areas and by reducing fragmentation. More particularly, the creation of biological corridors allows species (and hence genes) to move from one protected area to another, and so offers a wider range of options for species to adapt through migration to global stressors such as climate change. In addition, it makes it possible to manage natural processes that occur at scales beyond protected areas. Examples include water flows, pollination, and larval dispersal in marine systems.

The negative consequences of the isolation of protected areas through the establishment of fences and roads, along with edge effects that include poaching and the spread of epizootic diseases, have been an important driver of the establishment of conservation areas that span protected areas. The Kavango-Zambezi Transfrontier Conservation Area (KAZA), for example, in principle allows for the seasonal movement of large mammals between national parks and wildlife management areas (Figure 11.2) (Tshipa et al. 2017, Cushman et al. 2018).

11.3 Protected area design: economic principles

Consider how the design of protected areas based on ecological principles might be affected by the application of the economic principles described in Chapters 3 and 4. Recall, first, that the Hotelling arbitrage condition holds that a resource owner will be indifferent between conserving and converting a resource at a particular time if the proportional rate of change in the value of the conserved resource at that time is equal to the rate of return on the best alternative investment that could be made. Whether or not the resource carries a market price is immaterial. The proportional rate of change in value of the resource should reflect the expected change in the stream of net benefits of conservation to all people, whether those net benefits are monetized or not. If the conserved resource is priced in the market but has unpriced effects on others (positive or negative) the rate of change in its value should include any changes in those unpriced affects. In other words, it is the rate of change in the market value of the resource net of any externalities.

The Hotelling arbitrage condition is a particular application of the equimarginal principal, which holds that for a decision-maker to be indifferent between alternative courses of action the marginal net benefits of both

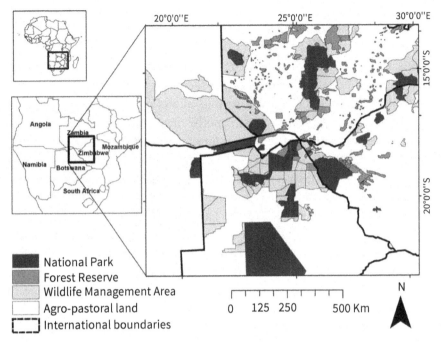

Figure 11.2 Area spanned by the Kavango-Zambezi Transfrontier Conservation Area (KAZA), showing the location of national parks, wildlife management areas, and forest reserves in Angola, Botswana, Namibia, Zambia, and Zimbabwe.
Source: Cushman et al. (2018).

courses of action should be the same. Since the arbitrage condition applies to assets, marginal net benefit refers to any change in the stream of services associated with a change in the asset. The arbitrage condition allows us to compare the marginal net benefits of maintaining a natural asset—an oil deposit, a forest, an ecosystem—in some state, or converting it to an alternative state. Indeed, it offers a quite natural way to think about the value of protected areas, including the value of listing or delisting protected areas.

Adding the equimarginal principle to the set of ecological principles invoked in the design of protected areas, however, changes one's perspective on the optimal size and location of protected areas, as well as the optimal level of protection. Simberloff's 1976 critique of the island biogeography approach to protected area design cited earlier included the following statement: "The cost and irreversibility of large-scale conservation programs demand a prudent approach to the application of an insufficiently validated theory." This recognizes that bigger may not always be better, and that cost matters. If the designation of protected areas is not an end in itself, but a means to an end—the conservation of threatened wild species—the nature and effectiveness of the protection offered is important. Every additional square kilometer designated for protection has an opportunity cost. There is a cost to those whose life and livelihoods are affected by the loss of access to the resources of the area, and a cost to those charged with the implementation of the protection program. Nor are those costs likely to be independent of the size of the protected area. There are certainly some economies of scale in protection, but both sets of costs would ordinarily be expected to rise as the size of the protected area increases beyond a certain point.

The point here is that the protection of an additional square kilometer of land or sea potentially confers benefits in terms of the number of species conserved, but this needs to be balanced again the opportunities forgone by committing resources to the acquisition of the necessary rights, the additional cost of conservation effort, and the net costs to those impacted by the change in rights. For the protection of an additional square kilometer of land or sea to be efficient, the value of the additional conservation outcomes secured should be at least as great as the additional costs incurred.

The debate, triggered by the theory of island biogeography, about the relative advantage of "single large" over "several small" protected areas has no clear resolution. If there is a consensus it is that factors other than the species area relationship are likely to determine which approach is to be preferred in particular cases. Ecologists point to the importance of the degree of connectedness of protected areas, their distance from source populations, the permeability of protected area boundaries, the dispersal characteristics of protected species and so on. The net benefits associated with different protected area strategies are likely to be affected by all of these considerations. They are likely to impact the costs of implementing a conservation program, of enforcing protected area access rues, of effects on people in surrounding areas, as well as the intended conservation outcomes of different strategies. If, taking all these factors into consideration, the benefits of protected areas are increasing in the size of the protected area, but the costs are increasing at a faster rate, there will be an optimal size to the protected area (Figure 11.3).

For A^* in Figure 11.3 to be optimal both $B(A)$ and $C(A)$ should be comprehensive. All socially relevant costs and benefits should be included—including the opportunities forgone to invest in conservation elsewhere. Up to this point the evidence is that protected areas have been designed taking account of selected benefits and costs only. A study in the early 1990s claimed that the size of protected areas and the resources made available to manage protected areas were typically less than optimal, since many of the benefits

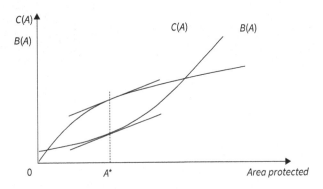

Figure 11.3 Net benefits of protected areas.

Net benefits are maximized at size A^*, at which the marginal gains in terms of conservation (and other) outcomes, $dB(A)/dA$, are equal to the marginal costs, $dC(A)/dA$.

were in the form of public goods that were underestimated, while the private costs were seen to be large by comparison (Dixon and Sherman 1990).

Since that time the range of associated benefits has increased to include a number of ecosystem services of public interest (other than habitat provision), along with the private benefits offered by, for example, the development of protected area-based ecotourism, or of recreational and commercial hunting and fishing. Similarly, the range of costs to communities affected by the loss of access rights has increased to include not only direct impacts on production in protected areas, but also the negative impacts on natural resources and the ecosystem services they offer outside of protected areas, along with less tangible cultural costs to local communities. In marine systems, protected areas take many forms including protected marine areas, no-take zones, marine sanctuaries, ocean sanctuaries, marine parks, fishery closed areas, fisheries refugia, and locally managed marine areas (Food and Agriculture Organization 2012). Aside from their conservation goals, marine protected areas may be a tourism resource, allowing people to access areas of high marine biodiversity such as coral reefs (Roberts et al. 2003), or a commercial fisheries resource, securing breeding grounds or fish nurseries (Palumbi 2002, Food and Agriculture Organization 2012).

Evaluation of the trade-offs involved in any particular set of benefits and costs makes it possible to identify the optimal size of an individual protected area, or the optimal structure of a network of protected areas. To illustrate the economic principles at work we take a very simple example of a marine protected area designed to yield benefits to an adjoining open-access fishery (Pezzey et al. 2000). Harvest, $H = qEN/K$, follows a Gordon-Shaefer model (in which fishers optimize the effort applied to harvesting a stock characterised by logistic growth). Harvest depends on catchability, q, effort, E, and fish stock size relative to the carrying capacity of the general system, N/K. Here K is normalized to one. Part of the fishery, K_R, is closed to fishing, leaving $K_F = 1 - K_R$ open. K_R can thus be thought of as the share of the whole area that is put under protection. The growth of stocks in the protected and unprotected areas, N_R and N_F, is assumed to depend on the density of fish in each area, N_R/K_R and N_F/K_F, and a larval pool that is assumed to be a homogeneously mixed product of fish stocks in both areas, $N_R + N_F$. Implicitly, all stocks are defined at a particular period. Omitting time subscripts for convenience, the change in the size of each stock from one period to the next can be written as:

$$\Delta N_R = r K_R \left(N_R + N_F \right) \left(1 - N_R / K_R \right)$$
$$\Delta N_F = r K_F \left(N_R + N_F \right) \left(1 - N_F / K_F \right)$$

For the fishery to be sustainable the amount harvested in each period should balance the change in the size of the open access stock in that period, implying that:

$$q E N_F / \left(1 - K_R \right) = r \left(1 - K_R \right) \left(N_R + N_F \right) \left(1 - N_F / \left(1 - K_R \right) \right)$$

Since the fishery is open access, rents are exhausted, and $pH = wE$—where p is the price of fish and w is the cost of effort. It follows that at the open access equilibrium

$$N_F / \left(1 - K_R \right) = w / pq$$

in which $w / pq < 1$ is the relative cost of catching fish. Defining $w / pq \equiv c$, these two expressions can be used to obtain the open access level of effort:

$$E^o = \left(r p \left(1 - c \right) / w \right) \left(c + \left(1 - 2c \right) K_R - \left(1 - c \right) K_R^2 \right)$$

allowing us to test the effect of changes in the proportional size of the protected area. The size of the open access fishery is maximized where the partial derivative of E^o with respect to K_R is equal to zero, implying that

$$K_R = \frac{1 - 2c}{2 \left(1 - c \right)}$$

It follows that $K_R > 0$ if and only if $c < 1/2$. At $c = 1/2$, $K_R = 0$. As c falls K_R rises, and as $c \to 0$, $K_R \to 1/2$. That is, the optimal reserve size depends on the relative cost of catching fish. If $c \geq 1/2$ the optimal reserve size is zero. If $c < 1/2$ the optimal reserve size is greater than zero. The share of the fishery that is optimally protected varies inversely with c, and rises to $1/2$ as c falls to zero.

In this simple example the only benefit of the protected area is to enhance catch in an adjoining fishery. This is an even more restrictive a goal for a protected area than the maximization of the number of wild species it can support. Intuitively, changing the goal would be expected to change the optimal size of the protected area. The cross-boundary effects of the protected area are also assumed to rest on the homogeneous dispersal of larvae across the whole system. This effectively abstracts from the question of where the protected area should be sited. Intuitively, again, incorporation of source-sink dynamics would be expected to change the optimal location of the protected area (Sanchirico and Wilen 2001, Sanchirico and Emerson 2002).

To optimize the design of protected area networks, conservation biologists have applied a range of programming methods that involve the specification of both conservation targets and a set of (linear) constraints on land use. An extension of the approach now allows protected area network planners to take account of differences in the cost of establishment of different levels of protection. The extension of the Marxan spatial planning tool to include a number of zones, for example, allows the optimization of networks of areas offering different levels of protection and involving different costs of establishment (Watts et al. 2009). To illustrate the approach, the authors applied the method to a multiple-use marine park in Rottnest Island, Western Australia, that included recreational fishing, recreational diving, and conservation objectives. They defined three zones: a high protection zone in which recreational fishing and diving were both excluded, a partial protection zone in which only recreational fishing was excluded, and a low protection zone in which both recreational activities were allowed. Given a conservation goal of at least 30% protection of all habitat types, a recreational goal of at least 80% of current usage, and assigned costs of implementation, the area was divided into three zones that satisfied all conservation and recreation targets at minimum cost, as in Figure 11.4.

Approaches of this type accordingly allow the design of cost-effective protected area networks. By identifying areas that satisfy conservation and ancillary use goals at least cost, they enable planners to make the most effective use of available resources. An important caveat is that the costs of implementation need to reflect the true social opportunity cost of resource use. Neglect of many of the external effects of protected areas means that current protected area networks are unlikely to be efficient. Nevertheless, there is evidence that

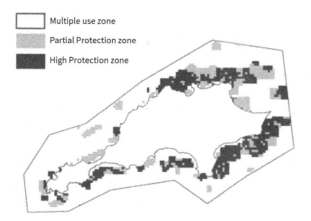

Multiple use zone

Partial Protection zone

High Protection zone

Figure 11.4 Optimal structure of protection in the Rottnest Island Marine Park, Western Australia.
Source: Watts et al. (2009).

current protected area design does reflect at least some of the more important principles involved.

A study of protected areas in 147 countries that investigated (a) elevation, slope, distance to roads and cities, and suitability for agriculture, and (b) the level of protection offered, found that most protected area networks are biased to higher elevations, steeper slopes, and greater distances to roads and cities, and that the bias was stronger the greater the level of protection offered (Joppa and Pfaff 2009). The authors of the study concluded that protected areas were being placed in locations where they could least prevent land conversion, and that the strictest access restrictions were being imposed in places where fewest people sought access. Nevertheless, their findings indicate that planners are indeed taking account of both habitat suitability and the cost of implementation. There is an obvious connection between the location of wildlife refugia and the level of human activity. The areas that are most likely to become wildlife refugia in the absence of protection are precisely the areas where human population and human activities are lowest. These are also the areas where the cost of establishing protected areas, in terms of the loss of access rights, production, and employment are lowest. Both factors favor selection of remote refugia as protected areas.

The trade-off between reserve size, location, and the effectiveness of protection is resolved—in the case of natural refugia—by the selection of areas that are not under pressure at the time they are listed. The remoteness and size of protected areas both have implications for the cost of protection, however, which limits the capacity to strengthen protection as pressure increases over time. For example, a 2009 evaluation of 270 wildlife counts in Kenya over a 30-year period found that wildlife populations had declined sharply, and that the rate of decline was similar in national parks, wildlife reserves, and nonprotected areas. This was ascribed to two main factors: poor coverage of seasonal ungulate migrations in national parks, and the difficulty of enforcement in large remote parks such as Tsavo East, Tsavo West, and Meru (Western et al. 2009).

A second consequence of the focus on areas that impose low costs on local resource users is that the representativeness of selected areas continues to be compromised. As of 2014, 36% terrestrial ecoregions had 17% coverage or more (the CBD terrestrial target), but 29% had less than 5% coverage, and 8% had less than 1% coverage. In marine systems, 20% of marine ecoregions had more than 10 coverage (the CBD marine target), while 46% had less than 1% coverage. New protected areas continue to be located less to assure representative coverage of the world's biomes, than to reflect the local opportunity cost of establishment (Watson et al. 2014).

11.4 Protected areas and the supply of ecosystem services

On the benefit side of the ledger, the publication of the Millennium Ecosystem Assessment prompted many to consider the wider range of benefits offered by protected areas established either to provide habitat for endangered wild species, or to protect charismatic landscapes. The Millennium Assessment itself had shown that along with biodiversity conservation, protected areas offered benefits including the regulation of water supplies and water quality, prevention of emissions of greenhouse gases that might have resulted from habitat conversion, and tourism potential (Millennium Ecosystem Assessment 2005). Since that time, increasing efforts have been made to calculate the value of ecosystem services generated by protected areas. While many have failed to address the additionality of protected areas—the increment in ecosystem services secured through designation of protected area status—others have not. Four sets of ecosystem services have been investigated in detail: carbon sequestration, water quality and water quantity, tourism and recreation and, at least in the case of marine protected areas, enhanced provision of foods.

Carbon sequestration. Carbon sequestration and the regulation of water supplies are both sensitive to rates of deforestation. Estimating the net impact of protected areas on deforestation is, however, complicated by the fact that the deforestation that would have occurred in the absence of protection cannot be observed, and because protection can displace deforestation from protected to unprotected areas. A 2005 study of deforestation rates in and around 198 IUCN Category 1 and 2 protected areas in the tropics in the last two decades of the twentieth century found that deforestation rates had increased in around 70% of the surrounding buffers, and that in South and Southeast Asia, where surrounding forests had been largely cleared by the early 1980, losses continued inside the protected areas (DeFries et al. 2005). A study of 49 tropical protected areas in the same year found that while the establishment of parks had reduced deforestation within park boundaries, increased rates of deforestation in surrounding areas had the effect of isolating protected areas (Naughton-Treves et al. 2005).

The question in both cases is whether deforestation rates were lower in protected areas, or higher in unprotected areas, than they would otherwise have been. While the answer to the question would be expected to be different in different parts of the world, there are certainly examples of protected area networks that have had the effect of slowing deforestation rates. A study of the effects of forest protection in Costa Rica between 1960 and 1997, for example, used matching methods to control for biases along observable dimensions and test for sensitivity to hidden biases. It found that protection had reduced deforestation by around 10%, while deforestation spillovers from protected to unprotected forests were negligible (Andam et al. 2008).

The carbon sequestration implications of changes in deforestation rates due to protected areas have been investigated in some of the most important systems. In the Brazilian Amazon, for example, expansion in the number and size of protected areas means that more than half of all remaining forests are now protected, and explains a substantial proportion of the regional reduction in deforestation rates. A study of the scope for protected areas in the region to reduce carbon emissions found that if all protected areas in the region were effectively enforced, they had the potential to avoid 8.0 ± 2.8 gigatons of carbon emissions by 2050 (Soares-Filho et al. 2010). Estimates of the value of carbon sequestration vary widely, and are highly sensitive to the social discount rate used. Simulations of the social cost of carbon using integrated assessment models range from $41.94 to $400.33 per metric ton of carbon in 2010 US dollars, the median being $137.26 per metric ton carbon (Hungate et al. 2017). The implication is that the carbon sequestered in fully protected areas in the Brazilian Amazon might be valued at around $1 trillion 2010 US dollars.

Fresh water provision. The impact of protected areas on water supplies lies in the effect of land cover on the seasonal quantity and quality of water available through water filtration, groundwater recharge, and the regulation of slow (subsurface) water flows. As with carbon sequestration, these services are sensitive to the impact of protection on deforestation rates. As with carbon sequestration, too, there are substantial differences between different protected areas and different regions. A major motivation for the establishment of many protected areas in the twentieth century was in fact the protection of watersheds through the conservation of vegetation.

The main goals of watershed protection are primarily the regulation of quick and slow flows together with erosion and sediment control. The benefits of watershed protection can therefore be measured in terms of runoff, streamflow, erosion, and sediment. They are influenced by land cover along with watershed characteristics such as soil, aspect, slope, elevation, precipitation, and temperature. To obtain measures of the value of watershed protection requires understanding of the connection between changes in land cover associated with protection and the provision of water-based services, such as the downstream production of foods, fuels, and fibers. A study of the value of watershed protection in Flores, Indonesia, for example, was able to calculate the marginal impact on producer surplus in different downstream areas by estimating the savings in water collection costs associated with watershed protection (Pattanayak 2004). The absolute value of the change in water flows in that case, up to 5,000 Indonesian rupiahs, was limited by the value of the foods, fuels and fibers produced by downstream farmers using that water. In other cases, the value of watershed protection can be much higher.

In perhaps the best-known case of watershed protection worldwide, land use and land cover in the Catskill Mountains in New York has been managed to provide a clean and reliable water supply for New York City for more than two decades. Protection of the watershed in 1996 at a cost of US$1–1.5 billion enabled the city to avoid building and operating a water filtration system that would have cost US$6–8 billion (Barbier 2007). Nor is New York City alone in benefiting from watershed protection. Around a third of the largest 100 cities around the world depend on protected areas for a significant part of their water supply (Stolton et al. 2015).

Tourism. Globally, protected area-based ecotourism is the fastest growing sector in one of the most rapidly growing industries. In 2016, tourism generally accounted for more than 10% of global GDP, of which nature-based ecotourism accounted for 6%. Tourism generally has been growing at an average of 4% over the last 25 years, while ecotourism has been growing at around 5%. Small island developing economies tend to be most reliant on tourism, but in low-income countries generally nature-based tourism is frequently second only to oil as a source of foreign exchange. In Ethiopia, Mexico, Nepal, Mali,

Kenya, Egypt, El Salvador, Thailand, and Costa Rica it accounts for more than 20% of total export receipts. Before the 2008–2009 recession visitation rates to protected areas worldwide showed strong growth in developing countries, but stable or even declining rates in the United States and Japan. Growth in the world economy since the recession has seen tourism return to high rates of growth—7% in 2017.

As with water, the added value of protection can be derived from the additional tourist expenditures it induces. If tourism revenues increase with increasing species richness or abundance, and if additional protection is associated with higher species richness or abundance, it is possible to calculate the marginal tourism revenue product of protection. While it would be possible to use hedonic methods to calculate the impact of differences in species richness or abundance on tourist willingness to pay for protection, most studies have opted for more direct survey-based approaches.

For example, a study of the value of World Heritage Site designation for the Sagarmatha (Mount Everest) National Park in Nepal used the contingent valuation method in a 2011 survey of international visitors' willingness to pay for access. A majority (63.8%) of visitors were willing to pay more than the existing entry fee, and prior knowledge of the World Heritage Site designation was found to contribute $16.39 to median willingness to pay for access (Baral et al. 2017). If entry fees were adjusted to capture this it would generate on the order of US $720,000. Similar studies in other parts of the world have been used to estimate willingness to pay for changes in park management regimes, park facilities, access restrictions, enhanced richness or abundance of the species in protected areas, changes in benefits to local communities, and other aspects of park governance.

11.5 Protected areas and poverty

In Chapter 10 we saw that income and wealth are important drivers of both the value assigned to nonmarketed environmental assets, and behavioral responses to changes in value. We also saw that a decision satisfying the Hotelling arbitrage condition can still involve winners and losers. Indeed, this may be critical to the successful implementation of the decision. As protected area strategies have been extended to include interactions across protected area boundaries and to take account of the impact of protected areas on the well-being of local communities, the question of how the benefits and costs of protected area designation and operation are distributed has become increasingly central.

The first serious attempts to take account of the distributional impacts of protected areas were the integrated conservation and development projects introduced in the 1980s. These were site-based conservation projects that included social or economic development goals. That is, they attempted to combine biodiversity conservation, community participation, and economic development for the rural poor. Initially the track record of integrated conservation and development projects was not good, with most failing to deliver on either goal. A 2004 review of the performance of a number of such projects concluded that they were inherently unlikely to succeed in their conservation goals. This was because biodiversity loss mitigation implies a long-term shift in the behavior of large numbers of people dispersed over large areas—a requirement that cannot be satisfied by short-term local projects. Nor were integrated conservation and development projects more likely to succeed in their development goals. Most projects mistakenly assumed that the provision of seed money would be sufficient to trigger transformative change (Wells et al. 2004).

The authors concluded that there were in fact few win-win options, and that a better approach would be to identify and negotiate the trade-offs involved in conservation, while broadening the remit of projects to:

- focus on broad landscapes that include protected areas as well as zones of more intensive human use;
- build alliances with and among local communities;
- build coalitions for conservation among key local and national stakeholders;
- engage local and sectoral government agencies;
- help communities develop and implement their own plans;
- explore the potential for local involvement in protected area management;
- support basic environmental education;
- raise awareness of the wider values of local biodiversity; and
- support selected pilot income-generating activities with local support.

A study of Madagascar's Ranomafana National Park found the present value of the opportunity cost to all local residents in the decade after the establishment of the park in 1991 to be $3.37 million (2004) US dollars. These were, however, unevenly distributed across households—the present value of costs per household ranging from $353 to $1,316. While $3.37 million was reported to be large relative to household incomes in the region, it was small relative to the wider conservation benefits of Ranomafana (Ferraro 2002).

A number of detailed studies have since investigated the impact of protected areas on the well-being of local populations. In Costa Rica, for example, changes in tourism, infrastructure, and ecosystem services associated with the establishment of protected areas were balanced against the output lost due to land-use restrictions to determine whether the impacts on local populations were positive or negative. The authors concluded that in that case protected areas reduced poverty, largely through the opportunities created by tourism. Changes in land cover were found to have no statistically significant impact on poverty, whether directly or through the establishment of roads, clinics, or schools (Ferraro and Hanauer 2014).

In Thailand, a study of the local impacts of strictly protected areas combined socioeconomic data from a poverty mapping study with satellite-based estimates of forest cover while controlling for factors driving both protection and development. As in Costa Rica, it was found that despite the opportunities foregone by imposition of land-use restrictions, the establishment of protected areas was associated with an increase in average consumption and a reduction in poverty rates. As in Costa Rica too, the explanation lay in the growth of tourism in and around the protected areas (Sims 2010).

Nor are these exceptional cases. A meta-analysis of data on 165 protected areas from 171 published studies revealed a positive relationship between conservation and socioeconomic outcomes, and between conservation outcomes and management regimes that empowered local communities, reduced economic inequality, and prioritized cultural and livelihood benefits. Protected areas that reported positive net socioeconomic benefits were generally managed for sustainable resource use rather than the preservation of wild species. At the same time, protected areas that reported positive conservation outcomes were more likely to deliver positive socioeconomic benefits to, and to implement comanagement regimes with, local communities (Oldekop et al. 2016).

This suggests is that the most effective protected area design is one that simultaneously addresses the need to protect threatened species, and the factors causing resource users to be a threat. A 2002 evaluation of marine protected areas noted that their effectiveness depended on interactions between biological, economic, and institutional factors. Marine protected areas that were motivated by threats to fish stocks, for example, were frequently ineffective due to the fact that they addressed the symptoms rather than the causes of overfishing (Sanchirico and Emerson 2002). The findings of Oldekop et al. (2016) indicate that the conservation objectives of protected areas are most likely to be met where protected area establishment is accompanied by the implementation of measures to provide local communities with alternative sources of income, and where protected area governance engages those communities in a meaningful way.

11.6 Summary and conclusions

This chapter reviewed the dominant approach to conservation since the late nineteenth century—protected areas. It described the historical evolution of protected areas and their design, from private hunting reserves to integrated conservation and development projects. It recapitulated the ecological principles involved in protected area design, and then discussed how conclusions reached on ecological grounds might be modified by adding the economic principles involved in the Hotelling approach. Specifically, we showed how adding the equimarginal principle to the set of ecological principles may change the optimal size and location of protected areas, as well as the optimal level of protection. There may be fundamental differences between protected areas designed around the ecological demands of preservation of particular species, and protected areas designed around the social value of all the resources contained in the area.

We have earlier seen that such differences have been a long-standing concern to conservation biologists. Recent updates to the US Endangered Species Act (ESA) that extend the use of economic data have rekindled that concern. The ESA revisions allow consideration of the economic impacts of species listings. This is not in and of itself a bad thing. Data on costs can help ensure the cost-effectiveness of targeted actions. Data on benefits can help prioritize those actions when resource constraints limit pursuit of all. The revisions in fact open the door to research findings on the wider and longer-term costs and benefits of biodiversity conservation (though we recognize the concerns that the revisions might mean decisions are motivated by politics rather than the best-available data on the benefits of conservation). We have seen that the most important of these intellectual developments on the benefits of conservation connect biodiversity, ecosystem functioning, and the production of ecosystem services—the benefits to people offered by ecosystems (Tallis et al. 2008).

While the ESA focuses on individual (endangered) species, it connects each to a supporting ecological community—"critical habitat," in the language of the Act. Valuation of the community of supporting species requires an understanding of the ways in which different species contribute to the persistence of the target species (Hanley and Perrings 2019). More particularly, it requires an analytical approach with roots in both theoretical ecological studies of the stability of meta-communities, and economic studies of financial market risks. If species are seen as the assets from which ecosystem services derive in uncertain environmental conditions, changes in their diversity may be analyzed using the tools of portfolio theory (Admiraal et al. 2013).

Long applied to the analysis of financial risk, portfolio theory has been used extensively in the choice of crops to manage environmental or market risk (Alvarez et al. 2017). The approach allows managers to select the combination of exploited species that either minimizes or contains risks. In recent years, the theory has been increasingly applied to the management of risk in a range of conservation problems (Matthies et al. 2019). Management of the risks facing species listed under the ESA requires the maintenance of a safe supporting system—a portfolio of supporting species (the rationale for those who favor multiple rather than single species listings, as occurs in Australia's Environment Protection and Biodiversity Conservation Act). Since the safe supporting system derives value both from its role in protecting listed species and from the production of other ecosystem services, including data on both should help prioritize among potential conservation sites.

A significant advantage of this type of economic approach to protected area design is that it allows conservation scientists to identify the wider and longer-term benefits to society of species protection. A critical element in the valuation of the benefits of conservation is the relation between performance and environmental conditions. Species that are seemingly redundant in current conditions may have an important role to play in future conditions. We have earlier seen, for example, that the in situ conservation of genetically dynamic landraces and crop wild relatives may not yield immediate benefits, but maintains the genetic stocks needed to enable crop varieties to respond to future changes in climatic conditions or the disease environment (Dempewolf et al. 2017). In an evolving system, a portfolio that keeps evolutionary options open is generally more valuable than one that closes evolutionary options off (Bellon et al. 2018). The economic approach recognizes this, and factors it into the valuation of protected natural resources, as well as the trade-offs between the area protected and the level of protection offered.

References

Admiraal, J. F., A. Wossink, W. T. de Groot, and G. R. de Snoo. 2013. More than total economic value: how to combine economic valuation of biodiversity with ecological resilience. Ecological Economics 89:115–122.

Alvarez, S., S. L. Larkin, and A. Ropicki. 2017. Optimizing provision of ecosystem services using modern portfolio theory. Ecosystem services 27:25–37.

Andam, K. S., P. J. Ferraro, A. Pfaff, G. A. Sanchez-Azofeifa, and J. A. Robalino. 2008. Measuring the effectiveness of protected area networks in reducing deforestation. Proceedings of the National Academy of Sciences 105:16089–16094.

Baral, N., S. Kaul, J. T. Heinen, and S. B. Ale. 2017. Estimating the value of the World Heritage Site designation: a case study from Sagarmatha (Mount Everest) National Park, Nepal. Journal of Sustainable Tourism 25:1776–1791.

Barbier, E. B. 2007. Valuing ecosystem services as productive inputs. Economic Policy 49:178–229.

Bellon, M. R., A. Mastretta-Yanes, A. Ponce-Mendoza, D. Ortiz-Santamaría, O. Oliveros-Galindo, H. Perales, F. Acevedo, and J. Sarukhán. 2018. Evolutionary and food supply implications of ongoing maize domestication by Mexican campesinos. Proceedings of the Royal Society B: Biological Sciences 285:20181049.

Chape, S., M. Spalding, and M. D. Jenkins. 2008. The world's protected areas. UNEP-WCMC in Association with University of California Press, Berkeley.

Cushman, S. A., N. B. Elliot, D. Bauer, K. Kesch, H. Bothwell, M. Flyman, G. Mtare, D. W. Macdonald, and A. J. Loveridge. 2018. Prioritizing core areas, corridors and conflict hotspots for lion conservation in southern Africa. PLoS One 13:e0196213.

DeFries, R., A. Hansen, A. C. Newton, and M. C. Hansen. 2005. Increasing isolation of protected areas in tropical forests over the past twenty years. Ecological Applications 15:19–26.

Dempewolf, H., G. Baute, J. Anderson, B. Kilian, C. Smith, and L. Guarino. 2017. Past and future use of wild relatives in crop breeding. Crop Science 57:1070–1082.

Di Franco, A., J. G. Plass-Johnson, M. Di Lorenzo, B. Meola, J. Claudet, S. D. Gaines, J. A. García-Charton, S. Giakoumi, K. Grorud-Colvert, and C. W. Hackradt. 2018. Linking home ranges to protected area size: the case study of the Mediterranean Sea. Biological Conservation 221:175–181.

Dixon, J. A., and P. B. Sherman. 1990. Economics of protected areas: a new look at benefits and costs. Island Press, Washington, DC.

Dudley, N., J. D. Parrish, K. H. Redford, and S. Stolton. 2010. The revised IUCN protected area management categories: the debate and ways forward. Oryx 44:485–490.

Ferraro, P. J. 2002. The local costs of establishing protected areas in low-income nations: Ranomafana National Park, Madagascar. Ecological Economics 43:261–275.

Ferraro, P. J., and M. M. Hanauer. 2014. Quantifying causal mechanisms to determine how protected areas affect poverty through changes in ecosystem services and infrastructure. Proceedings of the National Academy of Sciences 111:4332–4337.

Food and Agriculture Organization. 2012. The state of world fisheries and aquaculture 2012. FAO, Rome.

Hanley, N., and C. Perrings. 2019. The economic value of biodiversity. Annual Review of Resource Economics 11:355–375.

Hungate, B. A., E. B. Barbier, A. W. Ando, S. P. Marks, P. B. Reich, N. van Gestel, D. Tilman, J. M. Knops, D. U. Hooper, and B. J. Butterfield. 2017. The economic value of grassland species for carbon storage. Science Advances 3:e1601880.

IUCN. 2008. Protected areas. IUCN, Gland.

Joppa, L. N., and A. Pfaff. 2009. High and far: biases in the location of protected areas. PLoS One 4:e8273.

Matthies, B. D., J. B. Jacobsen, T. Knoke, C. Paul, and L. Valsta. 2019. Utilising portfolio theory in environmental research: new perspectives and considerations. Journal of Environmental Management 231:926–939.

Millennium Ecosystem Assessment. 2005. Ecosystems and human well-being: general synthesis. Island Press, Washington, DC.

Naughton-Treves, L., M. B. Holland, and K. Brandon. 2005. The role of protected areas in conserving biodiversity and sustaining local livelihoods. Annual Review of Environment and Resources 30:219–252.

Newmark, W. D. 1995. Extinction of mammal populations in Western North American national parks. Conservation Biology 9:512–526.

Oldekop, J., G. Holmes, W. Harris, and K. Evans. 2016. A global assessment of the social and conservation outcomes of protected areas. Conservation Biology 30:133–141.

Palumbi, S. 2002. Marine Reserves: a tool for ecosystem management and conservation. Pew Commission, Arlington, VA.

Pattanayak, S. K. 2004. Valuing watershed services: concepts and empirics from Southeast Asia. Agriculture, Ecosystems & Environment 104:171–184.

Pezzey, J. C. V., C. M. Roberts, and B. T. Urdal. 2000. A simple bioeconomic model of a marine reserve. Ecological Economics 33:77–91.

Ripple, W. J., and R. L. Beschta. 2012. Trophic cascades in Yellowstone: the first 15 years after wolf reintroduction. Biological Conservation 145:205–213.

Roberts, C. M., S. Andelman, G. Branch, R. H. Bustamante, J. C. Castilla, J. Dugan, B. S. Halpern, K. D. Lafferty, H. Leslie, J. Lubchenko, D. McArdle, H. P. Possingham, M. Ruckelshaus, and R. R. Warner. 2003. Ecological criteria for evaluating candidate sites for marine reserves. Ecological Applications 131:S199–S214.

Roberts, C. M., J. A. Bohnsack, F. Gell, J. P. Hawkins, and R. Goodridge. 2001. Effects of marine reserves on adjacent fisheries. Science 294:1920–1923.

Sanchirico, J. N., and P. M. Emerson. 2002. Marine protected areas: economic and social implications. Resources for the Future, Washington, DC.

Sanchirico, J. N., and J. E. Wilen. 2001. A bioeconomic model of marine reserve creation. Journal of Environmental Economics and Management 42:257–276.

Shears, N. T., and R. C. Babcock. 2003. Continuing trophic cascade effects after 25 years of no-take marine reserve protection. Marine Ecology Progress Series 246:1–16.

Simberloff, D. S., and L. G. Abele. 1976. Island biogeography theory and conservation practice. Science 191:285–286.

Sims, K. R. 2010. Conservation and development: evidence from Thai protected areas. Journal of Environmental Economics and Management 60:94–114.

Soares-Filho, B., P. Moutinho, D. Nepstad, A. Anderson, H. Rodrigues, R. Garcia, L. Dietzsch, F. Merry, M. Bowman, and L. Hissa. 2010. Role of Brazilian Amazon protected areas in climate change mitigation. Proceedings of the National Academy of Sciences 107:10821–10826.

Stolton, S., N. Dudley, B. Avcıoğlu Çokçalışkan, D. Hunter, K. Ivanić, E. Kanga, M. Kettunen, Y. Kumagai, N. Maxted, and J. Senior. 2015. Values and benefits of protected areas. Pages 145–168 in G. L. Worboys, M. Lockwood, A. Kothari, S. Feary, and I. Pulsford, editors. Protected area governance and management. ANU Press, Canberra.

Tallis, H., P. Kareiva, M. Marvier, and A. Chang. 2008. An ecosystem services framework to support both practical conservation and economic development. Proceedings of the National Academy of Sciences 105:9457–9464.

Tshipa, A., H. Valls-Fox, H. Fritz, K. Collins, L. Sebele, P. Mundy, and S. Chamaillé-Jammes. 2017. Partial migration links local surface-water management to large-scale elephant conservation in the world's largest transfrontier conservation area. Biological Conservation 215:46–50.

UNEP-WCMC and IUCN. 2016. Protected planet report 2016. UNEP-WCMC and IUCN, Cambridge and Gland, Switzerland.

Watson, J. E., N. Dudley, D. B. Segan, and M. Hockings. 2014. The performance and potential of protected areas. Nature 515:67.

Watts, M. E., I. R. Ball, R. S. Stewart, C. J. Klein, K. Wilson, C. Steinback, R. Lourival, L. Kircher, and H. P. Possingham. 2009. Marxan with zones: software for optimal conservation based land-and sea-use zoning. Environmental Modelling & Software 24:1513–1521.

Wells, M. P., T. O. McShane, H. T. Dublin, S. O'Connor, and K. H. Redford. 2004. The future of integrated conservation and development projects: building on what works. Pages 397–422 in T. O. McShane and M. P. Wells, editors. Getting biodiversity projects to work: towards more effective conservation and development. Columbia University Press, New York.

Western, D., S. Russell, and I. Cuthill. 2009. The status of wildlife in protected areas compared to non-protected areas of Kenya. PLoS One 4:e6140.

12

Conservation Beyond Protected Areas

In its rude beginnings the greater part of every country is covered with wood, which is then a mere incumbrance of no value to the land-lord, who would gladly give it to any body for the cutting. As agriculture advances, the woods are partly cleared by the progress of tillage, and partly go to decay in consequence of the increased number of cattle. . . . Numerous herds of cattle, when allowed to wander through the woods, though they do not destroy the old trees, hinder any young ones from coming up, so that in the course of a century or two the whole forest goes to ruin. The scarcity of wood then raises its price.

—Adam Smith, *The Wealth of Nations*, 1776

12.1 Introduction

Despite the rapid growth in the size and number of protected areas over the last three decades, 83% of the world's terrestrial surface and 93% of the world's oceans are still formally unprotected. In this chapter we consider the nature of the conservation problem outside of protected areas, the form that conservation takes, and how it reflects both the Hotelling principle and the protected area design principles described earlier. Aside from the threat to wild species in wild lands and capture fisheries, this covers conservation of domesticated species in agriculture, aquaculture, and forestry in areas subject to private, common, communal, and state ownership or control.

In Chapter 11 we saw that protected area networks are increasingly seen as part of a wider matrix, and that the success of conservation efforts in protected areas is increasingly recognized to depend on the relation between protected and unprotected areas. The more isolated protected areas are, the more limited they are in the number and type of species that can be maintained. The study of extinctions in national parks in the Western United States reported

Conservation. Charles Perrings and Ann Kinzig, Oxford University Press (2021). © Oxford University Press.
DOI: 10.1093/oso/9780190613600.003.0012

in Chapter 11 showed that conservation outcomes improved the more permeable the park boundaries were (Newmark 1995). The same author later
investigated the same problem in African parks, and reported that isolation
of protected areas due to the establishment of fences and roads, overhunting,
and disease restricted the movement of wildlife into and out of reserves, compromising the persistence of large mammal species (Newmark 2008). Few national parks are large enough to accommodate the range needs of migratory
species such as wildebeest or elephants within their boundaries, for example.
But by allowing the boundaries of national parks to be permeable, and by providing some limited protection in adjoining wildlife management areas, it is
possible to strengthen conservation outcomes.

In what follows we consider several dimensions of the conservation
problem outside of protected areas, covering the conservation of endangered
wild species in unprotected areas and especially in agricultural areas, the in
situ protection of the genetic diversity of livestock strains, crops and crop
wild relatives, and the ex situ protection of germ-plasm in zoos, arboreta, and
seed banks. We then connect these issues to the Hotelling approach, and draw
conclusions about the similarities and differences in conservation within and
beyond protected areas.

12.2 Conservation of threatened wild species outside protected areas

Historically, protected areas were established to achieve a number of goals.
The protection of threatened wild species and the representativeness of the
species and ecosystems covered were two among many different and sometimes conflicting objectives. The earliest national parks, such as Yellowstone
or Banff, were developed more to regulate development in charismatic
landscapes than to protect particular species. It is not therefore surprising
that existing protected area networks do not necessarily protect endemic
biota, and that the species and ecosystems they cover are not necessarily representative. In the United States, for example, there is a striking mismatch
between the distribution of protected areas, patterns of endemism, and
threatened species (Figure 12.1). While protected areas are primarily located
in the West, endemics and threatened species are primarily located in the
Southeast (Jenkins et al. 2015).

A similar mismatch between the distribution of protected areas and endemic
biota can be found in most regions, and most biomes. In the Mediterranean
biome, a global conservation priority, less than 5% of the endemic biota

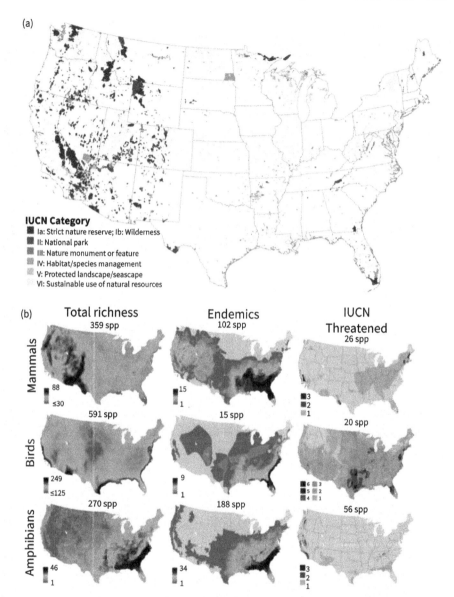

Figure 12.1 The distribution of protected areas in the United States (panel A), and species of mammals, birds and amphibians (panel B).
Source: Adapted from Jenkins et al. (2015).

falls within protected areas aimed at biodiversity. Such protected areas as do exist tend to be located in unproductive "leftover land" and do not represent endemic biota. In the Cape floristic region of South Africa, for example, protected areas tend to be located on high, steeply sloped land away from farms or forests, while endemics are frequently found in small remnants of natural habitat on private farmland, forests, or in urban areas. Elsewhere in the biome, a number of endemic species, including open-pasture endemics in the Mediterranean Basin, are found mainly in managed silvo-pastoral landscapes (Cox and Underwood 2011).

A study of the way that local ecological communities have responded to changes in land cover associated with land use, and to a range of other indicators of anthropogenic stress, has quantified the effects on local species richness and abundance. The study shows that in the most strongly affected habitats species richness has on average been reduced by more than 75%, while abundance has been reduced by around 40%. Globally, the authors estimate that richness has been reduced by 13.6%, and total abundance by 10.7% (Newbold et al. 2015). Figure 12.2 shows that the impact of land use on species richness and abundance is generally increasing in the intensity of use. The largest negative impacts are in urban landscapes and agricultural lands. Whereas the decline in local species richness and abundance in urban areas and pastures increases with the intensity of land use, in croplands and plantations intermediate levels of intensity can be more damaging than high levels of intensity.

From an economic perspective the question to be asked is when and where it would be efficient to induce landowners to do more to protect species richness and abundance. Consider the mediterranean biome. To get a sense of the scale of the problem, a study of unprotected natural and seminatural private lands that support native species and habitats was used to calculate the potential for conservation, using species-area curves generated from ecoregion-scale data on native plant and vertebrate species richness (Cox and Underwood 2011).

The authors concluded that Chile had the highest percentage of land in this category, and California/Mexico the least, but noted that if it were possible to conserve species on just 25% of this land, it would be sufficient allow persistence of more than 6,000 species. The implication is that if unprotected natural and seminatural lands were managed to allow persistence of native species, there would be "significant additional biodiversity gains" (Cox and Underwood 2011).

The most compelling attempts to answer the question are due to Polasky and colleagues, who have sought to evaluate what parts of particular landscapes are best treated as wildlife habitat. Their approach involves a number of steps. First, they define which parcels contain habitat for a species, and combine all adjacent parcels into habitat patches. Second, they calculate upper and lower bounds for the number of breeding pairs if all habitat patches were either completely connected or completely isolated, and calculate a connectivity score for the landscape based on the distance between patches and the dispersal

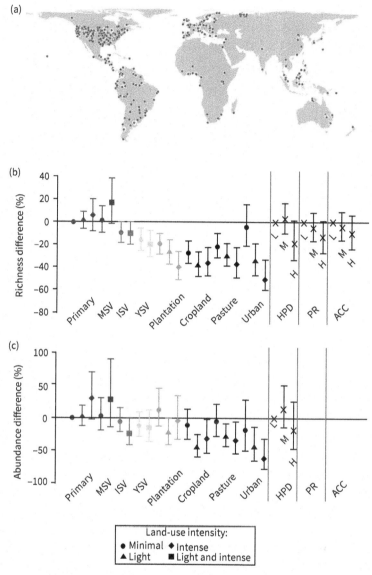

Figure 12.2 Modeled responses of the richness (b) and abundance (c) of local diversity to human pressures in selected sites (a).

Error bars show 95% confidence intervals. Responses are shown for land-cover types: primary vegetation (P); mature secondary vegetation (MSV); intermediate secondary vegetation (ISV); young secondary vegetation (YSV); plantation, cropland, pasture, and urban. Land-use intensity is categorized as minimal (circle), light (triangle), intense (diamond), or combined light and intense (square). Other anthropogenic stresses shown are human population density (HPD); proximity to roads (PR) measured by the log of the distance to the nearest road; and accessibility to humans (ACC) measured by the log of the travel time to the nearest major city). These are shown as fitted effects from a model with no interactions between continuous effects and land use, at the lowest (L), median (M), and highest (H) values in the data set.

Source: Cox and Underwood (2011).

ability for the species. Finally, they calculate the number of breeding pairs for a species using the connectivity score, and convert the number of breeding pairs for a species on the landscape into the probability that a species will persist on the landscape (Polasky et al. 2008).

This generates a biological score for the area: $B = \sum_{s=1}^{S} \pi_s$, where S is the total number of species, and π_s represents the probability that the sth species will persist on the landscape. The problem posed is then to maximize the biological score, subject to an acceptable level of net economic benefits (or to maximize net economic benefits subject to an acceptable biological score). Net economic benefits are defined as the net present value of commodity production plus conservation. Conservation is assumed to generate no economic return but to involve a management cost, although it is acknowledged that it might include, for example, the benefits of recreation and other ecosystem services. The net present value of land committed to all uses is thus the discounted stream of net benefits from economic uses plus the discounted stream of conservation costs: $E_j = \sum_{i=1}^{n} \sum_{j=1}^{m} w_{ij} V_{ij}$ where $w_{ij} = 1$ if parcel j is in land-use i and 0 otherwise.

The approach was applied to the Willamette Basin in Oregon, and used to identify combinations of land uses (including conservation) that lie on the production possibilities frontier—that is, that are efficient. For purposes of the study, biodiversity comprised 267 terrestrial vertebrate species, and the dominant alternative land uses were agriculture, forestry, rural residential, and conservation. Examples of land-use combinations on and off the production possibilities frontier are illustrated in Figure 12.3.

The main conclusions drawn by the authors were that it is possible to maintain a high level of biodiversity and generate large economic returns through land-use management. This is largely because some land uses, such as forestry, have the capacity to offer both high biological scores (due to the fact that many of the listed species are generalists) and high economic returns. Moreover, they concluded that securing habitat for most species could be achieved at low cost, but achieving habitat for the few species was likely to be very expensive. Since the lower slope of the production possibilities frontier is steep, there are large conservation gains to be had at low economic cost. But since the upper slope is flat, the last few conservation gains involve a high cost. Moving from land-use combination A to land-use combination D, for example, secures habitat for an additional 20 species, at a cost of US$2.4 billion. Moving from land-use combination D to land-use combination H secures habitat for an additional 8 species at a cost of US$25.3 billion.

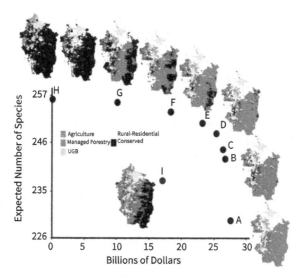

Figure 12.3 Willamette Basin: land-use patterns associated with specific points along the efficiency frontier (A–H) and the current landscape (I).

Compared to the current landscape, points on the efficiency frontier have less agriculture and more rural residential use. There is a shift from predominantly managed forest toward conservation land as the biological objective is emphasized more relative to the economic objective.

Source: Polasky et al. (2008).

Discussion of the instruments available to induce conservation of wild species on private land is deferred to the next chapter. Here we identify the conservation problems identified in the literature. These tend to be more targeted than those discussed earlier, and deal with persistence of particular species rather than the conservation of all extant species. Two categories of conservation problem are (a) the maintenance of habitat remnants important to the survival of endangered species, and (b) the establishment and maintenance of biocorridors between habitats important to the survival of endangered species. Both are driven by the fact that land conversion results in fragmented habitat, and hence in fragmented populations. Since local extirpations are common in fragmented habitats, recolonization following extirpation is important to the survival of fragmented populations. This requires, at minimum, habitat patches for breeding, plus biocorridors through the matrix. This is particularly important for endangered species, many of which are restricted both in their dispersal range and the kinds of habitat through which they can disperse (Fahrig and Merriam 1994).

For example, while the Eurasian lynx (Lynx lynx) has been listed by the IUCN as of "least concern" since 2008, it is still endangered in parts of its natural range. In the Czech Republic, for instance, the species was extirpated by the early twentieth century. Following reintroduction there now exist small but relatively unstable and disconnected populations. Since decisions to conserve the Eurasian lynx in the Czech Republic have few implications for the survival of the species elsewhere in its range, the conservation problem is essentially a national one. It includes both the maintenance of suitable habitat patches, and the connection of those patches. A study of the scope for connecting large mammals through the construction of biocorridors in the country identified areas of occurrence of the Lynx, areas suitable as habitat, and potential corridors connecting these areas (Figure 12.4).

Applying the approach developed by Polasky and colleagues to this problem, different biocorridor networks would have different economic costs and biodiversity benefits. Data on these costs and benefits could then be used to evaluate the trade-offs involved, making it possible for the Czech Republic to determine a habitat and biocorridor network that is optimal given its conservation priorities and the cost of alternative networks. Factors likely to be important to such decisions include the complementarity or substitutability of different habitat patches. Breeding, summer foraging, and overwintering habitats would be complements, while alternative summer foraging habitats would be substitutes. An optimal habitat and biocorridor network would give highest priority to protecting both complementary resources and the corridors connecting them, and lowest priority to protecting habitats that are close substitutes. The substitutability of habitats is an issue that is especially important in the implementation of the biodiversity offset schemes discussed in the next chapter, but it is worth noting that any conservation strategy confronts the same issue. When not everything can be fully protected the substitutability between sites is one of the main criteria informing site selection.

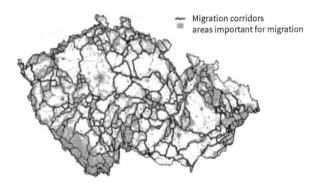

Figure 12.4 Occurrence (A), habitat suitability (B), and potential biocorridors (C) for the Eurasian Lynx in the Czech Republic.
Source: Adapted from Romportl et al. (2013).

12.3 Conservation in agriculture

In 2015 over 37% of the world's terrestrial surface was committed to agriculture, 25.2% in meadow and pasture, and 12.2% in arable land and permanent crops. The conversion of natural habitat to agricultural production is seen as the main driver of biodiversity loss in terrestrial systems (Millennium Ecosystem Assessment 2005a). While the loss of habitat has the most direct effects on species richness and abundance, these are amplified by the effects of fragmentation. Fragmentation reduces the size of the populations of plants and animals that can be supported, and makes them more vulnerable to variation in climate, resources, and the introduction of new species. In addition, agriculture affects biodiversity through the offsite effects of nutrient flows, pesticide applications, and the diversion of available water. The global flux of nitrogen, for example, has roughly doubled, and the global flux of phosphorus has roughly tripled over background levels since the development of agriculture (Millennium Ecosystem Assessment 2005b). Dead zones in the Gulf of Mexico and many other parts of the world are an offsite effect of nutrient applications in agriculture (Diaz and Rosenberg 2008). The global collapse of many pollinator species is a consequence of the rapid increase in application of neonicotinoid pesticides such as clothianidin, imidacloprid, and thiametoxam (Van der Sluijs et al. 2013, Van der Sluijs et al. 2015).

Although the off-farm threat to wild species posed by loss of habitat, habitat fragmentation, and the application of nutrients and pesticides are the problems that most exercise the environmental community, they are not the only conservation problems in agriculture. There are three conservation problems that relate more directly to on-farm resources are:

1. the genetic erosion and genetic vulnerability of cultivated species that has followed the widespread adoption of high-yielding varieties;
2. the loss or degradation of abiotic resources used in agricultural production; and
3. the incidental on-farm impact of agricultural production on noncultivated species.

In the last century, yield growth in agriculture has been driven both by the application of nutrients and pesticides and by plant breeding and genetic engineering. Both trends have had negative effects on agrobiodiversity: "the variety and variability of living organisms that contribute to food and agriculture in the broadest sense, and that are associated with cultivating crops and rearing animals within ecological complexes" (Jackson et al. 2007).

Agrobiodiversity comprises both beneficial and harmful species: modern crops, landraces, crop wild relatives, livestock breeds, pollinators, and decomposers on the one side, and crop and livestock competitors, pests, parasites, and pathogens on the other. Technological developments in agriculture have had important implications for both. The application of herbicides, fungicides, insecticides, biological control agents, microbial pesticides, and antibiotics has locally extirpated many crop and livestock competitors, predators, pests and pathogens. At the same time, the development, diffusion, and adoption of high-yielding crop varieties and more productive livestock strains has resulted in the disappearance of many landraces, wild crop relatives, and traditional livestock strains.

Genetic erosion and genetic vulnerability: in situ and ex situ conservation of plant genetic resources: More than 90% of global food supply now derives from high-yielding varieties of a small number of crops—wheat, rice, corn, oats, tomato, and potato—together with improved strains of five species of livestock—cattle, sheep, pigs, chickens, and ducks. Two implications of this are (a) an increase in the genetic vulnerability (decrease in genetic diversity) stemming from the widespread adoption of high-yielding varieties, and (b) the genetic erosion of landraces displaced in the process. Genetic vulnerability occurs if a widely planted crop is genetically susceptible to a pest, pathogen, or environmental hazard, raising the risk of widespread crop loss. The replacement of thousands of landraces with a small number of genetically uniform high-yielding varieties is thus a source of genetic vulnerability. Genetic erosion occurs as a result of the loss of individual genes or alleles, or combinations of genes or alleles such as those in locally adapted landraces. Genetic erosion within a species is generally caused by declining abundance. It follows that whereas genetic vulnerability is likely to be observed in the high-yielding varieties, genetic erosion is more likely to be observed in the land races and wild crop relatives left behind (Food and Agriculture Organization 2010).

The economic cost of the loss of landraces or wild crop relatives is the lost opportunity to use their genetic material to breed or engineer desirable traits in future crops. Most cultivated crops and many livestock strains already contain genetic material from wild crop relatives, landraces, or traditional livestock strains as a result of twentieth-century plant and animal breeding programs. The conservation problem in agriculture is to ensure that the raw material for future genetic engineering of plants, and future plant or animal breeding programs, is not lost. There are two dimensions to this. One involves the ex situ conservation of plant and animal germplasm in seed banks, zoos, aquaria, gene banks, arboreta, and botanical gardens. The other involves the in situ conservation of germplasm in farms or agrobiodiversity reserves—protected areas dedicated to the conservation of cultivated diversity and associated agricultural practices and knowledge systems (Food and Agriculture Organization 2010). The in situ conservation problem of landraces is distinct from the in situ conservation problem of wild crop relatives. Landraces can only be conserved on-farm, while wild crop relatives are mainly conserved if they happen to occur in established protected areas. Landraces are cultivated plants that are morphologically distinct, have some genetic integrity, but are also genetically variable and dynamic, and have distinctive properties in terms of yield, date of maturity, and pest and disease resistance. Their conservation in situ requires that they be planted in a wide range of conditions. Crop wild relatives, by contrast, are noncultivated taxa belonging to the same genus as current crops. There are between 50,000 and 60,000 species worldwide that fall into this category, around 700 of which are the primary and secondary genepools of the most important food crops.

The FAO Commission on Genetic Resources for Food and Agriculture has identified in situ conservation priorities for the most important wild relatives of 14 of the world's major food crops including: in Africa, finger millet (*Eleusine* spp.), pearl millet (*Pennisetum* spp.), garden pea (*Pisum* spp.), and cowpea (*Vigna* spp.); in the Americas, barley (*Hordeum* spp.), sweet potato (*Ipomoea* spp.), cassava (*Manihot* spp.), potato (*Solanum* spp.), and maize (*Zea* spp.); in Asia and the Pacific, wild rice (*Oryza* spp.) and the cultivated banana/plantain (*Musa* spp.); and in the Near East, the garden pea (*Pisum* spp.), wheat (*Triticum* spp. and *Aegilops* spp.), barley (*Hordeum spontaneum* and *H. bulbosum*), faba bean (*Vicia* spp.), chickpea (*Cicer* spp.), alfalfa (*Medicago* spp.), clover (*Trifolium* spp.), pistachio (*Pistacia* spp.), and stone fruits (*Prunus* spp.) (Maxted and Kell 2009).

Crop wild relatives still tend to be conserved in situ only as an incidental effect of the protection of other species. That said, there are a small number of reserves established specifically to conserve wild crop relatives. For example, the Erebuni Reserve in Armenia was established specifically to conserve wild relatives of wheat (*Triticum araraticum, T. boeoticum, T. Urartu*), rye (*Secale vavilovii, S. montanum*), and barley (*Hordeum spontaneum, H. bulbosum and H.glaucum*) (Food and Agriculture Organization 2010).

The ex situ conservation of plant genetic resources for food and agriculture takes the form of collections held by a variety of depositories worldwide, primarily genebanks (approximately 1,750) and botanical gardens (approximately 2,500). Collectively these depositories hold more than 7 million accessions. The pattern of accessions has Accessions in the 50 years after the First World War varied between 2,000 and 5,000 a year. In the 20 years after

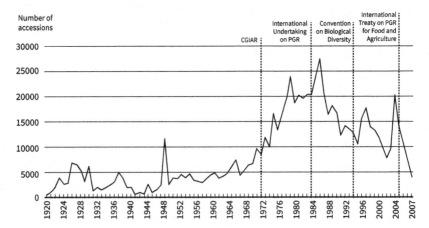

Figure 12.5 The number of accession to ex situ collections of plant genetic resources worldwide, 1920–2007.
Source: Food and Agriculture Organization (2010).

1968 the rate of accessions increased sharply, peaking at around 27,000 a year. Since that time, however, the rate of new accessions has fallen sharply, and by 2007 was back at levels not seen since the 1950s (Figure 12.5). Why?

Part of the explanation lies in the change the rights to crop genetic diversity claimed by nation-states. The growth in accessions by ex situ collections in the 1970s and 1980s was largely associated with the work of the 11 gene banks in the Consultative Group on International Agricultural Research (CGIAR) system, established to manage germplasm collections on behalf of the world community.[1] The CGIAR focused its collections on the landraces and wild crop relatives that supported development of the high-yielding varieties produced in first green revolution. Collectively, the centers maintain over 740,000 accessions of 3,446 species of 612 different genera. The CGIAR funding base includes national governments, philanthropic organizations, and a number of intergovernmental organizations, but it is nevertheless independent of all these organizations. It is also committed to making plant genetic material freely available to the world community. The principle on which the collections were founded is the same as that informing the first international agreement on plant genetic resources, the International Undertaking on Plant

---

[1] The CGIAR centers holding germplasm collections are Bioversity International; International Center for Tropical Agriculture (CIAT); Centro Internacional de Mejoramiento de Maíz y Trigo (CIMMYT); International Potato Center (CIP); International Center for Agricultural Research in the Dry Areas (ICARDA); the World Agroforestry Center (formerly ICRAF); International Crops Research Institute for the Semi-Arid Tropics (ICRISAT); International Institute of Tropical Agriculture (IITA); International Livestock Research Institute (ILRI); International Network for the Improvement of Banana and Plantain (INIBAP); International Rice Research Institute (IRRI); and Africa Rice (formerly WARDA).

Genetic Resources adopted in 1983: that plant genetic resources are a heritage of mankind and consequently should be available without restriction (Rose 2004).

In the decade after the International Undertaking came into force, that principle came under question. When the Convention on Biological Diversity came into force in 1993, it upheld a very different principle: that States have sovereign rights over their own biological resources (Convention on Biological Diversity 1993). This gave national governments the right to exclude others from accessing species within their jurisdiction, effectively ending the International Undertaking. The agreement that was to replace it, the 2004 International Treaty on Plant Genetic Resources for Food and Agriculture, was explicitly written to be compatible with the Convention on Biological Diversity. One effect of the change has been a marked reduction in the rate at which nation-states are depositing germplasm in the CGIAR collections. At the same time both the number of national genebanks and the size of national collections has been increasing.

At present, for major crops such as wheat and rice, a significant proportion of the genetic diversity of those crops is represented in ex situ collections. However, for many neglected and underutilized species, and for most crop wild relatives, the proportion of genetic diversity held in ex situ collections is extremely small. Since the resources available to support national collections in high biodiversity tropical countries are limited, the prospects for a significant improvement in this position are weak (Food and Agriculture Organization 2010).

The degradation of agricultural land: conservation of the resource base: The global rate of conversion of natural habitat to agricultural land has fallen in the last three decades, the total area under agriculture having stabilized at around 4.9 billion hectares or a little over a quarter of all ice-free land. There are, however, significant regional differences. In high-income countries there has been a net gain in forested area and a net loss of agricultural land. In low- and middle-income tropical and subtropical countries, by contrast, the extensive growth of agriculture has been associated with continuing forest losses. Around 7 million hectares of forest were lost annually in these countries in the first decade of this century—6 million hectares to agriculture (Food and Agriculture Organization 2016). The net result of this trend is a redistribution of agricultural land away from the temperate zones and toward the tropics. While this trend has implications for biodiversity in general, the conservation problem considered here is more limited. It is the protection of the value of the natural assets required for agricultural production—the soils, water resources, and species important to the production of crops or livestock, together with the ecosystem processes and the ecological functions that support crops or livestock.

At the turn of the century it was estimated that land degradation was harming around 2.6 billion people in over a hundred countries. It is a problem that particularly affects drylands, where some 73% of rangelands and 47% of marginal rainfed croplands are impacted (Gisladottir and Stocking 2005). Overall, around a third of the land currently in agriculture is characterized as moderately or severely degraded (Food and Agriculture Organization 2017). The form this takes varies considerably, but includes soil erosion (due to wind, water, or tillage), compaction, salination, the depletion of surface and groundwater stocks, and the on-site ecological consequences of fertilizer and pesticide use.

Most land degradation is a consequence of intensification of one kind or another. In some cases, intensification implies an increase in cropping frequency or in grazing pressure without any change in the underlying production technology. In slash-and-burn systems, for example, an increase in the frequency with which land is cleared for production increases water-borne soil erosion. Indeed, any reduction in the fallow periods in fallow systems has negative effects not only on tillage and water erosion, but also on stocks of soil nutrients. Similarly, in rangelands, an increase in the density of livestock or the frequency with which pastures are grazed increases both soil compaction and the rate at which forage is depleted. More generally, intensification involves a change in technology that may have mixed effects on the value of natural agricultural assets. In the 50 years before 2010, the area under irrigation increased by around 100%, global fertilizer use increased by around 500%, and global pesticide use increased by more than 1000% (Foley et al. 2011, Carvalho 2017) (Figure 12.6).

Irrigation has a number of consequences for natural agricultural assets. One is a direct effect on water resources. Currently, approximately 70% of global freshwater withdrawals are associated with irrigated agriculture. The proportion of renewable freshwater sources withdrawn annually is a measure of the impact of the growth of irrigated agriculture on the sustainability of water supplies. As Figure 12.7 shows, this is most severe in North Africa, the Middle East, and Central and South Asia. In such areas, where the value of irrigated agricultural land is frequently dependent on the stock of groundwater, declining water tables may imply declining land values.

The problem is exacerbated in places where groundwater reserves are treated as open-access, common-pool resources since individual users have no incentive to take account of the impact of their pumping decisions on others. In India, where groundwater depletion is a major issue in Punjab,

A Fertlizer use   B Pesticide use

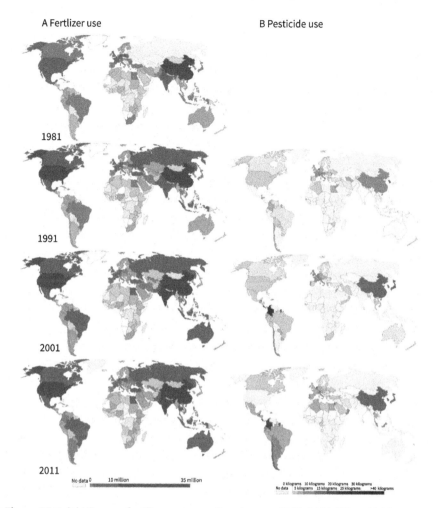

1981

1991

2001

2011

No data 0   10 million   35 million

0 kilograms 10 kilograms 20 kilograms 30 kilograms
No data   5 kilograms 15 kilograms 25 kilograms   >40 kilograms

Figure 12.6 (A) Nitrogen fertilizer consumption, tonnes, 1981–2011; (B) pesticide use per hectare of cropland, 1991–2011.

Total nitrogenous fertilizer consumption is measured in tonnes of total nutrient per year. Average pesticide application per unit of cropland is measured in kilograms per hectare per year.

Source: Food and Agriculture Organization (2018).

Haryana, and Rajasthan and where 89% of groundwater extraction is for irrigated agriculture, the net present value of irrigated agriculture under the existing open access regime has been shown to be 40% lower than an optimal regime involving the marginal cost pricing of the electricity used in groundwater pumping (Sayre and Taraz 2018).

Indirectly, irrigation may be associated with other effects that impact the value of natural agricultural assets. These include the salinization and waterlogging of soils and, where irrigation depends on groundwater, soil

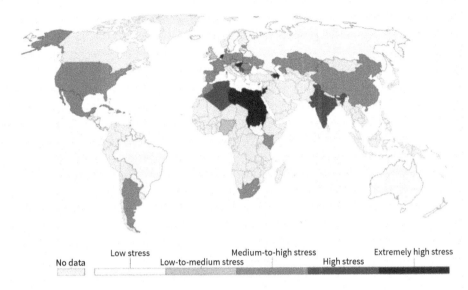

Figure 12.7 Freshwater withdrawals as a percentage of internal resources.
Annual freshwater withdrawals refer to total water withdrawals from agriculture, industry, and municipal/domestic uses. Withdrawals can exceed 100% of total renewable resources where extraction from nonrenewable aquifers or desalination plants is considerable.
Source: Ritchie and Roser (2019).

subsidence. In coastal areas the depletion of groundwater may also be accompanied by salt-water intrusion. The global annual cost of salinization of irrigated lands due to lost crop production has been estimated to be US$ 27.3 billion (Qadir et al. 2014), but as with waterlogging or soil subsidence the impact on land values tends to be quite localized. The impact may be very large, particularly where agricultural lands abut urban areas—the "sinking" of Venice a result of groundwater withdrawals in the last century being a case in point.

Water, wind, or tillage erosion similarly affect the value of agricultural land. In one of the best-known cases, the American Dust Bowl of the 1930s, agricultural land values were depressed in more-eroded counties relative to less-eroded counties, a phenomenon that persisted through the 1950s (Hornbeck 2012). Since the area of agricultural land currently affected by erosion is globally in the order of 40% (Foley et al. 2005), the effect on land values might be expected to be substantial. As with salinization, key questions for conservation are (a) how long the effects of erosion may be expected to last, and (b) whether the effects of erosion extend beyond the farm gate. The consequences of erosion for the value of assets is likely to be higher the longer the effects last, and the wider they are felt. In cases where soil erosion is irreversible, and involves external impacts hundreds or thousands of kilometers away from the site, the change in on-farm land values may severely understate the impact on asset values.

For similar reasons, the impact on land values of the growth in fertilizer and pesticide use may poorly approximate the change in the social value of assets. The dead zone in the Gulf of Mexico, for example, is a distant offsite effect of excess nutrient applications on farms in the Mississippi basin (Dodds 2006, Turner et al. 2008)—an effect that has been replicated in many other parts of the world (Diaz and Rosenberg 2008). It is not reflected in changes in private land values in the Mississippi basin. Pesticide applications also have effects that fail to be captured in private land values. Although the use of agrochemicals enhances productivity and hence farm values, agrochemical residues in soils in terrestrial and freshwater aquatic ecosystems, and in coastal marine systems, have long-lasting toxic legacy effects on both humans and other species. Globally, pesticide use has increased at around 11% per year in the last half century. At the same time, the range of pesticides has expanded to include organochlorines, organophosphates, carbamates, pyrethroids, growth regulators, and neonicotinoids (Carvalho 2017).

The effects tend to be widely distributed and long-lasting. Locally, organochlorines such as DDT and toxaphene (both still in use in parts of the world) remain in soils for years, and are transported by runoff to rivers and coastal systems contaminating and bioaccumulating in aquatic species. Globally, a range of pesticides including hexacyclohexanes, chlordane, toxaphene, organochlorine compounds, and organophosphates have also been found to volatilize, and be transported by atmospheric processes to higher latitudes. For example, chlorpyrifos, an organophosphate used in banana plantations Central America, has been transported as far as the Arctic icepack (Garbarino et al. 2002). While the use of persistent organochlorines has been phased out in many parts of the world, they remain in active use in several countries. As in the case of soil erosion, the legacy effects of such pesticides are still evident decades after the last stocks were used (Carvalho 2017). Nor is there any evidence that these effects have been captured in private land values.

The on-farm impact of agricultural production on noncultivated species: The last of the main conservation problems encountered in agricultural areas, the impact on noncultivated species, concerns the effects of agricultural production practices on the richness and abundance of species other than crops or livestock, and whether those species are targeted as crop and livestock pests, predators, or competitors or are incidentally affected by land clearance, water use, or the application of pesticides and fertilizers. There are several related processes.

First, the conversion of habitat compromises directly affected sessile species. The extensive growth of agriculture involves land clearance and the elimination of species affected by the resulting loss of habitat. This general process is recognized to be the primary cause of biodiversity loss during the Holocene (Millennium Ecosystem Assessment 2005a).

Second, conversion of particular pieces of land leads to the fragmentation of habitat, with direct effects on the size of the populations of wild species that can be supported. Habitat fragmentation is recognized to be a significant cause of biodiversity change, with the effect of fragmentation depending both on the size and remoteness of habitat fragments (Reed 2004).

Third, fertilizer, herbicide, and pesticide applications all have off-site effects on "downstream" ecological communities. As a measure of the scale of ecological impacts of fertilizer applications, the global flux of nitrogen has more than doubled, and the global flux of phosphorus has more than tripled over background levels (Elser 2011). Examples of the multiple off-site effects of fertilizer and pesticide applications include the dead zone in the Gulf of Mexico, and the effects of herbicides and pesticides on nontarget species in adjacent wildland ecosystems is another.

Fourth, the introduction of domesticated species in agriculture, and the accidental introduction of pests and pathogens, have led to establishment and spread of many invasive species, frequently with negative effects on native biodiversity (Perrings et al. 2010).

Fifth, wild biodiversity may be put at risk from gene flow from domesticated to wild species, or from cross-species transmission of infectious diseases. While many emerging epizootic and zoonotic diseases, such as SARS, Hanta virus, or COVID-19 have their origins in wild species brought into contact with domesticated species, the risks in fact run in both directions. Domesticated species may be an important source of risk to wild species.

In Europe, farmlands still provide the most important habitat for wild species. More than half of all bird species, for example, occur in the 174.4 million hectares of land committed to farming (about 40% of the total land area of the European Union). As elsewhere, agricultural intensification has had a number of impacts on wild species. A Europe-wide study of the impacts of agricultural intensification tracked the effects of the increased use of herbicides, pesticides, and fertilizers and the simplification of landscapes through crop specialization, removal of landscape elements, conversion of permanent pasture, land abandonment, and the expansion of early successional shrubs. The study found that resulting alterations in on-farm habitat had led to a decline in the richness and abundance of a wide range of species (Emmerson et al. 2016).

Among the best-known incidental impacts of the application of pesticides is the near-worldwide collapse of pollinator populations. While the pesticides of most current concern are neonicotinoids (a number of which are now banned in the European Union), this is not a new problem. In the 1950s, concern was being expressed about the impact of then-common pesticides on bee populations, including aldrin, calcium arsenate, chlordane, chlorthion, diazinon, dibrom, dicapthon, dieldrin, guthion, hemtachlor, lindane, metacide, and parathion (Anderson and Atkins 1958). The current pollinator crisis has many causes other than pesticides, including habitat loss, and pathogens such as the mite Varroa destructor and the deformed wing virus. But there is broad agreement both that neonicotinoids are heavily implicated in the decline of wild been populations, and that managed honeybees cannot compensate for this loss (Tylianakis 2013, Martin 2015).

From a conservation perspective, the problem lies in the fact that the privately optimal strategy for farmers may well be to ignore the impact of pesticides on wild bee populations. A recent study of the use of pesticides that harm wild bee populations found that whether or not farmers invest in wild been conservation depends on the availability of substitute pollinator services. Since the availability of commercial bees masks the decline in wild bee pollination, farmers have little incentive to conserve wild pollinators. In fact, if commercial bees are available, it may be privately optimal for farmers to allow the extirpation of wild pollinators (Kleczkowski et al. 2017). This is just one more case where the external effects of private decisions mean that the privately and socially optimal level of conservation differ.

Over the longer term, the application of pesticides has implications for the evolution of targeted and nontargeted species alike. Just as the application of antibiotics has led to the evolution of antibiotic resistant bacteria, so the application of pesticides has led to the evolution of pesticide resistant plants and insects. Insects typically evolve resistance to a new insecticide within 10 years, and plants typically evolve resistance to a new herbicide with 25 years. An attempt to indicate the cost of this process argued that if 10% of the agricultural output lost to pest damage in the United States were due to pesticide-resistant insects, this would imply an annual cost of up to $7 billion (in 2001 dollars, around $10 billion in 2018 dollars). At the same time, pest evolution results in an arms race between pesticide and pest, the cost of which is ultimately borne by all consumers (Palumbi 2001).

12.4 Habitat substitutability

Implicit in the on-farm conservation of biodiversity is the assumption that habitat patches may be substitutable. It is assumed that habitat lost through the creation of arable land or pasture can be substituted by habitat conserved in forest fragments or riparian zones, or habitat recreated through restoration programs. The implication is that the reallocation of natural habitat to more highly valued uses, at least at the margin, need not lead to a net loss of biodiversity. Species displaced through the conversion of an area of natural habitat in one location can be secured by the protection of an equivalent area of habitat in another location. This assumption is in fact essential to one of the instruments discussed in the next chapter, biodiversity offsets, which require a measure of equivalence between conserved and converted areas.

The conservation issue here concerns the substitutability and/or equivalence of habitat when the converted and conserved patches may be distant from one another, may impact different species, or may support different ecosystem services. The issue has attracted increasing interest as offsets and mitigation banks have become more popular, but it is in fact an important element of all conservation problems—whether inside or outside protected areas. The problem addressed at the level of an individual farm is essentially the same as the problem faced at the level of a country, a region, a biome, or the planet. The question of what to conserve and where embeds the question of how to compare the value of conservation in different locations.

In the case of biodiversity offsets, the question is posed as one about the equivalence of two areas. From a strictly ecological perspective equivalence is typically defined to be an equal value of one or more components of the ecological community impacted by conversion. In many cases this has been interpreted to mean a close match in habitat size and characteristics. For example, biodiversity offsets allowed to compensate for industrial development in the boreal forest of Alberta, Canada, are defined as "mitigation, conservation, or restoration strategies enacted in substitute forest areas so that no net loss of critical habitat occurs" (Dyer et al. 2008). Similarly, offsets established to mitigate risk to species listed under the Endangered Species Act in the United States focus on habitat suitable for the listed species (Ten Kate and Inbar 2008). In productive systems, the Canadian Fisheries Act of 2012 requires that any harm to fisheries habitat imposed by current use be fully offset. Although the 2012 Act abandons the principle that had been applied since the 1980s—"no

net loss of productive capacity of fish habitat"—the new fishery protection provisions still use productivity metrics. However, these are
decomposed to cover the main factors influencing productivity: loss of
habitat area, increased sediment concentration, reduced structure and
cover, increased nutrient concentration, decreased food supply, direct
mortality, change in temperature, increased noise, increased electromag-
netic field, reduced access to habitat, reduced dissolved oxygen, and flow
changes (Rice et al. 2015).

More generally, ecological equivalence is currently satisfied by establishing
the equivalence of a number of essential biodiversity variables: genetic composition, species populations, species traits, community composition, ecosystem
function, and ecosystem structure. Such essential biodiversity variables allow
comparison of sites across locations. Importantly, they are also taken to reflect
differences in the way people use the ecosystem services delivered by each
site (Gonçalves et al. 2015). From the Hotelling principle, we would expect
equivalence to reflect the broader range of benefits associated with conservation at different locations. While equivalence of type is mandated by, for
example, the US Endangered Species Act, equivalence of type is generally not
efficient. If it is used to identify offsets, for example, it can skew conservation
efforts to ecosystems of the same type as have been converted, which may not
correspond with local conservation priorities, be cost-effective, or deliver the
highest conservation benefits (Habib et al. 2013).

Recall that from an economic perspective, the substitutability of sites is
related to their relative capacity to produce a defined set of services. As we
saw in Chapter 7, the rate at which the biota at one site can be efficiently
substituted for the biota at another site is equal to the ratio between the marginal products of each site. If we are interested in the production of a defined
set of biodiversity benefits, then the substitutability of sites in the production
of those benefits is reflected in the shape of the lines describing the combinations of the two sites that yield a given level of benefits—the isoquants. Sites
would be perfect substitutes in this sense if they could be traded off one for
one in the production of benefits (implying a marginal technical rate of substitution of -1). They would be less than perfect substitutes if it took more
or less of one site to deliver some given level of benefits than of another site.
Where two sites are close substitutes or not may depend on how the benefits
are defined. The stricter the ecological equivalence between sites, the more
narrowly defined is the output of those sites, and the less likely it is to find
close substitutes. The more relaxed the ecological equivalence between sites,
the more broadly defined is the output of two sites, and the more likely it is to
find close substitutes.

12.5 Summary and conclusions

While the primary conservation instrument worldwide is the establishment of protected areas, we have seen that there are conservation questions to be asked and answered in every system, for every activity. We have focused on biological conservation, but we could just as easily have focused on the conservation of other resources. The principles to be applied are the same. This chapter identified the factors behind conservation challenges in biological production systems, particularly agriculture and aquaculture. It described the main methods currently used both to analyze the problem and to manage it, paying special attention to three issues: the genetic erosion and genetic vulnerability of cultivated species that has followed the widespread adoption of high-yielding varieties, the loss or degradation of abiotic resources used in agricultural production, and the incidental impact of agricultural production on noncultivated species.

The main difference in the biological conservation problem in production systems and protected areas concerns the mix of species involved. The set of species of interest in agroecosystems is quite different from that in protected areas. In both systems, however, an understanding of change in the expected value of the resources involved should take account both of the species targeted by resource managers, and those incidentally affected by management. It should also take account both of returns to assets owned and controlled by resource managers, and to assets incidentally affected by management. Just as protected area managers should take account of off-site impacts on the population affected by the protected area, so should farm managers take account of off-site impacts of farm operations. There are externalities in both cases, and those externalities affect the value of resources committed to either species preservation or agricultural production. The three issues addressed in this chapter are all examples of externality involving either wider or longer-term costs to others.

The final problem considered in the chapter, that of substitutability of habitat and ecological equivalence, is also relevant to the problem of protected area design. When there is insufficient land to achieve all society's species preservation goals, and when different parcels of land offer different sets of services, there are choice to be made about the best use to be made about each parcel. We know from previous chapters that the question of what to conserve and where embeds the question of how to compare the value of conservation in different locations. In the conservation literature, this is addressed through the concept of equivalence. We saw that it is generally interpreted to mean similarity across a range of attributes—genetic composition, species populations, species traits, community composition, ecosystem function, and ecosystem structure. While this approach allows biological comparison of different sites, we also saw that by the Hotelling principle, the equivalence should reflect the broader range of benefits associated with conservation at different locations.

References

Anderson, L., and E. Atkins. 1958. Effects of pesticides on bees: laboratory and field tests study the effects of agricultural pesticides on highly important pollinators of state's crops. California Agriculture 12:3–4.

Carvalho, F. P. 2017. Pesticides, environment, and food safety. Food and Energy Security 6:48–60.

Convention on Biological Diversity. 1993. United Nations Treaty Series, New York.

Cox, R. L., and E. C. Underwood. 2011. The importance of conserving biodiversity outside of protected areas in Mediterranean ecosystems. PLoS One 6:e14508.

Diaz, R. J., and R. Rosenberg. 2008. Spreading dead zones and consequences for marine ecosystems. Science 321:926–929.

Dodds, W. K. 2006. Nutrients and the dead zone: the link between nutrient ratios and dissolved oxygen in the northern Gulf of Mexico. Frontiers in Ecology and the Environment 4:211–217.

Dyer, S., J. Grant, T. Lesack, and M. Weber. 2008. Catching up: conservation and biodiversity offsets in Alberta's boreal forest. Canadian Boreal Initiative, Ottawa, ON.

Elser, J. J. 2011. A world awash with nitrogen. Science 334:1504–1505.

Emmerson, M., M. Morales, J. Oñate, P. Batáry, F. Berendse, J. Liira, T. Aavik, I. Guerrero, R. Bommarco, and S. Eggers. 2016. How agricultural intensification affects biodiversity and ecosystem services. Advances in Ecological Research 55:43–97.

Fahrig, L., and G. Merriam. 1994. Conservation of fragmented populations. Conservation Biology 8:50–59.

Foley, J. A., R. DeFries, G. P. Asner, C. Barford, G. Bonan, S. R. Carpenter, F. S. Chapin, M. T. Coe, G. C. Daily, H. K. Gibbs, J. H. Helkowski, T. Holloway, E. A. Howard, C. J. Kucharik, C. Monfreda, J. A. Patz, I. C. Prentice, N. Ramankutty, and P. K. Snyder. 2005. Global consequences of land use. Science 309:570–574.

Foley, J. A., N. Ramankutty, K. A. Brauman, E. S. Cassidy, J. S. Gerber, M. Johnston, N. D. Mueller, C. O/'Connell, D. K. Ray, P. C. West, C. Balzer, E. M. Bennett, S. R. Carpenter, J. Hill, C. Monfreda, S. Polasky, J. Rockstrom, J. Sheehan, S. Siebert, D. Tilman, and D. P. M. Zaks. 2011. Solutions for a cultivated planet. Nature 478:337–342.

Food and Agriculture Organization. 2010. The second report on the state of the world's plant genetic resources for food and agriculture. FAO, Rome.

Food and Agriculture Organization. 2016. State of the world's forests 2016: forests and agriculture: land-use challenges and opportunities. FAO, Rome.

Food and Agriculture Organization. 2017. The future of food and agriculture: trends and challenges. FAO, Rome.

Food and Agriculture Organization. 2018. Databases. FAO, Rome.

Garbarino, J. R., E. Snyder-Conn, T. J. Leiker, and G. L. Hoffman. 2002. Contaminants in Arctic snow collected over northwest Alaskan sea ice. Water, Air, and Soil Pollution 139:183–214.

Gisladottir, G., and M. Stocking. 2005. Land degradation control and its global environmental benefits. Land Degradation & Development 16:99–112.

Gonçalves, B., A. Marques, A. M. V. D. M. Soares, and H. M. Pereira. 2015. Biodiversity offsets: from current challenges to harmonized metrics. Current Opinion in Environmental Sustainability 14:61–67.

Habib, T. J., D. R. Farr, R. R. Schneider, and S. Boutin. 2013. Economic and ecological outcomes of flexible biodiversity offset systems. Conservation Biology 27:1313–1323.

Hornbeck, R. 2012. The enduring impact of the American dust bowl: short-and long-run adjustments to environmental catastrophe. American Economic Review 102:1477–1507.

Jackson, L. E., L. Brussaard, P. C. de Ruiter, U. Pascual, C. Perrings, and K. Bawa. 2007. Agrobiodiversity. Pages 1–13 in S. A. Levin, editor. Encyclopedia of biodiversity. Elsevier, New York.

Jenkins, C. N., K. S. Van Houtan, S. L. Pimm, and J. O. Sexton. 2015. US protected lands mismatch biodiversity priorities. Proceedings of the National Academy of Sciences 112:5081–5086.

Kleczkowski, A., C. Ellis, N. Hanley, and D. Goulson. 2017. Pesticides and bees: ecological-economic modelling of bee populations on farmland. Ecological Modelling 360:53–62.

Martin, C. 2015. A re-examination of the pollinator crisis. Current Biology 25:811–815.

Maxted, N., and S. P. Kell. 2009. Establishment of a global network for the in situ conservation of crop wild relatives: status and needs. FAO Commission on Genetic Resources for Food and Agriculture, Rome.

Millennium Ecosystem Assessment. 2005a. Ecosystems and human well-being: biodiversity synthesis. World Resources Institute, Washington, DC.

Millennium Ecosystem Assessment. 2005b. Ecosystems and human well-being: general synthesis. Island Press, Washington, DC.

Newbold, T., L. N. Hudson, S. L. L. Hill, S. Contu, I. Lysenko, R. A. Senior, L. Börger, D. J. Bennett, A. Choimes, B. Collen, J. Day, A. De Palma, S. Díaz, S. Echeverria-Londoño, M. J. Edgar, A. Feldman, M. Garon, M. L. K. Harrison, T. Alhusseini, D. J. Ingram, Y. Itescu, J. Kattge, V. Kemp, L. Kirkpatrick, M. Kleyer, D. L. P. Correia,

C. D. Martin, S. Meiri, M. Novosolov, Y. Pan, H. R. P. Phillips, D. W. Purves, A. Robinson, J. Simpson, S. L. Tuck, E. Weiher, H. J. White, R. M. Ewers, G. M. Mace, J. P. W. Scharlemann, and A. Purvis. 2015. Global effects of land use on local terrestrial biodiversity. Nature 520:45.

Newmark, W. D. 1995. Extinction of mammal populations in Western North American national parks. Conservation Biology 9:512–526.

Newmark, W. D. 2008. Isolation of African protected areas. Frontiers in Ecology and the Environment 6:321–328.

Palumbi, S. R. 2001. Humans as the world's greatest evolutionary force. Science 293:1786–1790.

Perrings, C., H. A. Mooney, and M. H. Williamson, eds. 2010. Bioinvasions and globalization: ecology, economics, management, and policy. Oxford University Press, Oxford.

Polasky, S., E. Nelson, J. Camm, B. Csuti, P. Fackler, E. Lonsdorf, C. Montgomery, D. White, J. Arthur, B. Garber-Yonts, R. Haight, J. Kagan, A. Starfield, and C. Tobalske. 2008. Where to put things? spatial land management to sustain biodiversity and economic returns. Biological Conservation 141:1505–1524.

Qadir, M., E. Quillérou, V. Nangia, G. Murtaza, M. Singh, R. J. Thomas, P. Drechsel, and A. D. Noble. 2014. Economics of salt-induced land degradation and restoration. Natural Resources Forum 38:282–295.

Reed, D. H. 2004. Extinction risk in fragmented habitats. Animal Conservation 7:181–191.

Rice, J., M. J. Bradford, K. D. Clarke, M. A. Koops, R. G. Randall, and R. Wysocki. 2015. The science framework for implementing the fisheries protection provisions of Canada's fisheries Act. Fisheries 40:268–275.

Ritchie, H., and M. Roser. 2019. Water use and sanitation. Our World in Data, retrieved from https://ourworldindata.org/water-use-sanitation.

Romportl, D., M. Andreas, P. Anděl, A. Bláhová, L. Bufka, I. Gorčicová, V. Hlaváč, T. Mináriková, and M. Strnad. 2013. Designing migration corridors for large mammals in the Czech Republic. Journal of Landscape Ecology 6:47–62.

Rose, G. L. 2004. The international undertaking on plant genetic resources for food and agriculture: will the paper be worth the trees? Pages 55–90 in N. Stoianoff, editor. Accessing biological resources: complying with the convention on biological diversity. Kluwer, Dordrecht.

Sayre, S. S., and V. Taraz. 2018. Groundwater depletion in India: social losses from costly well deepening. Journal of Environmental Economics and Management 93:85–100.

Ten Kate, K., and M. Inbar. 2008. Biodiversity offsets. Pages 189–203 in R. Bayon, N. Carroll, and J. Fox, editors. Conservation and biodiversity banking: a guide to setting up and running biodiversity credit trading systems. Earthscan, London.

Turner, R. E., N. N. Rabalais, and D. Justic. 2008. Gulf of Mexico hypoxia: alternate states and a legacy. Environmental Science & Technology 42:2323–2327.

Tylianakis, J. M. 2013. The global plight of pollinators. Science 339:1532–1533.

Van der Sluijs, J. P., V. Amaral-Rogers, L. Belzunces, M. B. Van Lexmond, J.-M. Bonmatin, M. Chagnon, C. Downs, L. Furlan, D. Gibbons, and C. Giorio. 2015. Conclusions of the worldwide integrated assessment on the risks of neonicotinoids and fipronil to biodiversity and ecosystem functioning. Environmental Science and Pollution Research 22:148–154.

Van der Sluijs, J. P., N. Simon-Delso, D. Goulson, L. Maxim, J.-M. Bonmatin, and L. P. Belzunces. 2013. Neonicotinoids, bee disorders and the sustainability of pollinator services. Current Opinion in Environmental Sustainability 5:293–305.

13
Conservation at the National Level

States have, in accordance with the Charter of the United Nations and the principles of international law, the sovereign right to exploit their own resources pursuant to their own environmental policies, and the responsibility to ensure that activities within their jurisdiction or control do not cause damage to the environment of other States or of areas beyond the limits of national jurisdiction.

—Convention on Biological Diversity, Article 3, 1993

13.1 Introduction

While protected areas are still the cornerstone of national conservation policy, it is increasingly recognized that they need to be complemented by policies designed to address conservation issues in nonprotected areas. In this chapter and the next we consider the wider range of conservation policies and instruments developed at national and international levels. The distinction between the national and international dimensions of the problem stems from the fact that the policy options are fundamentally different at the two levels. At the national level, governments have declared sovereign rights over the biota in land and sea areas under national jurisdiction, and have long-established rights to pass laws and regulations, to impose penalties for noncompliance with those laws and regulations, to assign property rights, and to levy taxes or grant subsidies. At the international level, none of these options are available except by agreement between nation-states.

Although we have come to take it for granted that national governments have authority to assign rights over the biota in a country—in the same way that they have historically had authority to assign rights over subsoil resources—this is a relatively recent phenomenon, largely driven by the evolution of intellectual property rights. As we saw in earlier chapters, the

Conservation. Charles Perrings and Ann Kinzig, Oxford University Press (2021). © Oxford University Press.
DOI: 10.1093/oso/9780190613600.003.0013

first international agreement about the diversity of terrestrial species, the International Undertaking on Plant Genetic Resources (1983), was grounded in the belief that plant genetic resources were a common heritage of humankind, and should therefore be available without restriction. Since that time, however, two things have changed. One is that nation-states have claimed rights to all genetic resources contained in areas of national jurisdiction. The Convention on Biological Diversity (1993), for example, is built around the principle that nation-states have sovereign rights over the biological resources within their boundaries, that authority to grant access to genetic resources rests with national governments, and that use of biological resources is subject to national legislation. The second is that nation-states have asserted the right to assign intellectual property rights to genetically modified resources, covering the results of both traditional plant and animal breeding and the genetic engineering of resources. As a result, the biodiversity in areas of national jurisdiction is increasingly seen as a national resource, access rights being regulated by national laws, and conservation priorities being determined by national policy (Perrings 2014). Trade-offs between, for example, the protection of ecosystems or landscapes and the assignment of mineral rights have become national policy decisions.

In this chapter we review the policies and instruments applied by national governments to the conservation of natural capital in areas of national jurisdiction. The motivation behind the majority of these instruments is to bring private and social resource values into alignment—at least at the national level. Since the overexploitation of natural resources is frequently associated with externalities of private resource use, incentive systems aim to confront resource users with the wider costs of their actions, or to compensate them for the wider benefits. The principles informing development of these instruments have been considered in earlier chapters. We have seen that alignment of the private and social value of natural resources, or environmental assets more generally, is necessary if they are to be conserved at socially optimal levels. We have also seen that there are many reasons why private natural resource users might neglect the wider and longer-term value of resources. The instruments described in the next section attempt to address this problem.

Sections 13.2–13.5 describe the main categories of instrument: the assignment of property rights, legal and regulatory restrictions, offsets, and economic incentives. The first three cover the assignment of property rights in biological resources, protective legislation, and biodiversity and environmental offsets. The last covers incentive systems including taxes, subsidies, agri-environment schemes, payments for ecosystem services, and penalties. A final section offers a summary and our conclusions.

13.2 Property rights

The allocation of property rights is a near-universal solution to the tragedy of (national) commons—the overexploitation of open access resources within some national jurisdiction. Almost every society has used the assignment of rights as the way to conserve resources under stress. In some cases, and at some times, rights have been preferentially assigned to private individuals or corporations. In other cases, and at other times, rights have been preferentially assigned to social groups, up to and including the nation-state. Whether rights have been retained by the collectivity or conferred on private interests has depended as much on political philosophy as on the biophysical properties of the resources at issue. The central question has not been whether to allocate property rights in overexploited resources, but which property rights to allocate: public rights (*res publicae*), private rights (*res individuales*), or group rights (*res communes*) (Cole 1999). We consider two sets of rights that are important in conservation: private or group rights to exploit common pool resources such as capture fisheries, and public rights to limit damage to endangered species habitat through the establishment of protected areas.

The Nobel prize winner Elinor Ostrom spent her life investigating the various property rights regimes established around the world to deal with common pool resources, many of which involve a mix of private and group rights. Her central conclusion was that there is no one-size-fits-all solution to manage common pool resources. Instead, people the world over have developed systems to fit the nature of the resource, the biophysical environment in which it is found, and the cultural and political characteristics of the society to which they belong. What all systems share, however, is the establishment of a set of rights and obligations, and some means of enforcing those obligations. This can be quite formal or very informal. Irrigation systems, for example, often involve quite complex governance mechanisms covering the rights that farmers have to water (how much water can be used and when), the enforcement of those rights, and sanctions for violations. In Nepal, farmer-managed irrigation systems have written rules that include penalties for farmers who fail to contribute to the upkeep and management of infrastructure (Joshi et al. 2000). In the United States, the lobster fishers of Maine have developed a governance system in which access rights are based both on a formal system of state licenses plus membership of a "harbor gang" that maintains a fishing territory for the use of its members. The harbor gangs comprise small group of fishers whose main function is to regulate competition within controlled sea areas (of 100 square miles or less). Regulation of nonmembers involves direct intervention—the cutting of traps. Regulation of members involves mutual restraint (Wilson et al. 2007).

While there is no unique property rights solution to common pool resource problems, Ostrom identified a number of characteristics shared by successful systems of common pool resource governance:

1. clear group boundaries;
2. governance rules adapted to local needs and conditions;
3. the participation of members in decisions to modify access rules;
4. external recognition of the rights of community members;
5. effective monitoring of members' behavior;
6. the use of graduated sanctions for rule violators; and
7. accessible, low-cost dispute resolution mechanisms.

A final characteristic—which Ostrom termed "nested tiers"—is that control of common pool resources is typically devolved to the lowest level possible. Where a resource system involves many localized resources, such as fishing areas, subcatchments, forest fragments, the most successful systems of governance involve a hierarchical structure of rights. Management of each localized resource is in the control of a local group, but the management of localized resources is coordinated across resources (Ostrom 2015).

Many private rights to common pool resources in the form of tradable quota or permits. This is most frequently seen in national marine fisheries, where fishers are assigned individual transferable quotas (ITQs) up to some total allowable catch. By 2013 there were around 200 rights-based programs in 40 countries. The main benefit of the approach is that it encourages efficiency. Less efficient fishers have an incentive to sell their quota to more efficient fishers, leading to the concentration of quota among the most efficient fishing enterprises. In New Zealand, for example, which has implemented an ITQ system since 1986, although there are more than 2000 quota owners, most quota are in the hands of just eight fishing enterprises (Hale and Rude 2017).

Aside from fisheries, the approach has been applied to both air and water pollution via emissions targets, and to the hunting of terrestrial wildlife (Tietenberg 2003, Schmalensee and Stavins 2017). Initial rights have been allocated in a number of ways: historic usage, lotteries, auctions, and a variety of administrative rules. The most common approach has been to allocate rights on the basis of current usage—grandfathering. While this has the advantage of improving the acceptability of new rights, it may encourage overuse in advance of the introduction of formal rights. To combat this, rights are frequently allocated based on historic rather than current use. To take a recent example, following the end of the EU milk quota in 2015, the Netherlands introduced measures to limit phosphate use in the dairy sector to take effect in 2018. Since dairy herds had been increasing since the end of the milk quota, phosphate quota were based on the number of cattle on farms not in 2018 but in mid-2015, when the phosphate plan was announced (Jongeneel et al. 2017).

A second set of rights that matter for conservation are public rights to protected areas. Unlike the rights to common pool resources discussed earlier, the establishment of protected areas usually involves acquisition of private or communal land by the government through eminent domain (the right of the state to take private property for a public purpose). Between 1990 and 2016 the proportion of national territory designated as protected areas more than doubled from 6.2% to 13.4%. In many cases this has involved a three-step process: extinguishing private rights to targeted land, placing that land in the public domain, and transferring the land into a protected area. By removing private access or use rights to threatened habitat, the process of establishing protected areas secures that habitat for endangered species. At the same time, however, it creates disaffection among expropriated landholders, and political pressures to exploit or overturn the process. Oil exploration, mining and development rights have been granted in many parks, and several parks have been "degazetted" or "denotified" (their status as parks has been terminated) (Veit et al. 2008).

13.3 Legal restrictions on land use

The framework within which national governments have developed instruments to promote the conservation of natural capital is provided by national legislation. In the United States, for example, the primary laws governing the conservation of wild species are the Endangered Species Act (1973), the Marine Mammal Protection Act (1972), and the Wild Birds Conservation Act (1992). We consider the first of these in more detail later, but a short description of its goal is to conserve and protect endangered and threatened species and their habitats. The Marine Mammal Protection Act prohibits the taking of marine mammals in US waters and by US citizens on the high seas, while the Wild Birds Conservation Act encourages wild bird conservation programs. The sustainable use of natural resources is covered by separate legislation. The Magnuson-Stevens Fishery Conservation and Management Act (1976), for example, governs marine fisheries in the US Exclusive Economic Zone. It aims to prevent overfishing, to rebuild depleted stocks, to conserve essential fish habitat, and to support the socioeconomic benefits of marine fisheries.

In Europe, there is a similar separation between legislation governing the protection of endangered species and that governing the exploitation of natural resources. National conservation legislation follows a number of European directives including the Habitats Directive (1992) on the conservation of natural habitats and wild fauna and flora Birds, the Zoos Directive (1999) on the keeping of wild animals in zoos, the Birds Directive (2009) on the conservation of wild birds, and the Regulation on Invasive Alien Species (2014) on the management of the introduction and spread of invasive alien species. So, for example, before BREXIT the UK Conservation (Natural Habitats, etc.) Regulations (1994) implemented the Habitats Directive in the United Kingdom, imposing restrictions on planning permissions likely to affect Special Protection Areas or Special Areas of Conservation—at least for the present. Legislation relating to the exploitation of natural resources is separate. Both the Common Agricultural Policy and the Common Fisheries Policy are supported both by EU regulations and national law.

Legislation in other parts of the world frequently combines the conservation of wild living resources with the sustainable exploitation of renewable natural resources. For example, in India the conservation and use of wild species is governed by the Wildlife Protection Act (1972), the Environment (Protection) Act (1986), and the National Forest Policy (1988). In China, the Law on the Protection of Wildlife (1988) aims to protect species of wildlife that are rare or near extinction, as well as to manage the utilization of wildlife resources, and to maintain "ecological balance." In South Africa, the Environment Conservation Act (1989) aims to protect ecological processes, natural systems, and biodiversity, and to mitigate the negative impacts of man-made structures, installations, processes, products or activities. But it also aims to promote the sustainable use of species and ecosystems, and to support environmental "improvements" that contribute to quality of life.

The Endangered Species Act: Perhaps the most well-known conservation legislation is the Endangered Species Act (ESA) (1973), which provides a framework for the conservation of endangered and threatened species and their habitats in the United States. The purposes of the act are "to provide a means whereby the ecosystems upon which endangered species and threatened species depend may be conserved" and "to provide a program for the conservation of such endangered species and threatened species." The Act is implemented by the Fish and Wildlife Service and the National Marine Fisheries Service, which are charged with undertaking a number of actions: (a) listing species as "endangered" or "threatened"; (b) designating critical habitats for the survival of species in these categories; (c) prohibiting activities that increase the likelihood of extinction; (d) creating and executing recovery plans for listed species; and (e) removing species from the list that may no longer be endangered or threatened.

Among the provisions of the Act that have proved to be most contentious are that priority to endangered or threatened species is without regard to taxonomic classification, and independent of the economic costs or benefits of recovery plans. A 1978 Supreme Court decision on the ESA (*Tennessee Valley Authority v. Hill et al.*) concluded that actions to prevent the extinction of a species should be implemented irrespective of cost. As a study of the economics of the ESA points out, however, this does not mean that there are no trade-offs to be made in the conservation of endangered or threatened wild species. Nor does it mean that the Fish and Wildlife Service and the National Marine Fisheries Service are not budget-constrained. In a world of finite resources priorities have to be set, and cost has to be a factor whether or not that is formally recognized in the wording of the Act.

Both the threat to species and the efficacy of protective measures depend on economic variables. Many of the land-use changes that cause loss of habitat, for example, are motivated by income-earning opportunities. Similarly, the choice among protective measures is necessarily driven by relative prices, and is necessarily constrained by agency budgets (Brown and Shogren 1998). A controlled study of the effect of ESA listing on the conservation status of endangered and threatened species found that whether a listed species recovered or not depended largely on the government funds made available to support recovery. Recovery programs for listed species that were supported by significant government funding were effective. Recovery programs for listed species that were not supported by significant government funding had little impact. In fact, the study found that absent significant government funding for recovery programs, species listed under the ESA fared less well than if they had not been listed (Ferraro et al. 2007).

A larger problem is that the many of the costs associated with listing under the ESA and with recovery plans are imposed on landholders. If the critical habitat identified for a listed species occurs on private land, the potential uses of that land are restricted—with inevitable implications for its value to the owner. This has, perversely, given landowners an incentive to avoid having their land designated as critical habitat for a listed species by degrading it in advance. It has also ensured that the designation of both private public lands as critical habitat is politically charged. Nonetheless, there are a number of species whose survival prospects have been improved through the habitat protection offered by the ESA. Among the most charismatic examples are the bald eagle, the whooping crane, the peregrine falcon, the gray wolf, and the grizzly bear. A number of species have been delisted. In some cases, such as the Eastern cougar, it is because the species has gone extinct. In others, such as the Hualapai Mexican vole, it is because the original listing decision was in error. However, many species have been delisted because they have recovered. Examples include the bald eagle, the Louisiana black bear, and the gray wolf (see Table 13.1).

There is less evidence that the ESA has been used to stop projects expected to harm listed species. On the contrary, a study of the effects of the implementation of the Act in the seven years after the 2008 recession found that

Table 13.1 Domestic species delisted under the Endangered Species Act due to recovery.

Common Name	Year listed	Year delisted	Common Name	Year listed	Year delisted
San Miguel Island Fox	2004	2016	Robbins' cinquefoil	1980	2002
Santa Cruz Island Fox	2004	2016	Tennessee purple coneflower	1979	2011
Santa Rosa Island Fox	2004	2016	Eureka Valley evening-primrose	1978	2018
Deseret milkvetch	1999	2018	Gray wolf	1978	2017
Lake Erie water snake	1999	2011	Island night lizard	1977	2014
Hidden Lake bluecurls	1998	2018	Brown pelican	1970	2009
Eggert's sunflower	1997	2005	Brown pelican	1970	1985
Gray whale	1994	1994	Arctic peregrine Falcon	1970	1994
Oregon chub	1993	2015	Palau ground dove	1970	1985
Louisiana black bear	1992	2016	Turquoise parakeet	1970	2017
Steller sea lion	1990	2013	Palau Owl	1970	1985
Magazine Mountain shagreen	1989	2013	American peregrine falcon	1970	1999
Lesser long-nosed bat	1988	2018	Palau fantail flycatcher	1970	1985
White-haired goldenrod	1988	2016	Tinian Monarch	1970	2004
Black-capped Vireo	1987	2018	Humpback whale	1970	2016
Concho water snake	1986	2011	Bald eagle	1967	2007
Maguire daisy	1985	2011	Delmarva Peninsula fox squirrel	1967	2015
Virginia northern flying Squirrel	1985	2013	Aleutian Canada goose	1967	2001
Modoc Sucker	1985	2016	American alligator	1967	1987
Johnston's frankenia	1984	2016	Columbian white-tailed deer	1967	2003

Source: (US Fish and Wildlife Service 2018).

despite widespread concern that it was stifling development, no project had been stopped or even substantially altered as a result of the ESA (Malcom and Li 2015). The law nevertheless continues to be challenged by those potentially affected by its provisions. It is currently subject to proposals to reverse the requirement that no account be taken of cost. While this would formalize what is currently a very informal (and imperfect) procedure for identifying cost-effective recovery programs, it could also open up the listing of a species to a much wider range of legal objections. There are also proposals to replace the ESA with a system much closer to the long-standing Conservation Reserve Program discussed in Section 13.5.

Access restrictions: A second set of instruments, frequently associated with user rights, are legal restrictions on the activities that are a source of conservation externalities. These are among the oldest instruments in use, and include open and closed harvest seasons, bag and catch limits, hunting and trapping licenses, and gear restrictions. The tradable quota discussed earlier are a modern form of an old instrument. They specify rights to shares in a legal cap on harvests. It is the cap that solves the problem of declining stocks, not the establishment of rights. By setting and enforcing a total allowable catch (TAC), for example, the stock which supports that catch is protected. There is some evidence that fish stocks in countries that implement tradable quota are less depleted than in countries that do not implement tradable quota (Costello et al. 2008), but many stocks that are managed through ITQs have been overfished (Beddington et al. 2007). If the TAC is either set too high or it is not enforced, the stock will not be protected. ITQs cannot protect against bycatch (including bycatch of protected species), impacts on food web dynamics, or disturbance of the benthic systems on the sea floor.

Restrictions on access are among the most widespread instruments used to conserve stocks of species targeted by hunters, gatherers, fishers, foresters, trappers and others. Indeed, the establishment of protected areas is simultaneously the establishment of generalized restrictions on access to protected habitat. Analogous instruments include emission caps, exclusion zones, and zoning restrictions. Zoning restrictions limit the range of land/sea uses possible in a given protected area. Where people are allowed to use the resources of the area, there will usually be limitations on the activities they are legally permitted to undertake in different places. For example, the Great Barrier Reef Marine Park in Australia has applied zoning for decades to allow multiple uses of the resource. Zoning offers high levels of protection in some areas while allowing a range of exploitative uses in other areas, including aquaculture, boating, diving, photography, fishing, collecting, research, shipping, and tourism (Day 2002) (Figure 13.1).

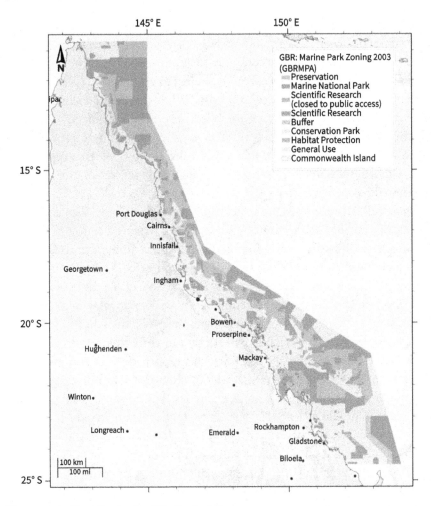

Figure 13.1 Great Barrier Reef Marine Park Zones.
Source: Great Barrier Reef Marine Park Authority (2018).

13.4 Environmental offsets

In the United States, the Endangered Species Act aims to contain the threat to listed species by requiring avoidance of damage to critical habitat where possible and the minimization of damage to critical habitat where it is not possible to avoid damage. In cases where there is little that can be done to minimize damage at some development site, however, biodiversity offset programs allow compensatory investment in habitat conservation at a remote site. More particularly, biodiversity offsets allow private developers whose actions threaten a listed species to mitigate the risk by buying credits

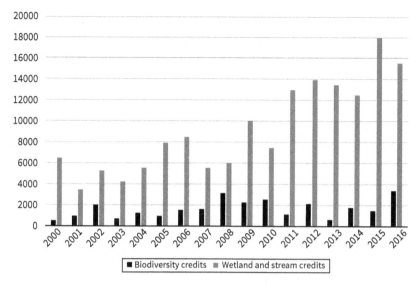

Figure 13.2 Volume of biodiversity, wetland, and stream credits transacted in the United States.
Source: Compiled from data derived from Bennett and Gallant (2018).

from biodiversity conservation banks that maintain habitat of different kinds. Wetland and stream offsets similarly allow developers aiming to drain, fill, or dredge a wetland or stream to meet their mitigation obligations under the Clean Water Act (CWA). Both programs have been in existence since the 1970s, but wetland and stream offsets are significantly more developed than biodiversity offsets (Figure 13.2). In 2016, the financial value of wetland and stream credits transacted was around US$3.5 billion. Biodiversity credits were less than one tenth of that amount in the same year (Bennett et al. 2017).

Biodiversity offsets in the United States are implemented as part of a requirement that developments affecting critical habitat should respect a number of conditions:

1. that there are no other viable alternatives within the region involving modified or noncritical natural habitats that are not critical;
2. that there are no measurable adverse impacts on (listed) species supported by the habitat;
3. that there is no reduction in the global/national/regional population of those species over a reasonable period of time; and
4. that robust, appropriately designed, and long-term biodiversity monitoring and evaluation are implemented (Business and Biodiversity Offsets Programme 2012).

Offsets should be designed to meet the last three of these requirements. As we saw in Chapter 12, one of the issues this raises concerns the ecological equivalence of the development and conservation sites. In the United States this has generally been interpreted to mean that the sites offer equivalent habitat for the particular species impacted by the development. So long as the legal requirement of developers involves protection of the species at the development site, that is the logical way to approach offsets. Development projects, in this case, comprise both a development site and an ecologically equivalent conservation site that together meet a conservation condition such as no net loss. The selected project should then be the combination of development and conservation sites that offers highest present social value, while satisfying the species-specific conservation condition.

No net loss is the central requirement of the European Union's biodiversity strategy, but it is increasingly being adopted elsewhere. It is also increasingly being interpreted to allow substitution between species, ecosystems, or landscapes. In this broader approach the loss of one species at the development site could be substituted by the conservation of another species at the conservation site. Allowing trade-offs between species, ecosystems, or landscapes is argued to offer two main benefits. First, it would allow the selection of conservation sites to be driven by wider regional priorities, rather than a strict interpretation of no net loss of a particular set of species. For example, it would make it possible for the conservation site to support rarer, or more endangered species than that affected on the development site. Second, it would allow the selection of compensatory conservation to be more sensitive to cost, so increasing the conservation benefits to be had from a given conservation investment (Habib et al. 2013).

A 2010 review of offset policies in a number of countries—the United States, the European countries, Australia, Brazil, and South Africa—found that while most countries had initially favored in-kind offsets located close to the development site, there was a tendency for this to be relaxed. The US conservation banking scheme largely requires in kind local mitigation, but the European Commission's Natura 2000 policy—which requires no net loss of biodiversity and ecosystem services through compensation or offsetting schemes—specifies only comparable functions at comparable proportions. Australian policies differ by state. Western Australia requires "like for like or better," but Victoria requires only that mitigation be commensurate. In fact, in-kind offsets are required only where vegetation losses in the development site are especially significant. The least restrictive of all current offset programs is Brazil's industrial offset program, which is flexible both as to the equivalence of development and offset sites, and their location (McKenney and Kiesecker 2010).

As the flexibility of offsets has increased, so has the need to be able to trade off conservation benefits of different kinds. In the conservation literature, the unit of account that allows different ecological functions to be compared is referred to as a "currency." It allows identification of offset sites based not on land area, but the ecological benefits to be had from each site. Given the currency, it is then possible to determine what is called a mitigation replacement ratio—the number of credit units provided through an offset to compensate one unit of loss at the development site. It follows that mitigation ratios will be sensitive to the compensation method chosen, whether the offset is in-kind or out-of-kind, whether it is of greater conservation significance, whether it is near or far, how long it will take to realize the conservation benefits, and the risk of offset failure (McKenney and Kiesecker 2010).

Of course, this is what any value system does. A unit of account allows decision-makers to compare different goods and services, so making it possible to assess the relative merits of actions that yield different bundles of goods and services. The currency referred to in the conservation literature is a unit of account for ecological benefits only, but it is a small step to identify a unit of account that spans both ecological benefits and the wider range of goods and services that people encounter. With such a unit of account, the Hotelling principle can then be employed to determine when a decision yields no net loss in value terms. Conservationists may have still have difficulty in using a monetary unit of account to decide on trade-offs among conservation options, but a conservation currency is really no different.

Finally, it is worth noting that biodiversity offsets are closely related to transferable development rights. The provision of an offset is a requirement on a developer whose actions are likely to have environmental costs. Transferable development rights are a mechanism for compensating landowners for forgoing development of part or all of their land. Landowners are given an option to sever the development rights from their land, and to sell these rights to another landowner for use at another location. Such rights can be used to widen the range of land uses available to the purchase, or to increase the density or intensity of land use. Once the development rights are sold, the seller's land is protected through a conservation easement or covenant (Panayotou 1994).

13.5 Economic incentives

Aside from regulatory requirements such as the obligation to mitigate residual damage through compensatory mechanisms such as offsets or in-lieu fees, environmental protection agencies have the capacity to offer private landholders a wide range of direct incentives to undertake in situ conservation or to mitigate the damage done to populations, ecological communities, or ecosystems. These include both carrots and sticks: subsidies and payments for ecosystem services on the one hand, and taxes, access charges, user fees, performance bonds, deposit-refund systems, and penalties on the other (Panayotou 2013). All involve price or price-like mechanisms designed to confront resource users with the full social cost of actions that threaten wild species, or to compensate those whose actions offer conservation benefits for either wild or cultivated species (Pascual and Perrings 2007, Ring et al. 2010).

From a conservation perspective, these mechanisms serve three rather different goals. The first is to encourage resource users to take full account of the wider consequences of their decisions, whether positive or negative. By altering the incentives to resource users, they can alter private behavior. The second is to reduce the cost of achieving a given level of conservation. Instruments of this kind can be used to minimize the cost of public good provision by engaging private landholders in the process. The third is to generate revenue that at least potentially, may be used to undertake or stimulate investment in conservation. In this section we discuss the main types of incentive mechanisms using examples.

Access fees: The most common economic incentives for regulating the pressure put on species, ecosystems, or landscapes are user, access, and license fees. As we saw in Chapters 4 and 11, the optimal level of access fees is equal to the marginal social cost of access, taking all effects into account. There is, however, little evidence that the fees currently in use are set in this way. In most cases, the conservation goal of the environmental authority is met through the establishment of an access restriction—the open and closed harvest seasons, bag and catch limits, hunting and trapping licenses, and gear restrictions referred to earlier—while the associated fee is treated as a revenue raising device. In cases where there are no access restrictions, or where access restrictions are not enforced, any gap between the access fee and the marginal social cost of access is problematic. Take stumpage fees or royalties in forestry, for example. Economists have argued for at least 30 years that destumping subsidies in agriculture, and concessional stumpage fees in forestry, have encouraged deforestation at excessive rates (Pearce and Warford 1993). The problem in such cases is that the landholder has an incentive to cut trees up to the point where the stumpage fee is equal to the marginal private benefit the tree, but no incentive to take account of the marginal impact of tree loss on habitat provision, soil erosion, water supply, or carbon sequestration.

There are good examples of access fees that are sensitive to the marginal external damage caused by one land use rather than another. Germany's differential land-use taxes are a case in point. Land uses are classified according to the social costs they incur, and range from the most environmentally beneficial (natural forest) to the most environmentally destructive (industrial site). Land taxes are sensitive to land-use class, and are increasing in the marginal environmental damage of land use. The tax implications of changing land use from natural forest to industry, for example, are greater than from changing land use from natural to managed forest. Such tax structures have at least the potential to internalize the environmental costs of land-use change. There are certainly instances of instruments of this kind in developing countries.

One reason why access fees frequently diverge from marginal social cost is their distributional impact. A fee that is trivial to some users may be prohibitive to others. If local landholders are poor, and if they depend on access to natural resources for their livelihoods, there may be a political argument for limiting access fees. In many countries this has given rise to the development of tiered access fee structures. In Zimbabwe, for example, conservation fees charged for daily access to Hwange game reserve are US$5.00 for locals, US$15.00 for nationals from the South African Development Community, and US$20.00 for nationals from elsewhere (Zimbabwe Parks and Wildlife Management Authority 2018). While these differentials may not match the income disparities between Zimbabwean nationals and nationals elsewhere, they provide at least partial compensation.

Agri-environmental payments: Agri-environment schemes in the United States and Europe have used payments to farmers as a means of achieving conservation goals since the 1980s. The US Conservation Reserve Program (CRP) was introduced in 1986, initially to address soil erosion caused by wind and water. A that time landowners signed CRP contracts for 10 to 15 years, receiving annual payments to undertake one of two conservation practices— one involving native species, the other involving non-native species (USDA 2015). Since then, the program has been expanded to include incentives to undertake actions targeting carbon sequestration, runoff of fertilizers and pesticides, the provision of bird habitat, and the support of pollinators. At present contracts are offered for 47 conservation practices. The aim in most cases is to retire erodible or otherwise environmentally sensitive cropland and pasture. By 2015 the program had enrolled 9.8 million hectares (down from the 2007 maximum of 14.9 million hectares) at an annual cost to USDA of $1.8 billion. Payments to farmers are capped by a "soil rental rate," which is a county-level estimate of nonirrigated cropland rental rates, modified by a parcel-specific soil productivity measure. These payments are highly variable nationally (see Figure 13.3). In 2012, while the average soil rental rate was US$126/hectare, the 10th and 90th percentiles were US$62/hectare and US$240/hectare respectively (Hellerstein 2017).

Initially, the CRP sought to elicit farmers' willingness to accept payments through an enrollment process that involved designated enrollment periods, called general sign-ups, during which landowners were able to offer fields they wished to enroll and to specify the rate at which they were offered (up to a maximum given by the assessed soil rental). USDA then selected which offers it wished to accept. Once the environmental goals of the program were expanded, a new form of continuous enrollment was introduced, under which landowners were able to offer land with high environmental benefits at any time of the year on a noncompetitive basis, receiving a fixed rental payment based on the parcel specific soil rental rate (Hellerstein 2017).

In Europe, agri-environmental schemes similarly pay farmers to take actions that either have a conservation goal or that maintain the countryside. Expenditures on agri-environmental schemes in Europe significantly outweigh expenditures on off-farm conservation. A 2015 study of agri-environmental schemes reported that EC spending on agri-environmental

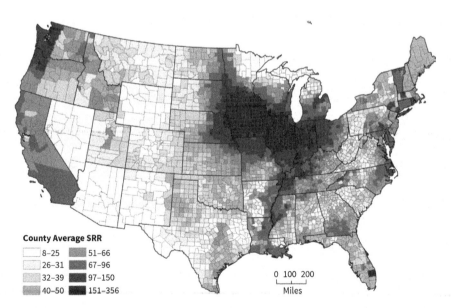

Figure 13.3 US Conservation Reserve Program county average soil rental rates (2012).
Source: Hellerstein (2017).

schemes in 2012, at €3.23 billion, was two orders of magnitude greater than spending on all Natura 2000 sites (Batáry et al. 2015). While particulars of agri-environmental schemes differ from one country to another, they share some common features. As in the CRP, farmers sign contracts of at least five years' duration to adopt specified "environmentally friendly farming techniques." Since 1992, all states in the European Union have an obligation to offer such schemes. The United Kingdom's Environmentally Sensitive Areas scheme, introduced in 1985, is an example. It aimed to conserve areas of landscape or wildlife value that were sensitive to changes in farming practices, and worked by offering payments to farmers to maintain or introduce environmentally beneficial farming practices over a contract period of five (later ten) years (Hodge and Reader 2010). In 2005 it was superseded by the Environmental Stewardship Scheme offering conservation incentives in 22 environmentally sensitive areas (approximately 10% of agricultural land). In most cases contract rates are fixed—and therefore more similar to CRP continuous enrollment than general signups.

Elsewhere, agri-environmental schemes tend to be on a much smaller scale, and to involve rather different payment schemes. In Australia, for example, agricultural support programs had been largely eliminated in the 1980s. However, from the 1990s a number of smaller-scale, federally funded projects were introduced offering payments to landowners for undertaking conservation investments. The most well-known of these, the Bush Tender program introduced in Victoria in 2000, invited landowners to submit proposals to protect areas of native vegetation on their property. Since then a range of tender-based projects have been implemented at national, state, and regional scales covering habitat provision, the protection of wetlands, forest conservation, the mitigation of salinity, and the protection of native vegetation. An evaluation of these programs found them to be generally more cost-effective than grant based programs offering similar benefits. Nevertheless, the level of funding of such projects has remained very small (Rolfe et al. 2017).

Agri-environmental payments are a particular example of payments for ecosystem services (PES). They tend to be older than most PES schemes, to be dominated by state or national funding, and to be more closely connected to the ownership of agricultural land. In recent years, a wider set of schemes has emerged that similarly engages land users through payments, but that is less dominated by state or national funding, and is less focused on agricultural land. Schemes of this sort have become an increasingly popular way to achieve the delivery of a wide range of environmental public goods outside of protected areas—especially in developing countries where property rights in land differ from the areas where agri-environmental schemes are strongest (Schomers and Matzdorf 2013).

Most PES schemes in developing countries focus on one of four main ecosystem services: carbon sequestration, watershed services, landscape amenity, and habitat provision (biodiversity conservation). They tend to take one of two main forms: smaller, more localized schemes involving direct transactions between suppliers and consumers of local environmental public goods, and larger state or national schemes aimed at the provision of global public goods. Both involve the provision of public goods that benefit people other than the landowners or landholders themselves: that is, where the members of one community enjoy positive spillovers from the public goods provided by another community (Ferraro and Kiss 2007, Wunder et al. 2008).

At the largest scale, the Reducing Emissions from Deforestation and Forest Degradation (REDD) scheme, negotiated in 2005 under the United Nations Framework Convention on Climate Change (UNFCC), is designed to compensate tropical countries that reduce carbon emissions due to deforestation and forest degradation, which account for around 10% of global emissions. At this scale, however, the principle of national sovereignty has been taken to mean that the UNFCCC can only offer reporting guidelines. The kind of contractual obligations that characterize most markets are missing. Since forests offer a number of benefits aside from carbon, however, schemes to reduce deforestation also have the potential to protect local water supplies, to reduce localized flooding and soil erosion, to regulate local climates, and to secure habitat for the protection of biodiversity that underpins locally important ecosystem services. This makes it possible to implement schemes in which macro-climatic regulation through carbon sequestration is an external effect of the provision of locally important ecosystem services.

One of the earliest examples, Costa Rica's scheme for forest conservation, makes flat payments to landowners for the conservation of forests, assumed to deliver four main services: the protection of watersheds, the conservation of biodiversity, recreation and amenity, and carbon sequestration. The last of these is designed to feed into the REDD scheme, but the first three are assumed to deliver local benefits. Payments are partially financed from a sales tax on fossil fuels, but the intention is that it should eventually be wholly financed by the beneficiaries of the environmental services it delivers. A number of downstream beneficiaries of watershed protection have entered into contracts with the scheme administrator, but less has been done to realize the benefits of biodiversity, recreation and amenity, and carbon sequestration. On the supply side, though, the scheme has had a substantial impact on the rate of forest loss (Börner et al. 2017).

The main questions about the impact of payment for ecosystem services schemes are whether the payment induces additional effort, whether payments are cost-effective, and what impact they have on the well-being of service providers. Additionality implies that the scheme generates a greater supply of the service than would have occurred anyway. Cost-effectiveness implies that the scheme delivers the service at least cost. In low-income countries, the third question has generally been taken to mean whether the scheme alleviates poverty. Many PES schemes have been launched in the belief that they would both contribute to the well-being of poor landholders and generate an additional supply of the targeted services—a win-win. Since the agri-environmental schemes in high-income countries are typically also vehicles for income transfers to farmers, a focus on poverty alleviation in low-income countries is entirely understandable. Nevertheless, by pursuing multiple objectives one may fail to deliver on any of them.

If a project generates multiple outputs, it is important that all outputs be considered. For example, a scheme managed for only one among several services delivered by the system can compromise those other services. Just as managing a forest only for timber supply can compromise water quality, flood risk, and soil erosion so managing the same forest only for carbon can compromise fire risk and habitat. Decisions that seem rational when only one service is considered are often inefficient when all services are considered. In the same way, if the payments associated with a scheme designed primarily to deliver ecosystem services also impact the income and wealth of participants, it is important that such effects are considered. But if the primary aim is ecosystem service delivery, then payments should be sufficient only to induce participation, and should be conditional on performance. Symmetrically, if the primary aim is to deliver income support to participants, then either ecosystem service provision is incidental and conditionality is irrelevant, or ecosystem services should be provided only up to the point that there is some additionality. It is not generally possible to maximize both ecosystem service provision and income transfers with a single payment scheme (Kinzig et al. 2011).

Schemes dedicated to the provision of ecosystem services have been shown to satisfy additionality. For example, a PES scheme was introduced in an area of Uganda that had been deforested at an annual rate of 2.7% between 2005 and 2010. The scheme offered landholders annual payments of 70,000 Ugandan shillings/hectare (about US$20.00) to conserve forest on their land. The scheme was implemented as a randomized controlled trial in 121 villages, 60 of which received payments for two years. Output was measured remotely as a change in land area covered by trees. Tree cover declined by 4.2% during the study period in treatment villages (below historic rates), compared to 9.1% in control villages. Despite the fact that deforestation rates in the control villages were substantially above historic rates, the study found no evidence that participants had shifted deforestation to controlled land. It concluded that the scheme satisfied additionality, if only during the course of the trial (Jayachandran et al. 2017).

Over the longer period, there is little evidence that payments for ecosystem services schemes that are effective in delivering ecosystem services are also significant contributors to poverty alleviation. A 2010 evaluation of the evidence suggested that while payments for ecosystem services schemes do have some potential to benefit poorer landholders, the improvements recorded in most cases tend to be very small relative to governments' poverty alleviation goals. Moreover, in cases where poverty alleviation is the primary goal of the scheme, they tend to be ineffective in delivering ecosystem services (Pattanayak et al. 2010).

Environmental performance bonds: Monitoring performance in PES schemes is frequently both costly, and a source of conflict with scheme participants. There are, however, a long-standing set of instruments that have been used to induce monitoring of the environmental effects of resource access. Performance bonds shift responsibility for controlling, monitoring, and enforcement to individual resource users who are charged in advance for the potential damage. Like any deposit refund system, environmental performance bonds require advance payments by logging and extractive industries that are sufficient to cover the environmental damage caused by their activities. Bonds are refunded if the realized damage is less than then value of the bond. Instruments of this kind encourage restoration in a cost-effective way. They also ensure that funds are available to restore damaged environments if bonded resource users fail to do so (Perrings 1989). Environmental performance bonds have been recommended as a market-based instrument to encourage sustainable forest logging while reducing monitoring costs (Leruth et al. 2001). More recently, they have been recommended as vehicles for assurance long-term monitoring and maintenance of carbon sequestration sites (Gerard and Wilson 2009).

Penalties for noncompliance: A final set of conservation instruments comprises penalties for noncompliance with environmental legislation or access restrictions. Penalties include more obviously price-like instruments such as fines for noncompliance, but also include custodial sentences and other punishments. The real value of the penalty corresponding to some offence depends on three things. The first is the nominal value of the penalty (the published penalty for the offence). The second is the probability that an offence will be detected, and that the offender will be arrested. The third is the probability that the offender, if arrested, will be convicted and face the published penalty. The second and third both depend on enforcement effort.

The headline "price" of illegal activity is the nominal penalty for that activity. Consider the problem of poaching in East, Central, and Southern Africa. As a way of deterring illegal hunting in the region, nominal penalties have been raised substantially. In 2017, for example, following a sustained and dramatic increase in the number of rhinos poached in Namibia, the country increased the penalties for the illegal hunting of both elephant and rhino from a maximum fine of N$200 000 (US$14,000), to a maximum fine of N$25 million (US$1.75 million) plus imprisonment for up to 25 years. Similarly, penalties for illegal hunting of other protected game (zebra, giraffe, klipspringer, impala, and hippo) were increased from a maximum fine of N$20 000 (US$1,400), to a maximum fine of N$10 million (US$700,000) plus imprisonment for up to 10 years. For second or subsequent convictions the maximum fine was increased to N$50 million (US$3.5 million) with imprisonment for up to 40 years. Other countries in the region have followed suit. In 2018, Kenya announced that as life imprisonment had failed to deter illegal hunting, it was introducing the death penalty for poaching.

The second and third elements in the real value of penalties—the probability of arrest, and the probability of conviction if arrested—reduce the real value of nominal penalties. There are no data on the probability of detection, arrest, or conviction for illegal hunting in Africa, but the growing volume of animal products reaching East Asian markets suggests that despite an increase in the commitment of resources to enforcement, it remains very low. A 2014 study of the deterrent effect of penalties in Africa argued that while intensifying enforcement effort was necessary, it was not sufficient to protect the most highly valued species. Rising animal product prices and deepening poverty in areas of supply had both increased the incentive to hunt illegally. The study suggested that the only solution to the problem was to address poverty in the supply areas, building both the incentives and the capacity within local communities to conserve wildlife (Challender and MacMillan 2014).

Elsewhere, there is strong evidence that investment in enforcement can be a very effective way of driving up the real value of penalties for noncompliance with environmental regulations. For example, a US study of enforcement on permit compliance under the Clean Water Act considered the impact of fines on future compliance. It found that when a state imposed fines on a firm for water pollution violations in one year, violations in the subsequent year by that firm declined on the order of 66%. More importantly, the deterrent effect of fines on other firms was almost as strong as the effect on the sanctioned firm.

The same study found that monitoring alone—monitoring not followed by prosecution for noncompliance—had no effect (Shimshack and Ward 2005).

13.6 Summary and conclusions

The array of instruments described in this chapter are all designed, in one way or another, to close the gap between the private and social costs and benefits of the many ways in which people use nature. The assignment of property rights and regulatory restrictions on behavior change the control that people have over natural assets, and the nature of their obligations to the community to which they belong. Taxes, access charges, user fees, performance bonds, and penalties confront resource users with the social cost of their actions. Agri-environmental schemes, subsidies, and payments for ecosystem services compensate landholders for the social benefits their actions confer on others. They do so imperfectly. Taxes, access charges, and user fees frequently fail to close the gap between the private and social cost of resource use, while subsidies and payments frequently fail to close the gap between the private and social benefits of resource use. Moreover, in some special cases, market interventions of these kinds make things worse, not better. Perverse subsidies in agriculture, forestry, and fisheries, for example, frequently increase effort in cases where effort should be reduced. But in principle, such instruments help people make decisions that better serve the interests of the wider society.

In terms of the general theory of conservation, pricing the services provided by environmental assets to reflect marginal social cost is necessary if the asset itself is to be correctly valued. Since resource users will conserve natural assets only if the expected growth in the value of those assets to them is greater than the expected growth in their value if converted, the aim of such instruments is to assure that individuals, households, and firms give due weight to the wider stream of benefits associated with assets in their control.

Not surprisingly, instruments that compensate resource users for public goods generated by land-use and land-cover choices are more popular than instruments that penalize resource users for costs imposed on others. The widespread adoption of payments for ecosystem services in recent years reflects this fact. Yet in many cases, the private value of environmental assets used in some way is greater than the value of the same assets to society. The clear-felling of private forests can, for example, lead to downstream flooding, landslides, and the siltation of rivers and dams. If forest managers do not carry these costs, the social value of the forest resource used in this way is less than its private value. Instruments that penalize forest managers for the adoption of clear felling can induce the adoption of management techniques that better conserve soils and water flows and enhance the public value of the asset.

Since many of the most important conservation challenges at the national level involve private land managers, it follows that instruments of this type are a critical part of the policy problem. Local and national governments have limited scope for managing privately owned natural resources, but they can use incentives to influence private behavior. Appropriately chosen incentives can lead private resource users to make the same conservation decisions that would be made by a social planner seeking to maximize some index of national well-being.

References

Batáry, P., L. V. Dicks, D. Kleijn, and W. J. Sutherland. 2015. The role of agri-environment schemes in conservation and environmental management. Conservation Biology 29:1006–1016.

Beddington, J. R., D. J. Agnew, and C. W. Clark. 2007. Current problems in the management of marine fisheries. Science 316:1713.

Bennett, G., and M. Gallant. 2018. Lessons learned on demand: demand dynamics of ecosystem markets in the United States. Forest Trends, Washington, DC.

Bennett, G., Gallant, M., and K. ten Kate. 2017. State of biodiversity mitigation 2017: markets and compensation for global infrastructure development. Forest Trends, Washington, DC.

Börner, J., K. Baylis, E. Corbera, D. Ezzine-de-Blas, J. Honey-Rosés, U. M. Persson, and S. Wunder. 2017. The effectiveness of payments for environmental services. World Development 96:359–374.

Brown, G. M., and J. F. Shogren. 1998. Economics of the endangered species act. Journal of Economic Perspectives 12:3–20.

Business and Biodiversity Offsets Programme. 2012. Standard on biodiversity offsets. BBOP, Washington, DC.

Challender, D. W., and D. C. MacMillan. 2014. Poaching is more than an enforcement problem. Conservation Letters 7:484–494.

Cole, D. H. 1999. Clearing the air: four propositions about property rights and environmental protection. Duke Environmental Law & Policy Forum 10:103.

Costello, C., S. D. Gaines, and J. Lynham. 2008. Can catch shares prevent fisheries collapse? Science 321:1678–1681.

Day, J. C. 2002. Zoning: lessons from the Great Barrier Reef marine park. Ocean & Coastal Management 45:139–156.

Ferraro, P., and A. Kiss. 2007. Direct payments to conserve biodiversity. Science 298:1718–1719.

Ferraro, P. J., C. McIntosh, and M. Ospinaa. 2007. The effectiveness of the US endangered species act: an econometric analysis using matching methods. Journal of Environmental Economics and Management 54:245–261.

Gerard, D., and E. J. Wilson. 2009. Environmental bonds and the challenge of long-term carbon sequestration. Journal of Environmental Management 90:1097–1105.

Great Barrier Reef Marine Park Authority. 2018. Zoning, permits and plans. GBRMPA, Townsville.

Habib, T. J., D. R. Farr, R. R. Schneider, and S. Boutin. 2013. Economic and ecological outcomes of flexible biodiversity offset systems. Conservation Biology 27:1313–1323.

Hale, L. Z., and J. Rude. 2017. Learning from New Zealand's 30 years of experience managing fisheries under a quota management system. The Nature Conservancy, Arlington, VA.

Hellerstein, D. M. 2017. The US conservation reserve program: the evolution of an enrollment mechanism. Land Use Policy 63:601–610.

Hodge, I., and M. Reader. 2010. The introduction of entry level stewardship in England: extension or dilution in agri-environment policy? Land Use Policy 27:270–282.

Jayachandran, S., J. De Laat, E. F. Lambin, C. Y. Stanton, R. Audy, and N. E. Thomas. 2017. Cash for carbon: a randomized trial of payments for ecosystem services to reduce deforestation. Science 357:267–273.

Jongeneel, R., C. Daatselaar, M. van Leeuwen, and H. Silvis. 2017. Phosphate production reduction decree of the Netherlands: impact on markets, environment and dairy farm structure. Wageningen Economic Research 2017-024, Den Haag.

Joshi, N. N., E. Ostrom, G. P. Shivakoti, and W. F. Lam. 2000. Institutional opportunities and constraints in the performance of farmer-managed irrigation systems in Nepal. Asia-Pacific Journal of Rural Development 10:67–92.

Kinzig, A. P., C. Perrings, F. S. Chapin, S. Polasky, V. K. Smith, D. Tilman, and B. L. Turner. 2011. Paying for ecosystem services: promise and peril. Science 334:603–604.

Leruth, L., R. Paris, and I. Ruzicka. 2001. The complier pays principle: the limits of fiscal approaches toward sustainable forest management. IMF Staff Papers 48:397–423.

Malcom, J. W., and Y.-W. Li. 2015. Data contradict common perceptions about a controversial provision of the US Endangered Species Act. Proceedings of the National Academy of Sciences 112:15844–15849.

McKenney, B. A., and J. M. Kiesecker. 2010. Policy development for biodiversity offsets: a review of offset frameworks. Environmental Management 45:165–176.

Ostrom, E. 2015. Governing the commons. Cambridge University Press, Cambridge.

Panayotou, T. 1994. Conservation of biodiversity and economic development: the concept of transferable development rights. Environmental and Resource Economics 4:91–110.

Panayotou, T. 2013. Instruments of change: motivating and financing sustainable development. Routledge, London.

Pascual, U., and C. Perrings. 2007. Developing incentives and economic mechanisms for in situ biodiversity conservation in agricultural landscapes. Agriculture, Ecosystems & Environment 121:256–268.

Pattanayak, S. K., S. Wunder, and P. J. Ferraro. 2010. Show me the money: do payments supply environmental services in developing countries? Review of Environmental Economics and Policy 4:254–274.

Pearce, D. W., and J. J. Warford. 1993. World without end: economics, environment, and sustainable development. Oxford University Press, Oxford.

Perrings, C. 1989. Environmental bonds and the incentive to research in activities involving uncertain future effects. Societat Catalana d'Economia: Annuari 7:160–167.

Perrings, C. 2014. Our uncommon heritage: biodiversity, ecosystem services and human wellbeing. Cambridge University Press, Cambridge.

Ring, I., M. Drechsler, A. J. Van Teeffelen, S. Irawan, and O. Venter. 2010. Biodiversity conservation and climate mitigation: what role can economic instruments play? Current Opinion in Environmental Sustainability 2:50–58.

Rolfe, J., S. Whitten, and J. Windle. 2017. The Australian experience in using tenders for conservation. Land Use Policy 63:611–620.

Schmalensee, R., and R. N. Stavins. 2017. The design of environmental markets: what have we learned from experience with cap and trade? Oxford Review of Economic Policy 33:572–588.

Schomers, S., and B. Matzdorf. 2013. Payments for ecosystem services: a review and comparison of developing and industrialized countries. Ecosystem services 6:16–30.

Shimshack, J. P., and M. B. Ward. 2005. Regulator reputation, enforcement, and environmental compliance. Journal of Environmental Economics and Management 50:519–540.

Tietenberg, T. 2003. The tradable-permits approach to protecting the commons: lessons for climate change. Oxford Review of Economic Policy 19:400–419.

US Fish and Wildlife Service. 2018. ECOS environmental conservation online system. US Fish and Wildlife Service, Washington, DC.

Veit, P. G., R. Nshala, M. Ocheing'Odhiambo, and J. Manyindo. 2008. Protected areas and property rights: democratizing eminent domain in East Africa. World Resources Institute, Washington, DC.

Wilson, J., L. Yan, and C. Wilson. 2007. The precursors of governance in the Maine lobster fishery. Proceedings of the National Academy of Sciences 104:15212–15217.

Wunder, S., S. Engel, and S. Pagiola. 2008. Taking stock: a comparative analysis of payments for environmental services programs in developed and developing countries. Ecological Economics 65:834–852.

Zimbabwe Parks and Wildlife Management Authority. 2018. Parks and wildlife management authority (tariff of fees) by laws, 2016. Zimbabwe Parks and Wildlife Management Authority, Harare.

14

Conservation at the International Level

For do not the ocean, navigable in every direction with which God has encompassed the earth, and the regular and the occasional winds which blow now from one quarter and now from another, offer sufficient proof that Nature has given to all peoples a right of access to all other people? Seneca thinks that this is Nature's greatest service, that by the wind she united widely scattered peoples, and yet did so distribute all her products over the earth that commercial intercourse was a necessity to mankind. Therefore this right belongs equally to all nations.

—Hugo Grotius, *Mare Liberum*, 1609

14.1 Introduction

Conservation problems that occur wholly within national jurisdictions are amenable to all of the instruments available to sovereign governments. Within national jurisdictions governments have the power to assign property rights, to pass laws regulating the behavior of people and to set penalties for noncompliance with those laws, to change the private costs and benefits of resource use by applying taxes or subsidies, and to check the market power of corporations. They can establish or disestablish protected areas. They can limit the uses made of resources in particular places through zoning restrictions or the use of licensing systems. They can restrict the times resources may be used through the designation of open and closed seasons. They can constrain environmental impacts by setting catch limits or quota, or by prohibiting or limiting the emission of pollutants to air, water, or soil. National governments have the power to compel private resource users to internalize the external environmental costs of their actions, or to compensate private resource users for the external environmental benefits they confer on others. They also have the power to mobilize the resources needed to secure provision of environmental public goods.

Conservation. Charles Perrings and Ann Kinzig, Oxford University Press (2021). © Oxford University Press.
DOI: 10.1093/oso/9780190613600.003.0014

None of these powers extend beyond the limits of national jurisdiction. At the international level there is no sovereign authority to internalize transboundary externalities through the assignment of property rights, through the promulgation of laws and regulations, or through the imposition of taxes. The conservation of ecosystems that either span national jurisdictions or extend beyond areas of national jurisdiction accordingly poses a special set of challenges. It requires the establishment of governance mechanisms that operate above national governments, and hence that involve some cession of national sovereignty. At a minimum, this involves the coordination of national action. More generally, it involves the negotiation of bilateral or multilateral agreements to cooperate in restricting the uses people make of environmental resources across or beyond national jurisdictions, or to invest in the provision of international environmental public goods. To date, nation-states have negotiated over 1,300 multilateral environmental agreements, and just under 2,300 bilateral environmental agreements (Mitchell 2019). Of these the most far-reaching are the framework agreements, including the Convention on Biological Diversity (CBD), the United Nations Framework Convention on Climate Change (UNFCCC), and the United Nations Convention to Combat Desertification (UNCCD).

The intergovernmental bodies established after the Second World War—the United Nations system (UN) along with the International Monetary Fund and the World Bank—provide a vehicle for cooperation between national governments in a number of areas, including the natural environment. Among UN agencies, the United Nations Environment Programme (UNEP), established in 1972, is charged with implementing UN activities on the environment, including support to UN member states seeking to develop environmental strategies at both national and international levels. This includes support for the development of multilateral agreements targeted at particular environmental issues. One other organization formed after the Second World War, the International Union for the Conservation of Nature (IUCN), is a network comprising both governments and civil organizations concerned with the environment. Along with UNEP, it performs important environmental monitoring work at the international level, particularly on threats to biodiversity. In recent years, the work of UNEP and IUCN in this area has been supplemented by the establishment of an international assessment body, the Intergovernmental Platform on Biodiversity and Ecosystem Services (IPBES).

The international governance of natural systems across and beyond national jurisdictions accordingly includes both a large number of specific agreements between nation-states, and a set of intergovernmental agencies charged with implementing particular programs. While the terms of bilateral and multilateral agreements have the status of international law, this differs markedly from national law. International law is sometimes described as "soft law" since there are no formal penalties for noncompliance with the terms of treaties. Since it is consent-based, compliance with the terms of agreements is purely voluntary. In such circumstances nation-states behave strategically, basing their behavior on the responses it is expected to generate.

The central characteristic of environmental assets that span national jurisdictions is that their use in one location has consequences for human well-being in other locations. In some cases, this follows from the fact that the geographical extent of a system spans several jurisdictions. For instance, pollution of (or water withdrawals from) a river that passes through several countries can have consequences for downstream users. Water withdrawals from the Colorado River in the United States, for example, have had severe consequences for consumers in Mexico, and for coastal ecosystems in the Gulf of California. In other cases, it follows from the fact that separate systems are linked by transport systems—roads, railways, canals, air and sea routes, and so on. For example, the transmission of infectious diseases that have emerged in one location to other parts of the world is generally caused by the movement of people or products along trade or travel routes. Similarly, the threat to endangered species in one part of the world is often exacerbated by the demand for products deriving from that species in other parts of the world. Indeed, the Convention on International Trade in Endangered Species of Wild Fauna and Flora (CITES) exists to ensure that international trade in wild plants and animals does not compromise the survival of the species.

In this chapter we consider the problem of conservation across and beyond national jurisdictions. This includes both environmental assets that may lie wholly within the areas of jurisdiction of more than one country, such as a river basin, and assets that necessarily lie beyond national jurisdiction, such as the general circulation system or the high seas. We address three important aspects of the problem. In the next three sections we consider the types of assets that fall into these categories, and what conservation challenges they face. In Section 14.5 we focus on the problem of strategic behavior, and the conditions under which strategic behavior by nation-states leads to the optimal level of conservation. In Section 14.6 we return to the institutions developed to provide transnational environmental public goods and to conserve resources across and beyond national jurisdictions. A final section offers a summary and conclusions.

14.2 Migratory species

We begin with environmental assets that span a small number of nation-states. Frequently encountered examples include straddling stocks of fish, migratory birds, and mammals. Migratory species are especially vulnerable because environmental changes anywhere along migration routes can threaten the survival of the species. They are particularly affected by the destruction or degradation of habitat at different points on their range, by overexploitation, and by disease. For example, an estimated 80% decline in the abundance of cerulean warblers—a species that migrates between Andes mountains in South America and the Appalachians in North America—is due in part to the loss of breeding habitat in the Appalachians as a result of strip mining, and in part to the conversion of wintering habitat in eastern slopes of the Andes to cattle pastures, coffee plantations, and coca plantations. Threats along migration routes are also important. In the United States, the extinction of the passenger pigeon and the near extinction of the American bison, were both due to overhunting on migration routes (Wilcove 2008).

Internationally, migratory marine species, including marine mammals, seabirds, turtles, sharks, and tuna, are among the most threatened of all species—21% are classified as critically endangered, endangered, or vulnerable. Most at risk are sea turtles—85% of which are threatened—but seabirds and migratory cartilaginous fish have also been negatively affected by environmental stresses along their migration routes (Lascelles et al. 2014). Around 11% of migratory birds are threatened or near threatened, with the conversion of habitat to agriculture in Africa, South Asia, and Southeast Asia being the most frequently cited causes (Kirby et al. 2008).

The protection of migratory species whose range extends across national borders is typically addressed through bilateral or multilateral agreements to coordinate conservation strategies in each jurisdiction, or to cooperate in the provision of jointly administered protected areas. The Kavango-Zambezi Transfrontier Conservation Area described in Chapter 11, for example, coordinates the management of national parks, wildlife management areas, and forest reserves in Angola, Botswana, Namibia, Zambia, and Zimbabwe, in part to protect migratory mammals such as elephants and wildebeest. Ventures of this kind are, however, the exception rather than the rule.

In most cases where the range of a species spans national jurisdictions, the treatment of species on either side of the border is very different. There is little attempt to coordinate conservation policy, or even to agree the threat status accorded species. In this respect, peripheral transboundary species—species whose range lies mainly in one country, but includes a small proportion in another country—are particularly at risk. A recent study of peripheral transboundary species in North America, for example, found very few instances where the treatment of the species is the same in both parts of its range. In many cases, species are assigned very different status on either side of the border, with management regimes varying accordingly. The Canadian lynx, for example, is treated as threatened in the United States, but is hunted in Canada. Similarly, the American black bear is endangered in Mexico, but is hunted in several border states in the United States (Thornton et al. 2017).

Differences in the level of protection offered species in different parts of their range is frequently a deliberate management strategy. Some 25% of peripheral transboundary species facing different levels of protection across their range are either migratory, or disperse over large distances. In some cases, the more protected area is treated as a source for the exploitation of animals in the less protected area. For example, marine protected areas may be managed as source for harvested fish species in adjacent to fishing grounds, and national parks may be managed as a source for hunting concessions in adjacent wildlife management areas (Sanchirico and Wilen 2001). In other cases, the added risks faced by individual animals moving between jurisdictions potentially compromises conservation objectives. The American black bear is cited as an example. This is particularly problematic where conservation aimed at the persistence of a meta-population depend on population connectivity across jurisdictions (Thornton et al. 2017).

For many migratory or long dispersing species, management across jurisdictions requires bilateral or multilateral agreement. One example in marine systems implements the provisions of the United Nations Convention on the Law of the Sea of 10 December 1982 relating to the conservation and management of straddling and migratory fish stocks: the Straddling Stocks Agreement. This establishes principles for the conservation of straddling stocks, and provides a framework for cooperation between nation-states in the optimal utilization of fish stocks (United Nations 1995). The agreement notionally covers stocks both inside and beyond the exclusive economic zones of member states. Specifically, it requires that conservation measures in areas under national jurisdiction should be compatible with measures applied in the adjacent high seas. It also requires mechanisms for compliance and enforcement on the high seas.[1] In practice, however, implementation of the terms of the agreement beyond areas of national jurisdiction is weak.

A second source of weakness in agreements established to protect migratory species, is the failure to attract participation from all states along migration routes. The 1979 Convention on the Conservation of Migratory Species of Wild Animals (CMS), for example, has 127 signatories, but large areas in North America and Asia are not covered (Figure 14.1). Since the agreement operates by identifying endangered or threatened species that require bilateral or multilateral agreements for their conservation and management, it only operates on species whose range falls within the jurisdictions of two or more member states.

An interesting example is the Wadden sea seal agreement between Germany, Denmark, and the Netherlands, which was signed two years after a Phocine distemper virus epizootic reduced the seal population by around 60%. It currently covers both the common and gray seals in the Wadden Sea, and aims to maintain a "favorable conservation status for the seal population" through the development of a joint management plan, research and

---

[1] Article 5 of the Straddling Stocks Agreement requires coastal States and States fishing on the high seas to:

  (a) adopt measures to ensure long-term sustainability of straddling fish stocks and highly migratory fish stocks and promote the objective of their optimum utilization;

  (b) ensure that such measures are based on the best scientific evidence available and are designed to maintain or restore stocks at levels capable of producing maximum sustainable yield, as qualified by relevant environmental and economic factors, including the special requirements of developing States, and taking into account fishing patterns, the interdependence of stocks and any generally recommended international minimum standards, whether subregional, regional or global;

  (c) apply the precautionary approach;

  (d) assess the impacts of fishing, other human activities and environmental factors on target stocks and species belonging to the same ecosystem or associated with or dependent upon the target stocks;

  (e) adopt, where necessary, conservation and management measures for species belonging to the same ecosystem or associated with or dependent upon the target stocks, with a view to maintaining or restoring populations of such species above levels at which their reproduction may become seriously threatened;

  (f) minimize pollution, waste, discards, catch by lost or abandoned gear, catch of nontarget species, both fish and nonfish species, (hereinafter referred to as nontarget species) and impacts on associated or dependent species, in particular endangered species, through measures including, to the extent practicable, the development and use of selective, environmentally safe and cost-effective fishing gear and techniques;

  (g) protect biodiversity in the marine environment;

  (h) take measures to prevent or eliminate overfishing and excess fishing capacity and to ensure that levels of fishing effort do not exceed those commensurate with the sustainable use of fishery resources;

  (i) take into account the interests of artisanal and subsistence fishers;

  (j) collect and share, in a timely manner, complete and accurate data concerning fishing activities on, inter alia, vessel position, catch of target and nontarget species and fishing effort, as set out in Annex I, as well as information from national and international research programmes;

  (k) promote and conduct scientific research and develop appropriate technologies in support of fishery conservation and management; and

  (l) implement and enforce conservation and management measures through effective monitoring, control and surveillance.

Figure 14.1 Parties and range states of the Convention on Migratory Species.
Source: United Nations Environment Programme (2018).

monitoring, and the creation of a network of protected areas. Signatories are required to limit takings of seals and to establish common standards for enforcement (Common Wadden Sea Secretariat 1990).

Other examples include the 2005 CMS West African Elephant memorandum of understanding (MOU) between 13 range states in the region. This MOU provides a framework for coordinating efforts by national governments and nongovernmental organizations to maintain and restore elephant populations and their habitats in West Africa. The region has less than 2% of all African elephants, and faces among the most extreme conservation challenges on the continent. Ninety percent of the elephant range has already been lost, and habitat loss continues. Remaining populations are small and fragmented, and threatened by construction of roads and railways, and conversion of habitat to livestock production (United Nations Environment Programme 2005).

The CMS has brokered agreements on migratory species from many genera. For example, the United Kingdom participates in separate agreements for the conservation of European bats, African-Eurasian migratory waterbirds, albatrosses and petrels, and cetaceans in the Baltic, North-East Atlantic, Irish, and North Seas. It has also ratified MOUs for the conservation marine turtles in the Indian Ocean, the aquatic warbler, migratory birds of prey in Africa and Eurasia, and cetaceans in the Pacific Islands Region. Nevertheless, the majority of bilateral or multilateral agreements to protect migratory species are directly negotiated between the affected countries without engaging the CMS. For example, the United States and Canada coordinate management of Pacific halibut through the International Pacific Halibut Commission (IPHC), established in 1923. The commission both establishes annual catch limits for the fisheries in US and Canadian waters, and sets the dates for the fishing season.

What is striking about the protection offered to migratory species whose range spans national jurisdictions is the linkage between the effort committed by nation-states to the development of effective agreements and value attached to the species concerned. In the case of Pacific halibut this is driven by a commercial fishery. In the case of the Wadden Sea seals it is driven by the value attached to the wider ecosystem. The Wadden Sea, a UNESCO World Heritage Site, is the world's largest continuous system of intertidal sand and mud flats, and a biodiversity hotspot hosting 12 million migratory birds and around 10,000 resident species of animals and plants, aside from the seals.

In Southern Africa, two transfrontier cooperative ventures aim to conserve charismatic megafauna and their dispersal fields. The 2002 agreement between Mozambique, South Africa, and Zimbabwe for the establishment of the Great Limpopo Transfrontier Park established a wildlife reserve that spanned all three national jurisdictions. Similarly, the 2011 agreement between Angola, Botswana, Namibia, Zambia, and Zimbabwe on the establishment of the Kavango Zambezi Transfrontier Conservation Area (KAZA) aimed to harmonize policies and management practices for the conservation of species that straddle the borders between them. In both cases the animals conserved are critical to tourism, and hence the economies of the signatory states.

By contrast, the West African Elephant MOU addresses a conservation issue that has lower priority for the countries involved. While there are a number of national parks that have elephant populations in Nigeria, Benin, Burkina Faso, and Ghana, they are both more isolated and contribute less to the economy than the better-known parks in Kenya, Tanzania, South Africa, Botswana, Namibia, Zimbabwe, and Zambia. As a result, fewer resources are committed to protection of the animals—principally against poaching—and less attention is paid to cross-border issues.

14.3 Transboundary and linked ecosystems

A second set of connections across jurisdictions involve linkages due not to the movement of species, but to hydrological and atmospheric flows. The impact of deforestation—which contributes around 10% of global carbon emissions—on the climate is a frequently cited source of such transboundary flows. This impact varies from one forest type to another. Most deforestation, as we have already seen, occurs in tropical forests, which generally store less carbon per hectare than temperate moist forests (Keith et al. 2009). But all deforestation contributes to the build-up of atmospheric carbon to some degree. The linkage between deforestation at one location and impacts elsewhere lie in the general circulation system. Air movements transport emissions from one country to all others. To address this, nation-states have entered into a number of agreements aimed at coordinating the management of national emissions. The most general of these is the 1992 United Nations Framework Convention on Climate Change (UNFCC) (United Nations 1992). The convention has evolved through repeated renegotiation in a succession of protocols, culminating in the 2015 Paris Agreement, which aims to hold emissions to within 1.5C above preindustrial levels.

Aside from the UNFCCC, a number of bilateral and multilateral agreements exist to minimize the effects of transboundary flows of a wide range of air pollutants. For example, the 1979 Convention on Long-range Transboundary Air Pollution covers emissions within the national jurisdiction of one state that negatively affect other states, but where it may not be possible to identify the source of emissions. It cites the principle that states have "the sovereign right to exploit their own resources pursuant to their own environmental policies, and the responsibility to ensure that activities within their jurisdiction or control do not cause damage to the environment of other States or of areas beyond the limits of national jurisdiction" (United Nations 1979). The convention requires cooperation and coordination in research and monitoring activity, but not in managing emissions—beyond encouraging adoption of best practices. Nor does it address the issue of liability for damage.

By comparison, the 1997 UN Convention on the Law of the Non-Navigational Uses of International Watercourses aims to secure the conservation of surface and groundwaters crossing international boundaries by imposing an obligation on member states to consider the effect of their actions on other states. It obliges countries to take reasonable steps to control damage due to pollution or the introduction of invasive species, to remedy damage to shared water resources, and to compensate sharing states for any loss (United Nations 1997). Partly because of the stringency of these obligations, the convention took over 17 years to come into force, and has still only been ratified by 36 states. Most of the world's 263 international river basins (Figure 14.2) are accordingly either not regulated through treaty, or are regulated through treaties entered into by countries that are not signatories to the convention.

Consider the case of the Colorado River, which flows through seven states in the United States and two states in Mexico, discharging into the

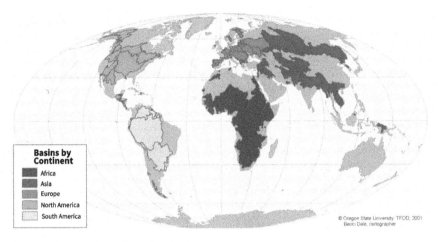

Figure 14.2 Transboundary river basins.
Source: Giordano and Wolf (2002).

gulf of California (Figure 14.3). The regulation of water flows into Mexico lies with the International Boundary and Water Commission (IBWC), a body established by treaty between the United States and Mexico in 1944 to regulate transboundary water issues. Under the 1944 treaty, the United States is obliged to provide Mexico with 1.5 million acre-feet of Colorado River water annually, which is approximately 10% of average flow. The treaty also established a hierarchy of water uses, in descending order: domestic and municipal, agriculture and stock-raising, electric power, industrial, navigation, fishing and hunting, other. There was no requirement to allocate water for ecological purposes, and no requirement to maintain water quality. Two related consequences of this were a progressive deterioration in the quality of water provided to Mexico, and the degradation of the Colorado delta wetlands.

By the mid-1960s salinity levels had risen to the point that Colorado River water in Mexico was unfit for human or livestock consumption, or for irrigation. An amendment to the agreement in 1965, Minute 218, required the United States to undertake some cleanup, but the problem remained. In 1973 a further amendment, Minute 242, obliged the United States to fund cleanup of salt-damaged Mexicali Valley lands and keep salinity levels of delivered water below a certain level. The state of the wetlands was not addressed until much more recently. In two further amendments, Minute 319 of 2012 and Minute 323 of 2018, the United States agreed to a number of measures aimed at restoring the wetlands. These include pulsed flows intended to simulate floods, to reconnect the river to its estuary, and to restore habitats along the

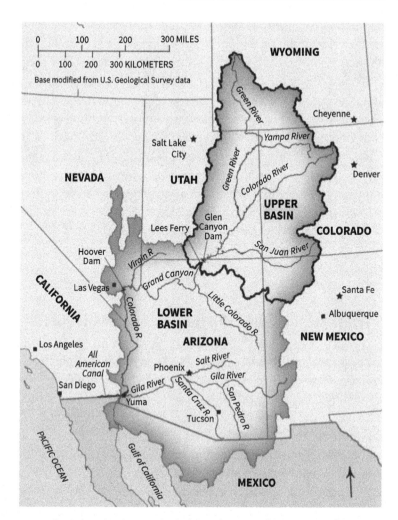

Figure 14.3 The Colorado River Basin showing the seven US States (California, Arizona, Nevada, Utah, Wyoming, Colorado, and New Mexico) and two Mexican states (Baja California and Sonora) affected by transboundary management.
Source: US Geological Survey (2014).

delta. The latest amendment also designates a quantity of water—210,000 acre-feet—specifically for environmental purposes.

The US-Mexico Water Treaty is slightly unusual in the asymmetry between the parties. This is reflected both in the initial agreement, and in successive negotiations over amendments. The salinity issue was not, for example, seriously addressed until Mexico threatened to bring the matter to the International Court of Justice. The central issues are, however, the same as in nearly every river basin agreement. These center on the obligations of upstream users to deliver water in sufficient quantity and of sufficient quality to meet the terms of the agreement. As in many river basin treaties, the eco-logical functions of stream flows have been neglected for most of the period the 1944 Water Treaty has been in force, and they remain a relatively minor consideration.

In river basin agreements where downstream users dominate, such as the Nile River Co-operative Framework Agreement between Egypt, Sudan, South Sudan, Rwanda, Tanzania, Uganda, Kenya, and Burundi, historic use rights have been employed to prevent upstream development wherever it threatens stream flow. If the value of downstream assets depends on stream flows at a certain level, and if upstream projects reduce stream flows, the resulting re-duction in the value of downstream assets is an external cost of the upstream projects. River basin agreements are then the forum in which to negotiate compensation.

14.4 Trade, travel, and the movement of species

A third category of transboundary flows between ecosystems are those medi-ated by trade or travel. There are two dimensions to this problem. One is the threat posed by the trade in endangered species to the survival of those spe-cies in the wild. The other is the damage done through the deliberate or ac-cidental introduction of harmful species through trade or travel. In the first case, trade exacerbates a conservation problem in the exporting country. Depletion of many plants or animals to satisfy demand for animal or plant products has been enough to threaten their survival. In the second case, it exacerbates a conservation problem in the importing country. The rapid ex-pansion of world trade and travel networks, and the growth in the volume of trade and travel within those networks have led to the movement of plants, animals, insects, and microorganisms between ecosystems at unprecedented levels (Hulme 2009).

In this section we focus on the second of these problems, but both are im-portant. The Convention on International Trade in Endangered Species of Wild Fauna and Flora (CITES) was developed to protect animals and plants whose survival is threatened by international demand both for live specimens and for the many wildlife products they yield. Currently, CITES protects nearly 6,000 species of animals and 30,000 species of plants thought to be at risk from trade. Examples include primates, cetaceans, sea turtles, parrots, corals, cacti, and orchids. Many other species traded in international markets are not themselves threatened, but have the capacity to threaten others. Not all species introduced to new ecosystems are able to survive, but some have the capacity both to establish and spread. And some of those are able to inflict significant harm to host systems and the people who benefit from those systems (Williamson and Fitter 1996). The coronavirus that has thrown the world into turmoil as we finalize this book is a good example.

Introduced species that both establish and spread, and that inflict serious damage to host systems, are referred to as invasive species. The USDA currently estimates that there are around 50,000 invasive species established in the United States, imposing costs of around $140 billion annually across agriculture, recreation and tourism. Some are new arrivals. Others have been in the United States for hundreds of years. Some, like kudzu and the zebra mussel, are extremely costly to control and impose significant damage to systems they invade. Others are more benign. Globally, the list of most damaging species introduced via trade or travel is dominated by pathogens—human, animal, and plant diseases. Examples of human diseases introduced this way include HIV/AIDS, several strains of highly pathogenic avian influenza, West Nile virus, SARS, and Ebola. Animal diseases include bovine spongiform encephalopathy and foot and mouth disease. Plant diseases include diseases of trees such as phytophtora ramorum, Dutch elm disease, citrus greening and diseases of crops, such as grey leaf spot. This list also includes disease vectors such as Aedes albopictus, the tiger mosquito, responsible for transmitting a number of viruses including Dengue fever and Japanese encephalitis. There are no estimates of the cost of all trade-related diseases, but the cost of a single pandemic—SARS—was in the order of $40 billion (Lee and McKibbin 2004).

Among other species, the global cost of invasive insects has been estimated at between $70 billion and $80 billion annually (Bradshaw et al. 2016). Of species imposing harm on host ecosystems, water weeds such as *Salvinia molesta* and *Eichhornia crassipes* spread via contaminated boats and equipment and have established in waterways in every continent, clogging irrigation and hydroelectric systems and compromising fisheries. Grasses such as cogon (*Imperata cylindrica*), introduced in the United States via packing material from Japan early in the twentieth century, have disrupted ecosystems in many temperate zones. The comb jelly (*Mnemiopsis ledyi*), introduced into the Black Sea through the ballast water of ships from the east coast of America and subsequently the Azov, Marmara, Aegean, and Caspian Seas, has had major effects on the whole ecosystem wherever it has invaded. In small island ecosystems, invasive species introduced either deliberately or accidentally by travelers or traders are the main source of population declines and species extinctions (Reaser et al. 2007). Within the United States, a 2005 study estimated the cost of invasive plants, animals, insects, and microbes to be in order of $120 billion (Pimentel et al. 2005).

Invasive species of all types are an externality of the closer integration of the global economy—the growth of trade and travel. Closer integration of the global economy means that the volume of world trade has grown significantly relative to world output. That is, a growing proportion of the goods and services produced worldwide involve international transactions. Global supply chain management has become a major issue for all companies sourcing materials or distributing their products internationally. Since every container of imports contains a sample of the organisms in the country of exports, the number of species introductions is expected to increase with trade volumes. At the same time, an increase in the speed of transport increases the likelihood that species moved this way survive the journey. Since there is a finite pool of species in any one country, the number of species introduced through any one type of trade along any one trade route should saturate at some point. However, the development of new trade goods distributed along new trade routes means that the rate at which new species are introduced is likely to continue to rise for decades to come (Perrings et al. 2010).

While the volume of trade affects the likelihood that new species will be introduced, the likelihood that introduced species will then establish and spread depends on the bioclimatic similarity of the ecosystems being connected, the ecological distance between them, the nature of the introduced species (the traits, such as high plasticity, that may make them invasive), and the invasibility of the ecosystems into which species are being introduced (including the effects of fragmentation and biodiversity loss). Species are more likely to establish and spread the greater the bioclimatic similarity between source and host systems, the fewer predators thy encounter, the more disturbed is the host system, and the traits of introduced species that given them a competitive advantage (Sakai et al. 2001). Generalists are more likely to establish and spread than specialists, particularly where host habitats have been disturbed. Although habitat specialists may be competitively superior to habitat generalists, habitat disturbance in host systems allows invasion by habitat generalists (Marvier et al. 2004). Among woody plants, for example, small mean seed mass, a short juvenile period, and a short mean interval between large seed crops are predictors of success in disturbed habitats (Rejmánek et al. 2004).

It follows that the vulnerability of a host system to invasion depends on a number of things aside from the volume and direction or trade, or the nature of trade pathways and transport systems. It depends on bioclimatic similarity to source systems, the characteristics of introduced species, and the degree to which host systems have been disturbed. Hitchhiker species that have no environmental effects when introduced along with trade goods in one bioclimatic zone might, for example, be extremely harmful when introduced in another bioclimatic zone. In the same way, species introduced with trade goods in bioclimatically similar host systems may become invasive in a more highly disturbed system, but fail to establish in one that is less disturbed. The invasive species externalities of trade tend to be location-specific.

The problem is currently addressed through a global trade structure that has lasted since the end of the Second World War: the 1947 General Agreement on Tariffs and Trade (GATT) administered by the World Trade Organization. The GATT recognizes that the introduction of potentially invasive species along with trade goods has at least the potential to harm importers. Article XX of the agreement accordingly authorizes countries to take action in restraint of trade wherever the importation of some commodity threatens human, animal or plant health. Since the 1990s, implementation of Article XX has been via separate agreements on animal and plant health (the 1994 Sanitary and Phytosanitary (SPS) Agreement) and human health (the 1996 International Health Regulations, IHR). These agreements establish the rules under which trade interdictions are allowed. Note, though, that the GATT, the SPS Agreement, and the IHR do not allow the external invasive species costs of trade to be negotiated between trading partners, or factored into national tariffs.

The fora in which trade externalities are currently being negotiated are not the broad agreements, but a growing number of bilateral and multilateral regional trade agreements (RTAs). By 2019 there were 291 such RTAs, accounting for well over half of all global exports of manufactured goods. Most are relatively small, but three—the European Union, US-Mexico Canada Agreement (USMCA) which replaced the North American Free Trade Association (NAFTA), and the Association of Southeast Asian Nations (ASEAN)—together account for over 55% of global manufactured exports. Many RTAs specifically address the environmental externalities of trade. For example, the USMCA includes a chapter on the environment, Chapter 24, together with a separate Agreement on Environmental Cooperation supported by a Commission that is charged with, inter alia, "promoting . . . where appropriate, the internalization of environmental costs and accountability for environmental harms." Under this agreement the parties retain the right to impose their own environmental laws, but agree not to use those laws as a disguised restriction on trade or investment.

Article 24.16 of the USMCA includes specific wording on the invasive species risks of trade:

1. The Parties recognize that the movement of terrestrial and aquatic invasive alien species across borders through trade-related pathways can adversely affect the environment, economic activities and development, and human health. The Parties also recognize that the prevention, detection, control and, when possible, eradication, of invasive alien species are critical strategies for managing those adverse impacts.

2. Accordingly, the Environment Committee established under Article 24.26.2 (Environment Committee and Contact Points) shall coordinate with the Committee on Sanitary and Phytosanitary Measures established under Article 9.17 (Committee on Sanitary and Phytosanitary Measures) to identify cooperative opportunities to share information and management experiences on the movement, prevention, detection, control, and eradication of invasive alien species, with a view to enhancing efforts to assess and address the risks and adverse impacts of invasive alien species (United States et al. 2018).

In many cases, the environmental issues addressed by RTAs go far beyond trade-related invasive species risks. The USMCA agreement, for example, calls for a work program that includes "the conservation, protection and sustainable management of wild flora and fauna and their habitats, and specially protected marine, coastal, and terrestrial natural areas, as well as buffer zones and corridors . . . [and] the conservation and protection of shared species, including migratory birds and their habitat."

14.5 Strategic behavior and transboundary conservation

As we saw in Chapter 8, if we are to understand when the signatories to a bilateral or multilateral agreement may be expected to cooperate in the provision of a transboundary public good and when they are not, we need to understand both the factors affecting demand for the public good, and the characteristics of the production function involved (sometimes called the supply aggregation technology). It is convenient to take the simplest possible case, in which a country considers whether or not to enter into an agreement with a neighboring state to engage in some environmental action that provides benefits to both, and the choice is not repeated. The net benefits to each country of participation (or not) in the agreement depend on the decisions of the other country. It follows that each country determines its best response to the level of commitment made by the other country. This will be selected from a Nash-Cournot reaction curve that defines one country's best response to the provision of a public good by the other country. Therefore a binary choice—between participation or nonparticipation—where there are two countries generates four distinct payoffs. These are net benefits to one country of participation or nonparticipation conditional on the decision of the other country to participate or not. The choice each country makes is thus conditional on the choice made by the other country. Behavior is strategic.

While a binary choice, two country problem is as simple as things get, it can still be very complicated. The range of possible strategies reveals five distinct collective action problems involving (a) coordination (where the risk lies in not being able to coordinate action), (b) disagreement (where the risk lies in failure to agree), (c) defection (where the risk lies in the incentive countries have to defect from the socially optimal outcome), (d) equity (where the risk lies in outcome inequality), and (e) instability (where the outcome of strategic interactions are unstable) (Holzinger 2008). In fact, the binary choice two country problem involves up to 78 strategically distinct games. While the most widely cited examples are defection problems such as the prisoners' dilemma, coordination and disagreement problems are also frequently encountered in international environmental negotiations (Touza and Perrings 2011).

The structure of payoffs depends on the production function or supply aggregation technology involved. The production function describes the way in which contributions by each country affects provision of the public good: the polar examples of public good production functions being additive, best-shot, and weakest link. If a public good is supplied via an additive function, for instance, the benefits to both countries depends on the sum of the efforts of each. Examples include the mitigation of climate change through carbon sequestration, or the abatement of atmospheric and water pollution. As we noted in Chapter 8, however, they also include the conservation of (homogeneous) habitat where the benefits offered scale with the area protected. In the case of best-shot and weakest-link public goods the benefits to both countries depends on contribution of either the most effective provider (best shot) or least effective provider (weakest link). An intuitive example of a best-shot public good is the provision of information on emerging infectious diseases. The benefits to all countries of national disease surveillance efforts is fixed by the best information provided. By contrast, an equally intuitive example of a weakest-link public good is the control of the same disease. The protection offered by national disease control to all countries is only as good as the protection offered by the weakest link in the chain.

Two other features of public good production functions turn out to be important to an understanding of international conservation efforts. One is that many conservation efforts involve either a step or threshold level of provision. The similarity between step and threshold public goods is that both offer no benefits until the step or threshold has been achieved. The difference is that while a step public good also offers no benefits for provision beyond the step, a threshold public good does offer benefits beyond the threshold. For example, a biocorridor linking subpopulations in a meta-community that spans national jurisdictions is a step public good. Since half a biocorridor is no biocorridor at all, provision below the step offers no benefit. But equally, once the corridor has been established, there is no further benefit to be had by extending it further. Other examples of step public goods are coastal defenses or levees, or the eradication of an infectious disease or an invasive pest. There are no benefits to any one country unless the biocorridor, defensive levee, or eradication program is complete, but there are also no benefits to provision beyond the step.

To see the difference between step and threshold public goods, consider the example of the control of an infectious disease. A necessary and sufficient condition for any infectious disease to be controlled is that the reproductive number $R0$ (the number of new infections created by one infection in a susceptible population) be brought below one. This forms the threshold. $R0 > 1$ ensure that the disease will spread. $R0 < 1$ ensures that it will eventually die out. However, effort to reduce $R0$ much below 1 is not wasted, since there are benefits to controls that end the disease more quickly. It is intuitive that analogous thresholds exist for species we wish to conserve rather than to destroy. The most common conservation thresholds are the critical minimum population sizes, or critical minimum habitat sizes, of endangered species. Below the threshold, a species is doomed to extinction. It follows that conservation efforts that fail to maintain the population of an endangered species above the threshold will necessarily fail. Yet conservation efforts that further boost the population beyond that point will still yield benefits (Touza and Perrings 2011).

A second important feature of public good production functions, of relevance to international conservation efforts, is that countries are frequently able to capture at least some of the benefits of public good provision. As we saw in Chapter 8, contributions to impure public goods yield both a noncapturable,

(a) Prisoner's dilemma

Community 2

Action	Cooperate	Defect
Community 1 Cooperate	3,3	1,4
Defect	4,1	2,2

(b) Chicken

Community 2

Action	Cooperate	Defect
Cooperate	3,3	2,4
Defect	4,2	1,1

(c) Assurance

Community 2

Action	Cooperate	Defect
Community 1 Cooperate	3,3	0,1
Defect	1,0	1,1

(d) Battle of the sexes

Community 2

Action	Cooperate	Defect
Cooperate	3,3	0,0
Defect	0,0	2,3

Figure 14.4 Nash equilibria in two-by-two nonrepeated games.

nonexclusive benefit to all parties, and a capturable, exclusive benefit to the provider. Since this capturable, exclusive benefit is frequently the main motivation for provision of the public good, it offers a potentially important way of influencing national conservation choices.

For our two-country case, the characteristics of the production technology are reflected in the payoff structure. Consider again the examples we saw in Figure 8.6. In the first of these examples, the prisoners' dilemma, comparison of the payoffs to each country conditional on the decision made by the other country show that the best strategy for each is to defect, even though this delivers fewer benefits to both countries together (the sum of payoffs) than any other strategy. There is a single Nash equilibrium (shaded). In the other games, there are multiple Nash equilibria (Figure 14.4).

To see how sensitive the outcome in such cases is to the payoffs to individual countries, consider the properties of assurance games. Weakest-link public goods always have the structure of assurance games, but so do many others. Such games differ from prisoners' dilemmas both in the lack of any dominant strategy, and in the fact that there is more than one Nash equilibrium. In this example cooperation and defection by the two countries are both Nash equilibria. Neither country has an incentive to change their strategy once it has been selected. If cooperation in this case meant participation in a transboundary conservation agreement, that agreement would be self-enforcing. Neither country would have an incentive to back out of the commitment.

Nevertheless, even though cooperation by both provides the highest payoff to all, defection by both is an equally stable strategy. What gives the game this property is the penalty to cooperation faced by each country if the other

(a) Prisoner's dilemma

Community 2

Action	Cooperate	Defect
Cooperate	3,3	1,4
Defect	4,1	2,2

Community 1 is labeled to the left of the Cooperate/Defect rows.

(b) Chicken

Community 2

Action	Cooperate	Defect
Cooperate	3,3	2,4
Defect	4,2	1,1

(c) Assurance

Community 2

Action	Cooperate	Defect
Cooperate	2,2	1,1
Defect	1,1	1,1

Community 1 is labeled to the left of the Cooperate/Defect rows.

(d) Battle of the sexes

Community 2

Action	Cooperate	Defect
Cooperate	3,2	0,0
Defect	0,0	2,3

Figure 14.5 An assurance game in which the benefit to one-sided cooperation equal the benefit to one-side defection.

defects. Consider a change in the structure of payoffs that saw the benefit to one-sided cooperation equal the benefit to one-side defection funded out of the gains from cooperation (Figure 14.5).

This would reduce the likelihood that the outcome would be defection. Since the payoff to cooperation by each country is no worse than the payoff to defection, regardless of which strategy the other country chooses, both countries are more likely to choose cooperation. The use of side payments of this kind to change the structure of payoffs from bilateral or multilateral agreements is increasingly common. For example, nonconditional payments to national governments under the REDD scheme are explicitly designed to secure their participation in agreements designed to mitigate the risks of deforestation-induced climate change. Moreover, even in a noncooperative setting, unilateral action by one country to alter the structure of payoffs to another can induce the second country to commit to a particular strategy. Now consider the case where the conservation decisions made by the two countries are sequential. Country 1 chooses first, country 2 second. The payoff structure can be written in the extensive form shown in Figure 14.6.

This is a choice about conservation of a transboundary threatened species. Country 1 decides based on the way they expect country 2 to respond. In this case, for example, if they choose to conserve the species, they know that they will get a payoff of 3 if country 2 also conserves, but a payoff of 0 if country 2 does not respond. They also know that country 2's best strategy will be to not conserve. Similarly, if they choose not to conserve the species, they know that they will get a payoff of 4 if country 2 then chooses to conserve the species

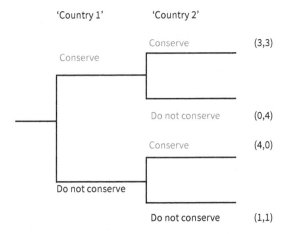

Figure 14.6 An extensive form of the prisoners' dilemma without shared pay-offs. Expectation of the second country's best response to each choice leads to mutual defection.

but only 1 if country 2 also refrains from conservation. They also know that country 2's best strategy will be to not conserve. It follows that country 1 will choose not to conserve the species if they choose first.

Now suppose that there is agreement to share the benefits of conservation no matter what the level of conservation undertaken, or which country undertakes it (Figure 14.7). The aggregate payoffs are the same as before (6 if both conserve, 4 if one chooses not to conserve, 2 if both choose not to conserve) but that payoff is now shared. That is, the scope for free-riding is removed.

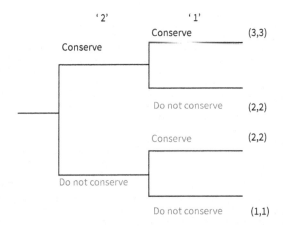

Figure 14.7 An extensive form of the prisoners' dilemma with shared pay-offs. Expectation of the second country's best response to each choice leads both countries to conserve.

If country 1 now chooses to conserve the species, they know that they will get a payoff of 3 if country 2 also conserves, but a payoff of 2 if country 2 does not respond. They also know that country 2's best strategy will be to conserve. Similarly, if they choose not to conserve the species, they know that they will get a payoff of 2 if country 2 then chooses to conserve the species but only 1 if country 2 also refrains from conservation. They also know that country 2's best strategy will be to conserve. It follows that country 1 will choose to conserve the species if they choose first.

Analyses of bilateral and multilateral environmental agreements using insights from the theory of games have identified several conditions that have to hold if they are to be effective (Barrett 2003, Barrett 2005). One is that agreements are likely to be more effective, the smaller the number of parties involved. There are different reasons for this, but one is the nature of the production function. For additive public goods in particular, the gap between the commitment a country is likely to make in isolation and the commitment it should make in a fully cooperative setting is increasing in the number of countries. Suppose, for example, that there are n symmetric countries, in each of which marginal benefits are decreasing and the marginal costs are increasing in the area committed to conservation. If the ith country acts in isolation it will equate its own marginal cost and marginal benefit of conservation. That is, it will increase the area committed to conservation up to the point where $MB_i = MC_i$. If the country were to cooperate with others, it would equate the marginal cost of conservation with the marginal benefit to all countries, increasing the area committed to conservation up to the point where $nMB_i = MC_i$. This is illustrated in Figure 14.8.

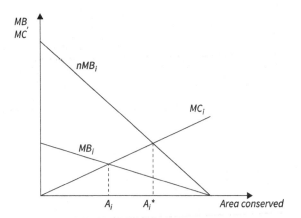

Figure 14.8 The difference between the noncooperative (A_i) and cooperative (A_i^*) level of conservation where there are n symmetric countries.

Source: Adapted from Barrett (1999).

Since the gap between the marginal benefits in the noncooperative and cooperative cases is increasing in the number of countries involved, so is the difference in the area of land committed to conservation and hence the cost of cooperation. Agreements are more likely to be effective the smaller the cost to each country of cooperation.

Other characteristics of effective agreements are that they evolve through repeated renegotiation, and that the parties have no incentive to renegotiate the agreement. Repeated games allow the parties to focus not on the short-term payoff to a single strategy, but on the long-term benefits of multiple strategies. They allow countries to use their strategic response to the choices made by other countries to penalize behaviors that reduce the long-term benefit to themselves. While one shot prisoners' dilemmas involve a dominant strategy in which both parties defect, repeated prisoners' dilemmas may lead to long-run cooperation. Unfortunately, however, repetition does not guarantee cooperation. It does not, for example, preclude the possibility that the parties will get locked into a cycle of repeated defection. The most effective treaties are thus not only repeatedly renegotiated, they are also evolutionary—in the sense that the number and type of parties to the agreement may change over time. If new parties come to the table it allows the introduction of new strategies which, if they demonstrate higher payoffs, can come to dominate the strategies adopted by existing parties.

14.6 Funding conservation as a global public good

The mechanisms used to assure cooperation in the conservation of transboundary species or ecosystems generally involve either penalties or payments to incentivize both participation in and compliance with the terms of bilateral or multilateral agreements. Successful agreements include either effective penalties/disincentives to defect from a precisely defined set of objectives, or payments to compensate parties for the costs of cooperation. These change the structure of payoffs in ways that make the cooperative solution the dominant solution. There are certainly examples of both penalties or compensation arrangements that have induced cooperation in multilateral environmental agreements (Perrings 2012).

Consider again the most general framework agreement on the conservation of species, the 1993 United Nations Convention on Biological Diversity (CBD). The objectives of the CBD are stated in Article 2 to be "the conservation of biological diversity, the sustainable use of its components, and the fair and equitable sharing of the benefits arising out of the utilization of genetic resources, including by appropriate access to genetic resources and by appropriate transfer of relevant technologies, taking into account all rights over those resources and technologies, and by appropriate funding" (United Nations 1993).

The reference to "fair and equitable sharing of the benefits" and "appropriate funding" underscore the central role of incentives in the CBD. The specific measures agreed for in situ conservation[2] are not costless, and absent compensation from elsewhere may be expected to lead to levels of conservation closer to the noncooperative than the cooperative outcome. Compensation for the added cost of cooperation means, at minimum, cover for the difference in the total cost of provision at national and global levels. This difference is generally referred to as the incremental cost of provision at the globally optimal level. Formally, incremental costs are the difference between the cost of provision that would be warranted taking account of only the national benefits it offers, and the cost that is warranted taking account of the global benefits it offers. Costs that are warranted by national benefits are those at which the

---

[2] Article 8 of the CBD requires countries to:

    (a) Establish a system of protected areas or areas where special measures need to be taken to conserve biological diversity;

    (b) Develop, where necessary, guidelines for the selection. establishment and management of protected areas or areas where special measures need to be taken to conserve biological diversity;

    (c) Regulate or manage biological resources important for the conservation of biological diversity whether within or outside protected areas. with a view to ensuring their conservation and sustainable use;

    (d) Promote the protection of ecosystems, natural habitats and the maintenance of viable populations of species in natural surroundings;

    (e) Promote environmentally sound and sustainable development in areas adjacent to protected areas with a view to furthering protection of these areas;

    (f) Rehabilitate and restore degraded ecosystems and promote the recovery of threatened species. inter alia, through the development and implementation of plans or other management strategies;

    (g) Establish or maintain means to regulate. manage or control the risks associated with the use and release of living modified organisms resulting from biotechnology which are likely to have adverse environmental impacts that could affect the conservation and sustainable use of biological diversity, taking also into account the risks to human health;

    (h) Prevent the introduction of. control or eradicate those alien species which threaten ecosystems. habitats or species;

    (i) Endeavour to provide the conditions needed for compatibility between present uses and the conservation of biological diversity and the sustainable use of its components;

    (j) Subject to its national legislation. respect. preserve and maintain knowledge, innovations and practices of indigenous and local communities embodying traditional lifestyles relevant for the conservation and sustainable use of biological diversity and promote their wider application with the approval and involvement of the holders of such knowledge, innovations and practices and encourage the equitable sharing of the benefits arising from the utilization of such knowledge. innovations and practices;

    (k) Develop or maintain necessary legislation and/or other regulatory provisions for the necessary protection of threatened species and populations;

    (l) Where a significant adverse effect on biological diversity has been determined pursuant to Article 7, regulate or manage the relevant processes and categories of activities; and

    (m) Cooperate in providing financial and other support for in situ conservation outlined in subparagraphs (a) to (l), particularly to developing countries.

marginal cost of provision are just balanced by the marginal benefits it offers to the country. Costs that are warranted by global benefits are those at which the marginal cost of provision are just balanced by the marginal benefits to global community—that is, that country plus the rest of the world.

To see this, consider the figure we have used to explore the optimal provision of public goods (Figure 14.9).

Absent any mechanism to compensate a country for the global benefits of local conservation, local conservation effort will be increased up to the point where the marginal local costs and benefits of conservation are equal—at C_L. Payment of at least the stippled area—the incremental cost of provision—is sufficient to induce local conservation effort at C_G, the globally optimal level. If local landowners were to receive the associated producer surplus of production at C_G, this would include the gray area.

A working example of payments equal (in principle) to incremental cost, at the international level, is the funding mechanism implemented by the Global Environment Facility (GEF). The GEF was established in 1991 as a pilot program within the World Bank to finance the protection of the global environment. In 1994 it was restructured, with involvement of the United Nations Development Programme (UNDP) and the United Nations Environment Programme (UNEP), as the permanent financial mechanism for the two main framework conventions: the CBD and the 1992 United Nations Framework

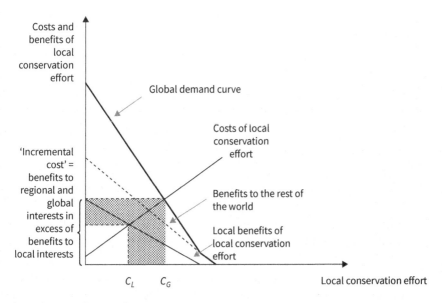

Figure 14.9 Incremental cost.
The incremental cost of increasing local conservation from the local (C_L) to global (C_G) optimum is indicated by the stippled area. The associated producer surplus is indicated by the gray area.

Convention on Climate Change (UNFCC). It has subsequently become the financial mechanism for two more international conventions: the 1994 United Nations Convention to Combat Desertification (UNCCD) and the 2001 Stockholm Convention on Persistent Organic Pollutants.

In principle, the GEF uses incremental cost to determine the amount to commit to local environmental projects that generate global benefits. Support for biodiversity conservation focuses on five areas: the management of biodiversity in productive landscapes and seascapes; the effectiveness of protected area systems; biodiversity policy, planning, and review; the implementation of the Cartagena protocol on biosafety; and the implementation of the Nagoya protocol on access and benefit sharing. Current priorities for wildlife conservation, for example, aim to support investments in the growth of wildlife populations; development of the wildlife-based economy; establishment of conservation areas, including Trans Frontier Conservation Areas (TFCAs) large enough to support ecologically viable populations and genetic diversity; and the realization of benefits for local communities from protected area management (Global Environment Facility 2019).

In practice, the countries receiving funds from the GEF have a lot of discretion in the spending of those funds. In recent years the GEF has reported a shift in national funding priorities away from protected areas and toward biodiversity management in productive landscapes. Whereas countries had consistently prioritized funding of protected areas in allocating their GEF resources, in the most recently completed replenishment period, GEF-6, 68% of funds were allocated to biodiversity management in productive landscapes and seascapes outside protected areas, and only 30% were allocated to protected areas.

While the GEF is the main single source of funds for the incremental cost of national conservation efforts that offer global benefits, it is not alone. A similar trend can be observed in the international expenditures of international nongovernmental environmental organizations like Conservation International, the World Wide Fund for Nature, The Nature Conservancy, and others. Support for protected area management has been displaced for support for intersection between conservation and development. The trend may have been lamented as a betrayal of the original remit of such organizations—biodiversity for biodiversity's sake—but it reflects a recognition that all conservation efforts involve opportunity costs, and that it is better to address the tradeoffs between conservation and development directly, than to leave them as externalities of a "pure" biodiversity conservation strategy.

14.7 Summary and conclusions

In Chapter 13 we saw that the main motivation for the development of property rights, a regulatory regime, and economic incentives at the national level is to align the private and social value of natural resources. If private resource users assign the same value to natural resources as the society to which they belong, their conservation choices will be socially optimal. The problem addressed in this chapter is that just as there may be a wedge between the private and social costs and benefits of economic activity within the nation-state, so there may be a wedge between the local and global costs and benefits of activities that span national jurisdictions. We saw that the closer integration of the global economy, like the flows that mark earth's general circulation system, means that many national activities generate spillovers that impact people elsewhere in the global system. Yet the international community has none of the levers that nation-states take for granted. It cannot assign property rights, pass laws and regulations, set penalties for noncompliance, impose taxes or subsidies, or pay for the provision of ecosystem services. At the international level, cooperation and coordination can only be achieved through negotiated bilateral or multilateral agreements, or sanctions for noncompliers.

This chapter considered a number of the issues that require a coordinated or cooperative international response: the conservation of migratory species, the management of transboundary flows of water and air, and biosecurity in the global system of travel and trade. It then considered the implications of strategic behavior between nations for coordination and cooperation between countries on these issues. Finally, it discussed the financing of international cooperation. Since coordination or cooperation depend on bilateral or multilateral agreements, the chapter identified which agreements apply in each case, and discussed their strengths and weaknesses.

As we saw in Chapter 8, the effectiveness of agreements intended to deliver public goods at the international level is highly sensitive to the nature of the game. The control of invasive pests or pathogens, for example, is typically a weakest- or weaker-link public good. The protection enjoyed by all countries is only as good as the protection offered by the least effective country. In principle, games of this kind should induce matching behavior. All parties may be expected to do only as much as the least effective country. Yet where the local costs of ineffective international controls are high, each country has an incentive to do better. The agreements established to deal with such problems—the International Health Regulations, the Sanitary and Phytosanitary Agreement, the International Plant Protection Convention—therefore all contain terms that allow individual countries to invest resources in building capacity in less effective countries. At the same time, however, they stop short of allowing collective preventive action.

The only vehicle allowing collective funding of local efforts to strengthen biosecurity, or the capacity to conserve resources offering potential benefits to others, is the Global Environment Facility. The chapter described how the GEF works, and what it tends to invest in. While the incremental cost principle that notionally informs allocations with the GEF is consistent with the Hotelling approach to conservation, it is worth noting that funding levels are such that individual countries are unlikely to commit the resources to local conservation that are warranted by the global benefits of that conservation. The 2020 COVID-19 pandemic has further tested the resolve of individual countries to take decisions based on a calculation that includes the benefits to other countries. At the same time, we conclude that bodies like the GEF or the WHO have an increasingly critical role to play in managing local actions that confer either global benefits or costs.

References

Barrett, S. 1999. Montreal versus Kyoto: international cooperation and the global environment. Pages 192–219 in I. Kaul, I. Grunberg, and M. Stern, editors. Global public goods: international cooperation in the 21st century. Oxford University Press, New York.

Barrett, S. 2003. Environment and statecraft: the strategy of environmental treaty-making. Oxford University Press, Oxford.

Barrett, S. 2005. Managing the global commons. Task Force on Global Public Goods, Stockholm, Sweden.

Bradshaw, C. J., B. Leroy, C. Bellard, D. Roiz, C. Albert, A. Fournier, M. Barbet-Massin, J.-M. Salles, F. Simard, and F. Courchamp. 2016. Massive yet grossly underestimated global costs of invasive insects. Nature Communications 7:12986.

Common Wadden Sea Secretariat. 1990. Agreement on the conservation of seals in the Wadden Sea. Common Wadden Sea Secretariat, Wilhelmshaven, Germany.

Giordano, M. A., and A. T. Wolf. 2002. The world's freshwater agreements: historical developments and future opportunities. Pages 1–8 in A. T. Wolf, editor, Atlas of International Freshwater Agreements, UNEP, Nairobi.

Global Environment Facility. 2019. GEF-7: biodiversity strategy. GEF, Washington, DC.

Holzinger, K. 2008. Treaty formation and strategic constellations: a comment on treaties: strategic considerations. University of Illinois Law Review 1:187–200.

Hulme, P. E. 2009. Trade, transport and trouble: managing invasive species pathways in an era of globalization. Journal of Applied Ecology 46:10–18.

Keith, H., B. G. Mackey, and D. B. Lindenmayer. 2009. Re-evaluation of forest biomass carbon stocks and lessons from the world's most carbon-dense forests. Proceedings of the National Academy of Sciences 106:11635–11640.

Kirby, J. S., A. J. Stattersfield, S. H. Butchart, M. I. Evans, R. F. Grimmett, V. R. Jones, J. O'Sullivan, G. M. Tucker, and I. Newton. 2008. Key conservation issues for migratory land-and waterbird species on the world's major flyways. Bird Conservation International 18:S49–S73.

Lascelles, B., G. Notarbartolo Di Sciara, T. Agardy, A. Cuttelod, S. Eckert, L. Glowka, E. Hoyt, F. Llewellyn, M. Louzao, and V. Ridoux. 2014. Migratory marine species: their status, threats and conservation management needs. Aquatic Conservation: Marine and Freshwater Ecosystems 24:111–127.

Lee, J. W., and W. J. McKibbin. 2004. Estimating the global economic cost of SARS. Pages 92–109 in S. Knobler, A. Mahmoud, S. Lemon, Alison Mack, S. Sivitz, and K. Oberholtzer, editors. Learning from SARS: preparing for the next disease outbreak: workshop summary. National Academies Press, Washington, DC.

Marvier, M., P. Kareiva, and M. G. Neubert. 2004. Habitat destruction, fragmentation, and disturbance promote invasion by habitat generalists in a multispecies metapopulation. Risk Analysis: An International Journal 24:869–878.

Mitchell, R. B. 2019. International Environmental Agreements Database Project (Version 2018.1). University of Oregon, http://iea.uoregon.edu/.

Perrings, C. 2012. The governance of international environmental public goods. Pages 54–79 in E. Brousseau, T. Dedeurwaerdere, P.-A. Jouvet, and M. Willinger, editors. Global environmental commons: analytical and political challenges in building governance mechanisms. Oxford University Press, Oxford.

Perrings, C., H. A. Mooney, and M. H. Williamson, editors. 2010. Bioinvasions and globalization: ecology, economics, management, and policy. Oxford University Press, Oxford.

Pimentel, D., R. Zuniga, and D. Morrison. 2005. Update on the environmental and economic costs associated with alien-invasive species in the United States. Ecological Economics 52:273–288.

Reaser, J. K., L. A. Meyerson, Q. Cronk, M. De Poorter, L. Eldrege, E. Green, M. Kairo, P. Latasi, R. N. Mack, and J. Mauremootoo. 2007. Ecological and socioeconomic impacts of invasive alien species in island ecosystems. Environmental Conservation 34:98–111.

Rejmánek, M., D. M. Richardson, and P. Pysek. 2004. Plant invasions and invasibility of plant communities. Pages 332–335 in E. van der Maarel, editor. Vegetation ecology. Blackwell, Oxford.

Sakai, A. K., F. W. Allendorf, J. S. Holt, D. M. Lodge, J. Molofsky, K. A. With, S. Baughman, R. J. Cabin, J. E. Cohen, N. C. Ellstrand, D. E. McCauley, P. O'Neil, I. M. Parker, J. N. Thompson, and S. G. Weller. 2001. The population biology of invasive species. Annual Review of Ecology and Systematics 32:305–332.

Sanchirico, J. N., and J. E. Wilen. 2001. A bioeconomic model of marine reserve creation. Journal of Environmental Economics and Management 42:257–276.

Thornton, D. H., A. J. Wirsing, C. Lopez-Gonzalez, J. R. Squires, S. Fisher, K. W. Larsen, A. Peatt, M. A. Scrafford, R. A. Moen, and A. E. Scully. 2017. Asymmetric cross-border protection of peripheral transboundary species. Conservation Letters:e12430.

Touza, J., and C. Perrings. 2011. Strategic behavior and the scope for unilateral provision of transboundary ecosystem services that are international environmental public goods. Strategic Behavior and the Environment 1:89–117.

United Nations. 1979. Convention on long-range transboundary air pollution. United Nations Treaty Collection, New York.

United Nations. 1992. United Nations framework convention on climate change. United Nations, New York.

United Nations. 1993. Convention on biological diversity. United Nations, New York.

United Nations. 1995. Agreement for the implementation of the provisions of the United Nations Convention on the Law of the Sea of 10 December 1982 relating to the conservation and management of straddling fish stocks and highly migratory fish stocks. United Nations, New York.

United Nations. 1997. Convention on the law of the non-navigational uses of international watercourses. United Nations, New York.

United Nations Environment Programme. 2005. Memorandum of understanding concerning conservation measures for the West African populations of the African Elephant (Loxodonta africana). UNEP, Nairobi.

United Nations Environment Programme. 2018. Convention on the conservation of migratory species of wild animals. UNEP, Nairobi.

United States, Mexico, and Canada. 2018. Agreement between the United States of America, the United Mexican States, and Canada. Office of the United States Trade Representative, Washington, DC.

US Geological Survey. 2014. Colorado River Basin. USGS, Washington, DC.

Wilcove, D. S. 2008. Animal migration: an endangered phenomenon? Issues in Science and Technology 24:71–78.

Williamson, M., and A. D. Fitter. 1996. The varying success of invaders. Ecology 77:1661–1666.

15

Conservation in the Future

A state of nature, properly understood, involves men living together according to reason, with no-one on earth who stands above them all and has authority to judge between them. . . . no political society can exist or survive without having in itself the power to preserve the property—and therefore to punish the offences—of all the members of that society; and so there can't be a political society except where every one of the members has given up this natural power, passing it into the hands of the community in all cases.

—John Locke, *Second Treatise on Government*, 1689

15.1 Introduction

The Hotelling arbitrage condition, which lies at the core of the general theory of conservation discussed in this book, requires decision-makers to form an expectation about the rate of growth in the value of a resource when conserved, relative to the rate of growth in its value when converted. The arbitrage condition is forward-looking. In this final chapter we consider the factors likely to influence the value of species and ecosystems to individual users and the wider community in the years to come. We also take a forward look at the factors likely to drive a wedge between the value of ecosystems to individual users or individual communities and to the rest of the world. Many of these factors have been discussed at length in preceding chapters. They include the public good nature of many ecosystem services, the incompleteness of markets or other mechanisms for negotiating the environmental impacts of private behavior, and the fact that many of the impacts of private decisions are both distant in time and space and fundamentally uncertain. Here we consider how global environmental and socioeconomic trends are likely to affect the future value of conserving environmental resources both to individual communities and to global society. We also consider how changes in the interconnectedness or integration of the global system are likely to alter the

Conservation. Charles Perrings and Ann Kinzig, Oxford University Press (2021). © Oxford University Press.
DOI: 10.1093/oso/9780190613600.003.0015

footprint of local actions, and hence the scale at which conservation decisions should be made.

The notion that the closer integration of the global system has implications for the footprint of local decisions is not new. We have, for example, already considered some of the consequences of what came to be known as the Columbian Exchange—the spread of both beneficial and harmful species that followed Columbus's voyage to the Americas in 1492. The introduction of American crops such as maize, potato, tomato, and tobacco to the Old World was paralleled by the introduction of European, African, and Asian crops such as wheat, citrus, rice, coffee, and bananas to the New World. More notoriously, the introduction of American diseases such as Chagas disease, syphilis, and pinta to the Old World was paralleled by the introduction of European diseases such as bubonic plague, cholera, influenza, leprosy, malaria, measles, smallpox, typhus, and yellow fever to the New World. Few journeys before or since have had as widespread and long-lasting impacts as Columbus's journeys to the Americas. By irreversibly breaking the isolation of the New World, they widened the pool of people potentially affected by the trade in goods and services—for good or ill.

The process of global integration has continued since then. It has not always been smooth. Intense rivalry between imperial powers has led to conflict, the disruption of markets, and the suspension of cooperation between nation-states. The two world wars are cases in point. But the integration of the global economy nevertheless continues, as does the development of mechanisms for coordination and cooperation between nation-states. Global governance systems remain rudimentary, but the number of bilateral and multilateral agreements between nation-states continues to rise. There are certainly differences in the degree to which individual countries are integrated into the global economy. Exports of goods and services in the most outward-looking, highly integrated states (Luxembourg, Hong Kong, Singapore) were above 175% of GDP in 2017. In larger, less outward-looking states the corresponding figure is much lower: less than 12% for the United States, for example, and less than 10% in the poorest developing states such as Sudan, Ethiopia, and Afghanistan. Overall, however, the integration of individual states into the global economy is increasing. Between 1960 and 2017 world exports as a percentage of GDP more than tripled.

In what follows we consider the nature and implication of trends such as this, focusing on implications for the level at which conservation decisions need to be made. We do so through the lens of a particular principle of governance: that of subsidiarity. This principle holds that decisions should be taken at the lowest level possible. It is only where decisions taken at some level fail to take account of the wider or longer-term implications of the decision, that a higher-level authority should become involved. Higher levels of government should play a subsidiary role to lower levels of government, becoming involved only where lower levels of government are not competent to address the problem.

The subsidiarity principle has wide application. It is, for example, formally embodied in the 2007 Treaty on European Union (the Lisbon Treaty), which currently fixes the constitutional basis of the Union. It limits the right of the European Union to intervene to issues that cannot be dealt with effectively by member states. By the subsidiarity principle, the European Union can intervene only if an issue lies outside the competence or capacity of member states, either because of the scale of the actions needed, or because of the scale of the effects of those actions. In the United States, the principle (although not the word) is embedded in state's rights in the Constitution. The principle is also espoused by the Roman Catholic Church. It appears in at least two papal encyclicals—one in 1891, and one in 1931—both asserting that government should undertake only those actions that are beyond the capacity of individuals or communities acting independently.

In the present context, the subsidiarity principle implies that the decisions about how to use environmental resources should be made at the lowest level possible. This is the lowest level at which all significant spatial and temporal impacts of resource use can be accounted for in resource use decisions. It is important to note that even though the principle asserts the rights of local agencies to make decisions about resources within their jurisdiction, it also asserts the duty of higher levels of government to intervene when local agencies are unable to discharge their responsibility. The principle cuts both ways. In the European Union, for example, the principle requires Union intervention in all cases where environmental impacts include transboundary effects. Since member states are unable to address issues such as ozone depletion, climate change, biodiversity change, or transboundary air and water pollution, the regulation of such issues requires EU involvement (De Sadeleer 2012).

The chapter uses the principle to evaluate the implications of current environmental and socioeconomic trends for the conservation of nature and natural resources. Drawing on the 2019 global assessment of biodiversity and ecosystem services and the World Bank's forecasts of the global economy, it evaluates the main biodiversity-related environmental and socioeconomic trends. It then considers the consequences of these trends for the appropriate scale at which to make conservation decisions.

15.2 Environmental trends

In 2019 the Intergovernmental Science-Policy Platform on Biodiversity and Ecosystem Services provided an assessment of current environmental trends and projected the likely consequences of these trends for species, ecosystems, and the goods and services they provide (IPBES 2019). Their central finding is that anthropogenic disruption of most natural systems is still increasing and that this has far-reaching consequences for biodiversity, and hence the capacity of the planet to provide a range of critical ecosystem services. They note that more than three quarters of the earth's land surface has now been significantly altered by human action. Land has been converted to a range of human uses including the production of foods, fuels, fibers, and the supply of freshwater. Habitats have been fragmented by an increasingly dense network of roads, railways, canals, electricity, and oil corridors, and have been stressed by the effects of human emissions to land, water, and air. Two thirds of the oceans have been impacted to some degree, with effects on coral reef systems being particularly severe. The main consequences of habitat disruption has been a decline in the abundance of native species in most biomes, estimated to be at least 20% since 1900, and an associated increase in the extinction probability of many.

The human drivers of current trends in land-cover change are the billions of individually innocuous but collectively damaging decisions. These have led to the extensive growth of agriculture, which now occupies more than one third of the terrestrial land surface; the expansion of cities, which have doubled in area in less than three decades; and the extension of infrastructure. Aside from land-cover change, other factors include decisions affecting the direct harvest of both terrestrial and marine species, water capture and use, emissions of pollutants, invasive species, and climate change.

The criterion adopted by the Intergovernmental Science-Policy Platform on Biodiversity and Ecosystem Services for evaluating land degradation in any location is the difference between the current state of the system and its "natural" state, where the natural state is defined as that existing before the Holocene (before 10,000 years ago). While those undertaking the assessment found such a definition to be intuitive, it has a number of rather obvious problems. Some of these are noted in the assessment, including the fact that the Holocene is associated both with particular climatic conditions and with increasing human influence on land cover. Disentangling the two effects is extremely difficult. More importantly, if the baseline for measuring environmental degradation is the natural state of the system, all anthropogenic environmental change is degrading. Degradation and change are synonymous.

The implication is that the highest value of the system is when it is in a natural state. This is, to say the least, problematic.

If we nevertheless use the IPBES criterion, we would expect the extent of land degradation to differ between high- and low-income countries. IPBES observes that a greater proportion of land in high-income countries has been impacted by these drivers, but that the rate of change has slowed in recent decades, and in some cases has even been reversed. By contrast, a smaller proportion of land is impacted in low-income countries, but the rate of change is much higher. Most future land degradation (by this criterion) is expected to occur in Central and South America, sub-Saharan Africa, and Asia. It is estimated that less than one tenth of the Earth's land surface will be unimpacted by these drivers by 2050—primarily deserts, mountainous areas, tundra, and the poles (IPBES 2018a).

Figure 15.1 shows four measures of the ways in which human actions are degrading habitats, biodiversity, and soils. Panel (a) shows the degree to which humans have appropriated production of biomass. It measures human

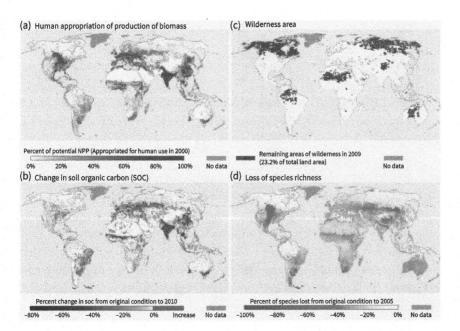

Figure 15.1 Measures of human impacts on biodiversity, habitat, and soils relative to pre-existing conditions.

The degree to which humans have appropriated production of biomass is indicated in panel a. The decline in soil organic carbon is indicated in panel b. Parts of the land surface that can be considered as wilderness are indicated in panel c, and levels of species loss, estimated for all species groups, is shown in panel d.

Source: Adapted from IPBES (2018a).

controlled biomass as a proportion of the biomass that would have been produced by plants in natural conditions. The higher the proportion, the darker the shade. For areas of intensive agriculture, the proportion of biomass production controlled by humans is 100%.

Panel (b) shows the decline in soil organic carbon relative to pre-Neolithic conditions—conditions before settled agriculture. It is a measure of the degree to which soils have been degraded. Panel (c) shows remaining wilderness areas. Areas are defined as wilderness if ecological and evolutionary processes operate with minimal human disturbance. In all other areas, the same processes are significantly impacted by human activity. Panel (d) shows levels of anthropogenic species loss relative to pre-existing (pre-Holocene) species composition. Loss is measured as the percentage of all species groups that been extirpated by 2005.

On the longest time scales, climatic shifts such as that observed in the Holocene and other interglacial periods are driven by the Milankovitch cycles, and especially by the eccentricity of the earth's orbit around the sun (on 100,000 year cycles), and its obliquity or axial tilt (on 40,000 year cycles). As we would expect from the current latitudinal gradient, warmer periods on such timescales have been found to be associated with higher levels of biodiversity (Mayhew et al. 2012).

On shorter time scales, the climate change that is due to anthropogenic greenhouse gas emissions is argued to have a range of impacts on biodiversity and ecosystem functioning—some positive, but most negative. Mean temperatures have increased by approximately 1.0°C over preindustrial levels, and the rate of change is accelerating. In the last 30 years, mean temperatures have risen by around 0.2°C per decade. There has been an increase in the frequency and intensity of extreme weather events, and the associated "natural" disasters of floods and droughts. Sea levels have risen by 16 to 21 centimeters since 1900, and the rate of increase is accelerating. In the last 20 years, sea levels have risen by more than 3 millimeters per year. These changes have been shown to have far-reaching effects on species distributions, population dynamics, community structure, and ecosystem functioning. They have also been shown to have significant effects on managed systems—agriculture, forestry, aquaculture, and fisheries.

Climate change also has the potential to amplify the impacts of other industrial pollutants that more directly affect biomass at regional scales, such as sulphates and nitrates. The trend in emissions of both these pollutants is, however, different in different parts of the world. Figure 15.2 shows global atmospheric sulphate emissions in 1980 and 2000, and projects emissions to 2030.

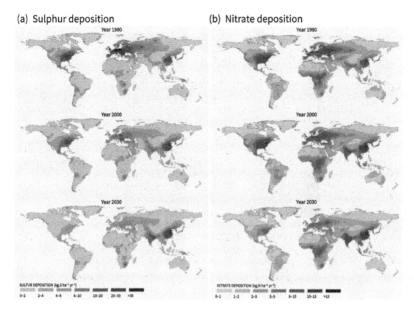

Figure 15.2 Total sulfur and nitrate deposition.

Panel A: Total sulfur deposition in kg S ha⁻¹ yr⁻¹ for 1980, 2000 and 2030. Panel B: Total nitrate deposition in kg N ha⁻¹ yr⁻¹ for 1980, 2000, and 2030.

Source: IPBES (2018a).

In 1980, atmospheric sulfate and nitrate depositions were highest in eastern North America, Europe, and East Asia due to intensive fossil fuel use. By 2000, sulfate deposition had decreased in North America and Europe as a result of pollution control measures, but had increased in East Asia, and South Asia, where the effects of industrial growth were less constrained by pollution control measures. By 2030 both sulfate and nitrate depositions are expected to fall in Europe and North America, but are expected to continue to increase in sub-Saharan Africa, East Asia, and South Asia (IPBES 2018a).

While the threats to species depend most directly on habitat loss and fragmentation, industrial emissions—and particularly greenhouse gas emissions—are expected to make the problem worse. Around 47% of terrestrial mammals and 23% of birds identified by the IUCN as threatened are negatively affected by climate change in some part of their distribution. Particular populations have either declined or have been locally extirpated—unable to adapt to a changing climate, or to disperse to areas with suitable climatic conditions. For example, around half of all coral reefs have been lost in the last 150 years due to a combination of climate change and other factors, but the recent acceleration in losses appears to be largely climate-driven (Figure 15.3).

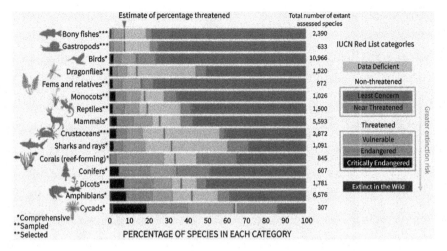

Figure 15.3 The proportion of assessed species threatened with extinction.

The figure shows the percentage of species threatened with extinction in taxonomic groups that have been assessed comprehensively, or through a sampled approach, or for which selected subsets have been assessed, by the International Union for Conservation of Nature (IUCN) Red List of Threatened Species. Groups are ordered according to the best estimate for the percentage of extant species considered threatened (shown by the vertical lines), assuming that data deficient species are as threatened as nondata deficient species.

Source: Adapted from IPBES (2019).

The ecological consequences of these trends vary across time and space. The hotspots of endemic species subject to high levels of stress have lost more than 20% of species present in the early Holocene. Elsewhere, whether species have been extirpated from areas subject to large human impacts depends largely on their traits. Large, slow growing habitat specialists and top predators are declining. Small, fast growing generalists are becoming more abundant, and are frequently spreading beyond their original distribution.

The extirpation of large herbivores and predators has changed the structure and functioning of many ecosystems, altering fire regimes, patterns of seed dispersal, and nutrient availability, among other things. The growth and spread of small, fast-growing generalists has similarly changed host systems in fundamental ways. In a sample of 21 countries it was found that invasive alien species have increased by around 70% in the last 50 years, with negative impacts on native species, especially endemics, and especially on islands. As we have earlier noted, many of the most harmful invasive species are pathogens. Indeed, just one pathogen, *Batrachochytrium dendrobatidis*, has already driven a number of amphibian species to extinction, and threatens around 400 more. The same process is steadily reducing differences between ecological communities in different places, simultaneously reducing the genetic diversity that is the source of the evolutionary potential of species, and increasing their vulnerability to common stresses (IPBES 2019).

In human-dominated systems such as agroecosystems, the homogenization of both cultivated plants and animals, and of pests and pathogens, is especially marked. IPBES records a significant decline in the diversity of cultivated domesticated plants and animals generated through plant and animal breeding since the Neolithic revolution. The adoption of high-yielding varieties in since the 1960s has led to a decline in the pool of genetic variation that underpins food security. Around 10% of livestock breeds and around 3.5% of domesticated birds have gone extinct in this period. Many landraces and crop wild relatives are currently under threat (Perrings 2018).

One consequence of anthropogenic stress reported by IPBES is the rapid evolution of species. A process that has been widely recognized in pest species—viruses, agricultural insect pests, and weeds—is now being observed in a much wider range of animals, plants, fungi, and microorganisms. Just as it has been understood that insects, weeds, and pathogens evolve resistance to insecticides, herbicides, and anti-viral and anti-bacterial treatments, it is now observed that fish populations evolve to mature earlier under intensive harvesting, other species evolve seasonally earlier reproduction under warming climatic conditions, mosquitoes evolve resistance to control efforts, and so on.

The rapid evolution of invasive species is especially important. Invasions are often characterized as rapid evolutionary events. Invasive populations have been found to be genetically dynamic. Genetic drift has, for example, been found to alter the genetic structures of invasive species in ways that strengthen their capacity to establish and spread, but also to induce an evolutionary response in native species. More generally, a number of genetic attributes have been shown to promote invasion success, including additive genetic variance, epistasis (or interaction genetic variance), and hybridization. With enough additive genetic variance, a species can adapt to the environmental change involved in its relocation from one place to another. But even without much additive genetic variance, hybridization of invasive populations with either natives or other invaders frequently results in novel genotypes, allowing faster growth, greater size, or increased aggressiveness. Weeds that have hybridized with crops genetically engineered to be pesticide-resistant has, for example, led to the emergence of pesticide-resistant weeds. Indeed, allopolyploid hybridization in plants (which results in fertile hybrids) has, in some cases, led to hybrids that are reproductively incompatible with either parental species—leading to instantaneous speciation (Lee 2002).

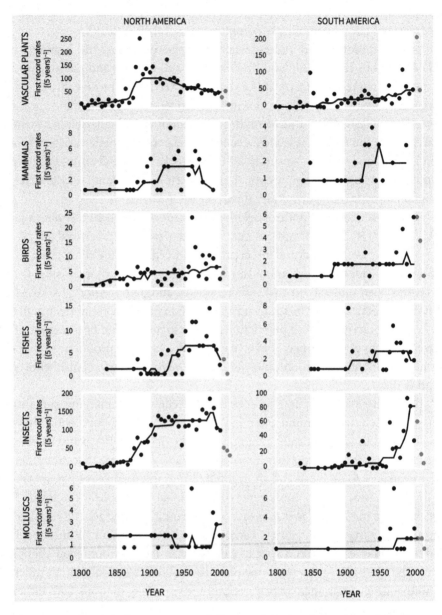

Figure 15.4 Trends in the appearance of alien species in North America and South America from 1800 to 2000.

Source: IPBES (2018b).

The introduction, establishment, and spread of species around the globe as a byproduct of trade and travel is a process that is expected to continue for the foreseeable future. The economic drivers of this trend are described in the next section. The ecological consequences include the effects described earlier: the loss of native species, the rapid evolution of invaders either in response to environmental changes or as a consequence of hybridization, and the homogenization of ecosystems. It is, however, a process that plays out in different ways across space and time.

Globally, 37% of all recorded introduced species that had established in a host system were observed for the first time after 1970. For birds, more than half of all naturalized introductions were recorded for the first time after 1950. The process is new, and is still unfolding. If we consider the rates of appearance for different species groups, however, we see that some groups appeared earlier than others, and increased at faster rates, but also that patterns vary by region. An assessment of the process in the Americas finds that most species groups appeared earlier and increased more rapidly in North America than in South America, but also that rates of appearance of at least some species groups (vascular plants and mammals in particular) are now declining in North America while still increasing in South America (Figure 15.4).

15.3 Economic trends

A second set of trends involves changes in the structure of the global economic system. Globalization is a process that has its roots in the migrations that populated the world over millennia, but is generally thought about as a more modern phenomenon linked to the growth of empires in the Mediterranean region, the Middle East, and Asia, and to the establishment of trade routes and to the spread of cultures, ideas, and religions over the last 3,000 years. The process has been intermittent, rather than continuous, and marked as much by war as by trade. Incidental effects of the military campaigns that underpinned the Roman and Mongolian empires, for example, included both the establishment of secure land trade routes, and the diffusion of ideas and technologies. In the late fifteenth and early sixteenth centuries, exploratory sea voyages by Christopher Columbus, Vasco da Gama, and Ferdinand Magellan laid the basis for a new global trade regime in which the strategy pursued by the dominant players in Europe was mercantilism—the pursuit of national wealth through the maintenance of positive trade balances. Mercantilist strategies were at once the motivation for colonial expansion, the development of a colonial trade in natural resources and human beings, and a cause of war between rivals. While mercantilism had been largely dismantled by the nineteenth century, the imperial rivalries that were one of its main legacies resurfaced in the world wars of the twentieth century.

The term "globalization" itself was not widely used until the 1980s, and most studies of the process focus only on the recent past—the last 50 years. In this period globalization has had four main dimensions: trade flows, capital movements, migration and the movement of people, and information flows or the dissemination and diffusion of knowledge. The closer integration of the global economic system implies increasing flows of any or all of these things. To capture the process a number of indices have been developed. One of these, the KOF globalization index, uses a set of 42 variables spanning the economic, social, and political dimensions of globalization.[1] The index differs from others in distinguishing between real flows and the conditions that enable flows to take place. Real flows are reported in what is called the "de facto" index, while the regulator environment is reported in the "de jure" index.

---

[1] Exports and imports of goods (% of GDP); exports and imports of services (% of GDP); average of the Herfindahl-Hirschman market concentration index for exports and imports of goods (inverted); average of the prevalence of nontariff trade barriers and compliance costs of importing and exporting; income from taxes on international trade as percentage of revenue (inverted); unweighted mean of tariff rates; number of bilateral and multilateral free trade agreements; sum of stocks of assets and liabilities of foreign direct investments (% of GDP); sum of stocks of assets and liabilities of international equity portfolio investments (% of GDP); sum of inward and outward stocks of international portfolio debt securities and international bank loans and deposits (% of GDP); sum of capital and labor income to foreign nationals and from abroad (% of GDP); prevalence of foreign ownership and regulations to international capital flows; Chinn-Ito index of capital account openness; number of bilateral investment agreements (BITs) and treaties with investment provisions (TIPs); international incoming and outgoing fixed and mobile telephone traffic in minutes (% of population); secondary income paid and received; gross inflows and outflows of goods, services, income, or financial items without a quid pro quo (% of population); arrivals and departures of international tourists (% of population); inbound and outbound number of tertiary students (% of population); number of foreign or foreign-born residents (% of population); fixed telephone and mobile subscriptions (% of population); percentage of countries for which a country requires a visa from foreign visitors; number of airports that offers at least one international flight connection (% of population); total used capacity of international internet bandwidth in bits per second (% of population); patent applications by nonresidents filed through the Patent Cooperation Treaty procedure or with a national patent office (% of population); exports of high R&D intensity products in current US$ (% of population); share of households with a television set; individuals using the internet (% of population); quantification of the legal environment for the media, political pressure that influences reporting, and economic factors that affect access to news and information; exports and imports of cultural goods defined as in UNESCO (2009) (% of population); exports and imports of personal, cultural, and recreational services (% of population); applications to register a trademark with a national or regional intellectual property (IP) office by nonresidents in percentage of all applications; number of McDonald's restaurants (% of population); number of IKEA stores (% of population); ratio of girls to boys enrolled in primary education level in public and private schools; human capital index based on the average years of schooling and an assumed rate of return to education; quantification of aspects on freedom of expression and belief, associational and organizational rights, rule of law and personal autonomy, and individual rights; absolute number of embassies in a country; personnel contributed to UN Security Council Missions (% of population); number of internationally oriented nongovernmental organizations (NGOs) operating in that country; number of international intergovernmental organizations in which a country is member; international treaties signed between two or more states and ratified by the highest legislative body of each country since 1945; number of distinct treaty partners of a country with bilateral investment treaties (BITs).

The economic dimensions of globalization include both trade and capital flows (trade in goods and services and foreign direct investment) and the regulatory environment that enables or limits those flows (customs duties, taxes, trade, and investment restrictions). The social and political dimensions of globalization are similarly divided into real and enabling phenomena. For example, tourist numbers and human migration would be real flows. Visa restrictions would be regulatory. The number of embassies and international NGOs would be real, and membership of international organizations and multilateral or bilateral agreements would be regulatory.

At the global level, the KOF index shows that the interval since 1970 can be divided into three periods. Between 1970 and 1991, and from 2008, globalization increased at a relatively modest rate. Between 1991 and 2008 globalization increased at a much more rapid rate. Moreover, the rate at which the enabling conditions for closer integration increased in this period (the de jure index) was much higher than the rate at which real flows increased (the de facto index) (Figure 15.5).

Three aspects of globalization that are particularly important for the conservation of natural resources are (a) international flows of goods and services, (b) international mobility and migration, and (c) international flows of capital. We consider these in turn.

International flows of goods and services: While the connections between all economies have become tighter over time, there are still substantial differences between countries based on their size, their wealth, and their

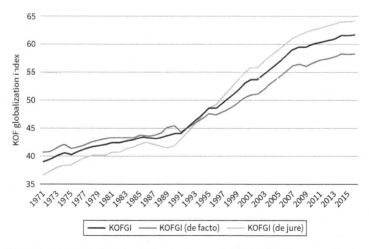

Figure 15.5 The KOF globalization index for the world, including the overall index, the de facto index, and the de jure index.
Source: Gygli et al. (2019).

income. Figures 15.6 and 15.7 record imports and exports of goods and services as a percentage of GDP for high-income, upper-middle-income, lower-middle-income, low-income, and highly indebted poor countries since 1960. These are principal elements of the KOF globalization index, and like the world index, all income groups show that a similar temporal pattern of modest growth before 1991, and rapid growth between 1991 and 2008. However, they also show striking differences in the exposure of high- and low-income countries to the global markets.

The heavily indebted poor countries (the poorest group of countries) and low-income countries both imported a much higher proportion of goods and services than either the middle- or high-income countries throughout the interval 1960–2016. A better indicator of dependence on foreign markets is the propensity to export, usually measured by the ratio of exports to GDP. In the early part of the same interval, the poorest countries also exported a higher proportion of goods and services than either the middle- or high-income

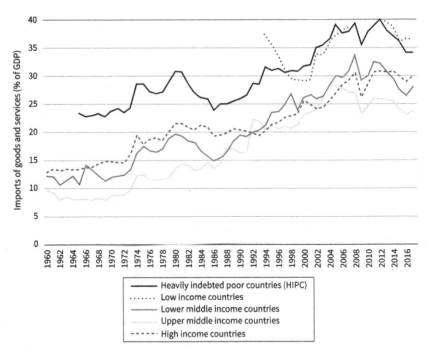

Figure 15.6 Imports of goods and services as a percentage of gross domestic product, by income group.

Includes the value of merchandise, freight, insurance, transport, travel, royalties, license fees, and other services, such as communication, construction, financial, information, business, personal, and government services. Excludes compensation of employees and investment income (formerly called factor services) and transfer payments.

Source: World Bank (2018).

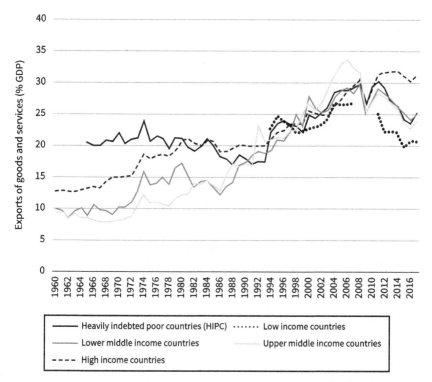

Figure 15.7 Exports of goods and services as a percentage of gross domestic product, by income group.

Includes the value of merchandise, freight, insurance, transport, travel, royalties, license fees, and other services, such as communication, construction, financial, information, business, personal, and government services. Excludes compensation of employees and investment income (formerly called factor services) and transfer payments.

Source: World Bank (2018).

countries. In later years, however, even though the propensity of the poorest countries to export continued to rise, the difference between low-, middle-, and high-income countries diminished, largely due to falling commodity prices.

What does differentiate exports from low-, middle-, and high-income countries is not the ratio of exports to GDP, but the composition of exports. Whereas exports from middle- and high-income countries tend to be dominated by services and manufactured goods, exports from many low-income countries are generally dominated by natural resources and agricultural products. Figure 15.8 shows agricultural and natural resource dependence by country as at 2016. Oil and mineral exporters in the Middle East show up as being most dependent, but regions where agriculture is a principal activity—such as Latin America and sub-Saharan Africa—also register high levels of export dependence.

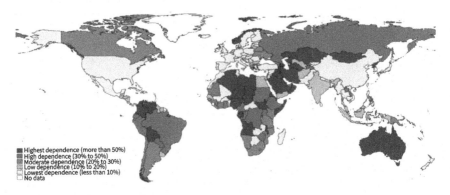

Figure 15.8 Export dependence on agriculture and natural resources.
Source: United Nations Conference on Trade and Development (2018).

Where the trade flow data look different from the KOF globalization index is in the period after 2008. For all income groups imports have been falling as a percentage of GDP, and for all except the high-income countries, exports have been falling as a percentage of GDP. This is due both to changes in commodities prices, and changes in enabling conditions. The World Bank's 2019 report on global economic prospects notes that the rise in protectionist sentiment in recent years could slow or even reverse the trend toward globalization. New tariffs and import restrictions have been put in place in high-income countries, and the probability for even tighter restrictions on trade is thought to be high. Trade growth has slowed more rapidly than expected, and the intensification of trade disputes is thought to "threaten the stability of the rules-based global trading system and undo the beneficial effects of trade liberalization and global integration achieved during decades of multilateral cooperation" (World Bank 2019c). At least from an economic perspective, the period since 2008 involves a reversal of the globalization trends of the last 50 years. Declining trade flows have been accompanied by declining enabling conditions. The KOF de facto and de jure indexes for trade flows reflect this trend (Figure 15.9).

Mobility and migration: The dimension of globalization that has stimulated the sharpest reaction is the movement not of goods but of people and, specifically, increasing levels of out-migration from developing countries. There are a range of consequences to both short-term and long-term movements of people. Many of these consequences are positive, but some are negative. Take short-term movements of people associated with either business travel or tourism. While both are a source of economic benefits to receiving countries, they also involve costs. For example, business travelers and tourists are both important in the transmission of infectious diseases

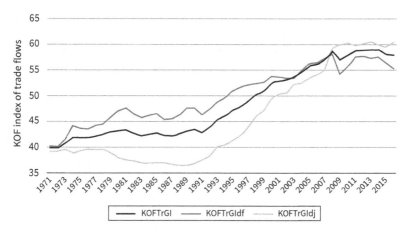

Figure 15.9 The KOF globalization index for world trade flows, including the overall index, the de facto index, and the de jure index.
Source: Gygli et al. (2019).

across international borders. Neither the costs nor the benefits of short-term movements of people are evenly distributed across countries. Figure 15.10 reports tourist arrivals to different groups of countries between 1995 and 2017. It shows both that total tourist arrivals have been consistently increasing (by over 150% in the period), and that the largest number of arrivals has consistently been recorded by high- and upper middle-income countries. That is, both the benefits and the costs of short-term movements of people accrue to the richest countries.

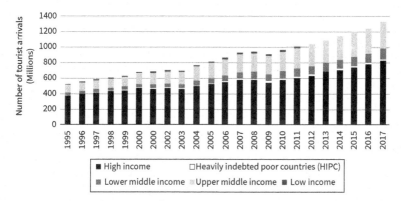

Figure 15.10 Tourist arrivals 1995–2017.
Indicates the number of people who travel (not for work) to a country other than their usual residence, for a period not exceeding 12 months.
Source: Data derived from World Bank (2019d).

Long-term movements of people—migration—are similarly unevenly distributed across countries, both numerically and in terms of their impacts. Migrants are defined by the United Nations as people who change their country of usual residence, and migration is measured by the change in the stock of migrants—the number of people residing in a country other than their country of birth. Although some countries record annual migration flows, most do not. In 1980, the global stock of international migrants was 102 million. Over the next 20 years it rose to 173 million, and by 2017 it stood at 258 million. At that level 3.4% of the world population were classified as migrants, compared to 2.3% in 1980. Although the rate of growth in migration slowed after the 2008–2009 recession, for most of the period since 1980 the average annual rate of growth in migration has been around 2.7% (Pew Research Center 2019).

As with import and export propensities, the source and destination of migrants reflects income and wealth differentials. North America, Europe, and Oceana receive more migrants than they supply. Asia, Latin America and the Caribbean, and Africa supply more migrants than they receive. The largest concentrations of migrants are found in Asia (80 million) and Europe (78 million). The smallest are in Oceana (8 million) and Latin America and the Caribbean (10 million). North America (58 million) and Africa (25 million) lie in between. The largest sources of migrants are also Asia (110 million) and Europe (64 million). The smallest are Oceana (2 million) and North America (5 million). Latin America and the Caribbean, and Africa, each supply around 39 million.

In the years since the recession the most rapidly growing source of migrants has been Syria, where civil conflict has led nearly 7 million people to emigrate. The next most rapidly growing source of migrants is sub-Saharan Africa, and especially countries where there have been long periods of conflict: Sudan, Southern Sudan, Eritrea, and the Central African Republic. While the destination of most sub-Saharan African migrants has been other countries in the region, the proportion moving to Europe and the United States increased substantially between 1990 and 2017. Looking ahead, a worldwide survey of migration intentions shows that half of adults planning to migrate in the future currently live in eight African countries (Nigeria, the Democratic Republic of the Congo, Sudan, Egypt, Ethiopia, Ghana, Algeria, and Côte d'Ivoire), four Asian countries (India, Bangladesh, China, and Pakistan), three Latin American countries (Mexico, Colombia, and Brazil), two Middle Eastern countries (Islamic Republic of Iran and Iraq), and two European countries (Italy and Spain) (Global Migration Data Analysis Centre 2018).

From an environmental perspective, sudden-onset disasters and conflict are increasingly important determinants of the displacement of people within countries—what is referred to as internal displacement. While there are no data on the direct connection between internal displacement and international migration, it is clear that there is some correlation between the two. Most internal displacement occurs in low- and lower-middle-income countries in high-risk environments that share three characteristics: high levels of exposure to natural hazards, high levels of socioeconomic vulnerability, and low levels of coping capacity (Figure 15.11).

Of the 24.2 million people displaced by natural disaster, 66% were located in China, India, and the Philippines. Proportionately, however, the greatest burden was carried by island states, especially Cuba and Fiji, as well as the Philippines. Most displacements are weather-related and involve either storms or flooding, with small island states being especially vulnerable. Patterns of displacement due to conflict and violence are different. In 2016, 69% of the 6.9 million people displaced by conflict and violence were located in Africa and the Middle East.

While there are few data on the relation between internal displacement and international migration, there is a clear correlation between internal displacement in one year and refugee status in the next for at least those countries

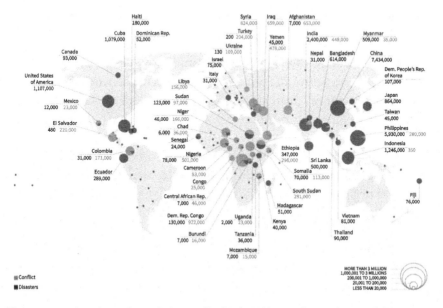

Figure 15.11 Numbers of people internally displaced by conflict and natural disasters in 2016.

Source: Internal Displacement Monitoring Centre (2017).

where civil conflict has been ongoing for a number of years. The connection between displacement due to natural disasters and international migration is less well established.

In the longer term, the expectation is that environmental change and conflict will be associated with increasing large-scale involuntary migration. This is expected to take one of four forms. First, an increase in the frequency and magnitude of extreme weather events, such as hurricanes, is likely to result in increasing internal and international displacement. Second, a climate-induced reduction in the sustainability of natural resource-based livelihoods, such as agriculture and forestry, is expected to lead people to relocate. Third, an interaction between climate change and conflict is expected to amplify the conflict-related displacement of people. Fourth, regional scale changes in habitability is expected to lead to larger scale population movements. Rising sea levels, coastal inundation, the salinization of low-lying aquifers and soils, and the loss of other water sources are expected to lead to large-scale movements of people away from areas that are no longer habitable. These trends are, in turn, expected to lead to a change in the governance of international migration (Warner 2018).

Capital movements: Aside from international flows of goods and services, and of people, one other economic trend likely to affect future conservation involves capital flows. Direct investment by wealthier countries in the exploitation of natural resources in poorer countries, frequently colonies, was a hallmark of globalization in the postmercantilist era. While many former colonies have diversified away from mining, forestry, and agriculture, it is still the case that much foreign direct investment in poorer economies is still targeted at the extraction and processing of primary products.

Foreign direct investment is also significant through the fact that it gives the investor in one country either direct control or at least significant influence over an enterprise in another country. Formally, foreign direct investment includes the equity that secures control and influence, as well as related investments and reverse investments or disinvestments. The latter are recorded as negative magnitudes. To show global trends in foreign direct investment over the last 50 years, Figures 15.12 and 15.13 report net inflows of foreign direct investment in low-, middle-, and high-income countries both as a percentage of GDP, and in billions of current US dollars. The two figures reveal the same striking global trend: an increase in aggregate foreign direct investment at rates well beyond the increase in global imports and exports in the same period. But they also reveal marked differences between richer and poorer countries. While the value of foreign direct investment into high-income countries is several times the value of foreign direct investment into

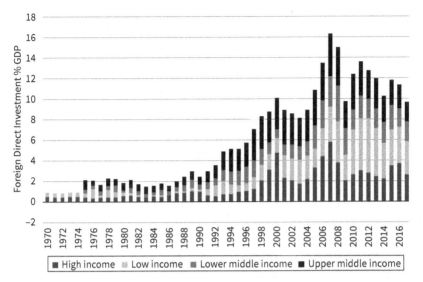

Figure 15.12 Foreign direct investment, net inflows 1970–2017, as a percentage of GDP by income group.
Source: World Bank (2019a).

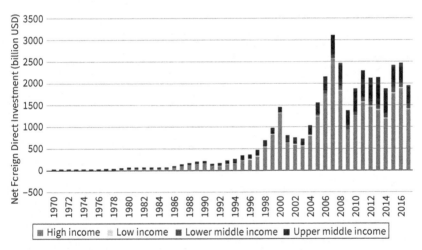

Figure 15.13 Foreign direct investment, net inflows 1970–2017, measured in billions of current US$ by income group.
Source: World Bank (2019b).

all other countries combined (Figure 15.13), it nevertheless makes a much smaller relative contribution to the economy. As Figure 15.12 shows, foreign direct investment as a percentage of GDP is highest in low- and middle-income countries, and (in general) lowest in high-income countries. The exceptions are the years immediately preceding the 2001 and 2008 recessions. In both 2000 and 2007 foreign direct investment into high-income countries spiked to unprecedented levels. In the years following the recession, foreign direct investment in low- and middle-income countries has been declining both in value and relative to GDP, but remains much higher than in the years before 2000.

We consider the environmental implications of these trends later in this chapter. The points to note here are (a) that the greater exposure to foreign direct investment in low-and middle-income countries means that a larger share of the production decisions made in those countries are taken by nonresidents, and (b) that because foreign direct investment in low- and middle-income countries is almost exclusively geared to the production of goods and services for export, it reinforces the trend toward more tightly integrated international markets.

15.4 The population affected by conservation decisions

So what do these trends imply for conservation in the future? Recall that the subsidiarity principle holds that conservation decisions should be taken at the lowest level possible, which is the lowest level that captures all significant costs and benefits of the decision. If the decision to conserve or convert a particular tract of land has no implications for the welfare of nonresidents, for example, the decision should be left to the residents alone. Nobody else is a stakeholder in the decision, and nobody else should be involved in the decision. But if the decision does have implications for the welfare of nonresidents, then the same principle implies that the decision should be taken at a level that encompasses the impacts on nonresidents. Similarly, if the decision to conserve or convert the land has no implications for the future welfare of either residents or nonresidents—if the effects of the decision are ephemeral—then the decision-makers should be permitted to take only current costs and benefits into account. But the decision has implications for future generations of either residents or nonresidents, then the decision framework should encompass the impacts on future generations.

It follows that the subsidiarity principle requires an understanding of the population affected by any decision—not in law, but in fact. The population affected by a decision establishes the scale at which the decision should be taken. It is the constituency of stakeholders. If it spans more than one jurisdiction, then the decision should be taken by a body spanning those jurisdictions.

In the European Union or the United States, the subsidiarity principle implies that if the action of one state has implications for the welfare of the residents of other states, then the decision should be taken at the level of the Union (Europe) or the federation (United States).

While land-use/land-cover change is always local, it frequently has off-site consequences for the welfare of people who are distant in time and space. Forest clearance in sub-Saharan Africa, for example, has potential consequences for the emergence of zoonotic and epizootic diseases; for the emission of carbon dioxide, and therefore for the stabilization of the global climate; for the amount and distribution of rainfall in other parts of the world; for off-site flooding and the siltation of rivers locally; for the survival probability of the species displaced from a part of their habitat, and for the functions and processes of the ecosystem disrupted in the process. Many of these consequences are externalities of the decisions behind land-use/land-cover change, and so are ignored by the decision-makers. But the population affected by the decisions—the constituency of stakeholders—includes everyone impacted by emerging infectious diseases, by changing temperatures, rainfall, sea levels, flood and fire regimes, by the declining diversity of displaced forest species, and by the loss of locally important ecological functions.

The environmental and economic trends described earlier have several characteristics that bear on the population affected by land-use/land-cover decisions at different scales. Three are especially important.

Small decisions: First, the most challenging environmental trends reflect the cumulative impact of small decisions to conserve or convert land that, taken in isolation, appear to have few implications for the welfare of others. Systemic changes in the climate, like the global decline in biodiversity, the dispersal of invasive species and the homogenization of ecosystems, are the consequence of billions of small land-use/land-cover decisions, all individually rational, all individually innocuous, but cumulatively harmful. Each decision, evaluated from the perspective of the subsidiarity principle, has so few consequences for the welfare of others that none feel the need to identify, let alone engage, the constituency of stakeholders. Yet cumulatively, the same decisions fail the subsidiarity test. They have impacts that extend well beyond the decision-makers themselves.

In 1966, the economist Alfred Kahn identified what he called "the tyranny of small decisions" as a potential source of market failure. The market failure lies in the fact that the cumulative effects of many small individually innocuous decisions frequently generates harmful outcomes that none of the decision-makers would welcome (Kahn 1966). A classic example of the tyranny of small decisions, published two years later, is Garret Hardin's "tragedy of the commons" (Hardin 1968). While the actions of each person with access to Hardin's commons may be individually rational, the cumulative impact of those decisions is harmful to all.

Many of the public bads resulting from agriculture or industry are a consequence of small decisions that are largely unregulated. As we have seen in earlier chapters, addressing this problem requires intervention in even small decisions not case-by-case, but by the development of incentives designed to affect each class of decisions. Identifying the marginal social cost of decisions within a particular class in turn requires understanding of the population affected by that class of decisions. In the extreme case, the appropriate level at which to take land-use/land-cover decisions that cumulatively affect the global population is the global level.

Small worlds: Second, the introduction and spread of invasive pests and pathogens, the diffusion and adoption of common agricultural technologies, and the homogenization of both managed and impacted ecosystems reflect a seemingly irreversible process—the increasingly close integration of the global economic system. The dispersal of both beneficial and harmful species and the homogenization of ecosystems are direct results of the growth of trade and travel within an increasingly highly connected global network of transport routes. As exports and imports rise relative to GDP, so does the likelihood that the exchange of goods and services results in the introduction, establishment, and spread of harmful pests and pathogens. As the market reach of major seed and pesticide companies expands, so does the likelihood that farmers will plant the same seeds, apply the same pesticides, and select for the same pests. As the network of air transport routes expands, so does the likelihood that emerging infectious diseases will have pandemic effects.

The characteristics of the network are crucial. Studies of the role of the air transport network in the transmission of recent diseases, such as the 2003 SARS and 2009 H1N1 pandemics, have shown that the relevant concept of distance in the air transport network depends both on the time and distance associated with distinct routes, but also on the volume of traffic along different routes. Probabilistic measures of effective distance have been calculated that equate smaller passenger volumes with larger distances, and vice versa. The effective distance between any two nodes in the network is the shortest path by this measure. Simulations of the global spread of infectious disease, using the effective distance between transport nodes, show that diseases spread along the shortest path tree as simple waves. The simulated spread of a disease originating in Hong Kong is illustrated in Figure 15.14. Spread across the air transport network, modeled as the shortest path tree from Hong Kong, is shown in the upper panel, while the corresponding geographical spread is shown in the lower panel. Analysis of the spread of actual pandemics reveals closely related patterns. Both SARS and H1N1 were shown to have spread as linear functions of effective distance. The patterns of COVID-19 have yet to be established as we write, but may be expected to be similar.

Air transport networks, like many socioeconomic and biological networks, are referred to as small world networks. Small world networks have two important characteristics. One is that they have small characteristic path lengths. The other is that they are highly clustered. The small characteristic path lengths in small world networks means that effects can propagate through the network rapidly. The clustering indicates a degree of regional specialization or focus. Individual clusters are subnetworks in which most nodes are directly connected, while connections between clusters are made via hubs—or nodes of high degree. It has been shown that if connections between people both confer benefits and impose costs, and if people choose which connections to make, then small world networks emerge as a natural response to variation in the costs and benefits of connections (Jackson and Rogers 2005).

The important point here is that the way the risks of biodiversity change propagate across the global system depends both on the pathways between different parts of the system—the structure of the network—and on the volume of movements along pathways. Globalization means both that different parts of the world are expected to become more closely linked through the trade and transport network, and that the volume of flows along trade and transport pathways are expected to increase. Understanding the properties of the underlying network, as well as patterns of trade and travel, make it possible to identify both regional and distant effects of local decisions. The clustered

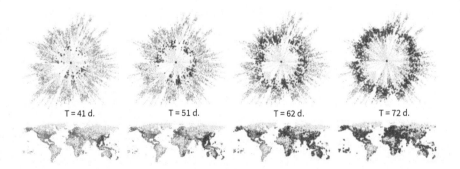

Figure 15.14 The simulated spread of an infectious disease originating in Hong Kong across the air transport network, modeled as the shortest path tree (effective distance) from the origin.
Source: Reprinted in grayscale from Brockmann and Helbing (2013).

characteristic of small world networks means that regional effects propagate to the global system via hubs, such as seaports, international airports, and so on. The hubs effectively filter such effects, potentially helping to contain the propagation of risk in either direction. It follows that the clustering within small world networks can help determine the scale at which decisions with wider impacts should be taken.

Distant ownership: Third, all of the economic trends identified earlier are highly sensitive to income and wealth. Trends in foreign direct investment flows as a proportion of gross domestic product show that low-income countries are increasingly dependent on economic activities that are directed by non-nationals. While this trend has brought with it benefits in the form of access to technologies and markets that would otherwise be closed and has generated local employment opportunities, it has also come at a cost. Much foreign direct investment has focused on the exploitation of land and natural resources. For example, large-scale land acquisitions in sub-Saharan Africa aimed at increasing food production have generated employment opportunities, and contributed to the provision of public goods, but a review of recent studies of the impacts of such investments concludes that compensation has not generally covered the loss of benefits to those who depended on the natural resources impacted by the process (Hufe and Heuermann 2017). One reason for this relates to the weak regulation of the local environmental effects of foreign direct investment.

The evidence on the environmental impacts of foreign direct investment is mixed. A long-standing debate on the incentive effects of weak environmental regulations is largely unresolved. There is evidence that an increase in pollution abatement costs associated with the production of particular commodities in developed economies is positively correlated with an increase in imports of those commodities from developing economies (Levinson and Taylor 2008). This is at least consistent with the pollution haven hypothesis, by which foreign direct investment is argued to flow to countries where environmental regulations are weaker and abatement costs lower. But there is also some evidence that foreign direct investment that embodies cleaner technology than that required by local environmental regulations confers an environmental benefit—the pollution halo hypothesis (Elliott and Zhou 2013). What is clear is that the geography of investment in polluting industries alters the geography of the associated pollution burden. The evidence is that trends in foreign direct investment have increased pollution in developing countries and reduced pollution in developed countries (Solarin and Al-Mulali 2018).

Implicit in the pollution haven debate is a different question. By definition, foreign direct investment implies that control over production decisions lies with those whose principals (owners or shareholders) are not residents of the host country. The implicit question is whether changes in patterns of ownership over capital assets in a country lead to changes in the treatment of the environmental externalities of production decisions. Are foreign owners of farms, game ranches, hunting concessions, or tourist operations more or less likely to take account of the local impacts of their activities than domestic owners? Interestingly, most of the evidence for the pollution halo hypothesis relates to pollutants with global effects (such as carbon dioxide), rather than local effects (such as nitrates or sulfates). But since the implicit question has not been formally tested, we cannot draw any firm conclusions.

The general point is that foreign direct investment trends imply a change in the identity of the stakeholders to local decisions. Trends in the number of people converting habitat, and trends in the structure and volume of trade and travel, both alter the population affected by local decisions. So too do trends in foreign direct investment. Since the right scale of decisions to conserve or convert land should reflect the population affected by those decisions, all three trends are relevant.

15.5 The optimal scale at which to conserve and the governance of conservation

Throughout this book we have considered the factors to be taken into account in deciding whether or not to convert or conserve a particular asset—a landscape, a habitat, a species or community of species, a mineral resource, a water body, and so on. The Hotelling principle has allowed us to say that assets should be conserved only if the expected rate of growth in their value when conserved is at least as great as the expected rate of growth in their value when converted. The value of conservation is conditional both on the amount of conversion that has already taken place, and the range of external effects of the conversion decision. The implications of our discussion of recent trends is that the social costs of habitat conversion may be rising much more rapidly than the private costs of land conversion, leaving a greater and greater wedge between the social and private marginal net benefits of conservation. The gap between the conservation that private individuals would choose, and the conservation that society desires, is widening.

By the subsidiarity principle, private landholders should be left to choose the level of conservation that is optimal for them only if the direct and indirect effects on others are negligible. Where the cumulative impact of private conversion decisions is substantial, and where the external costs or benefits of private conservation decision are impact others, the choice to conserve or convert should be made at a scale that spans the affected population—the constituency of stakeholders. Whether to protect a village landmark is likely to be a problem only for the village. Whether to protect a species endemic to the village landscape is likely to be a problem for the world.

The challenge for governance is to engage the constituency of stakeholders in an environment comprising existing entrenched institutions, political structures, legal and customary rights and obligations, social norms and conventions, and so on. Existing legal and customary rights typically privilege particular groups and places while discriminating against other groups and places. They also embody rules and procedures that limit the capacity to make changes to meet changing conditions. The result is that efforts to change systems of governance tend to be slow, and to be easily blocked or diverted. We close by reconsidering four cases where current trends indicate a change in the socially optimal scale of conservation. We identify the implications for governance, and note at least some of the issues to be addressed. All are examples of the tyranny of small decisions—a problem frequently encountered in the supply of additive or multiplicative public goods. All require intervention at scales that transcend current institutions.

Forest conversion: Deforestation is known to be a major driver of both climate change and biodiversity loss, as well as a range of more localized impacts on rainfall, flooding, and fire regimes. The impact of deforestation on climate change stems from the fact that the world's forests contain more carbon that all exploitable reserves of coal, oil, and gas. Carbon is lost in the process of deforestation, and gained in the process of afforestation or forest growth. Forests currently sequester around 28% of all emissions caused by the combustion of fossil fuels. It follows that deforestation both contributes directly to greenhouse gas emissions, around 13%, and reduces the capacity of forests to sequester atmospheric carbon. A combination of afforestation/reduced deforestation has the potential to remove 18% of CO_2 from the atmosphere by 2030 (Intergovernmental Panel on Climate Change 2018).

Deforestation is also heavily implicated in the loss of biodiversity. Although tropical forests cover only 10% of the world's terrestrial surface, they house around two thirds of all the world's species. Deforestation, and particularly tropical deforestation, therefore has larger consequences for species loss than the conversion of other habitats. One attempt to project the consequences of continued tropical forest loss assumes loss at the current rate until primary forests are lost. At that rate of loss, projected species extinction rates are two or more orders of magnitude higher than extinction rates recorded in four of the five previous mass extinction events (Alroy 2017).

While there are many drivers of deforestation, most are linked to the conversion of forests to other uses, mainly agriculture. The proximate causes of deforestation include both large-scale conversion to oil palm or other plantations or to commercial cash crops, and small-scale conversion to food crops, frequently through some variant of slash-and-burn production. Land conversion occurs particularly rapidly where road construction opens up new areas of forest, and so is often linked to the infrastructural development associated with new mines. Wildfires, particularly in partially converted systems, are increasingly implicated.

Underlying causes include the population growth that stimulates demand for agricultural land, and that encourages shorter and shorter fallow cycles in slash-and-burn systems, and the economic growth that stimulates demand for commercial crops such as oil palm, sugar cane, soy bean, coffee, coca, cacao, rubber, and bananas. The underlying causes also include the property-rights regimes that allow open access to forest resources, while limiting security of land tenure.

The process is one in which billions of small decisions, each having trivial consequences for either climate or the survival of forest species, cumulatively drive the two most severe global environmental challenges of our time. Land conversion is always a local process, locally enabled or regulated, and driven by local benefits and costs. The cumulative impacts it has that are distant in both time and space are never factored into the decision to convert. While landholders may themselves be impacted by changes in temperature, precipitation, flood, and fire that are cumulative effect of land conversion, they do not take those effects into account in making their own decisions.

By the subsidiarity principle it is clear that devolving land conversion decisions to the landholders themselves leaves all others at risk. Engaging local institutions in the process through the establishment of local property rights or local zoning restrictions can bring at least some of the off-site impacts of land conversion to the attention of landholders. But many local and regional governments have as little interest in the more distant consequences of local land-use decisions as the landholders themselves. Most national land-use change is still small relative to global land-use change. And the right of nation-states to determine land use within their jurisdiction is seen as an issue of national sovereignty.

Although the framework agreements on climate change, desertification, and biodiversity contain language on the obligation of individual nation-states to avoid harm to others, no one country is willing to cede sovereignty over land use. In these circumstances, the closest states have come to agreeing restrictions on land use is the Reduced Emissions from Deforestation and

Forest Degradation (REDD+) scheme initiated in 2005. The scheme is intended to encourage developing countries to reduce emissions and through forest management option that are, at least in part, funded by developed countries. In practice, however, developing countries are free to make their own unrestricted decisions on land use. The principle of subsidiarity has, ironically, been invoked by nation-states to limit the capacity of REDD+ to do more than suggest guidelines for reporting forest resource management. While an objective reading of the principle suggests that the wider constituency of stakeholders should be represented in national land-use decisions, this looks unlikely to happen in the foreseeable future.

Landraces and crop wild relatives: One of the main conservation issues in agroecosystems is the in situ conservation of the landraces and wild crop relatives. Landraces are traditional crop varieties that are typically well adapted to local conditions. They are also the primary source of the genetic material used to produce modern crop varieties that are not only high-yielding, but also resistant to drought, pests, and disease. They are conserved both through national and international ex situ collections of plant genetic material such as the Consultative Group on International Agricultural Research (CGIAR) collections, and through on-farm or conservation. Since landraces are genetically dynamic—evolving in response to changes in environmental conditions—ex situ collections can only be kept up to date if farmers continue to cultivate landraces in situ. The problem confronting society is that farmers have little incentive to plant landraces instead of modern, high-yielding hybrids (Bradshaw 2017, Phillips et al. 2017). For each farmer the individually rational choice is to substitute high-yielding varieties, but every decision to plant high-yielding varieties in place of traditional varieties increases the genetic erosion of those traditional varieties.

The declining genetic diversity of landraces due to displacement by modern varieties is now well established. For example, the genetic pool of lima bean landraces in Mexico was shown to have declined by 72% in the three decades after 1979 due to allelic displacement (Martínez-Castillo et al. 2012). Similar results have been found for tetraploid wheat, sorghum, and maize (Perrings 2018). What makes this of social concern is that landraces are readily adaptable to human and natural selection, and thus an important source of rare alleles. The loss of alleles in the courses of the genetic erosion of landraces is also the loss of the capacity to adapt to changing climatic or environmental conditions.

For a crop like maize, widely planted across the world, this makes the in situ conservation of maize landraces and wild maize relatives such as Teocinte a global concern. The constituency of stakeholders are producers and consumers of maize and maize products everywhere. Put another way, the genetic externalities of farmers' planting decisions in the center of origin of maize, Mexico, have a global reach. Although there are no good estimates of the value of externalities that involve uncertain loss of adaptive capacity, varietal development opportunities, or heightened vulnerability to disease and other environmental stresses, it is clearly large (Lipper and Cooper 2009).

Authority to intervene in farmers' planting decisions lies with the state. The two international agreements concerned with the conservation of land races and wild crop relatives are the 2001 International Treaty on Plant Genetic Resources for Food and Agriculture (the Plant Treaty) and the 1992 Convention on Biological Diversity. Both assert that states have sovereign rights over biological resources that fall within their jurisdiction (Convention on Biological Diversity 1992). Neither gives states an incentive to contribute material to the international ex situ collections, but instead encourages them to build national ex situ collections. Since most states place a low priority on in situ conservation of landraces, landraces have a low profile in national collections. Indeed, landraces and wild relatives together account for only 16% of holdings in national collections, compared to 72% of holdings in the international CGIAR collections.

While the goals of the Plant Treaty are the conservation and sustainable use of plant genetic resources for food and agriculture and the fair and equitable sharing of the benefits arising out of their use, implementation is subject to national priorities. Article 5 of the Plant Treaty aims to promote in situ conservation of wild crop relatives and wild plants for food production, including in protected areas, but it is conditioned on national laws and policies (International Treaty on Plant Genetic Resources for Food and Agriculture 2009). In recent years, national policies have been primarily focused on the results of modern plant breeding and genetic engineering (Santilli 2012).

Implementation of Article 5 can be achieved by changing the incentive structure to farmers using methods of the kind described in Chapters 9 and 12, such as targeted compensation payments or contracts for the conservation of particular crops (Narloch et al., 2011). What resources are committed to encouraging in situ conservation of landraces and wild crop relatives in any one country depends, at present, on that country. By the subsidiarity principle, leaving in situ conservation decisions to the nation-state potentially compromises the welfare of a much larger community. There are mechanisms available to channel resources to individual countries to make investments in the global public interest. The Global Environment Facility is a case in point. But the decision to make those investments lies with the nation-state. Even though the conservation of maize landraces confers benefits to consumers worldwide, the Mexican government, for instance, has no incentive to take account of conservation benefits beyond Mexico. In the absence of international payments for the conservation of landraces in Mexico, too few resources will be committed to the problem (Perrings 2018).

Marine capture fisheries: In marine systems, unlike terrestrial systems, there is a consensus that overexploitation of capture fisheries is more important as a proximate cause of biodiversity loss than habitat loss, climate change, pollution, disease, or invasive species. A study of catches in all 64 large marine ecosystems (LMEs) in the second half of the twentieth century reported an accelerated rate of fisheries collapse. Cumulative collapses had affected 65% of all species fished, and 29% of species harvested at the end of the century were in a state of collapse (Worm et al. 2006). Nor has the trend reversed in this century. The most recent FAO assessment of fish stocks concluded that the share of fish stocks within biologically sustainable levels has declined from 90% in 1974 to 69% in 2013 (Figure 15.15). That is, 31% of fish stocks were overfished. In marine capture fisheries beyond areas of national jurisdiction, as in Garret Hardin's village commons, the tyranny of small decisions lies behind the continuing decline in marine biodiversity.

There is also a consensus about the underlying causes of biodiversity loss: the lack of effective governance mechanisms, particularly in areas beyond national jurisdiction. Within the exclusive economic zones of nation-states, fisheries are at least partly regulated. Beyond the exclusive economic zones, fisheries are effectively open access—there is nothing to exclude fishers from the resource, and no incentive for them to conserve stocks. While the subsidiarity principle would suggest that harvesting decisions in the high seas should be made at the highest level, there is no system of governance that would allow multilateral control over private fishing effort.

This is despite the fact that there are a number of multilateral agreements aimed at the regulation of marine resources in sea areas beyond national jurisdiction. The most important agreement on the management of high seas resources is the 1982 UN Convention on the Law of the Sea (UNCLOS), currently ratified by 167 states (though not the United States). This agreement formalizes states' rights to marine resources within and beyond the 200 nautical miles that defines the exclusive economic zone, and to mineral resources within the continental shelf. Although the agreement notionally offers special protection to highly migratory species and marine mammals, it has not proved to be an effective deterrent to the overexploitation of both.

Nor are other agreements more effective. A number of countries have, for example, signed up for a code of conduct for fisheries beyond areas of national jurisdiction—the FAO Code of Conduct for Responsible Fisheries—though compliance is purely voluntary. The code includes an agreement to promote

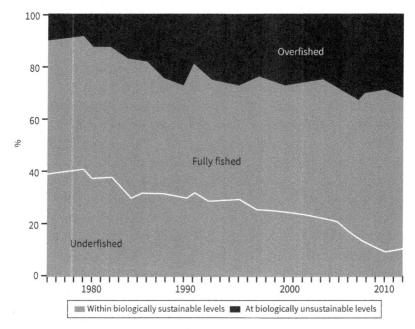

Figure 15.15 Global trend in the state of world marine fish stocks monitored by FAO (1974–2013).
Source: Food and Agriculture Organization (2016).

compliance with international conservation and management measures by fishing vessels on the high seas, but is not legally binding on signatories. The establishment of Regional Fishery Management Organisations (RFMOs) to address specific conservation and management issues associated with high seas fisheries is a step toward the governance of fisheries beyond national jurisdiction, but these organizations have been largely unable to limit illegal and unreported fishing in the area.[2] Part of the difficulty is that Article 87 of UN Convention on the Law of the Sea affirms the principle of the "freedom of the high seas," and

---

[2] Regional Fishery Management Organizations:

FAO Bodies: APFIC Asia-Pacific Fisheries Commission, CECAF Fishery Committee for the Eastern Central Atlantic, CWP Coordinating Working Party on Fishery Statistics, GFCM General Fisheries Commission for the Mediterranean, IOTC Indian Ocean Tuna Commission.

RECOFI Regional Commission for Fisheries, SWIOFC South West Indian Ocean Fishery Commission, WECAFC Western Central Atlantic Fishery Commission.

Non-FAO Bodies: AAFC Atlantic Africa Fisheries Conference, CCAMLR Commission for the Conservation of Antarctic Marine Living Resources, CCSBT Commission for the Conservation of Southern Bluefin Tuna, COREP Regional Fisheries Committee for the Gulf of Guinea, PPS South Pacific Permanent Commission, CTMFM Joint Technical Commission for the Argentina/Uruguay Maritime Front, FFA South Pacific Forum Fisheries Agency, IATTC Inter-American Tropical Tuna Commission, IBSFC International Baltic Sea Fishery Commission, ICCAT International Commission for the Conservation of Atlantic Tuna, ICES International Council for the Exploration of the Sea, IPHC International Pacific Halibut Commission, IWC International Whaling

specifically "freedom of fishing." The RFMOs have some capacity to develop policies for member states, and are playing an increasing role in monitoring illegal, unreported, and unregulated fishing in their areas of competence, but they do not have the capacity to limit nonmembers. Indeed, there is nothing that can legally be done to constrain noncontracting parties (Barrett 2005).

An area of marine management that offers some conservation benefits for fisheries is the establishment of marine protected areas (MPAs). Most MPAs are established within areas of national jurisdiction, so allowing enforcement to occur. MPAs established in spawning areas of high species richness, for example, have been shown to enhance catches in adjoining areas. In recent years nongovernmental conservation organizations have promoted the establishment of marine protected areas in sea areas beyond national jurisdiction, in part as a way of protecting against the decline of epipelagic fisheries. Absent a collective commitment to the governance of the high seas, however, marine-protected areas beyond the exclusive economic zones suffer from the same limitations that affect other initiatives in sea areas beyond national jurisdiction.

The governance of high seas resources, like the governance of environmental issues that span national jurisdictions, depends on agreements between nation-states. Just as the objectives of multilateral agreements are limited by the interests of nation-states, so are the resources available to intergovernmental bodies charged with implementing multilateral agreements. The governance of the high seas is vulnerable on both counts. Since all countries are affected by the decline in high seas resources, the subsidiarity principle implies that private harvesting decisions in sea areas beyond national jurisdiction should be consistent with global interest in the conservation of stocks, in turn implying the establishment of a regulatory regime and incentives implemented at the global level.

Emerging infectious zoonoses: Finally, as we have already seen, of the main effects of the growth of trade and travel has been an increase in the rate at which pests and pathogens have been spread. The development of new trade routes has led to the introduction of new species either deliberately or accidentally. The growth in the volume of trade along existing routes has increased the frequency with which (a) new species are introduced along that route, and (b) existing

Commission, NAFO Northwest Atlantic Fisheries Organization, NAMMCO North Atlantic Marine Mammal Commission, NASCO North Atlantic Salmon Conservation Organization, NEAFC North-East Atlantic Fisheries Commission, NPAFC North Pacific Anadromous Fish Commission, OLDEPESCA Latin American Organization for the Development of Fisheries, PICES North Pacific Marine Science Organization, PSC Pacific Salmon Commission, SEAFO South East Atlantic Fishery Organization, SPC Secretariat of the Pacific Community, SRCF Sub-regional Commission on Fisheries, WCPFC Western and Central Pacific Fisheries Commission, WIOTO Western Indian Ocean Tuna Organization.

species are reintroduced along the same route. The cumulative number of new introductions along a particular route is a concave function of the volume of imports on that route. In other words, trade-related introductions of new species from a particular area eventually attenuate. The more bioclimatically similar are the countries connected by a particular route, the greater the likelihood that species introduced via that route have established and spread. Indeed, there is strong evidence for the role of trade and travel in the spread of many new diseases of humans, animals, and plants, including West Nile, SARS, a number of highly pathogenic avian influenzas, and a series of key livestock diseases (Jones et al. 2008). The current COVID-19 pandemic is just the latest in a long line of novel zoonoses spread through trade and travel.

The decisions that lie behind infections in traded animals or plant, or among travellers, span all of the factors contributing to risk in production, distribution, and consumption of traded goods and services. Decision-makers balance the marginal private costs and benefits of biosecurity measures—the cost and benefits to them of an additional unit of effort. The cost of disease includes any liability the decision-maker has for damages to others. If decision-makers are not legally liable, or are legally liable but the probability of enforcement is low, decision-makers will not take the wider consequences of their own behavior into account. That is, disease risk to others is an externality of their actions (Perrings et al. 2014).

Since the control of infectious disease is a weakest- or weaker-link public good, the risk to all depends on the level of biosecurity effort chosen by the least effective of all producers, distributors, or consumers. If one quarantine facility, one importer, or one producer fails to contain an introduced pathogen, the fact that all others may do so is irrelevant. Nonetheless, the likelihood that poor biosecurity by any one decision-maker triggers an outbreak also depends on the general biosecurity environment. If one person is infected in conditions that include overcrowding, poor sanitation, low levels of hygiene, and low levels of personal health, for example, an outbreak is more likely than if there is no overcrowding, good sanitation, and high levels of hygiene and health. The tyranny of small decisions, in this case, lies in the fact that the cumulative effect of individual biosecurity decisions is a level of disease risk that few decision-makers would welcome.

Because of the high costs of infectious disease, most countries implement public health policies designed to limit the social costs of potentially harmful private behavior. National policies, such as mandatory vaccination regimes and other sanitary and phytosanitary measures, seek to reduce the risk to all residents of production and consumption decisions at home. National inspection and interception regimes seek to protect residents, and national biota against the risks posed by imports and inbound travelers. At the same time, national disease surveillance and monitoring efforts, such as those undertaken by the US Centers for Disease Control or the US Department of Agriculture's Animal and Plant Health Inspection Service, provide decision-makers with information on the current status of a wide range of human, animal, and plant health risks.

Internationally, the World Trade Organization (WTO) and its constituent agreements, particularly the General Agreement on Tariffs and Trade (GATT) and the Sanitary and Phytosanitary (SPS) Agreement, give national governments the right to interdict trade temporarily to protect food safety and animal or plant health within their jurisdiction. The SPS Agreement and its supporting agencies (the Codex Alimentarius Commission for food safety, and the World Organization for Animal Health), along with the International Plant Protection Convention, provide a framework within which countries can intervene in trade on animal and plant health grounds. For human health, the 2005 International Health Regulations (IHR), administered by the World Health Organization (WHO), similarly authorize actions that disrupt trade or travel to particular countries.

Of all the conservation issues covered in this book, the management of infectious human, animal, and plant diseases comes closest to reflecting the most important property of the subsidiarity principle: that where decisions cannot be taken locally without risk to others distance in time and space, decisions will be taken at higher—national, regional, or global—scales. It is also the issue where nation-states come closest to ceding sovereignty to a supranational body. This is, of course, because many nations place a high enough value on human health that they are willing to cede some of their sovereign authority. The arguments contained in this book suggest that society should be placing a much higher value on biodiversity than it currently does, for reasons that include, but extend beyond, human health. These arguments also suggest that protection of that biodiversity will require coordination at supra-national levels. There is still the possibility for positive trends in this direction—if societies can learn to value biodiversity appropriately, and organize in the service of protecting that value.

References

Alroy, J. 2017. Effects of habitat disturbance on tropical forest biodiversity. Proceedings of the National Academy of Sciences 114:6056–6061.

Barrett, S. 2005. The theory of international environmental agreements. Pages 1457–1516 in K.-G. Maler and J. Vincent, editors. Handbook of environmental economics. North-Holland, Amsterdam.

Bradshaw, J. E. 2017. Plant breeding: past, present and future. Euphytica 213:60.

Brockmann, D., and D. Helbing. 2013. The hidden geometry of complex, network-driven contagion phenomena. Science 342:1337–1342.

Convention on Biological Diversity. 1992. United Nations, New York.

De Sadeleer, N. 2012. Principle of subsidiarity and the EU environmental policy. Journal for European Environmental & Planning Law 9:63–70.

Elliott, R. J., and Y. Zhou. 2013. Environmental regulation induced foreign direct investment. Environmental and Resource Economics 55:141–158.

Food and Agriculture Organization. 2016. The state of world fisheries and aquaculture. FAO, Rome.

Global Migration Data Analysis Centre. 2018. Global migration indicators 2018. International Organization for Migration, Berlin.

Gygli, S., F. Haelg, N. Potrafke, and J.-E. Sturm. 2019. The KOF globalisation index: revisited. Review of International Organizations. ETH, Zurich.

Hardin, G. 1968. The tragedy of the commons. Science 162:1243–1248.

Hufe, P., and D. F. Heuermann. 2017. The local impacts of large-scale land acquisitions: a review of case study evidence from Sub-Saharan Africa. Journal of Contemporary African Studies 35:168–189.

Intergovernmental Panel on Climate Change. 2018. Global warming of 1.5° C: An IPCC special report on the impacts of global warming of 1.5° C above pre-industrial levels and related global greenhouse gas emission pathways, in the context of strengthening the global response to the threat of climate change, sustainable development, and efforts to eradicate poverty. Intergovernmental Panel on Climate Change, Geneva.

Internal Displacement Monitoring Centre. 2017. Global report on internal displacement. IDMC, Geneva.

International Treaty on Plant Genetic Resources for Food and Agriculture. 2009. Food and Agriculture Organization, Rome.

IPBES. 2018a. The IPBES assessment report on land degradation and restoration. Montanarella, L., Scholes, R., and Brainich, A., editors. Secretariat of the Intergovernmental Science-Policy Platform on Biodiversity and Ecosystem Services, Bonn, Germany.

IPBES. 2018b. The IPBES regional assessment report on biodiversity and ecosystem services for the Americas. Rice, J., Seixas, C. S., Zaccagnini, M. E., Bedoya-Gaitán, M., and Valderrama N., editors. Secretariat of the Intergovernmental Science-Policy Platform on Biodiversity and Ecosystem Services, Bonn, Germany.

IPBES. 2019. Summary for policymakers of the global assessment report on biodiversity and ecosystem services of the Intergovernmental Science-Policy Platform on Biodiversity and Ecosystem Services. Intergovernmental Science-Policy Platform on Biodiversity and Ecosystem Services, Bonn, Germany.

Jackson, M. O., and B. W. Rogers. 2005. The economics of small worlds. Journal of the European Economic Association 3:617–627.

Jones, K. E., N. G. Patel, M. A. Levy, A. Storeygard, D. Balk, J. L. Gittleman, and P. Daszak. 2008. Global trends in emerging infectious diseases. Nature 451:990–993.

Kahn, A. E. 1966. The tyranny of small decisions: market failures, imperfections, and the limits of economics. Kyklos 19:23–47.

Lee, C. E. 2002. Evolutionary genetics of invasive species. Trends in Ecology & Evolution 17:386–391.

Levinson, A., and M. S. Taylor. 2008. Unmasking the pollution haven effect. International Economic Review 49:223–254.

Lipper, L., and D. Cooper. 2009. Managing plant genetic resources for sustainable use in food and agriculture. Agrobiodiversity, Conservation and Economic Development 170:27–39.

Martínez-Castillo, J., L. Camacho-Pérez, J. Coello-Coello, and R. Andueza-Noh. 2012. Wholesale replacement of lima bean (Phaseolus lunatus L.) landraces over the last 30 years in northeastern Campeche, Mexico. Genetic Resources and Crop Evolution 59:191–204.

Mayhew, P. J., M. A. Bell, T. G. Benton, and A. J. McGowan. 2012. Biodiversity tracks temperature over time. Proceedings of the National Academy of Sciences 109:15141–15145.

Narloch, U., A. G. Drucker, and U. Pascual. 2011. Payments for agrobiodiversity conservation services for sustained on-farm utilization of plant and animal genetic resources. Ecological Economics 70:1837–1845.

Perrings, C. 2018. Conservation beyond protected areas: the challenge of landraces and crop wild relatives. Pages 123–136 in V. Dayal, A. Duraiappah, and N. Nawn, editors. Ecology, economy and society. Springer, Singapore.

Perrings, C., C. Castillo-Chavez, G. Chowell, P. Daszak, E. Fenichel, D. Finnoff, R. Horan, A. M. Kilpatrick, A. Kinzig, N. Kuminoff, S. Levin, B. Morin, K. Smith, and M. Springborn. 2014. Merging economics and epidemiology to improve the prediction and management of infectious disease. Ecohealth 11:464–475.

Pew Research Center. 2019. Origins and destinations of the world's migrants, 1990–2017. Pew Research Center, Washington, DC.

Phillips, J., J. Magos Brehm, B. van Oort, Å. Asdal, M. Rasmussen, and N. Maxted. 2017. Climate change and national crop wild relative conservation planning. Ambio 46:630–643.

Santilli, J. 2012. Agrobiodiversity and the Law. Earthscan, London.

Solarin, S. A., and U. Al-Mulali. 2018. Influence of foreign direct investment on indicators of environmental degradation. Environmental Science and Pollution Research 25:24845–24859.

United Nations Conference on Trade and Development. 2018. Key statistics and trends in international trade 2017. United Nations, New York.

Warner, K. 2018. Coordinated approaches to large-scale movements of people: contributions of the Paris Agreement and the global compacts for migration and on refugees. Population and Environment 39:384–401.

World Bank. 2018. Data bank, world development indicators. World Bank, Washington, DC.

World Bank. 2019a. Foreign direct investment, net inflows (% of GDP). World Bank, Washington, DC.

World Bank. 2019b. Foreign direct investment, net inflows (BoP, current US$). World Bank, Washington, DC.

World Bank. 2019c. Global economic prospects: darkening skies. World Bank, Washington, DC.

World Bank. 2019d. International tourism, number of arrivals. World Bank, Washington, DC.

Worm, B., E. B. Barbier, N. Beaumont, J. E. Duffy, C. Folke, B. S. Halpern, J. B. C. Jackson, H. K. Lotzke, F. Micehli, S. R. Palumbi, E. Sala, K. A. Selkoe, J. J. Stachowicz, and R. Watson. 2006. Impacts of biodiversity loss on ocean ecosystem services. Science 314:787–790.

Index